A CONCISE HISTORY OF ART

A CONCISE
HISTORY OF ART

GERMAIN BAZIN

CONSERVATEUR EN CHEF
AU MUSÉE DU LOUVRE

with 717 illustrations
16 plates in colour

THAMES AND HUDSON
LONDON

FIRST ENGLISH EDITION TRANSLATED FROM THE FRENCH BY
FRANCIS SCARFE WITH ADDITIONS AND REVISIONS

PREFACE

Anyone trying to write a short history of art is liable to find his work being compared with Solomon Reinach's famous *Apollo* which served as a manual for several generations of students. At all events the task has become remarkably more complicated since the time when Reinach wrote his 'manual' in 1905. Since that date many civilizations have been more fully explored or even freshly discovered. The great Hellenist confined himself to the art of the West, and as his title *Apollo* suggests, his main purposes was to expound the 'Greek miracle' with all its antecedents and consequences. Reinach's work covered mainly the ancient Mediterranean and the Renaissance. But since then we have discovered another 'miracle' which might well be called the 'barbarian miracle', taking the word 'barbarian' in the same sense as the Greeks and Romans did. The primitive civilizations are now admired as they could not possibly have been fifty years ago, and since then we have also discovered the arts of the East. Moreover, we now recognize certain other values to be as fertile as the classicism to which Reinach devoted his researches, in particular the baroque which in his day was still ignored or condemned as a sign of decadence.

The reader may be surprised to find certain variations in the way the different chapters of this book are planned. All those dealing with ancient civilizations or with pre-Columbian archaeology or the Far East, contain an historical introduction which appeared superfluous in the case of the Western civilizations, whose history is sufficiently well known. In the case of the Far East, it appeared advisable to add some account of the religions of the countries concerned, without which it would be hard to understand the artistic works of races whose outlook is so unlike our own.

5

This book is an historical work, designed to give the uninitiated reader as many precise ideas and established facts as possible. The remarks which introduce each chapter can be read separately, and in each case they provide a short critical and aesthetic survey. In the conclusion the reader will find an outline of the various ways in which the work of art has been interpreted, from the time when modern man first turned his eager attention to this particular product of human genius.

The illustrations were chosen to accompany the text, but occasionally they diverge from it, especially those accompanying the prefatory remarks and the conclusion: in such cases the plates are intended to bring out resemblances or historical perspectives, and offer the reader the most direct evidence of whatever unifies or distinguishes the characteristic forms of different civilizations.

The author's aim has been to consider the work of art from a genuinely universal, impartial point of view, as something which transcends the limitations of time and place. Whilst he does not claim to have succeeded, he will feel rewarded if his efforts made in that direction are recognized. But unless he has no roots at all, who can hope to escape from his own time, or ignore the claims of the civilization in which he was reared?

GERMAIN BAZIN

CONTENTS

Preface 5

Acknowledgements 9

  I *The Origins of Art* 11
    Prehistoric and Protohistoric Cultures 12

  II *Primitive Artistic Civilizations* 23
    1 Egyptian Civilization 30
    2 The Civilizations of Western Asia 38
    3 The Aegean Civilizations 50
    4 The Art of the Nomads 54
    5 The Pre-Columbian Civilizations 57
    6 The Arts of the 'Uncivilized' Peoples 63

  III *The Classical Civilizations of the Mediterranean* 67
    1 Greece 74
    2 The Roman World 101
    3 Eastern Resistance 112

  IV *Earliest Forms of Christian Art* 119
    1 Early Christian Art in Rome 125
    2 Byzantine Art 131
    3 Western Art in the Early Middle Ages 141

  V *The Rise of the West* 151
    1 Romanesque Art 157
    2 Gothic Art 172

  VI *Islam* 205
    The Evolution of Muslim Art 209

VII *European Art in the Fifteenth Century* 223
  1 The Renaissance in Italy 228
  2 Late Gothic and the Renaissance in Europe 250

VIII *The Renaissance in Europe in the Sixteenth Century* 271
  1 Italy 276
  2 The Spread of the Renaissance in Europe 293
  3 The Minor Arts 314

IX *The Baroque Period* 317
  1 Baroque Europe 323
  2 The Resistance to Baroque 355

X *The Nineteenth-Century Crisis* 393
  1 Art in France 399
  2 Western Art outside France 415
  3 The Minor Arts 425

XI *The Civilizations of the Far East* 427
  1 Indian Art 433
  2 The Expansion of Indian Art 448
  3 Chinese Art 453
  4 The Expansion of Chinese Art: Japan 467

XII *Art Now* 471
  1 The Revolution in Architecture 476
  2 The School of Paris 485
  3 The National Schools 503
  4 The Minor Arts 517

Conclusion 521

Index 535

ACKNOWLEDGEMENTS

The publishers wish to thank the following for kindly allowing them to illustrate works in public or private collections, or for placing photographs at their disposal:

Ashmolean Museum, Oxford (pl. 565); Caisse Nationale des Monuments Historiques, Paris (pl. 338); Messrs. A. C. Cooper, Ltd., London (pl. 489); Herbert Felton, Esq., London (pl. 244); Brinsley Ford, Esq. London (pl. 489); Monsieur Jean Gilbert, Paris (pl. 686); Mrs. G. F. Luttrell, Dunster, Som. (pl. 406); Musée du Louvre, Paris (pl. 503); Museum of Fine Arts, Boston, Mass. (pl. 562); National Buildings Record, London (pl. 405); National Gallery, London (pl. XII); Señor G. M. Ojeda (Photo Club), Burgos (pl. 252); Monsieur L. Ollivier, Paris (pl. 337); Miss Catherine M. Powell, London (pl. 684); Royal Academy of Arts, London (pl. 406); Hon. Julian Salmond, Salisbury (pl. 490); Messrs. Walter Scott Ltd., Bradford (pl. 243); Edwin Smith, Esq., London (pl. 170); Tate Gallery, London (pl. 563, 684, 685); Victoria and Albert Museum (Crown Copyright), London (pl. 407, 561); Wadsworth Atheneum, Hartford, Conn. (pl. 663); Wallace Collection, London (pl. 486).

All other photographs reproduced in this volume are identical with those in the French and German editions.

I. THE ORIGINS OF ART

The earliest known products of human genius enable us to grasp the creative impulse behind works of art at the very source. The perfection of the statuettes of the Gravettian hunters period, and the masterpieces of Magdalenian cave-art show that primitive man had no inner urge to express some preconceived notion of 'beauty' through the medium of forms. Art is only one of the many expressions – though perhaps it is the most specific – of the unique genius which drives man to repeat the creative act of the demiurge in everything he does, so that he must needs excel himself from century to century. If the Gravettian carvings have such a dynamic sense of form, and if the animal figures painted in the French and Spanish caves are perfect works of naturalism that no later civilization could surpass, it is because primitive man, in making them, was convinced that he was genuinely creating. For him the image was no mere imitation. It had the same living faculties as the being of which it was a model, a double. It was thus a work of magic by which man asserted his mastery over the world. We know that our ancestor of the old Stone Age (the Palaeolithic) painted or carved natural forms with no intention of making a 'work of art': he intended, rather, to ensure the fertility of his prey, to entice it into his traps, or to acquire its strength for his own purposes. The primitive artist was a magician whose drawing had all the virtue of a magic spell, an incantation. If he gave so much attention to the living truth, it was in order to make shapes as lifelike as possible and endow them with the actual qualities of the creature. Thus the vivid naturalism of those early images can be traced to that desire to identify himself with the world, which distinguishes man from all other forms of life. The animal is bound to the natural order and is doomed to be merely one of its blind forces. Man, on the contrary, has an innate awareness of the surrounding world, thanks to which he can break free of it while ceaselessly striving to rejoin it in thought or action. Primitive man was deeply involved in the natural world, and lost none of its inherent energy. Not a thought nor deed of his failed to contact some power in the universe. Man's entire activity was aimed at skilfully intervening in the play of natural forces, in the hope of preserving a balance, attracting 'good' and repelling 'evil' powers.

If works of art appeared so late in Palaeolithic times, it was by no means because man was incapable of making them. The earliest Palaeolithic 'industries' of the Chellean, Acheulian and Mousterian periods show a craftsmanship that could well have been applied to art. But a long period was no doubt necessary before man could acquire a creative grasp of the forces underlying the world. The discovery and evolution of language, in itself, is an artistic operation in which verbal forms have to be invented and perfected. Naming things is the first creative act. To the primitive mind, the name has a magic power which identified it with the object. Thus man had slowly to bring his mental picture of the world into focus, before he could make his inner vision even more effective by reproducing the shapes he saw in nature. But at last certain 'magicians', who were no doubt of a race with an exceptional plastic sense, thought of extending their verbal spells, and giving them more evocatory power, by first of all painting images of the things or creatures they wanted to control. The profound knowledge of nature that can be seen in these works was not the result of the artists' disinterested contemplation, but was drawn from an intimate acquaintance with animal life, learnt in the daily drama of the hunt. Perhaps this explains why human images were so few and relatively crude: the drawing of the human figure was not an integral part of the primitive system of magic. As these paintings, drawings and engravings were executed without a model, often in the depths of gloomy caves and by the light of the feeblest of lamps, the primitive artist needed a marvellous memory to inform his creative imagination with such a power of synthesis. The artist-magician had to enter into a ritual trance, during which he 'emptied' his own soul by an act of intense mental concentration: he then evoked the supernatural powers which identified him with the bison, mammoth, horse or deer, until he was possessed by the soul of the animal itself and could then portray its image on the wall of his cave.

The study of the origins of art has a surprise in store, for the highest level of art was reached when man was living in this primitive state of the Old Stone Age, at a time when conditions had been made arctic or sub-arctic by the advance of the glaciers. From the Neolithic period onwards, civilization tended to become almost entirely materialistic in its outlook. There was a gap of several thousands of years between the cave art of the Magdalenian era (the final era of the Old Stone Age) and the first great civilizations of South-West Asia and the Nile valley.

PREHISTORIC AND PROTOHISTORIC CULTURES

Though its chronology is not firmly established, it is safe to say that the long prehistoric era during which man left little or no account of himself, lasted for hundreds of thousands of years – perhaps about 500,000. In the Palaeolithic phase, the largest part of man's prehistorical development, men existed by hunting and fishing, making most of their tools by chipping stone, especially flint. They lived in isolated tribes always in close contact with animal life. In the final most recent periods (Upper Palaeolithic) men built summer huts and also, in regions where rock-shelters were not available, winter houses half-dug into the ground.

1 Stags. Rock-Drawings, Lascaux (France). Upper Palaeolithic

Man's elementary equipment did not change drastically in the Mesolithic phase (Middle Stone Age). In the Neolithic phase (New Stone Age), the age of the greatest refinement of stone tools, there were swift changes in man's development, and towards 5,000 B. C., in the Near East, human effort was increasingly and ever more rapidly directed towards civilization, that is to say the framework of an organized society: industrial specialization involving endless improvements in tools; the emergence of new techniques such as pottery and mining (for flint); the development of trade; the discovery of agriculture; the domestication of animals; and permanent, collective settlements on land or lake.

The Upper Palaeolithic Period

The oldest examples of art date from the first millennia of Upper Palaeolithic times, a long period of the East-West migration of *Homo Sapiens* into Europe, where he replaced less advanced stocks. His rupestral art in the naturalistic style, consisting of carvings, drawings, paintings and engravings on rock-faces, is found concentrated in the south-west of France and in northern Spain, and is therefore know as 'Franco-Cantabrian'.

Aurignacian invaders and settlers (named after the French site at Aurignac, Haute-Garonne) first evolved drawing, engraving and painting. In early cave-works (e.g. La Pileta cave, Malaga) animals are silhouetted in pure profile, with only one leg to represent a pair and no indications of detail.

Gravettian mammoth hunters from Russia and Eastern Europe (named after the rock-shelter of La Gravette, Dordogne) carved, especially out

13

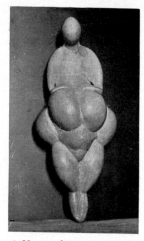

2 *Venus of Willendorf.*
Upper Palaeolithic. Vienna

3 *Venus of Lespugue. Upper*
Palaeolithic. Saint-Germain

of mammoth ivory, small figures which have been found over a wide
area in Eurasia. Some are of women apparently suffering from the fatty
degeneration known as 'steatopygia' still found among remnants of the
Bushmen in South Africa. While some of these statuettes tend to be
representative (Willendorf, Austria, pl. 2), others (Lespugue, France,
pl. 3) are almost geometrically stylized. It is not known whether this
three-dimensional vision came before or after the portrayal of shapes on
a flat surface. In south-western France and northern Spain the Gravet-
tians developed Aurignacian traditions of painting, their pictorial art
reaching a climax in the admirable paintings of the Lascaux cave in the
Dordogne (pl. 1, 6), discovered in 1940.

The ill-defined Solutrean period (named from the site at Soluté,
Saône-et-Loire) is known for leaf-shaped flint tools of astonishing refinement, and for a very few carvings of animals in relief on rock-faces
(the frieze of horses along the rock-shelter of La Chaire-à-Calvin,
Mouthiers; frieze of horses, ibexes, etc., at Roc de Sers, Charente). Such
sculpture was continued in the Magdalenian period (named after the
rock-shelter of La Madelaine, at Les Eyzies, Dordogne), for example in
the splendid equestrian frieze of Cap Blanc, in the Dordogne, and the
frieze of bison, horses, ibexes and female human torsos of Angles-sur-
l'Anglin. The 30,000 years or thereabouts of the Magdalenian period
(to be compared with a probable span of 50,000 years for the preceding
Aurignacian and Gravettian periods) were rich in artistic expression.
Sculpture ranged from the large, originally coloured, friezes to small
objects in reindeer-horn (pl. 4). The same material was also engraved or
incised (pl. 5). However, the pictorial arts became dominant, reaching

14

4 *Bison. Fragment of a Spear-Thrower from La Madeleine (France).*
Upper Palaeolithic. Saint-Germain

their peak in the polychrome animals of the famous caves of Altamira and Castillo (Santander, Spain), Font-de-Gaume (Dordogne), and Marsoulas (Haute Garonne).

The Abbé Breuil's investigations enable us to trace the evolution of this mural art from the simple line-drawing of Aurignacian times to the final polychrome painting, which is late Magdalenian. Whether incised or drawn on rock surfaces naturally covered in soft clay with the finger or 'brush', the line was at first of even thickness, and was only modulated later. Next a tinge of red ochre or black manganese was added, silhouetting the outline of the animal's body. At a later stage the brush or graving-tool would be run over all the finer points in order to bring out the movement, the pelt, or details of anatomy always, though, without the slightest hint of the picturesque. In the advanced

5 *Reindeer on Reindeer-Antler from Loret (France). Upper Palaeolithic.*
Saint-Germain

6 *Rock-Paintings of Animals, Lascaux (France). Upper Palaeolithic*

7 Hunting Scene, Cueva Remigia (Spain). Upper Palaeolithic

Magdalenian technique the painter finally blended his tones to reproduce the graded colouring of the hide or fur. All these various stages were dictated by a growing urge towards naturalistic truthfulness, yet such a virtuosity was achieved that the painter's hand marked the line down as boldly as a Pisanello, seeking and finding the clear-cut elegance of the arabesque. This thoroughbred art, the product of thousands of years of evolution and intense research, vanished from the Franco-Cantabrian areas while it was still at the height of its perfection, and with hardly a sign of any fall in quality. This may be explained by the amelioration of the cold climate of the Ice Age and the consequent disappearance of the hunter's quarry, which had occasioned Upper Palaeolithic art in all its remarkable forms.

During the Capsian period (named after the site at Gafsa, the *Capsa* of antiquity, in Tunisia) which began during the later Palaeolithic phase and continued into the Mesolithic, the Hamitic peoples of Africa produced a rock-art comparable with that of South-West Europe. Our present inadequate knowledge of the geology and prehistory of Africa makes it hard to settle the time-scale of the engravings and paintings of the Atlas and Sahara regions, or of Egypt, Lybia, Nubia and Rhodesia.

However, this art seems to have extended into the historic period. Here we find two distinct styles. In addition to the naturalistic manner, not unlike the Magdalenian, there was also an expressionistic and schematic form of art in which human and animal figures were grouped in dramatic actions (pl. 8). In Magdalenian art the figures were usually separate, and no such complexity of action was attempted. Drawings of the human figure, similarly grouped, are plentiful in the above regions. For the first time the artist had set himself the task of mastering the fundamentals of dramatic composition, and in this he succeeded all the more impressively as his diagrammatic treatment avoided the picturesque; the artist created the impression of whirling *vectors* of movement, pushing his systematization almost to the point of abstract draughtsmanship, the magical figures becoming pure 'signs'.

The peculiar Upper Palaeolithic rupestral art of eastern Spain (pl. 7) is to be related to this aspect of Capsian art, rather than to the developed

Magdalenian art, although it was influenced by art north of the Pyrenees. Thus, from very ancient times, man found a source of artistic inspiration in abstract art as well as in naturalism.

The Neolithic Period

Though it survived in Africa and Scandinavia, the early naturalistic art came to an end in the Franco-Cantabrian region in the Mesolithic period (about 10,000 B.C.) in the Azilian phase. The painted pebbles of the great cavern of Mas d'Azil (Ariège) are evidence of an art verging on the abstract, which was to prevail throughout the Neolithic period. Ceramics, which appeared in early Neolithic times, developed rapidly with the later (Bronze Age) invention of the potter's wheel and was no doubt favoured by the expansion of agriculture.

In the Neolithic and Chalcolithic stages (the latter being so named because during it metals were first used), mankind developed a rudimentary form of architecture which was sometimes impressive in its effects. Such Megalithic (large stone) monuments were usually constructed with colossal, unwieldy pieces of stone, and were intended for burial or for ritualistic purposes. The burial chambers consisted of upright stones weighing several tons each, serving as supports for slabs that were laid across them, the whole being finally covered (though not in all cases) with a mound of earth or small stones. They are of three main types: dolmen, a table-arrangement of stones with no passage leading in; passage grave, a rectangular or more or less circular tomb approached through a narrow stone passage; and gallery grave, a covered passage serving as a long burial vault. These underground tombs spread from the Eastern Mediterranean

9 Ritual Circle, Stonehenge. Neolithic

in the third and second millennia B.C. to France, Spain, Portugal, Great Britain and Northern Europe.

Huge arrangements of standing stones, whether set in straight lines as at Carnac in Brittany, or grouped in circles as at Avebury, Arbor Low and Stonehenge (pl. 9), in England, formed impressive sanctuaries which must have required enormous human effort and, at the same time, a fairly advanced social order.

Protohistory

A major event in the history of human techniques was the discovery and use of metals. These seem to have been valued at first for their preciousness. After learning how to obtain gold and silver, and then copper in the raw state (Chalcolithic period), man shaped them with hammers before he discovered the art of casting. The discovery of the blending properties of tin so as to form alloys, enabled him to harden copper, making possible its industrial use in the form of brass and bronze.

The eastern regions of the Mediterranean made the greatest creative contribution. In the third millennium the rise of the Elamite, Sumerian and Aegean historical civilizations coincided with the development of bronze metallurgy, which itself began about 3,500 B.C. The peoples of Central, Western and Northern Europe now emerged from their pre-historical stage to enter what is called the 'protohistorical' phase; for although they left no written records of their history, certain echoes of it survive in the traditions handed down by the peoples of the Near East. In any case, so far as metallurgy was concerned they depended on the Mediterranean, for merchants of the Eastern Mediterranean not only exported bronze articles to the West, but imported eastwards the tin they needed for its production. Metallurgical techniques also found their way into Central Europe through the Caucasus route by which the Near Eastern empires went in search of ore. It is not easy to give any strict chronology of the diffusion of metals, for although a relative time-scale may be clearly distinguished, there are no definite, epoch-making dates for the earlier periods. Copper side by side with tools of polished stone was widely in use in the second half of the fourth millennium B.C., while the same phenomenon is to be found in the Aegean area at the beginning of the third millennium, and in the Western Mediterranean by about 1900 B.C. Bronze was in common use in the Near East in the first half of the third millennium, in the Aegean about 2300 B.C., and in the West about 1500 B.C. As for iron, this was still a rare metal in the Near East in the first half of the second millennium. Nevertheless, by 1400 B.C. iron working techniques were evolved in Asia Minor, the centre of dispersion. In the West the Iron Age, which lasted for two thousand years, falls into two periods: the Halstatt period, taking its name from a site in Austria, which lasted roughly from 1000 to 500 B.C.; and the La Tène period (named after a site in Switzerland), from 500 B.C. to the Christian era.

The protohistoric Bronze and Iron civilizations extended over a considerable area, notably Italy, Spain, Gaul, the British Isles, Central and Northern Europe, Scandinavia, the Urals and the Altaï mountains. The epoch of La Tène corresponded with the westward expansion of the Celts. Although some anthropomorphic sculptures of this period have been found (in France, at Roquepertuse and Entremont; in Czechoslovakia, at Msecké-Zehrovice), the artistic activity of the above peoples showed itself mainly in domestic articles such as terra-cotta vessels (pl. 10), gold vases and jewellery. Whereas the creative imagination of the Mediterranean and Asiatic races found an endless source of inspiration for their plastic art in nature itself, the peoples of Central and Northern Europe seem to have derived more satisfaction from the abstract. The decorative range of their weapons and pots did not go beyond a few non-representational signs, such as the sacred horns of the bull, the double axe symbolizing thunder, the solar disc and its many derivatives – the wheel, the rowel, the star, the S, the spiral and double spiral (pl. 712), the swastika and the symmetrical cross. The head of the horse and swan were also solar symbols.

II. PRIMITIVE ARTISTIC CIVILIZATIONS

The artistic maturing of the Magdalenians was an isolated phenomenon. For thousands of years the people of Northern, Central and Western Europe, plunged in the obscurity of prehistory until our era, remained static in simple tribal groupings with not a glimmer of political or cultural genius. This entirely materialistic civilization spread as far as the Bosphorus, where the seven superimposed cities of Hissarlik in Troas (unearthed in the 1870s by the German scholar Schliemann – one being the site of Homer's Troy), reveal a striking poverty of the artistic instinct at a time which saw the rise of great neighbouring civilizations.

It was in the Mediterranean area that man made his first great efforts to emerge from his natural state. By inventing systems of politics, culture, religion, industry and commerce, he considerably extended both his practical and intellectual progress. Three great centres of civilization may be distinguished from the Neolithic period onwards, before 3000 B.C. These were in the Nile valley, Mesopotamia (Tigris and Euphrates basins) and the Aegean. All these civilizations were inspired by an heroic resolve to embody their idea of the world in enduring works. The various races who created them seem to have been blessed with a marvellous plastic imagination, and there is nothing – not even the most abstract of concepts – to which they failed to give a concrete form, a figure.

The magical, unorganized setting in which primitive man had lived was now set in order. Man became immune from the elemental powers he so much feared, by personifying them. He worshipped gods; he was no longer in contact with mere things, but with beings he could name, pray to and evoke. Beneficent and maleficent things now tended to crystallize into the abstract qualities of good and evil. The medicine-man gave way to the priest, an intermediary between man and god. Man's relationship to the visible or invisible world became regulated by a code of doctrines and practices; that is to say, religion.

Meanwhile the countless figures with which the Egyptians and Mesopotamians covered their monuments still remained profoundly imbued with the sense of the supernatural which had guided the hands of Magdalenian artists. No civilization carried to a higher point than did the Egyptian the belief in the identity of the image with its original. The host of illustrations, through which we can learn the smallest details of Egyptian life, were meant to add the support of reality itself to the objects and people who had to accompany the dead so as to allow them, in the after-life, to lead the same kind of existence as in their earthly state. These images are replicas – 'doubles' – of the articles and beings they represent, on which magic formulae conferred all the properties of the original model. The invention of images was then, properly

23

10 Burial-Urn. Hallstatt Period. Stuttgart

speaking, a creation; so that in the Nile valley the sculptor was known as 'He-who-keeps-alive'. In Mesopotamia this faith in the power of the image did not result in such a coherent system of imitation, but it was none the less present to the mentality behind the civilizations which succeeded each other in the Tigris and Euphrates valleys. Why did conquering princes so carefully cut the heads off the statues of defeated kings if not to rob them of that power of survival after death which in those days was guaranteed by an effigy? At the beginning of the Sumerian civilization in the first Ur dynasty, apparently it was not enough to paint or sculpt the likeness of a dead man's friends on the walls of his tomb, as was the custom in Egypt: they were actually put to death in the course of bloody funeral rites – wives, princes and servants followed their overlord into death, complete with their weapons, jewels, chattels and chariots of war. Belief in the 'double' later put an end to such holocausts.

This faith in the realness of images brought in its train a whole system of plastic conventions which, more or less empirical in Mesopotamia, assumed in Egypt a rational and sacred character. In order to have the maximum of real power, the image had to reproduce the model in its entirety and not with the incompleteness of our normal vision. The parts on the second and third planes, which remained hidden owing to the foreshortening of perspective, were therefore reproduced with the same fidelity as those which were fully visible. This explains the strange canon of the human figure, observed in religious art in Egypt for thirty

24

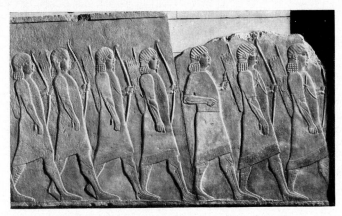

11 Warriors. Assyrian Relief. About 7th c. B.C. Paris

centuries, by which a head seen in profile, but with one eye full-face, is planted on a trunk seen from the front, and the trunk set on two legs shown in profile in a walking position (pl. 12). Thus all parts of the human body were represented from the angle at which they appeared most complete. Figures of men who in reality were *seen* in depth, one behind the other, were portrayed each one complete, either in Indian file (pl. 11) or superimposed in ranks (pl. 14 a).

The herdsman milking a cow was represented next to the animal but not against it, so as not to hide its body. In the same way offerings brought to a king by slaves would be portrayed above the basket supposedly containing them. At Khorsabad the famous winged bulls of the palace are shown with five legs, so as to appear equally 'complete' from both front and side (pl. 13). These mighty figures, like those of some of the cows at Hathor in Egypt, are not properly speaking built in the round, but are no more than a profile and a frontal view put together. The artists of those early civilizations had no spatial conception of objects. The sense of depth was as alien to them as the idea of perspective; some objects were portrayed flat while the profile of others was reduced according to the composition, the composition being dictated according to a moral hierarchy in which no account was taken of the relative sizes of the things themselves. Thus a man was always bigger than a tree, and even too big to enter his own house (pl. 14 a, 14 b). Integral realism, dictated by the needs of magic, obliged the artists to defy appearances. They did not see things from a distance as they appear to us, but saw them only as they knew them to be: the object they portrayed was not a spectacle for them, but they identified themselves with it by a process of empathy. Following their hand, their eye rested simultaneously on all the object's planes; they deliberately ignored the fact that certain

25

parts of a thing are farther away than others. Statuary was therefore usually presented head-on, with none of the play of line or forms that would give it spatial life (pl. 63). The name 'law of frontalism' has been given to this slavish convention which makes the statue completely static, giving it the inertia of mere architectural material.

In the images imposed on surfaces – bas-reliefs, paintings – the works were based on the side-view, silhouetted shadow-fashion against the wall; the details of the model were indicated diagrammatically by the chisel, rather than sculpted, and the main outline thus kept all the expressive strength that was characteristic of the cave-art of earlier times.

The architecture of all the primitive civilizations aspired to the colossal. It would appear that from the beginning, thanks to the multiple and combined efforts afforded by slave-labour, man intended his creations to rival those of nature itself. The Egyptian, in the same way as the Mexican or the Hindu, built mountains of stone in the form of pyramids, while the colossi of the Nilotic sculptors are rocks given forms and faces. All of them, Egyptians, Mycenaeans and Peruvians, exploited gigantic materials, while the Mesopotamians, for whom stone was in short supply, built their palaces on artificial hills of dried clay. It seems as though the poorer man was in technical resources, the more he tried to persuade himself of his own supernatural strength. In the art of bonding materials several races – such as the Mycenaeans and some Peru-

12 Egyptian Wood-Carving.
About 2700 B.C. Cairo

13 Winged Bull from Khorsabad.
Assyrian. 7th c. B.C. Paris

14a Schematic View of a fortified Town. Assyrian Bas-Relief

14b Schematic View of a Garden. Egyptian Papyrus. London

vian tribes – used stones of unequal sizes and shapes which they assembled as in a jig-saw puzzle (pl. 44). The Greeks called this the 'Cyclopean' style of building. However, at a very early stage the Egyptians and Sumerians developed a regular style, which the Romans later called *opus quadratum;* this notion of a wall made of identical and interchangeable parts (bricks and stones) implies a great effort of reasoning.

The image maker of the Nile valley, like the Sumerian, carefully polished the hardest of stones, as once the artist of the New Stone Age had done. Till the decline of the ancient world Egypt prolonged Neolithic art in the manufacture of vases of hard stone, in which Egyptian craftsmen had excelled from the outset.

All Egyptian art may be seen emerging from that technique. Nilotic sculptors first extended their activities from vases to stelae (needles) which they erected over royal tombs. They then took to polishing granite doors for their brick sanctuaries. It was at the beginning of the Memphitic period that they first dared to set up temples and tombs entirely of stone, which they used in enormous slabs. These obelisks were honoured as images of the deity in the temples of the sun during the Memphitic Empire (pl. 15). The menhir had the same function among the Western barbarians, and we know that in Sumeria they worshipped *betyles* of stone, perhaps symbols of the Earth-Mother in her least perishable form. This explains why these artists often showed a religious respect for the original shape of rough stones, which they simply improved with a little abrasion (pl. 16, 17).

It might be asked whether the inclination for mural art, so pronounced in Egypt but also found in the post-Sumerian civilizations of Asia, was a continuation of prehistoric cave-art. Do not the *mastaba* and the pyramid artificially reproduce the prehistoric cave inscribed with images? The second Theban Empire in its turn began to seek subterranean shelter

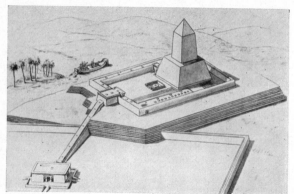

for its tombs, and certain Asiatic civilizations (Hittite and Persian) showed a special interest in carving natural rock-faces in the same way as the prehistoric civilizations of the Fezzan and the Sahara had done earlier.

The Egyptian technique of hollow-relief recalls that of engraving in caves, and in both cases, before becoming an independent art, painting was used only as an auxiliary to the carved outline. There is a thread of continuity between the cave-art of Africa which, unlike the European, was pursued well into the historic period, and the mural art of Egyptian civilization, which without doubt had its roots in prehistoric Africa.

The significance given to animals in religion and consequently in art, is another characteristic which links the first civilizations to prehistoric times. At first, brute strength seemed to man to be an attribute of divine power. The lion, the eagle, the bull and the snake played an outstanding part in primitive mythologies. They are to be found in Egypt (at first totemistic) as symbols or, rather, as incarnations of gods. In Mesopotamia they were closely identified with the divinities of the heavens or the underworld. The artists of the Nile, Tigris and Euphrates therefore became adept at the portrayal of animals, like their Magdalenian predecessors. Moreover, the bodies of animals, fused together in daring syntheses, gave rise to what amount to theological and plastic speculations.

This chapter, in which we have tried to discount geographical and temporal factors, so as to give a proper assessment of a primitive stage in the history of forms, must also include some study of the so-called 'pre-Columbian' civilizations. In the strictest sense some of these remained at the Stone Age; others discovered bronze but none of them iron, and the Mexicans erected their enormous stone structures with stone implements. No other evolved civilization shows so pathetically the material and psychological obstacles that had to be overcome by primitive man in order to raise his standard of life. We can only admire how those

16 Code of Hammurabi.
About 1700 B.C. Paris

17 Menhir from Les Maurels
(France). Neolithic. Rodez

mysterious races, notwithstanding their backwardness which was no doubt caused by their isolation, managed in spite of their crude technical development to create civilizations superior in some respects to what the Conquistadors were to build on their ruins.

As for the Bronze and Iron Ages, which in Western Europe are shrouded in the mist of prehistory, in the Mediterranean they produced historical civilizations rivalling those of Egypt and the Chaldeans. While we recall that iron was imported from Asia, we are still at a loss to say who invented the alloy of tin and copper – in itself too pliable – which resulted in a far tougher metal, bronze, while facilitating its industrial use owing to the much lower temperature required for casting. No doubt it was via South-West Asia that bronze slowly reached the Mediterranean, where local absence of tin deposits made its use costly and confined it to articles of luxury. For a long time in Egypt and Sumeria it was used only sparingly for statuary, being applied in the form of thin foil on a wooden core, the head alone being cast. The Indo-Europeans, who towards 2000 B.C. invaded the Mediterranean basin and fought and conquered the great powers of the period, no doubt owed their victory to their superior bronze and iron weapons, together with the domestication of the horse. During those ages of metal, the most skilful and highly evolved form of civilization was the Aegean which developed in Crete and later in Argolis from 3000 B.C. to 1130 B.C. It produced no statues, preferring personal articles to durable creations in stone. It excelled in making weapons, jewels, and pottery which were exported all over the East and to some parts of the West. This civilization recalls – though this time it was by the sea – the nomadic habits of those mounted tribes who were rearers of horses. Metal was better adapted than stone to the conditions of a wandering existence that encouraged them to produce only small objects such as jewels, personal finery, and trappings for harness. It was during the second millennium, well before historic times, that these nomad races entered the history of art. In certain sites of Central Asia we are beginning to find the oldest specimens of what is now termed 'steppe' art, which after absorbing the influence of the zoomorphic style from Chaldea was to invade the whole of Northern Europe where it held sway until something like A.D. 1000. In style and spirit this art, which gave exclusive attention to the portrayal of animals, must be studied as a rival to the primitive artistic civilizations rather than – as is usually done – as a prelude to the Middle Ages of the West.

The spirit of the Stone Age and the ages of metals is not dead today. It continues to inspire certain communities in Africa, Oceania and America, whose way of life (though degenerating all the time) perpetuates that of prehistoric man. The artistic output of these peoples will therefore take its proper place at the end of this chapter.

1. EGYPTIAN CIVILIZATION

Historical Background

Invulnerable on account of its position, with its desert hinterland and its redoubt on the Upper Nile which thrice in the course of history enabled its national unity to be restored, Egypt developed a highly skilled civilization which for thirty centuries maintained a political, cultural and artistic tradition unique in the history of the world. This unshakable tradition, almost devoutly preserved, accounts for its strength and greatness but at the same time for its monotony, though in those long centuries its subtle variations do show a gradual evolution.

The first artistic manifestations of Egyptian civilization – those of the pre-Dynastic era (before 3200 B.C.) and the Thinite era (1st and 2nd dynasties, after about 3200 B.C.) – show its close relationship to the neighbouring Sumerian civilization, perhaps because Egypt fell under its influence or because they both sprang from some common source. The Memphitic Empire or Old Kingdom (3rd to 11th dynasties, 2778 B.C. –2065 B.C.) carried out in the Delta region the most grandiose constructions to be found in Egypt, the Pyramids, which are the burial-places of the Pharaohs Cheops, Chephren and Mycerinus (4th dynasty, 2723 B.C. – about 2563 B.C.). At that time art was exclusively funerary, while domestic buildings were made of perishable materials, crude bricks of

18 Sphinx and Pyramid of Cheops

sun-baked clay, or wood. Statuary, relief and painting appear to have
been already properly established. After a period of anarchy Egypt was
formed anew, and the second period of its history is known as the Middle
Kingdom, the city of Thebes in Upper Egypt giving its name to the new
dynasties (11th to 17th dynasty, 2065 B.C.–1580 B.C.). Temples remained
of modest dimensions and funerary architecture continued to predomi-
inate. The task of recreating Egyptian unity fell to the 18th dynasty,
after it had been compromised by the Hyksos invasion. This dynasty
founded the New Kingdom (18th to 25th dynasty, 1580 B.C.–1085 B.C.),
which was the most brilliant phase of Egyptian art. In this period the
wealthy pharaohs, the lines of Emenophis and Ramses, built imposing
temples (Luxor and Karnak, near Thebes), while there was a tendency
to hollow out tombs in hypogeal form in the cliff-face of the Valley of
the Kings. Painting developed and became a completely independent
art tending to take the place of low-relief in funerary works. The
decorative arts were flourishing, as we can see from the tomb of
Tutankhamen. In the first millennium Egypt was several times invaded
and lost its independence. Only the dynasties established in the delta
at Saïs managed to maintain Egyptian civilization (Saïte period, 26th
dynasty, seventh and sixth centuries B.C.). Conquered by the Persians
in 525 B.C., then by Alexander, and on the latter's death passed over
to Ptolemy (Ptolemaïc period, 285 B.C.–21 B.C.), Egypt, although open
to Hellenic influence, never ceased to develop its native art which,
though it never regained vitality, was piously respected by the Romans
who were the last conquerors of the Nile valley in ancient times.

The Nile valley was the cradle of mankind's earliest social syntheses, and witnessed the first great human endeavour in the art of building. The country's wealth in stone materials, as well as the determination to make the dwellings of the dead last for ever, favoured the birth and progress of architecture. The longing for immortality inspired the first of these works, the Old Kingdom tombs called *mastabas* (shaped like the *frustum* – horizontal section – of a pyramid), and pyramids (pl. 18). The pyramid is, indeed, the most elementary architectural form, the one which most suggests stability and durability. Egypt had inherited from primitive times the taste for the gigantic which stresses the mightiness of man's creations (the Pyramid of Cheops, the largest of all, is 475 feet high, 738 feet wide, its base covers almost 13^1/$_2$ acres and its volume is over 2,500,000 cubic metres). On the outside there is a chapel in which the priest celebrated the funeral rites; it is decorated with mural images, carved or painted, and it has a 'false-door' ostensibly leading into the *serdah* containing the numerous 'doubles' which were intended as material support for the deceased king's soul in the after-life. The corpse, embalmed in the form of a mummy, was deposited in a crypt hollowed-out in the soil or built into the main structure.

After many experiments, the Egyptian temple took its final form in the New Kingdom (pl. 22). It was nothing less than a stone replica of the royal palace, which was made of wood and clay. Like the palace itself, it comprised three sections, the first reserved for introduction, the second for reception, the third for private life *(harem)*. The stone temple was built inside an enclosure of crude brick. There were two monumental 'pylons' or towers (pl. 19), themselves preceded by two obelisks (monolothic needles of stone), leading to a courtyard surrounded by colonnades

19 Pylons of the Temple of Khons, Karnak. 11th c. B.C.

20 *Courtyard of the Temple of Ammon, Luxor. About 1375 B.C.*

(pl. 20); the great pillared chamber (hypostyle hall) was a sort of throne-room in which the image of the god was shown to the crowds when it emerged in its galley on feast-days; behind it the private quarters were composed of treasure-rooms and sacristies, grouped round the *naos* or sanctuary which enveloped in secrecy and darkness the statue which was the god's 'double'.

Egyptian architecture was hindered in its development by its under-estimation of the arch; though it was not totally unknown or ignored, it was exploited only rarely and incidentally. Nilotic building was based on the system of 'flat-arching', which consists of holding roofs by means of slabs laid on supports. The solidity of the whole rested on the inertia of horizontally superimposed materials; and as stones, unlike wood, cannot take great weights without breaking, the Egyptian had to add the numerous supporting pillars which encumber the interiors, in order to be able to roof spaces of any size (pl. 22). As was later the case with Christian churches, though not with Greek temples, the Egyptian temple was essentially an enclosed space; closed from the outside and partly covered in from above, it hid its mystery behind long blank walls, keeping all its wealth of effects for the inside. The lighting of hypostyle chambers was supplied diagonally by skylights or lantern-lights obtained by giving extra height to the central naves. Its dominant feature of horizontality gave full expression to the notion of immobility to which all Egyptian art was devoted. The stones, well cut, were assembled by means of internal or flush jointing: by a careful coursing which hid the joints the Egyptians strove to give the effect of monolithic blocks. Owing to his urge for strength and his desire to build for all time, the Nilotic architect also made liberal use of massive materials sometimes weighing as much as five hundred tons (as in the high temple of the Pyramid of Chephren).

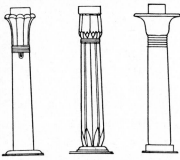

21 *Egyptian Columns (Palm, Lotus, Bell Capitals)*

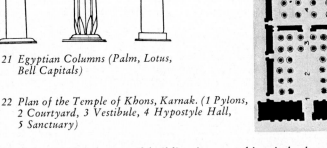

22 *Plan of the Temple of Khons, Karnak. (1 Pylons, 2 Courtyard, 3 Vestibule, 4 Hypostyle Hall, 5 Sanctuary)*

Though he created the art of building in stone, his mind, always after realism, stopped the Egyptian from inventing abstract forms that would have suited the raw material which he was the first to exploit in a rational manner: he contented himself with transposing into harder materials those earlier forms of architecture – in wood, compressed earth or clay – which remained in use for domestic purposes. The walls and towers (pylons) kept the sloped form which was given to mud or brick walls to prevent them from falling; the corners were decorated with a stone beading reminiscent of the sheaves of rushes used for binding dwellings of beaten earth; while the cornices had that splayed form characteristic of the tops of palm-trees. As for the columns themselves, whether palm-shaped, lotus-shaped or bell-shaped (pl. 21), their structure was that of the ancient supports made of sheaves of reeds or rushes, tied together and crowned with floral devices.

Sculpture

The Egyptian sculptor rarely made use of soft stone such as limestone. He preferred the hardest materials such as granite, basalt and porphyry, which are most durable and can be polished. During the thirty centuries of Nilotic civilization statuary never managed to break free from the 'law' of frontality. With the head always on the axis of the bust, and the arms glued to the sides, the statue has all the appearance of being an accessory of architecture. Under the Old Kingdom, sculpture showed a powerfully synthetic modelling and an intensely realistic vision which inspired the greatest masterpieces of that art (pl. 24, 63). But this experi-

23 'Lady Tui.' New Kingdom. Paris

24 Head of a seated Scribe.
About 2400 B.C. Paris

25 Head of a Queen.
About 1360 B.C. Paris

mental movement was checked during the first Theban Empire, when it gave way to a classicism rejecting individual characteristics and inclining more towards an ideal of impersonality. This evolution was very much accentuated until the academicism of the second Theban Empire, when an ideal of ease and gracefulness admirably expressed the peaceable nature of the race (pl. 23). The initiative of an heretical pharaoh, Amenophis IV (about 1378 B.C.–1360 B.C.), brought about a revolution in the figurative arts that almost freed Egyptian art from the static style to which dogma had hitherto condemned it.

Challenging all previous sacred conventions, the sculptors and painters of Tell el Amarna (Amenophis IV's new capital) tended to portray forms according to expressionist and mannerist principles (pl. 25, 704). Unfortunately this movement was stifled. The accesion of the weak pharaoh, Tutankhamon, who at once re-established the traditional religion and restored power to the priests of Amon, reduced art once again to a theological convention. The ephemeral restoration of the Saïte period breathed new life for a short time into moribund Egyptian sculpture, when it passed through a phase of archaism, renewing the elegant tradition of the New Kingdom and drawing some inspiration from the realism of the Old.

Mural Art

This title covers sculptures in low-relief as well as paintings, which are only an economical imitation of them. The term 'bas- (low-) relief' does not apply very well to mural sculptures, especially in the Middle Kingdom period, when, by making a deeply incised outline, the Egyptian sculptor produced a flat sculpture which did not project beyond the wall's surface and on which he then chiselled minor detail. The con-

26 Hunting and Fishing. Relief from Sakkara. 6th Dynasty

ventions governing such compositions with figures have been described in the introductory pages of this chapter. In portraying human beings the face, always impersonal, played no part in the movement, while gesture was always subordinated to a rhythmic cadence that gave it a priestly solemnity. In portraying animals the artist, no longer inhibited by the same theological discipline, could give free rein to his genius for observation (pl. 26).

Curiously enough, the female figures were always more supple and alive than the male; alone of all the pre-Hellenic peoples, the Egyptians succeeded in expressing the voluptuous grace of the feminine body. The execution of bas-reliefs by specialized teams of workers who carved the details once the overseer had worked out the general composition, explains many an imperfection. The colouring of the paintings was extremely sober: red or yellow ochre, a little green or blue. Following a convention established in the infancy of Egyptian art, male bodies were painted red, and female ones yellow.

The Minor Arts

The dry Egyptian soil, preserving whatever sank into it (except iron, owing to the presence of silica), has yielded thousands of specimens of domestic objects, many of them executed in luxurious style by the

*27 Gold Funerary Mask
of Tutankhamon
18th Dynasty. Cairo*

artists of the Nile valley and destined for the after-life of important personages. The lucky find of the tomb of the Pharaoh Tutankhamon (pl. 27), still intact, has yielded us royal furnishings of incredible richness. The Egyptians had good taste in finery, the men even more than the women adorning themselves with costly ornaments which often had some magic property or showed their social status. Artists excelled in the working of such jewels, using hard gems set in gold or sometimes in silver, which was both rarer and more valuable. But the purely realistic mode of thought of the Egyptians hampered them in the invention of a decorative system: they reproduced the forms of animals and human beings and even those of architecture, breast ornaments, for instance, taking the shape of a temple tower (pylon) and earrings that of the lotus-type column. The hold of architecture on all the other arts is typical of highly organized societies, in which artists work in teams under the supervision of a foreman or chief who, in his turn, has to carry out the instructions of the priesthood.

2. THE CIVILIZATIONS OF WESTERN ASIA*

While Egypt was pursuing its unchanging course, Mesopotamia, a frontierless region exposed to envious neighbours on account of its wealth, suffered many historical and ethnical vicissitudes, which now make it hard to follow the histories of successive civilizations in those parts. None the less, the creative impulse of the Sumerians was so strong that we can trace its development through the numerous feudalities and empires of which this 'land of two rivers' became the theatre.

As for the most part these peoples took little care of their burial-places, archeological evidence remains scarce. The earliest artistic works of this civilization go back to the Eneolithic period and are to be found on the site of Susa at Shush, in Elam, in Iran and at El Obeid, in Mesopotamia (fourth millennium B.C.). Under the name of 'Chaldean civilization' scholars used to mark out the 'high period' of Mesopotamia,

* I have adopted the short chronology (brought forward by about 300 years) established by Dr Contenau which agrees with that proposed for Egypt by M. Gilbert.

comprising: the 1st Ur dynasty in Sumeria (about 2700 B.C.), which left admirable specimens of the goldsmith's craft in its tombs; the Semitic dynasty set up towards 2450 B.C. at Agade by Sargon the Elder, who united the land of Sumeria with the Semitic land of Akkad (in Syria), and who also founded Babylon (about 2450 B.C.); the period of the Guti invasions (about 2250 B.C.), when the sheperd-king *(patesi)* Gudea held court at Lagash (pl. 35) – a city whose site has yielded important works now to be seen in the Louvre; the 3rd Ur dynasty, destroyed by Elamite invaders towards 2000 B.C.; the 1st Babylonian dynasty (1830–1530 B.C.), which with Hammurabi represents perhaps the peak of Chaldean civilization. Many people imagine that the Assyrian Empire (beginning of first millennium down to 612 B.C.) with its seat at Nineveh sums up Mesopotamian civilization on account of the important remains which have been found there and its reputation for cruelty; it is on the contrary no more than the expression of its decadence. Achaemenian Persia (sixth to fourth century B.C.) was the political and artistic successor of the Assyrians. In Persia, Mesopotamian art was to lose something of its origins by imbibing the Classical Greek influence. Moreover, the principles of Chaldean art nourished more or less all the peoples of Western Asia, both Semitic and Aryan. Having little gift for original artistic creation, the latter turned to it for inspiration and at the same time helped to sustain it in their periods of success (Hittites, Kassites, Kingdom of Mitanni). The radiation of Mesopotamian civilization spread very far, since towns of the third millennium, showing a distinctively Sumerian character, have been found in the Indus valley (excavations at Mohenjo-Daro and Harappa).

The Chaldean Genius

Whatever may be the attributes common to the two civilizations of the Nile and the Euphrates, of which much has been made by the historians, the genius of the Mesopotamian peoples is strikingly opposed to that of Egypt. An agricultural nation, peaceful in outlook, the Egyptians lived in close contact with the out-door world; the beneficent action of the Nile waters inspired them with an optimistic notion of natural powers, which gave them a belief in the immortality of the soul as well as a deep love of nature, both of which informed their art. Positivistic and with little bent for abstraction, they delighted in the reproduction of natural forms. Egyptian art is one of observation.

Although the flooding of the Tigris and Euphrates, which man learnt to control, gave Mesopotamia at that time a social structure not unlike that of the Nile valley, yet for reasons which perhaps have something to do with ethnical factors of which we know nothing, the races who first occupied these regions did not adopt the same naturalistic optimism.

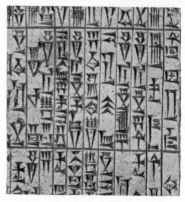

28 *Hieroglyphs. 5th Dynasty.*
Cairo

29 *Cuneiform Writing from the Code*
of Hammurabi. About 1700 B.C.
Paris

If they recognized the benefits of nature – and worshipped it in Ishtar their goddess of fertility – they considered human life to be threatened by demonic powers that had to be exorcised with the aid of magic. Little given to realism, which would have encouraged them to imitate their neighbours, they had an extraordinary gift for abstraction, which made them arithmeticans and astronomers. The genius of each of these two peoples was perfectly expressed in their technique of writing (pl. 28, 29). Egyptian hieroglyphic writing was only an abridged transcription of the forms of natural things; the belief in the identity of the 'double' obliged Egypt right through its history to cling to this cumbersome pictographic method, which in any case was primarily reserved for sacred use. On the other hand, at an early stage, in their cuneiform script the Mesopotamians worked out a syllabic system of abstract symbols, intended for everyday use, and this rapidly made their tongue the language of diplomacy in the East. Art itself became for them a 'script', that is to say not a collection of naturalistic shapes, but a system of signs. The Mesopotamian artist imposed a series of schematizations and metamorphoses on the elements he borrowed from nature, creating purely imaginary forms which, compared with the supernatural powers they evoked, had a sign-value rather than a replica-value as in Egypt.

The oldest expressions of this faculty for abstraction are the admirable prehistoric funerary vases found at Susa and Elam (pl. 30). The animal shapes on the vases from the oldest stratum, called 'Susa I', are geometrically stylized and thus achieve a most elegant decorative effect, comparable with the Rhodesian cave-paintings or with the first Greek vases (pl. 100). But the real source of this art is to be found in glyptics. For writing-purposes the Mesopotamians used cylinders covered with hollowed-out carvings which, when rolled on a slab of damp clay, gave

30 Cup in baked Clay from Susa. End of 4th millennium B.C. Paris

31 Sumerian cylinder-seal Impression (detail). End of 4th millennium B.C. Paris

an imprint in relief. These cylinder-seals, which were signets or else magic formularies, were used for all kinds of business or religious purposes. Unlike the monuments of the major arts they have survived in large numbers, and their study can teach us the whole of the evolution of the Mesopotamian aesthetic. From the beginning of Sumerian art these cylinder-seals reveal, already highly organized, the whole formal system of Mesopotamian art.

By skilfully combining animal forms suggested by the ibex, ass, lion, bison, eagle, snake and other beasts, the artists invented 'monsters', that is to say imaginary constructions (pl. 31). While Egyptian monsters remain mere composite entities of an architectural quality, those of Mesopotamia derive an astonishing unity from the nervous energy of their structure, and these imaginary creatures are extraordinarily alive. By ringing the changes on these monstrous shapes by different methods of composition – superimposing, fusing together, antithesis, symmetry and synthesis – the Sumerians created what amounts to a plastic language capable of infinite variation. This vocabulary of forms was to have important repercussions on the history of mankind, whereas Egyptian art reached a dead end and had no successors, which is quite usual with naturalistic art that can only prolong its own perfection by sterile imitation.

This play of metamorphoses on animal themes, invented by the Mesopotamians, was to prove an excellent source of training for others and to be most fertile imaginatively. Iranian, Scythian, Sarmatian, Turanian, German, Viking, Byzantine, and lastly Romanesque artists, were to delve freely into this mine of ideas, enriching it with endless original variations.

In architecture, by their use of vaulting, the Mesopotamians were to give the world a principle infinitely richer in possibilities than the flat roofing of the Egyptians. It required the mathematical mind of the Sumerian to dare project a keyed arch into space, with its radial arrangement of wedge-shaped stones, and its stability assured by nothing more than the force of gravity. From the time when it was applied along with all its implications by the Parthian and Sassanian builders, this principle was to revolutionize architecture and dominate building throughout the West, from Roman times to the Christian Middle Ages.

The Mesopotamians were thus great innovators, great initiators of artistic culture, and no doubt the Egyptians themselves were indebted to them in the initial stages. But whereas Egyptian art was ultimately to become a dead letter, the Mesopotamian plastic code was to remain a living language over many centuries.

Architecture

The scarcity of wood and stone obliged the Mesopotamians to build in baked brick – or often merely sun-dried brick – for which the silt from rivers gave them plenty of excellent material. Softened by centuries of rain these great heaps of clay now form hillocks (called *tells* by Arabs) which alone serve to break the monotony of the plains.

The most important invention of the Mesopotamians was the true vault. If like many primitive peoples they also made it with superimposed horizontal layers, each jutting out further than the one below (corbelling), which results in a 'false vault', they more frequently built it on the radial principle; tunnel-vaults bonded in this way have survived from the Sumerian period (tomb of a king in Ur). Assyrian bas-reliefs give evidence of the use of the semi-circular and elliptical cupola, but as no such domes have come down to us we cannot say whether the corbel or radial method was used.

32 Palace of Sargon II, Khorsabad. 713–707 B.C.

33, 34 Ishtar Gate, Babylon, and Bas-Relief from the Gate. 7th–6th c. B.C.

Vaulting increases the possibilities of clearance without recourse to detached struts to ease the overhead weight; but on the other hand it puts a lateral strain on its supports and thereby demands strong shoring which the Mesopotamians usually effected by the enormous thickness of their brick walls. For the stability gained from mere weight and mass in the flat-roof or lintel system, the vault substitutes a system of counter-strains which makes the structure an active organism. If the Mesopotamians did not carry this principle to its obvious conclusions, none the less they deserve credit for its invention.

Unlike the Egyptians, with their spiritual preoccupations, the Mesopotamians gave their architectural skill mainly to temporal undertakings. As well as fortresses they built grandiose palaces that were practically royal cities, as proof of the monarch's power (Sargon's palace at Khorsa-bad covers 25 acres, pl. 32). Mesopotamian architecture impresses us as monarchic and military, whereas the Egyptian was entirely religious.

The royal palaces were built on hillocks some 30 or 50 feet high which protected them from floods. They formed a rather confused collection of chambers, grouped in blocks round courtyards in the same way as Arab palaces to this day (pl. 32). First there came the reception-halls, then came the private apartments, and lastly public rooms. The palace also contained a building for worship known as the ziggurat. It consisted of seven rectangular storeys of decreasing size, painted in different colours and surmounted by a chapel which also served as an astronomical observatory. The corners of the palaces, like those of the ziggurat, were set according to the cardinal points of the compass. The rooms, though numerous, were of small dimensions – for the Mesopotamian made little use of detached pillars because he had neither wood nor stone to spare. The interiors were lit only by the door. From the outside the palace offered nothing but blank walls, often relieved by buttresses which pro-

35 *Statue of Gudea.*
About 2250 B.C. Paris

36 *Relief of Ur-Nina (detail).*
About 2400 B.C. Paris

duced some play of light and shade. The principal ornament was a monumental gateway, opening under a long vault between two towers and guarded by two winged bulls with human faces *(kheroubin)* (pl. 13) which served as propitiatory geniuses. These porchways were also used for meetings. In Assyrian and neo-Babylonian days they were decorated with composition in low-relief or painted clay (pl. 33, 34), arranged in tiered rows round the walls.

The Mesopotamians also discovered the principles of military architecture which, passing from the Arabs to the Byzantines and thence to the Crusaders, survived until the introduction of gunpowder. For the simple passive resistance achieved by the mere thickness of walls, which the Egyptians relied on, the Mesopotamians substituted active resistance. The square towers jutting into the compounds enabled connecting walls to be covered by cross-fire. They were decorated with merlons – embattled parapets between embrasures – which could shelter look-outs who fired from the space between the battlements. A series of courtyards each commanding the other increased the obstacles to be overcome by the attacker, who could never turn an overrun enclosure against the garrison. Finally the complex internal communications, with numerous narrow defiles and tortuous passages, further delayed the beseiger's progress. The Hittites improved on this system by building round keeps, better protected from the flanks and more difficult to sap, which had walls sloping at the foot so that projectiles hurled from the battlements would rebound on the enemy (fortress at Zendjirli).

The oldest works of sculpture of the first Ur dynasty *(Relief of Ur-Nina, Stele of the Vultures,* Louvre) are still close to the graphic technique of the cylinder-seals. On the bas-relief showing Ur-Nina and his family the figures, all alike, but with their names carved on their skirts to identify them, are little more than calligraphic symbols (pl. 36). Realism is to be found in the *Stele of Naram-Sin* (Louvre, Agade dynasty) on which the artist skilfully portrayed different actions in a battle. The excavations at Lagash have revealed the only great works of Chaldean sculpture in the round that are so far known to us, those depicting the shepherd-king Gudea (pl. 35). Carved in diorite and carefully polished, works such as this reach a degree of perfection, a synthesis which must have been the result of a long evolution of the stages of which nothing is yet known. The compactness of the statue concentrated within itself and its muscular vigour give an impression of power never achieved by the sculptures of the Old Kingdom in Egypt, in whose works the expression of energy was tempered by serenity and spiritual detachement. Scarcely emerging from the block of stone of which it was made, the Sumerian statue retains all the crude power of rock; it is a menhir in human form. This menhir quality is even more noticeable and was no doubt intended, in the famous *Code of Hammurabi* (Louvre, 1st Babylonian dynasty) in which we can also see writing mixed with sculpture as in certain statues of Gudea (pl. 16, 29).

37 Relief at Carchemish. Hittite

The Hittite bas-reliefs (at the sites at Boghaz-Keui and Carchemish, pl. 37) are transitional between Chaldean and Assyrian art. Long series of figures are shown in low-relief on the palace-walls of the Assyrian kings, and displayed at the foot of the wall and not as friezes at the top. This arrangement seems to have first occured to the Mitannites who in Upper Mesopotamia had unlimited supplies of rock, so scarce in Chaldea. The abundance of this material (a gypsum-like alabaster, unsuitable for building but soft and very easy to shape) allowed the Assyrians full scope for bas-reliefs, as we see from the excavations on the site at Nineveh. Reliefs from the Palaces of Ashurnasirpal (883 B.C. –859 B.C.) and Sennacherib (705 B.C.–681 B.C.) can be seen in the British Museum in London, and from the Palace of Assurbanipal at Khorsabad, in the Louvre. The Assyrian king's custom of abandoning their predecessor's palace and building one of their own favoured the development of sculpture. It has been calculated that if they were placed end to end, the panels discovered at Assurbanipal's palace at Khorsabad would stretch for 1¼ miles (p. 38).

The great Assyrian creations are, in historic times, the first examples of artistic undertakings of a purely monarchical character, in other words exclusively devoted to the glorification of a ruler. The art of the Egyptian pharaohs, even at the time of the Rameses, was always conditioned by a religious outlook. The Assyrian kings made images neither for temples nor for tombs, but for their own palaces in the way that Louis XIV was to do in modern times. Those long, monotonous processions in which the king made such a frequent appearance, were intended to stress the wealth, warlike qualities, hunting prowess and cruelty of the sovereigns who for centuries imposed their reign of terror over all Western Asia,

38 Army of Assurbanipal (669–626 B.C.) on the March. London

39 Relief from Agar Quf. 7th c. B.C. Bagdad

and whose refinements of torture were surpassed only by the civilizations of the Far East. Technically these bas-reliefs, whose very number suggests that they must have been hastily carried out, show a profound decadence especially in the portrayal of the human figure. They reduced this to a play of arbitrary forms with none of the power and noble significance of the Egyptian canon. The limbs are badly articulated, the gestures mechanical and lacking in truth, the faces set like masks. The sculptors always sacrificed life to their cherished notion of superhuman strength, while their instinct for abstraction led them to treat details (beards, curling hair, the folds of clothing, jewels) as decorative themes elaborated for their own sake. All these elements were assembled without being brought into harmony with the main composition, which makes the whole thing a kind of puzzle. Here we see in embryo all the characteristics of the hieratic style so typical of the Asiatic monarchies, which were later adopted in Byzantine art. The principles of the composition of animated scenes followed the conventions described at the beginning of this chapter; it is to be noted, however, that in Assurbanipal's time a certain sense of perspective began to emerge. The different features of the composition were sometimes arranged in depth, each hiding something of the other; but this progress towards optical truth remained unusual and was not part of general practice.

The real distinction of Assyrian art was in the representation of animals. The Assyrians' innate love of hunting and cruelty (being a people who by comparison with the Sumerians show a relapse into barbarism) helped them to understand the secret workings of animal psychology, much as primitive man had done. The intense truthfulness to life of their animal figures contrasts with the conventional style in which they portrayed human beings (pl. 39). All the expressions of the hunted animal, as it flees or stands at bay or roars with pain under the arrow or spear, were rendered by Assyrian sculptors with a savage vitality unknown to the Egyptians. The peaceful, pastoral Egyptians were too used to the company of domestic animals, which they painted and sculpted so admirably, to have as much understanding of the ways of wild beasts.

The Art of Achaemenian Persia

Political successors to the pharaohs and to the kings of Nineveh and Babylon, the Achaemenian dynasties (539 B.C.–331 B.C.) inherited a mixed tradition. These rulers of the greatest empire of antiquity prior to Rome built castles in keeping with their wealth, such as those at Parsargadae (Cyrus, 539 B.C.–529 B.C.), at Persepolis (Darius, 521 B.C. –486 B.C., and Xerxes, 486 B.C.–465 B.C.), and at Susa, (Artaxerxes II, 404 B.C.–358 B.C.). For the first time in Asia, these palaces were built

40 *Capital from Artaxerxes II's Palace, Susa. Early 4th c. B.C. Paris*

41 *Stirrup Jar. Late Minoan I*

of stone, though brick was used with it. They consist of an extraordinary number of rooms all built on a colossal stone foundation, the finest rooms being called *apadanas* or throne-rooms, in the hypostyle manner borrowed from Egypt. The *adapana* of Artaxerxes II at Susa, which covered nearly 8,375 square feet, rested on 36 columns $63^{1}/_{4}$ feet in height. These columns were in the form of a fluted shaft topped with a double series of scrolls, bearing a capital made of two bulls back to back, borrowed from Assyrian art (pl. 40). Other forms such as palm-shaped cornices were taken from Egypt. The Achaemenian buildings were all for secular purposes: the highly spiritual character of the Mazdean or Mazdakite religion forbade the use of temples and considered them as pagan. The fire-cult was celebrated on simple open-air altars *(pyrea)*. The 'kings of king's' also had luxurious tombs built in their honour, some of them being hollowed into rock after the manner of the Egyptian *hypogea* (tombs at Persepolis and Naqsh-i-Rustam).

The figurative and decorative art of the Persians evolves directly from Assyrian art, of which it retains all the monarchical character, much modified however by an element of placidity in keeping with the spirit of Persian civilization, which was one of the most humane of ancient times. At Persepolis and Susa we find the same long rows of soldiers and subject peoples as in Nineveh. The Persians made bas-reliefs in stone or enamelled terra-cotta (friezes from the palace at Susa, in the Louvre, pl. 133) which the neo-Babylonian Empire (625 B.C.–539 B.C.) had already used with great effect. Here the realistic portrayal of animals begins to disappear: the winged bulls and Achaemenian gryphons assume more heraldic, emblematic characteristics. The style of these sculptures has lost the barbarous strength of Assyrian works, and, already influenced by the Greek plastic arts, tends towards a decorative elegance.

3. THE AEGEAN CIVILIZATIONS

Historical Background

We call those civilizations 'Aegean' which from about 3000 B.C. to the twelfth century B.C. flourished on the shores of the Aegean, in the island of Cyprus, the Cyclades, Crete and the Peloponnese, where the Achaeans, after conquering Crete, continued its tradition for some time. This civilization was based essentially on the industry and commerce of metallurgy, and the Aegean invaders, who came from Asia Minor, brought copper with them from about 3000 B.C. and by about 2300 managed to perfect its use by alloying it with tin, thereby producing bronze. While the Cycladic islanders were beginning to experiment with sculpting in marble, the Cretans, who began to rule the seas from quite an early date, created a highly skilled civilization comparable with those of the same period in Egypt and Mesopotamia, but one which had an extraordinarily modern flavour; for this nation of seafarers, merchants and industrialists seems to have been singularly free from that obsession with deity which governed every thought and act of the Egyptians and Mesopotamians.

Minoan Art

The Minoan civilization, so named by Sir Arthur Evans who discovered it in Crete, flourished on that island from roughly the end of the fourth millennium till 1400 B.C. It was destroyed by the Achaeans, who came from Argolis (Peloponnesus), people of Indo-European stock who inherited the Aegean love of the sea and for a short time only (1400 B.C. –1200 B.C.) imposed themselves on the semi-barbarous 'Mycenaean' civilization, which the German Schliemann discovered in the Peloponnese.

As with most of the peoples of the Bronze Age, the Cretans made few images of the gods – from which sculpture draws its chief inspiration – and busied themselves mainly with industrial products.

Ceramics and metal-work were the principal occupations in Crete. The Cretans excelled in the working of precious metals as well as bronze, and exported silverwork, gems, gold, weapons, bronze ingots, to Asia Minor, Egypt, Peloponnesus (see the gold vessel found at Vaphio, south of Sparta, pl. 42), and also to the West. With them, ceramics had none of the crude industrial character it had with the other Bronze Age peoples (Hissarlik pottery); the prestige of metal was so great that potters began by imitating bronze vessels, giving the pots slim or gracefully curved shapes and covering them with a dark glaze. Artists prized elegance of

42 Gold Cup from Vaphio. 1580–1450 B.C. Athens

contour and relied on painting for decorative purposes (2400 B.C.–2200 B.C.). The vases of the Kamares style (about 1800 B.C.–1700 B.C.) bear geometrical patterns. Among the finest are the vases of the Middle Minoan III period (1700 B.C.–1580 B.C.) and those of the Late Minoan I (1580 B.C.–1450 B.C., pl. 41) in which realistic motifs are used, taken from floral or marine forms (cuttle-fish, octopus, coral, nautilus, sea-urchin, anemone, actinia); but the geometrical impulse took over again in the Palace style (Late Minoan II, 1450 B.C.–1400 B.C.).

The art of painting, probably begun on terra-cotta, found free expression in the frescoes adorning Cretan palaces. The imagery is borrowed from everyday life (dancing, bull-fighting), from nature (dolphins, flying-fish, flowers) and from more conventional designs (double-spiral, pl. 43). The bull, which left evidence of its importance in the Greek legend of the Minotaur, figures very frequently. The style is one of great ease, full of lively realism. Inspired by Egyptian and Sumerian art it is none the less more subtle and worldly; its jovial expressionism, its humorous, worldly realism foreshadow the hedonism of the Greeks, who were to deliver mankind from its fear of supernatural powers.

Cretan art has left no large-scale sculpture. The only works in the round, which are well-executed, are earthenware figurines (snake-goddesses) and figures in bronze or carved in hard stones. These were all for domestic decoration.

After the year 2000 B.C. the Minoans built great towns and palaces (Knossos, Phaestos, Hagia Triada, Mallia) where a very carefully planned system of sewers and canals and the size of store-rooms and cellars show an awareness of town-planning problems. The Minoan palace, composed of suits of rooms grouped round inner courts, was no doubt influenced by Mesopotamian palaces. The complexity of the lay-out of the chambers was perhaps responsible for the Greek myth of the labyrinth. These buildings were made of stone and wood, while numerous

43 Fresco from the Palace of Tiryns. 1400–1200 B.C. Athens

44 Lion Gate, Mycenae. 1400–1200 B.C.

isolated supports were used. The column appeared about 2000 B.C., with its shaft narrower at the base than at the top. The cushion-capital is thought to be a forerunner of the Doric style.

Mycenaean Art

The Achaeans who destroyed Cretan civilization inherited its might, but unlike the Minoans these hardy pirates were of a quarrelsome and war-like temperament, as Homer reminds us in the *Iliad*. Their warlike

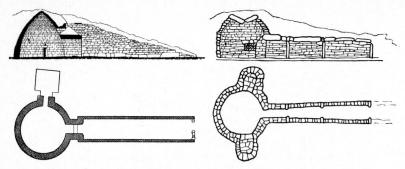

45 *Treasury of Atreus, Mycenae*　　46 *Neolithic Grave, Portugal*

instinct led to the construction of the strongholds at Mycenae and Tiryns (pl. 44). Owing to their colossal stonework, made of irregular blocks in what the Greeks called the 'Cyclopean' style, these buildings belong even more to megalithic architecture than they do to the Cretan Palace style, although their masonry is more regular. Their tombs (Treasury of Atreus at Mycenae, pl. 45, and the Tomb of Orchomenus), like certain Celtic or Celto-Iberian burial-places (Tomb of Alcalar, Portugal, pl. 46), consist of a covered passage leading to a burial chamber, the latter being hut-like in shape and topped with a sort of cupola made of slabs superimposed corbel-wise.

The decorative art of the Achaeans, so far as we can see from what has survived, appears to have been inspired by the Cretan, of which it is a degenerate form. Like the Cretans they knew the crafts of metal-work and had a great taste for silver and gold trinkets.

4. THE ART OF THE NOMADS

Central Asia, an immense reservoir of human energy, has never ceased pouring hordes of nomads into Euro-Asia. They were always ready to swoop like birds of prey on the pastoral settlers who built up the great historical civilizations of China and South-West Asia. These mounted barbarians had a vast territory to overrun in every direction. In the wide strip of the steppes from Budapest to Mongolia every race was represented with all its tribes: in the eastern steppes there were the Turco-Mongols (Ordos, Avars, Huns, Turks), while the western steppes were inhabited by peoples of Indo-European stock (Scythians and Sarmatians in central Russia, Satians [Saces] and Sogdians in Turkestan). But whatever their origins, their similar way of life imposed similar characteristics both in space and time on their chosen forms of artistic expression. As their nomadic habits restricted them to making small

47 Gilded bronze Plaque. Scythian

chattels, such as carpets (almost all of which have disappeared), gold ornaments and trinkets (buckles, sword-hilts, brooches, discs and badges for sword-belts) or harnessings for chariots and horses, they perpetuated the customs of the Bronze Age. As with the Magdalenian hunters, the animal represented the primordial power of nature for these tribes of hunters and shepherds: they gave something of the living suppleness of the animal to their ornamentation, which was all composed of curves and counter-curves to which the malleability of metals, whether gold, silver or bronze, readily lent itself. However, if their imagination was capable of creating an original style, their ornamental and zoomorphic art derives from the more civilized arts of Mesopotamia. It was by way of Iran – the great historic point of focus and communication between South-West Asia and the steppes, and melting-pot for so many races – that the tribes of the steppes came to know the ornamental style of the Sumerians and Elamites.

48 Plaques of cloisonné Gold-Work from the Grave of a Saxon Chieftain, Sutton Hoo. About A.D. 650. London

*49 Bronze funerary
Statuette. Luristan. Paris*

*50 Wooden Staff from the Death-
Ship of Oseberg (detail).
About A.D. 850: Oslo*

Excavations in the Luristan mountains, which form the frontier between Mesopotamia and Persia, have done much to enable us to understand how this intricate compounding of forms came about, by revealing
to us the art of the earliest Iranian settlers who had formed communities
by the eleventh century B.C. After their nomadic phase they still retained
their skill in the arts of metalwork; in their standards and their trappings
for harness they transposed into bronze with wonderful elegance the
monstrous, intertwined heraldic forms of the Chaldean cylinders
(pl. 49). Among these tribes of the steppes (Ordos, Huns, Scythians),
in daily contact with animal life, the zoomorphic style lost its monstrous
character and showed a renewal of realism, though this was soon affected
by the passion for ornament which filled the barbarians with a longing
for fantasy, their nomadic way of life luring their imagination into a
perpetual, onward flux.

It is their tombs which have revealed this art of the steppes. Graves
were covered by mounds called *kurgans,* in which the tribal chiefs were
buried with their wives, servants, horses, chariots and jewels in the same
way as in the oldest Ur dynasties, which they were no doubt imitating.
These have been examined especially in the steppes of Siberia and
southern Russia, which were inhabited by the Scythians some centuries
before the Christian era. The Scythians created a dramatic art in which
animals are entwined together in furious combat, such violent themes
resulting in fine modulations of pattern (pl. 47).

While Scythian art became debased by its contact with the Greek
goldsmiths of the Black Sea region, a new zoomorphic art began to appear
in Central Asia: that of the Sarmatians, which spread as far as China
in the Han period (202 B.C.–A.D. 265) and which appeared in graves

in south Russia in the Christian era. Sarmatian art spread to other hordes which were to invade the West, notably the Germans, Huns, Goths and Franks. Among these latter races this form of art tended to become increasingly aniconic (imageless) and abstract, losing sight of the animal realism of its origins. They favoured interlaced patterns, a kind of indecipherable ornamental knot, as well as cloisonné work in gold, the setting of glass beads or gems (garnets, sapphires, emeralds) in gold, and inserting gold filigree into another metal (known as damaskeening). They might well have been influenced by the fine gold craftsmanship of the Sassanians or Sassanids, who came to Persia after the Seleucids (A.D. 227–641). However, the jewelry of the Ordos and Scythians seems to suggest that the steppe tribes knew this technique earlier. These Nordic barbarians made much use of an ornamental system derived from the circular motif (wheels, helixes, spirals, roses, six-petalled marguerites, swastikas) which the Sumerians had invented. This abstract art, which consists of handling any living form as a purely ornamental motif, was to flourish once more among the Scandinavian Vikings until the ninth century A.D. (Death-ship of Oseberg, about A.D. 850, pl. 50). It also gave vitality to the first artistic productions of the Christianized West – those of the Franks, Merovingians and Saxons (pl. 48) and more especially the Irish monks of the seventh and eighth centuries (pl. 162). It was one of the sources of Romanesque art, and, as such, of fundamental importance in the advance of the arts in the Western world.

5. THE PRE-COLUMBIAN CIVILIZATIONS

The Pre-Columbian Mentality

The cultures which flourished on the American shores of the Pacific ocean before the European conquest were historically contemporary with our own Christian era, and yet even more than the older civilizations of Egypt and Mesopotamia they remained deeply enslaved to the primitive mentality. In no other part of the world did any civilized race remain longer at the mercy of terrifying supernatural powers; nowhere did man have a more tragic awareness of his fragility in a hostile world. He imagined he was on earth only to pay blood-tribute to deities lusting for death and murder, and the sun itself had to be fed its daily ration of human blood in order to continue on its course. The terrors of the Millennium left a memorable scar on our own civilization, so that we can only imagine what the psychology of such a race as the Aztecs, who were plunged every fifty-two years into despair lest the world come to an end, must have been. The ritual sacrifice of young women, children or captured enemies – for warfare often had no other purpose than to

51 Frieze of Plumed Serpents from the Temple of Xochicalco. Aztec

replenish the altars – has left the Aztec civilization with a gruesome reputation.

Although they were more humane, the civilizations of Peru and Bolivia also practised, though with a little more restraint, similar liturgical sacrifices. But no other evolved civilization made death the very principle of a cosmological, magical or religious system. As though the survival of the species in a terrifying universe could only be ensured by the sacrifice of an enormous number of its members! Those who were privileged to live had themselves to pay the horrible levy, being obliged for instance to make blood gush from their ears, or to draw a string covered with thorns through a hole pierced in their own tongue.

The works of the Peruvians are certainly imbued with some humane spirit, but this was never the case with the images made in Central America. The gods represented by the Maya, the Toltecs and Aztecs are all monsters, while the men are in the image of their gods. No art has ever symbolized so dynamically the inhumanity of a hostile world, no race ever erected such figures as these of the demoniacal powers that primitive man imagined to govern the world.

The strange formal structure of these pre-Columbian works – whose only parallel is to be found in old Chinese bronzes – is made up of a jumble of features all imbricated onto each other without the slightest continuity (pl. 51). The introduction of some unifying principle, of some ordered sequence in the chaos of appearances is the very hall-mark of rational thought, which has the capacity of projecting intellectual, guiding lines into the manifold discords of the world. The Egyptians and Sumerians had this gift, which expressed itself in their art through the still entirely intuitive conception – of which the Greeks became fully aware – of the unifying principles that govern the various elements of which a work is composed, by subjecting it to the laws of rhythm, cadence and proportion. In an Egyptian composition all the gestures are interrelated with the continuity of an arabesque (pl. 26). Sharp breaks

52 *Temple called 'The Castle', Chichen Itza. Maya*

constantly disturb the unity of Aztec reliefs which have a chaos of forms taken from all the kingdoms of nature, the only rhythm relating them to one another being something like what is found in savage dances consisting of a series of frenzied shudders. It is a kind of seismic rhythm, crude energy in action, uncontrolled by any intellectual power.

These races are the only ones to have knowingly given artistic expression to the mentality of primitive man, hurled into a universe whose powers he knew not how to harness, through works which for grandeur and beauty invite comparison with those of Sumeria and Egypt. They show us the highest level of civilization that is attainable by mankind without the aid of reason, without that marvellous instrument of the mind, which in different ways made possible the scientific and philosophical awakening of India, China and the Mediterranean peoples. They were also retarded perhaps by their isolation on a continent cut off from the great centres of the world's civilizations. Yet with no more than the most rudimentary tools, the pre-Columbians sought and contrived to overcome by energy alone a universe that appeared more hostile to man there than in any other part of the globe.

Historical Background

The two empires of the Aztecs and Incas, which dominated the greater part of civilized America at the time when the Spaniards arrived there, succeeded for a long time in concealing the rich complexity of the civilizations they had enslaved. In fact these two empires were both agents of political unification (like the Roman Empire) which were creative mainly at the material level, but which in spiritual matters depended on those they had conquered.

Pre-Columbian America may be divided into two main spheres of influence: Central America, and the Pacific side of South America.

Central America comprises the present territories of Mexico and the Republics of Honduras and Guatemala. The numerous cultures that flourished in this region had several elements in common, notably the use of the terraced pyramid as a base for the sanctuary; the ritual game of *pelota;* the frequency of human sacrifice; the use of hieroglyphic writing; the calendar based on eighteen months of twenty days, making cycles of fifty-two years. The two most creative races of this region were the Toltecs and the Maya. The birthplace of the Maya, who appear to have reached the higher degree of culture, was in Honduras and Guatemala, where in the early centuries of our era they built numerous townships which are now being unearthed in the forest by archaeologists (Uaxactum, Palenque, Quirigua, Copan). After a time of decadence the Maya Empire revived towards the end of the tenth century A.D. in the Mexican peninsula of Yucatan, and its greatest period lasted for two hundred years (987–1191, cities of Uxmal, Mazapan, Chichen Itza, Kabah, etc.). The empire fell owing to civil war; in the eleventh and twelfth centuries the neighbouring Toltecs seized Chichen Itza and created a mixed art, Maya-Toltec, which shows a great profusion of forms.

The high plateau of Mexico was a very active centre of civilization right from early times. Several peoples settled on the shores of Lake Texcoco, now dried up, the site of Mexico City. Several centuries before our era one of these tribes founded the city of Teotihuacan, which fell into decay in the tenth century A.D., about the time when the invading Toltecs built the city of Tula. The Toltecs paid particular honour to the god Quetzalcoatl, the green-plumed serpent, who was god of the wind then later god of the arts and of civilization (pl. 51). It is not certain at what date (perhaps the thirteenth century) the Aztecs, coming from the north, settled on the central plateau; the date when Mexico City (Tenochtitlan) was built is variously put at 1325 or 1370. Their principal deity was the cruel god of war, Huitzilopochtli, whose thirst for human blood surpassed all others'.

On the two ocean slopes of Central America lived satellite peoples of the Toltecs, Maya and Aztecs: on the Atlantic shore were the Zapotecs (city of Monte Alban) and Mixtecs (city of Mitla, founded in the fifteenth century), while on the Gulf of Mexico were the Totonacs (sites of Tajin, Cempoala, between sixth and twelfth centuries).

The cultures of South America are less known owing to the absence of written evidence, since the peoples there had no system of writing. They have been revealed mainly by burial-places containing excellent pottery and utensils. Their chronology is still obscure. It is usual to distinguish between the pre-Inca and Inca cultures. The Andean plateau (Peru and Bolivia) was the birthplace of American metallurgy, gold, silver, copper, then bronze. The Aymara built the gigantic monuments of Tiahuanaco to the south of Lake Titicaca. On the Peruvian coast, several peoples succeeded each other in an order which is difficult to establish chronologically: in the north, the Chimu (site of Chanchan); in the centre the builders of the city of Pachacamac near Lima; in the south, those who modelled the fine works in terra-cotta since discovered on the sites of Ica and Nazca. In the twelfth century the Kichua appeared, sunworshippers who established, over different races occupying a region over 2,500 miles long, a vast empire with a very advanced material civilization: the empire of the Incas which was to be destroyed by the Spaniards.

Architecture and Sculpture

The architecture of the pre-Columbian peoples has proportions which strive after great monumental effects, but its range of expression is limited by the absence of the vault and the rarity of the disengaged pillar. The tribes of Central America (Aztecs, Toltecs, Maya, Zapotecs) erected their monuments on artificial terraced mounds, and, for religious purposes, they built high pyramids, step-wise with tiled facings (pl. 52). The summit was reached by way of four steep staircases, giving access to the sanctuary containing the idol and the sacrificial altar. These monuments were often on a colossal scale: the Pyramid of the Sun at Teotihuacan still measures 212 feet in height and covers an area of 53,820 square yards, with a frontage of 700 feet. The largest of these remains yet found, the Pyramid of Quetzalcoatl at Cholula, 1,463 feet

53 Gateway into the Palace of Labna. Maya

54 Stele of Peidras Negras, Guatemala. Maya

wide, has a far greater volume than the Pyramid of Cheops in Egypt. The architects who built the palaces show a preference for halls, long rather than wide, so as to limit the span of beams and slabs for roofing. The most highly developed and richest architecture was that of the Maya, who were the only ones who dared build corbelled 'vaults' (pl. 53) and made frequent use of the detached support.

The Andean region has kept intact a much larger number of civil and military buildings. The monuments of the Peruvian coast, built in adobe (dried clay), have left very few remains (Chanchan). On the plateau, on the contrary, are to be found enormous works dating from the pre-Incan and Incan periods: paved roads, huge walls crossing the mountains, strongholds, palaces and temples. The city of Cuzco (in Peru) stands to this day on the foundations of the Inca city. The pre-Incas made free use of colossal monoliths (Gate of the Sun, Tihuanaco). Both polyhedral and regular stonework was so carefully assembled that today it is impossible to insert a pin between the interstices. The stones were often bound with copper cramps.

Sculpture was rare with the Peruvians, but the Central Americans made considerable use of it both in isolated carvings and for facing walls. The figures are ferocious, composite monsters, of which the best known is Quetzalcoatl, the plumed serpent (pl. 51). In the sunken reliefs they are accompanied by a background of geometrical patterns. The finest school of monumental sculpture was that of the Maya (pl. 54). Whereas the Toltecs and Aztecs followed the ideographic conventions common to primitive peoples, only the Maya came anywhere near optical truth in their construction of the human figure; the rhythmical beauty of their works sometimes recalls Greek art.

The Minor Arts

The pre-Columbian peoples excelled in the minor arts such as textiles, the working of hard stones and precious metals, which they lavished on their monuments (Temple of the Sun at Cusco), and especially ceramics (pl. 55, 56). The finest Central American ceramics are the burial urns of the Zapotecs, with their statuesque lines and flamboyant ornamentation,

55 *Chimu Vase from Peru.
Paris*

56 *Nazca Vase from Peru.
Paris*

and the smiling heads of the Totonacs; these works witness the ascendancy of sculpture over the other arts, which is normal in an artistic society governed by its feeling for the monumental. The Peruvian potters, on the other hand, sought curves better adapted to the needs of the vase, of which numerous specimens have been preserved undamaged in tombs. In polychromatic tones, on red or black slip, the Ica pots are adorned with a geometrical pattern, and those of Nazca with a demoniacal symbolism not unlike that of Central America. The anthropomorphic Chimu pottery perfectly adapts realistic observation to the curve of the vase, and their works are the only human representations to be found in the Americas. The Chimu potters, and above all those who made the earlier Chimu or Mochica pots, with their red foundation, left some admirable portraits. The later Chimu pots, with their black ground, show a withering of realistic inspiration.

6. THE ARTS OF THE 'UNCIVILIZED' PEOPLES

In the tropical zones, far removed from the great centres of civilization, peoples of negroid race who go about naked under the hot sun, pursuing a primitive way of life, still give the work of art the sacred and magical meaning that it had in earliest times. These peoples form two great cultural groups, dispersed across Africa and in the chain of islands scattered across the Pacific, from Australia to Madagascar and Easter Island.

Though these races have no known historical relationship, they hold in common an aesthetic notion which exalts the painted or sculpted form into a revelation from the beyond, a sign fraught with supernatural powers. This is true not only in the case of ancestral images, fetishes and totems evoking beneficent spirits and evil demons, or the masks used for ritual dances and ceremonies, but also in the case of objects of everyday use whose stylized patterns have symbolic value (for instance, figureheads on Polynesian canoes); for primitive man lives at all times in contact with the beyond. The attitude of the negroid or Oceanic artist is thus anti-realistic. When he evokes the form of a bird, a crocodile or a human being, he is pursuing an idea, not an image, accentuating some traits, stylizing the lines and volumes; the visual truth of the object is profoundly affected by his sense of magic and mystery. Contrary to the practice of primitive or barbarian peoples of the white race, in negro and Oceanic art the human figure plays a preponderant role because of the ancestor-worship they have in common. The mask is the essential object of these civilizations: the wearing of the mask produces a veritable transfer of personality in the man who assumes it. In funeral or ritual ceremonies, which are masked dances, the primitive man ensures the passing-over of the deceased ancestor, or else possesses himself of his virtues.

This art is also characterized by having no history. Objects collected by explorers before the contact of modern civilization caused rapid decay in native cultures, are objects in actual use whose origins have long been forgotten. Only some parts of Africa are able to provide any historical perspective. The African continent, cut off like an island, seems to have had no communication worth mentioning with the Mediterranean civilizations or with those of Asia, except in the North, which was conquered by Islam, and in Egypt, where a highly skilled civilization developed, and in Abyssinia, which, converted to Christianity, pursues to this day the primitive Christian art from Egypt, known as

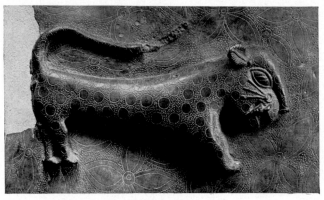

57 Bronze Plaque from Benin. 16th c. A.D. Paris

58 Bark Painting of Fish
from New Guinea. Paris

59 Wooden Statuette from the
Belgian Congo. Tervueren

Coptic art. Cave-paintings whose traditions go back perhaps to a period contemporary with those of France and Spain have been discovered in the north-west Sahara and in Rhodesia. In the latter region ruins of towns have been discovered, such as Zimbabwe, built apparently by the Bantu, probably in about the fifteenth century. Finally, the ancient Kingdom of Benin, on the Ivory Coast, whose zenith seems to have been in the sixteenth and seventeenth centuries, produced – no doubt under certain Mediterranean influences – admirable anthropomorphic and zoomorphic objects in bronze and ivory (pl. 57). The most productive negro artistic civilizations at present are to be found in Central Africa, in the Sudan, on the Guinea Coast and in the Congo region. African art, which devoted itself chiefly to wood-carving, is full of grandiose and tragic meaning which shows itself in a harsh and dry stylization, giving priority to the straight line over the curve, and the whittling-down of the statue into clear-cut geometrical volumes (pl. 59). It is these characteristics which appealed to the Fauve and Cubist painters of our own period.

Oceania has produced works which are more suggestive, less element-ary and have a more mystical and poetical meaning. The Oceanic native has a particular bent for whorls of curves and spirals (pl 60) and on this basis makes very subtle formal patterns, whereas the forms of African art are always dramatically isolated from each other. These patterns are, incidentally, not unrelated to those of pre-Columbian art. The stylistic interpretation of the Oceanic artist is even farther from nature than that of the African. He is a sculptor, but he also has the painter's temperament, which expresses itself in paintings on bark (pl. 58) and

60 Carving for the Entrance to a House from New Guinea

in the colourings of masks and statues. The art of the Pacific offers great variety from island to island. The finest works are to be found in Melanesia, New Caledonia, the Solomon Islands, the New Hebrides, New Zealand and the Marquesas. Easter Island, the last link in the chain of islands stretching towards America, has some five hundred monolithic statues of unknown origin, in the human image.

The Red Indians of North America show no signs of the same artistic gifts as the peoples of the same race in the centre and South of the continent. In the Rio Grande, in New Mexico, the Pueblos culture is a derivative and provincial centre of the aristocratic civilizations of Central America. These peoples have left towns built in stone on a semi-circular plan, sheltered under rocks or at the foot of cliffs. Farther to the north the Indians have remained in the nomad state, and they are painters rather than sculptors, making coloured patterns in feathers or paint.

In South America, in the upper Amazon as well as on the Atlantic coast, primitive peoples carried on a degenerate form of pre-Columbian art, sometimes mingled with influences that appear to have come directly, across the chain of islands, from Polynesian art.

III. THE CLASSICAL CIVILIZATIONS OF THE MEDITERRANEAN

The Egyptian, Mesopotamian and Aegaean civilizations are the work of the Semitic and Asiatic peoples established in the Mediteranean basin or in Western Asia long before 3000 B.C. The Indo-Europeans who gradually infiltrated into the Mediterranean, mainly after 2000 B.C., spent a long period as parasites of the civilizations they came to overthrow. For over ten centuries neither the Mitannites, the Kassites nor the Hittites made anything really original. The Achaeans battened on the cultural remnants of the Cretans and later the Persians, on whom fell the mantle of the Assyrians, made little more than a pale imitation of the royal art of Nineveh.

However, in the course of that protohistorical phase of the Aryan peoples, a slow assimilation was being accomplished, a blending of elements that was to produce the miracle of Greece. Whether they were pushed back by the Dorian invasion, which was the last wave of Aryan migration to penetrate Greece proper towards the year 1200, or whether in the preceding centuries they had fled from the misery caused in their own cities by social crises of their own making, whether they came from the North, or rather, as some now think, from the Middle East, the Hellenes, who almost immediately proved to have great talent for trading, gradually established colonial centres in both the Eastern and Western Mediterranean and as far north as the Hellespont. They settled more especially in Asia Minor where they founded the numerous cities of Ionia which, succeeding to the Aegaean 'thalassocracy' or maritime state, gradually supplanted the Phoenicians' hegemony of the seas and by way of reaction excited the rivalry of the mother cities, Athens and Corinth.

Compared with the ancient great powers, now in ruin, of Egypt and Mesopotamia, or with the Iranian empires of the Medes and after them the Persians who took up all their traditions, the Hellenes who were produced by the ferment of successive migrations represented all the youthful energies of the universe in the seventh and sixth centuries B.C. In them the Aryan genius emerged from its long obscurity, to accomplish one of the most vital revolutions of mankind and lay the foundations of the modern world.

The Greeks broke with the magical bond which had made man, ever since his origins, a power inseparable from the world about him. However mature they were, an Egyptian or Mesopotamian still had the feeling of being no more than a cog in the immense mechanism of the cosmos, so that man's intelligence, the privilege of his species, could do no more than propitiate the play of occult forces by bringing some divine

61 Assurbanipal hunting Lions. 7th c. B.C. London

power into action. In order to rise above nature, man has to identify himself with god; the pharaoh assured life and after-life to his subjects by uniting the human and divine in his own person.

We shall never be able to fathom the tremendous effort human genius had to make to upset a scheme of things based on traditions thousands of years old, in order to stand alone, aware of its new-found strength, face to face with the universe. From then on man no longer tended towards self-identification with the spirit of nature, but tried to transcend it by means of reason, so that he could draw knowledge and power from its laws. The creative act, carried out by primitive man only when he believed himself possessed by some demiurge, was now to become pure creativity. Man stopped being the creature of God, and began to create God in his own image. The Greek Pantheon brought under its roof all the personifications of the faculties and attributes of the human soul: intelligence (Athena), sensibility (Aphrodite), the aggressive instinct (Ares), the genius of trade (Hermes), the creative gift (Apollo), lyric power (Dionysus); even the cruder instincts, which subconsciously still link man with the beasts, found an idealized image among the demigods. Everywhere man began to project his own dimensions into a world suddenly reduced to a new scale. Order was imposed on chaos, for human intellect thought it could discover some law of harmony in the world, some pre-established system. Foreshadowing the spirit of modern discoveries, Pythagoras saw the essence of things in a mechanics which reduced all phenomena to the norm of numbers.

Man's freedom from those shackles which had enslaved him to the laws of the universe broke out somewhat naïvely in archaic statues, evoking a psychological expression which was hitherto unknown to the art of mankind – the smile, a symbol of euphoria, the 'hieroglyph of

68

62 Chariot Race. Ionic Relief. End of 6th c. B.C. Istanbul

happiness' as it has been called, which expresses the joy of pure creation and of free discovery (pl. 71, 72).

The magic touch now gave way to rational knowledge, but the latter had not yet felt that austere renunciation which is characteristic of modern times. The Greek did not reject the supernatural but transposed it into images and mythology. There is as much difference between mystery and myth as between night and day. Not that myths entirely stopped being objects of belief (though for enlightened minds this was to be the case, and the gods of Olympus quickly became the divinities of fable); but such belief was no longer placed in blind powers, holding sway over the universe, but rather in concepts. Primitive religions were born of fear. Greek religion, or rather mythology, sprang from the union of reason with poetry which is perhaps the very essence of the Greek miracle. It was as much through the songs of poets as through theological speculation that the confused legends of primitive times gradually syncretized into cycles of anthropomorphic myths. Eager to pour the world's every aspect into the mould of ideas, the Greek imagination personified everything, the most abstract concepts as well as nature's material forms, all the data of the mind, of history and natural philosophy; and, what is more, all these allegories were given a human face. The Greeks thought of everything either as concepts or figures. Any study of man's historical evolution will show that there is not a human attitude, whether of the senses or intellect, whether personal or social, that did not find its first representation in some Greek myth. The universe crystallized itself for them in shapes, in a vast system of anthropomorphic images which became an endless source of speculation for the plastic arts, poetry and drama.

The artists of that civilization saw before them an immense field of activity unknown to the Mesopotamians and which the Egyptians had scarcely touched: the discovery of man. The human figure was about to

Evolution of the Athlete in Sculpture

63 *Mycerinus. Egyptian, 4th Dynasty. Boston*

64 *Athlete (by Polymedes of Argos).*
1st half of 6th c. B.C. Delphi

65 *Apollo from Tenea. 1st half of 6th c. B.C.*
Munich

66 *Apollo. End of 6th c. Athens*

dethrone the animal from the sway it had held so long over the imagination and works of the first civilizations. Conscious of his physical weakness, man had at first worshipped the unerring mechanism of instinct to be found in the beasts, and he gave it all his admiration, although he alone enjoyed the privilege of intellect. Formerly man had had to borrow some animal attribute in order to become godlike; but now it was the animal that was translated into man, and the monsters of Greek mythology – centaurs, sirens, satyrs – are all animal forms promoted to the human plane, the plane of intelligence.

This discovery of man was made in two stages: first physically, then morally. It took no less than three centuries to gain experience of the

70

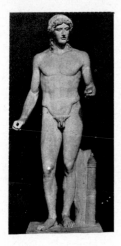

67 The Cassel Apollo (after
Phidias?). 2nd half of 5th c.
B.C. Cassel

68 The Diadumenos (after
Polycleitus). 2nd half of
5th c. B.C. Athens

69 Agias (School of Lysippus).
2nd half of 4th c. B.C.
Delphi

70 The Borghese Gladiator (by
Agasias of Ephesus). Early
1st c. B.C.

human body as such: the sixth and fifth centuries B.C. for male anatomy,
the fourth century for the female. After the stadium the artists went on
to explore the gynaeceum. Then, having painfully mastered the knowledge of the body, they applied it to expressing the soul. This great
investigation into the passions, which they began in the fourth century,
ended in the Hellenistic period in an inquiry which, passing beyond
Greek man, was directed on to the yet uncivilized world.

The work of art was delivered from that bondage to magic which
had made it the slave of narrow conventions by turning it into a means
of controlling the supernatural powers. It first became a simple illustration of myths, then very soon an end in itself. The image emerged from

71

71 *Head of Apollo from Thasos. 6th c. B.C. Copenhagen*
72 *Head of a Figure from the Temple of Aphaia, Aegina. Early 5th c. B.C.*
73 *Head of the Doryphorus (after Polycleitus). 5th c. B.C. Naples*

the sorcery of the temple's darkness to glitter in the sunshine, and as an ornament of cities offered itself as a spectacle to all and sundry, and not only to a few initiates. Costly to produce and carried out by free and paid men, it escaped from that obsession with the gigantic that had been served so well in Egypt and Assyria by hordes of slaves. It was now made to the scale of cities and not of empires. Not that it stopped aspiring to grandeur, but this quality was now sought by the Greeks in matters of proportion and not of dimension.

The conventions which for thousands of years had paralysed the free portrayal of the forms in nature had therefore no excuse for survival. There was no longer any question of endowing the image with the maximum magical power by giving it the largest possible number of attributes of the model. Any resemblance was drawn from mere external appearance. For the first time natural forms were represented as they are seen by the eye, that is to say in their spatial truth, with the fore-shortening which deforms them, and in the perspective which hides them or reduces their size. The Greeks' great plastic discovery was that of depth. After defining plane-geometry they laid down the principles of stereometry. Their rationalistic turn of mind was necessary to understand that unlimited space could be reduced to a three-dimensional system.

The intuitive naturalism which prevailed in primitive times became, in Greek art, a rationally planned realism; but it found its own limits in the idealism which led the Hellenes to see an expression of universal order in everything. The Greeks rigorously defined all the ideas of proportion, measurement, composition and rhythm which shape every form – whether abstract like a temple or realistic like a statue – accord-ing to the laws of number. In their aesthetic all the parts of a whole

Face in Sculpture

74 *Head of Hermes (after Praxiteles). 2nd half of 5th c. B.C.*
75 *Head of Meleager (after Scopas). 4th c. B.C. Rome*
76 *Head of the Borghese Gladiator (by Agasias of Ephesus). 1st c. B.C. Paris*

are in keeping with each other, proportioned according to a common scale: what we call a 'relationship' and what the Greeks called a 'canon', meaning a rule. This canon or standard is the formal principle from which component elements may be deduced according to a series of inter-relationships: for instance, the statue was based on the *dactyl* or width of the finger, while the entire temple depended on the width of the column. This secret order which governs the world and which constitutes beauty had to be reflected externally in art, while the philosopher strove to define its principles. Freed from the magical or theological bondage of its origins, art at last drew its whole mission from itself, much as science did, each of them aiming at the discovery of harmony, that is to say, ultimately and beyond all accidental discords, the pursuit of unity.

The name 'classicism' has been given to this realism which tended towards abstraction and was governed by a philosophy that reduced all things to the measure of man. It had such a universal validity that Greek civilization has remained alive while all its predecessors have long since become extinct.

Hellenism emerged from and returned to the East. The Greek genius was born in Asia Minor. Rich from the start, though still bearing traces of the experiments of the Egyptians, Cretans, and Mesopotamians, it quickly shed them and expressed itself in all its purity in the fifth century B.C., in a few cities of the Greek mainland and particularly Athens, that tiny strip of land which will always glitter like a diamond on the map of the world. Perhaps it was an increased infusion of Hellenic blood, from the ethnical contribution of the Dorian invasions, which produced this crystallization. Once rigorously defined this philosophical and plastic culture was to become the ferment from which future civilizations were to rise. In the Hellenistic period Ionia again took the first place, while Greece, fertilized once again from contact with the East, came into contact with Asiatic mysticism, and brought the speculative and rationalistic instrument it had created to bear on alien metaphysical systems – a synthesis from which Christian dogma was to emerge. The Greek plastic code, conceived in order to express the serenity of deified man, showed its adaptability by conforming to the new spiritual disquiet. Greece gave Rome the spiritual support which enabled it to base its material empire on the foundation of a powerful culture. Rome turned the classical sense of unity into the tool of politics, borrowing from Asiatic Greece that 'imperial' spirit which the latter had inherited from the earlier monarchies. Even Rome's genius for engineering (its main claim to greatness in the domain of the arts) derived from the wealthy cities of Ionia, which the Arabs so thoroughly destroyed that nothing was left but a few bones.

The powerful impulse of Greek genius remained active in time and space. It went to enrich the complexity of Byzantine art. In the West it still remained an unseen presence until it brought about the dawn of the Renaissance. Recent excavations have shown the astonished world that Hellenism spread as far as the Indus, and that Indian art received a definite impetus from the example of Greece.

1. GREECE

The Evolution of Greek Art

The evolution of Greek art has been divided into three periods: Archaic, Classical and Hellenistic. Its beginnings and maturity were dominated by two rival principles, the Doric and Ionic, in which the ancients themselves saw the masculine and feminine principles of Greece. The Ionic, springing from the contact of Asian Greece with the East, favours grace, elegance and wealth of ornament; while the Doric, which originated in Greece proper and in western Greece, tends towards severity and rigorous observance of proportions.

1. The Archaic period, during which Greece was emerging from the protohistorical period and slowly developing towards maturity, covers a period of several centuries (1200 B.C.–450 B.C.) and has been sub-divided as follows:

a) The Geometrical phase lasted from the fall of Mycenae to the eighth century B.C. – five hundred years of darkness which have been called the 'Greek Middle Ages', during which art and civilization languished as a result of the Dorian invasion. It has been called 'geometrical' owing to the decorative pattern found on ceramics discovered in Atica, Boeotia,

77 Doric Capitals of the Temple of Apollo, Corinth

Laconia and in the Archipelago, and also the 'cubist' style of carved idols found in the Cyclades. The temples at that time were built in crude clay and wood, with architectonic patterns in modelled and painted terracotta.

b) The Archaic phase, which lasted from 700 to 500 B.C., showed the preponderance of the Asian Greeks, which is very marked in their ceramics (workshops at Rhodes, Cyclades, Corinth and Attica) as well as in sculpture, which was already developed by the early sixth century in the form of statuary and monuments *(Naxian Sphinx,* Treasury of Cnidos at Delphi, Temple of Artemis-Gorgo at Corfu, painted limestone relief of the Hecatompedon in Athens). The same century witnessed the first stone temples: the Doric style developed in Greater Greece (Sicily and southern Italy, sites of Selinunte, Syracuse and Paestum), at Corinth (Temple of Apollo) and in the Peloponnese (Heraion at Olympia). Though few traces of the Ionic style remain, we know that it developed contemporaneously in the cities of Samos, Miletus, Ephesus in Asia Minor.

c) The pre-Classical phase (500 B.C.–450 B.C.). The conquest of Ionia by the Persians was to bring about a momentary eclipse there. Architecture flourished in southern Italy, then called 'Greater Greece' (Selinunte, Paestum, Segesta, Agrigentum in Sicily) and in the sanctuaries of Greece itself (Delphi, Olympia). This was the great period of the Archaic Doric, yet the Ionic spirit still inspired such monuments as the Treasury of the

78 Ionic Capital of the Prophylaea, Athens

Siphnians, at Delphi while the Corinthian style appeared in Sicily. The workshops of Attica took the lead in ceramics. Then, in the course of the sixth century and the first half of the fifth, masculine and feminine types of statuary began to develop, inspired respectively by the Doric and Ionic principles. In the first half of the fifth century monumental sculpture broke free from Archaism with the pediments of the Temple of Aphaia at Aegina, the Auriga at Delphi and the decoration of the Temple of Zeus at Olympia, which is the triumph of the Doric spirit.

2. *The Classical period* (second half of fifth to fourth century) was the period of equilibrium and maturity, dominated entirely by Greece proper. Towards 450 B.C. the Attic Myron and the Argian Polycleitus brought the athletic type to its perfection, the one in the expression of movement, the other by establishing the canon of athletic proportions. The great initiative of Pericles, who with Phidias as his master-of-works undertook to rebuild the Acropolis from its ruins after it had been burnt down by the Persians, was to make Athens the artistic centre of the Greek world. The Doric style found its perfect expression in both architecture and sculpture with the Parthenon which was inaugurated in 438 B.C. and of which Ictinus and Callicrates were the architects and Phidias the sculptor. The Propylaea (437 B.C.–432 B.C.) combines the Doric and Ionic styles, but the Temple of Nikè Apteros (Athene Nikè) by Callicrates (inaugurated 421 B.C.) and the Erechtheum (407 B.C.) are in the Ionic.

The Athenian hegemony emerged shaken from the Peloponnesian wars. In the fourth century the great architectural undertakings were already

79 Corinthian Capital from the Tholos, Epidauros

80 The Parthenon seen from the North. Inaugurated 438 B.C.

shifted to Asia Minor, which cultivated the Ionic style and showed an Asiatic preference for the colossal (Artemision at Ephesus, Didymeion at Miletus, Mausoleum of Halicarnassus). A new architectural form appeared transposed into wood, that is to say, the theatre (Epidaurus and Athens). Meanwhile Greece kept its pre-eminence in sculpture with Scopas of Paros, Praxiteles of Athens and Lysippus of Sicyon. The arrival of Polygnotus of Thasos in Greece gave great impetus to painting, the imitation of which led to the decadence of the art of ceramics which had been flourishing.

3. *The Hellenistic or Alexandrian period* (third century till the Christian era) dates from the dismembering of Alexander's Empire (323 B.C.) which created great prosperous kingdoms in Asia while transferring the seat of Greek art to the East. New cities such as Pergamum in Anatolia, Alexandria in Egypt, Antioch in Syria, all of which were cosmopolitan in character, furthered the fusion of Hellenism with the East which is peculiar to the Hellenistic period of this civilization. The Doric decayed, and the Corinthian took the lead. From the third century we see the development of official architecture – colonnades, meeting-rooms *(bouleterion)*, libraries, museums – while large urban agglommerations were built of which the thoroughly explored ruins of Pergamum give us a fair

81 *The Erechtheum on the Acropolis, Athens. Inaugurated 421 B.C.*

idea. Sculpture derived from Lysippian expressionism, which developed towards pathos and realism. The frieze of the Altar of Pergamum (formerly Berlin Museum) of the second century encouraged the 'pathetic' style which was further exploited by the Rhodes school (second and first centuries B.C.). The city of Pompeii, buried in the year A.D. 79 by the eruption of Vesuvius, reveals an Italian reflection of Hellenistic art at the domestic level. The only surviving paintings of ancient times come from this site, and from Delos and Rome.

Architecture

The Greeks inherited flat-roof building. They knew nothing of the possibilities of covering great spaces to be realized by means of the vault; and yet they accomplished a profound revolution in monumental art. A slave to massive walls, the architecture of previous civilizations had to limit itself to such expression of mere strength as could be obtained by colossal dimensions: the monuments of the Nile and the Euphrates were still little more than ordinary buildings coated with decoration. They were derived from the mud-wall which remained the basis of Mesopotamian construction methods until the end, and which the Egyptians continued to imitate in stone even after they had abandoned it. The Greek temple, on the contrary, had its origins in the wooden edifice, wood being a material allowing of large gaps in construction. The column of the hypostyle halls of the Nile was a fragment of wall, whereas that of the Greeks derived from the stake. Building in stone, the Greeks had the idea of masking the nakedness of the full wall with a colonnade which looked far less heavy, and broke the monotonous surface of blanks walls by vertical effects which were further accentuated by fluting. They thus invented a gamut of monumental expression by alternating solids and spaces, carried and carrying parts; while by bringing relative dimensions into play (height, width, thickness) in the component elements such as the support (column), the interval (between columns) and the carried surface (coping, etc.), their genius was able to achieve those effects of rhythm and harmony which properly constitute architecture in the real sense, that is, something the Hellenes thought of as a science of numbers.

All Greek monumental art derives from the column. The entire proportions of the temple depended on its strength and slimness, and the relationship between the diameter and height of the column – a relationship known as the 'module' – thus governed the entire edifice. With their scrupulous love of clarity and unity the Greeks reduced the expressions of architecture to three, which were nobility, grace and sumptuousness, to which corresponded the three 'orders', the Doric (pl. 77), Ionic (pl. 78) and Corinthian (pl. 79). These orders differed the one from the other in their proportions as well as in certain elements in their decoration: the Doric capital, with its unadorned moulding, frankly and robustly expresses the architectonic function of the support (pl. 80), while the volutes of

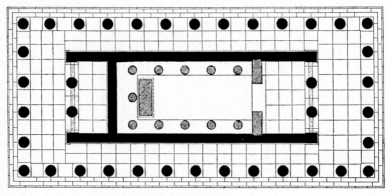

82 Plan of the Temple of Hephaestos, Athens

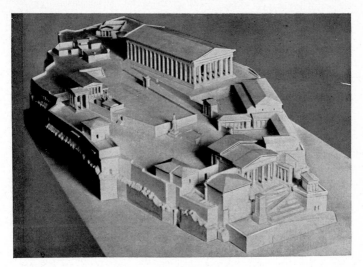

83 Reconstruction of the Acropolis

the Ionic capital suggests an elegant impression of elasticity (pl. 81). The acanthus leaves decorating the Corinthian capital contribute an element of ornamental luxury (pl. 79). Originating in Asia, which always favoured serial decorations (Assyrian and Persian friezes), the Corinthian and Ionic orders always have, on their entablature, a sculptured frieze showing a continuous pattern. The Doric order best corresponds with the Western mind, which inclines towards sharpness of definition: the rhythm of the columns and intercolumniation is repeated in the entablature by the alternating of fluted triglyphs and sculptured metopes. The Parthenon is the most perfect of all Greek temples, representing the golden mean between the somewhat heavy strength of the first Doric temples and the fragile gracefulness of the Ionic. With a length of 240 feet and 110 feet wide, it was build according to the Doric order, but has a continuous frieze (on the upper part of the wall inside the colonnade), as in the Ionic order.

The Greeks further enriched the expressive range of architecture by creating a system of ornamental moulding which was extremely simple and logical, dispersed about the monument in such a way as to underline its divisions and define the proper function of each element. Greek monuments were constructed with the greatest care from blocks of marble of moderate size, assembled with scientific skill. The walls were built entirely of ashlar without the use of cement, solidity being guaranteed by sheer weight, though the blocks were often bound with bronze clamps. Greek temples delight us now by the beauty of their marble which glitters in the sunshine, but their architects often embellished them with effects of colouring. This polychromy, applied to all the adornments of the

84 Theatre, Epidauros. 4th c. B.C.

Archaic temple constructed in limestone, was more discreetly done when they adopted marble, and was used only to emphasize the main members of the edifice.

The fundamental expression of Greek architecture was the temple (pl. 82). Temples were every city's pride, and were often built either alone or in groups at the highest point in the city, where stood its earliest centre, the Acropolis (pl. 83). The Greek temple, of much smaller dimensions than the Egyptian, usually comprised a blank rectangular wall, with a single or double colonnade *(peristasis)* running all round. Inside, the image of the god was kept in the *naos* or *cella* which was frequently divided into a nave and two aisles: this was preceded by a vestibule *(pronaos)* and followed by a sacristy or treasury *(opisthodomos)*. The rooms were all somewhat feebly lit through the roof. At the front and back (façades) the gently sloping gable-roof made two triangular sections, the pediments, which were decorated with sculptures. All the other monumental undertakings of Greek architecture such as the meeting-room, the market *(agora)*, the portico *(stoa)* incorporated colonnades. The house consisted of a number of rooms grouped round a peristyle containing a garden: unlike the temple, which was a public monument, the house was conceived from the inside, centring on the interior. The Greeks also invented the theatre which they built with an extraordinary simplicity and economy of means. Backing against a hill, the theatre had three main parts: a large segment of a circle with tiers of seats for the spectators, a circular orchestra for the chorus, a proscenium in front of the *skene* or decorated back-wall, for the actors (pl. 84).

82

The drawback of Greek architecture is its monotony. The monumental perfection attained in the fifth century left little scope for invention in the following centuries. Like all those forms of architecture that lack the arch or vault, Greek architecture could only exploit a limited number of possibilities both at the structural level and by way of harmonic effects. By their use of the arch the Romans were able to give the architect a far wider field of action.

Sculpture

Greek sculpture evolved in such a logical way, and with such a complete exploitation of its plastic and human potentialities, that it is rightly considered as being the most perfect example of the creation of a style.

After the abstract idols sculpted in marble in the Cyclades in the Bronze Age (pl. 85) and without showing any obvious connection with them, sculptors began in the seventh century B.C. to raise the problem of the male type *(kuros)* and the feminine type *(kore)*. The votive and religious statues gave them the pretext for 'still' statuary. Starting from Egyptian frontality, in the course of the sixth century they loosened its stiffness and began to animate their works by exploring anatomical truth as well as volume and movement. Modelling at first showed a geometrical tendency which had little relationship to internal structure; then gradually it began to express what was beneath the surface. Originally the statue was thought of as a front and profile, symmetrically assembled on a strictly vertical axis; then gradually it became a volume turning in space. Workshops all over the Hellenic Mediterranean contributed their share to this slow apprenticeship. The Peloponnese seems to have played a major part in perfecting the naked athlete, a most austere expression of concentrated strength (pl. 64–70). It was Ionia that created the feminine type, with a rather affected charm, whose transparent linen drapery *(chiton* and *himation)* hints at the body's lines. The naked *kuros* served as an experiment for the discovery of anatomical modelling, whereas the *kore* was the basis for discovering draped modelling. At first incised schematically over the volumes, gradually the folds of the dress began to be modelled

85 *Marble Lyre-Player from Amorgos. Bronze Age. Athens*

83

in hollows and convexities and gave vigorous expression to the reliefs of the figure. The preference given in the fifth century to the monumental *peplos* of Dorian wool, replacing the Ionic linen garment, was to advance this evolution which was completed by Athens. Overcome towards the year 550 B. C. by the 'Levantine' grace of the emigrant Ionians, Athens was to absorb this influence and at the beginning of the fifth century created the grave but unsevere style which was to become its own.

The evolution of 'still' statuary found its perfect fulfilment in the fifth century with the Peloponnesian Polycleitus, who about 445 B.C.–440 B.C. expressed the Dorian ideal of the athletic figure in his bronze *Doryphorus*

86 *Athena, Hercules and Atlas. Metope from the Temple of Zeus, Olympia. 5th c. B.C.*

*87 Dying Warrior from the East Pediment of the Temple of Aphaia, Aegina.
5th c. B.C. Munich*

(lance-bearer), which the Greeks called the 'Canon' because the sculptor executed it according to the proportions which he himself had described in an aesthetic treatise of that name. In this work, conceived as the expression of the ideal beauty of the human body, all the problems of volume and anatomy were solved scrupulously but without the slightest stiffness, the harmonious composition of the gestures giving the impression of living suppleness (pl. 73).

It was in monumental sculpture in low-relief that 'mobile' statuary seems to have developed, and it sprang from the need for learning how to group together several figures participating in some common action. Sculpture had been distributed as a uniform adornment but with no particular order, on mural surfaces in Egypt and Assyria; but now it was to become closely involved in the rhythm of the architectur. It was set at vantage-points where architectonic expression needed the balance of relief, such as the metopes between the triglyphs of the Doric temple (pl. 86), the pediments of the façades, the continuous frieze of the Ionic order. The pediments of the Temple of Aphaia at Aegina (about 500 B.C. –480 B.C., Glyptothek, Munich) were the first victory for monumental expression, but still show no more than independent or juxtaposed statues, conceived on the frontal or profile plane (pl. 72, 87). But in the metopes and pediments of the Temple of Zeus at Olympia (472 B.C. –456 B.C.) the figures are associated one with the other by the rhythm of the action and the cadence of the total composition (pl. 86); the three-quarters stance is attempted but not without constraint from recent memories of Egyptian frontality which curbs the natural swing of the torso in rotation. On the west pediment, in Apollo checking the struggle of the

88 Apollo from the West Pediment, Olympia. 5th c. B.C.

Centaurs and Lapithae (pl. 88), the 'Olympian' quality appears for the first time; Olympia is the culminating point of the Dorian spirit.

The sculpting of marble in low-relief had favoured a freer expression of gestures, because the forms remained attached to the background or

89 Zeus or Poseidon of Histiaea. Bronze. About 470 B.C. Athens

were applied to it as in the case of the pediments. It was the use of bronze which, being both stronger and less heavy, was to help the statue in the round to solve the problem of movement. A gesture like that of the outstretched arms in the *Zeus of Histiaea* (about 470 B.C., National Museum, Athens, pl. 89) could never have been thought of in marble. In his famous *Discus-Thrower* (*Discobolus*, about 460 B.C.–450 B.C., pl. 90) Myron contrived the canon of movement, just as Polycleitus in his *Doryphorus* had expressed the canon of repose. A synthesis between the contraction and relaxation of muscular effort at speed, this work finds the principles of its harmony in the balance of opposites.

90 Myron. The Discus-Thrower (after an early replica). About 460–450 B.C.

All these efforts converged towards Phidias, who from both the moral and plastic point of view represents the supreme expression of the Greek spirit. It was he who gave the most perfect form to that Greek notion of divinity which is known as 'Olympian', a kind of super-humanity whose

*91 Aphrodite and Dione from the East Pediment of the Parthenon.
About 447–432 B.C. London*

serenity is untouched by earthly cares. In his famous religious statues in
gold and ivory (called for that reason 'chryselephantine') – *Zeus of Olympia* and *Athena Parthenos* – the colossal dimensions (the *Zeus* being
45 1/2 feet in height) as well as the precious sheen of the material, still
contained something of the old, magical notion of the deity. But in the
monumental sculptures of the Parthenon, the divinity is conceived of in
terms of heroic man. In this group (447 B.C.–432 B.C.) in which Atticism
brings together Doric gravity and Ionic grace, Phidias achieved a perfec-

*92 Phidias. Fragment from the Frieze of the Panathenaea on the Parthenon.
London*

93 Victory removing her Sandal. Temple of Nikè Apteros. Late 5th c. B.C.

tion of harmony which no artist has ever surpassed. Each item, taken by itself, is a fluid composition of happily counter balanced volumes, while the twist of the bodies in space is accomplished with all the ease of real life. At the same time the figures are related to each other according to

94 Cresilas. Head of Pericles. Berlin

the principles of an harmonious rhythm. The two pediments *(Birth of Athena* and *Dispute between Athena and Poseidon,* pl. 91) and the ninety-two metopes contain restricted compositions which had to conform with geometrical requirements. The frieze which unfolds at the top of the walls under the colonnade, on the other hand, is a continuous

95 *Venus of Milo.*
Early 3rd c. B.C. (?). Paris

pattern of related forms, developing like the theme of a melody in music (pl. 92). This is one of the greatest undertaking in all sculpture: 350 human figures, 200 animals (horse and beasts of sacrifice) portray in heroic style the procession of the Panathenaea. Composed of youths on horseback, magistrates, musicians, Athenian maidens, every four years such a procession came to offer the statue of Athena, protectress of cities, a new veil which had been woven specially for her.

The late fifth century lived on the strength of the Phidian aesthetic, which was observed particularly by the sculptors of grave-columns at the Ceramus cemetery (reserved for heroes). The anonymous author of the caryatids of the Erechtheum (between 420 B.C.–413 B.C.) subjected the *korai* (Maidens) to the architectonic requirements of the support. The sculpted parapet of the Temple of Nikè Apteros at Athens (towards 410 B.C., pl. 93) accentuates the Ionian gracefulness of feminine figures. Meantime Paeonius achieved for the Temple of Zeus at Olympia, between 450 B.C. and 420 B.C., an instantaneous glimpse of movement in his *Nikè* (Victory) caught in full flight as she descends from Olympus (original still at Olympia). This effort was renewed in about 450 B.C. by the anonymous author of the Nereids dancing on the sea, discovered at Xanthos (now in the British Museum). With his bust of Pericles, Cresilas created the heroic type of portrait, reduced to the head and bust (pl. 94).

Of the great masters of Greek sculpture, only Phidias is known to us by original works, for, like the masterpieces of Myron and Polycleitus, those of the fourth century were pillaged by the Romans and have disappeared, while scholars have great difficulty in identifying later copies by which they are known.

Between the idealism of the fifth century and the naturalism of the Hellenistic period, the fourth century came as a period of crisis in Greek sculpture. It marks the transition from the mythological to the human. Scopas (very damaged remains of the Temple of Athena at Tegea, in the Peloponnese, about 386 B.C.–370 B.C.) accomplished a revolution by introducing into the Greek plastic code the portrayal of passion violently affecting the body and filling the face with anguish, which hitherto had remained imperturbable even in the moments of action, grief or death (pl. 75). Praxiteles, who first dared to portray the

96 *Zeus fighting the Giants. Altar of Pergamum. Between 197–159 B.C. Berlin*

feminine body entirely naked (the *Cnidian Aphrodite*) was the refined product of the Athenian decadence. He transformed the athlete into the adolescent; moreover the hips of his adolescents, who appear somehow lethargic, destroy the statue's proper balance and drive the sculptor to the use of supports *(Apollo Sauroctonus, Lycian Apollo, Resting Satyr,* etc.*).* An over-anxiety for gradation, no doubt to be blamed on the influence of painting, weakens the modelling which becomes too smooth and fluid, as can be seen from the *Hermes of Olympia,* no doubt made later (pl. 74). In the time of Alexander, the bronze-worker Lysippus, born at Sicyon in the Peloponnesus, kept a taste for athletic figures, characteristic of his Doric origins; but, obeying the spirit of his age, he debased the Polycleitian squareness by lengthening the proportions (making the body eight times the head, instead of seven). He upset the firm stance of the statue with unstable postures, caught or 'snapped' with a suddenness which twists the bust and gives the whole body an angular uneasiness *(Agias of Delphi,* pl. 69, *Resting Hermes, Athlete with the Strigil).* Forgetting the support which the wall formerly afforded, the statue was now fully modelled from all angles, three-dimensionally, the over-analysis of the anatomy giving the modelling a knotty and episodic appearance detracting from the expression of strength. In the Ionic tradition, which was increasingly active, the Asiatic background seems to have inspired artists to a luxurious fleshiness, well expressed in the statue of the king

97 Dionysus visiting Icarus. Hellenistic. London

(Mausoleum of Halicarnassus, British Museum, about 450 B.C.) and the *Venus of Milo* (Louvre, perhaps beginning of third century, pl. 95), the latter being one of the most sensual marbles left to us by Greek art.

In the Hellenistic period the Greek plastic code sacrificed every effect of harmony to expressionism and naturalism. The sculptor began to explore the whole gamut of human expression: suffering, death, sleep, laughter, voluptuousness, tenderness, instinct, physical infirmity, old age and infancy. In Alexander's time portrait-sculpture became more individualistic under the influence of painting, while landscape found its way into relief and sometimes became its sole theme (pl. 97).

Hellenistic art glorified brute strength. It created the type of Hercules, a circus-athlete with overgrown muscles, and also showed an interest in types of long-haired barbarians (statues of dying Galatians or Gauls). The beautiful athletes of the Classical period now became professionals of the stadium: *Running Athlete* or *Borghese Gladiator*, Louvre, first century, pl. 70, 76). Sometimes, on the other hand, they became effeminate to the point of hermaphroditism. But baroque feeling and a heightened realism in the representation of volumes and draperies also have their place, as in the noble *Winged Victory of Samothrace* (Louvre, about 180 B.C., pl. 98).

The largest group of work surviving from that period was the altar built at Pergamum for Eumenes II (197 B.C.–159 B.C.) on which a 'frieze' 390 feet long, arranged as a plinth in the manner of the Persians and Assyrians, portrayed a *Gigantomachia* (Battle of Gods and Giants, pl. 96, 106). This work was in the Berlin Museum before the recent war. The projection of the forms, excessively emphasized, and the chaotic movement

98 Winged Victory of Samothrace. About 180 B.C. Paris

of the attitudes, the draped form pronounced to the point of inflation, the melodramatic play of muscle, and the convulsed faces, express all the passions of strife, suffering and death. The taste for pathos led to the composing of groups of statuary bringing together a number of figures in some violent action (group known as the *Farnese Bull,* Naples Museum). The school of Rhodes carried on the traditional theatrical style of Pergamum, which was still very much alive in the famous *Laocoon* group (about 50 B.C., pl. 708) which was the last great work of Greek plastic art. Discovered in Rome in the sixteenth century it had a profound influence on Michelangelo.

Painting and the Minor Arts

Mutilated remains help us to reconstitute the history of Greek sculpture, with many gaps, and painted works of art have likewise disappeared, apart from a few specimens of the later decadent period at Pompeii, Delos and Rome (pl. 99). The latter are extremely beautiful in spite of their clumsiness which was due to mediocre executants. We will thus always remain ignorant of the art of the great painters of antiquity: Polygnotus, Zeuxis, Parrhasios, Apelles. However, we can gain some idea of what the general evolution of Greek painting was like, from the mark it left on an industrial art, that of painted ceramics. The considerable number of specimens (found in tombs) of these products, which were exported all over the Mediterranean, amount to an enormous collection of forms which, better than any other figurative art, enables us to reconstitute the life, customs and general evolution of styles in Greece. Study of the vases shows us that painting was freed from primitive constraints earlier than sculpture, and this increases our regret for the loss of so many great works.

99 Scenes from the Odyssey. Fresco from a House on the Esquilino. Rome

100 *Amphora from the Dipylon. Athens*

Before the seventh century the enormous Attic vases of the Dipylon (cemetery near one of the gates of Athens) show ceramics to have been under the same influence of the geometrical style as were the temple idols of the Cyclades (pl. 100). The triangular stylization of the human body recalls that of the pottery of Susa in the fourth millennium and certain cave-paintings of prehistoric Africa. This bent for rectilinear stylization, so unlike the fluid formalism of the Cretans, appears therefore to have been the manner of the Doric

101 Corinthian Wine-Jar (detail). Late 7th – Early 6th c. B.C.

primitives. We have already seen from sculpture that the Doric spirit always maintained a tendency towards squareness (Polycleitus and Myron). More clearly than sculpture, ceramics prove that the curvilinear style came from Asia by way of Ionia. The pots made in the workshops of Rhodes, Boetia and Corinth in the eighth and seventh centuries were decorated with dark figures on a light ground, set out in a continuous frieze and composed of animals seen either naturalistically or with a touch of fantasy, and of Phoenician or even Assyrian origin (pl. 101). The seventh century introduced scenes from everyday life which at first were mingled with animal adornments. The growing influence of Athenian ceramics which were to flood markets hitherto in the hands of the Corinthians, freed vases from Oriental influences.

102 Brygos. Bottom of a Drinking-Vessel. About 490–480 B.C. London

103 Death of Talos. Bowl from Ruvo. 1st half of 4th c. B.C.

104 Exekias. Achilles and Ajax playing Dice (detail of an Amphora).
2nd half of 6th c. B.C.

Athens used a process of black figures on a red ground (about 650 B.C. –500 B.C.) and, abandoning the lay-out according to zones, adopted the metope style of composition, that is to say rectangular panels blocked out in light red, to take the mythological scenes which were introduced at that time. The lines of the drawing were incised on the black surface of the figure with no attempt at modelling. The beauty of arabesque and elegance of silhouette, the life-like gestures, show that painting was already far in advance of sculpture which was still under the tyranny of the block's mass. A daemonic life animates these figures, which suggest the vitality of the Homeric poems (pl. 104).

The potter Nikosthenes or his colleague Andokides is credited with the invention of the process of depicting red figures on a black ground, towards the end of the sixth century. The light tint of the figures enabled the painter to work them with the brush, to analyse the modelling, perspective, foreshortening, play of light and shadow. The increasing influence of painting pushed the artist towards naturalism at the cost of beauty in decorative style, the figure being no longer conceived as a silhouette but according to the inner modelling. The finest red-figure vases are those of the so-called 'Severe' or 'Archaic' style (late sixth century to about 460 B.C.). Euphronios, the potters Brygos and Douris signed some magnificent pieces in which the balance between realism and style anticipates the harmony of Phidias (pl. 102). Naturalism was stressed

105 Achilles slaying Penthesilea. 5th c. B.C. Munich

after the arrival in Athens in 470 B.C. of the painter Polygnotus of
Thasos, who introduced perspective effects and psychological expression
into his painting (pl. 105). About 450 B.C. saw the beginnings of the 'Fine'
style period in ceramics: the aesthetic of Phidias made itself felt in painting and led to a certain degree of academism. During the period of the
Ornate style which began in about 420 B.C., its chief exponent being
Meidias, ceramics was invaded and led astray by the imitation of painting; compositions included too many figures and became confused, the
modelling suggested volumes (pl. 103) and, emulating the painter, the
potter began to transgress the decorative laws of his medium – all these
defects being further accentuated in the ceramics of southern Italy, whose
development coincided with the decadence of Athenian pottery after the
Peloponnesian War. The Greek ceramic works nearest to painting that
have survived are the funerary *lekythos* or oil-jars which had a white

ground; drawn in firm outline on a limewash background, the figures must have been made in imitation of those found in stucco paintings. The beauty of design of some of the fifth century *lekythos* only increases our regret for the loss of works by the great masters themselves, since so many of those known to us were from the hands of humble craftsmen.

The Greeks had a particular bent for the monumental arts and

106 Greek Cameo. 4th c. B.C. Paris

produced little in the way of the minor arts, with the exceptions of pottery for which they invented some admirable forms, peculiarly suitable for the various functions of the vase, and a decorative style of considerable beauty. The Greek disregard for comfort did not encourage the making of everyday things and furniture, except in the Hellenistic period. Miniature sculpting on bronze was only a reflection of large-scale sculpture, but their bronze mirrors have some beautiful incised drawings. Sober in their tastes, the Hellenes paid little attention to finery, at least in the Classical period. Some fine examples of silverware have survived from the Hellenistic period. Hellenistic artists made some excellent intaglios from hard gems for use as seals, and in Alexander's time they invented cameos (pl. 106), onyx stones cut in relief in which the different coloured layers of the material are skilfully exploited. Their genius for sculpture also came out in the minting of their coinage, the best specimens of this art being produced not at Athens but at Syracuse (pl. 107).

2. THE ROMAN WORLD

Historical Background

In the central region of Italy (Tuscany and Latium), Etruscan art, which came before that of Rome, was a kind of provincial extension of Greek art. It sought and found its happiest inspiration in Ionia during the Archaic period (late seventh century B.C. to first half of fifth). The Classical stream (second half of fifth century to fourth) was more banal. The rapid degeneration of this art from the third century produced neo-primitive forms heralding the plastic style of the late Empire, that of the early Middle Ages, or certain aspects of modern art.

The Etruscans imported a great quantity of Attic vases, and imitated the designs on them in the frescoes of their own underground tombs. This

107 Decadrachm from Syracuse. Late 5th c. Paris.

they did with a primitive touch, but with a narrative sense remote from the classical spirit, which has something of the Asian sensibility while foreshadowing Roman realism. The Romans were to inherit some of their gift for portraiture. Besides paintings and works in clay (pl. 108), the Etruscans left some fine archaic bronzes (pl. 109). Those structures of theirs that are known to us (city walls, municipal works) are interesting because they show a very precocious use of the arch formed of wedge-shaped stones when it was still unknown to the Greeks.

The Roman art of the Republican period saw a slow infiltration of the Greek aesthetic into Etruscan models. This carried all before it in the last years of the Republic, when the Roman aristocracy were fired with enthusiasm for conquered Greece and vied with each other for originals or copies of the masterpieces of Greek art. Caesar began the great transformation of Rome into the Imperial capital, by enriching it with great monuments: a forum (pl. 110), a theatre, the Basilica Aemilia, the Basilica Julia, the Curia Julia. What is called 'Augustan' art emerged from a great Greco-Roman synthesis of political theory; for Augustus wanted to found a Roman classicism in both literature and art which would be worthy of its Hellenic model and which would become the typical culture of the Empire. The architect Vitruvius Pollio condensed the principles of this classicism in a treatise on architecture written between 25 B.C. and 23 B.C. Augustus had numerous monuments erected in Rome: a forum (pl. 110), triumphal arches, the Theatre of Marcellus, several temples including that of Mars the Avenger, and the Ara Pacis (Altar of Peace, pl. 120). This was the beginning of that great period of building which was to spread all over the Empire and bring so many peoples the benefits of Roman government, peace and comfort. The burning of Rome in the year A.D. 64 enabled Nero – whether he was responsible for the disaster or not – to make the city more healthy and build himself an immense palace (the Golden House). In the first century of our era Vespasian founded the amphitheatre later called the 'Colosseum', which was finished by Titus and had a storey added by Domitian (pl. 111). The Antonine period was one of active building all over the Empire. Hadrian, thoroughly steeped in Greek culture, tried to perpetuate the images of the finest Hellenic works of architecture in his villa at Tivoli (A.D. 127–134) and rebuilt the Pantheon (A.D. 131–124, pl. 113). His enormous mausoleum

108 Apollo of Veii (Clay Figure from a Pediment). Etruscan. Rome

109 Bronze Chimaera from Arezzo. Etruscan. About 500–475 B.C. Florence

was later incorporated in the Castel Sant' Angelo. Another great fire in Rome in A.D. 191 enabled Septimus Severus and Caracalla to undertake among other things the Baths of Caracalla (A.D. 212–216), one of the masterpieces of Roman architecture. This activity continued until the fall of the Empire (Basilica of Constantine or Maxentius, A.D. 310–312). The whole of the Roman world was covered with monuments. Provence has some very fine ones dating from the first and second centuries (arch and theatre at Orange, amphitheatre at Nîmes, pl. 112, and Arles) and Germany from the fourth (baths, basilica and Porta Nigra at Trier, pl. 115). Africa has ruins of fine buildings at Timgad, Sbeitla and El Djem, while on the confines of the Empire Asiatic Balbec was enriched with colossal monuments. As for Pompeii and Herculaneum, the two cities of the campagnia which were buried by Vesuvius in A.D. 79 and rediscovered in the eighteenth century, they are a Western offshoot of Hellenistic rather than of Roman art.

Architecture

It was in the domain of architecture that the genius of the Romans found its most powerful expression. Prolonged peace, the wealth accruing from intense commercial activity, the public works commissioned by an administration anxious for the public welfare combined with the Roman taste for comfort, all created an enormous demand for building all over the Empire.

For religious undertakings the Romans drew inspiration from the Greek temples and from certain Etruscan traditions, showing a preference for the Corinthian order. They also used the Tuscan order which was an Etruscan interpretation of the Greek Doric. They innovated especially in

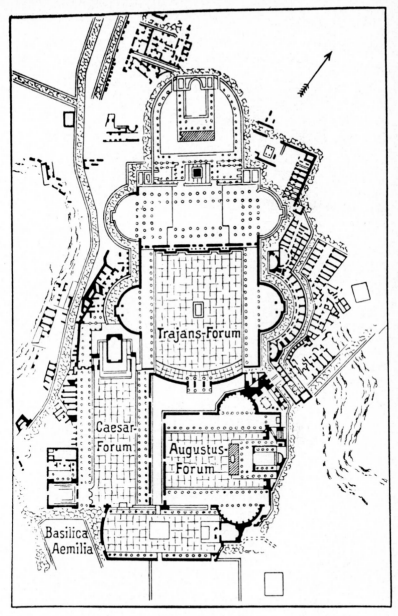

110 Plan of the Imperial Forums (restored). Scale approx. 1 : 5000

111 *Colosseum, Rome. Flavian*

civil engineering, making buildings which were functionally perfect. The adoption of the arch facilitated the creation of new types of monuments (pl. 113), called into being by the development of public ceremonies and social needs; the possibilities of spanning gaps with arches and vaults, which they made with remarkable skill and science, allowed them to make buildings with the immense roofed spaces required for holding large meetings. Abandoning the Greek manner of building with blocks of dressed but uncemented stone, they adopted a system of building in brick or rubble, having invented a cement of exceptional firmness. This base of brick or rubble they overlaid with marble facings, superimposing the Greek orders one on the other just as they wished (pl. 111), and giving no thought to relating decoration to structure as the Greeks had done. On their strong supports of brick or cement they set huge arches and vaults: domes, tunnel-vaults and 'cross-arches' or groin-vaults. All these principles seem to have come from Asia Minor, and a better knowledge of the Hellenistic cities would perhaps reduce the number of Roman inventions, many 'Roman' architects being of Greek origin, anyway.

112 *Amphitheatre, Nîmes*

113 Interior of the Pantheon, Rome (after an old print). Hadrianic

For ceremonial purposes the Romans took from the Hellenistic culture the memorial column and triumphal arch with one or three archways (pl. 118). For public works they also took the basilica from the East; this was a building with a nave, or nave and aisles, often ending in an apse, which they perfected and used as an exchange, a covered market or for the magistracy. The forum was a public place surrounded by arcades used for business purposes, and decorated with memorials and works of art. They took the theatre from the Greeks, but transformed it by building it on open ground, the hemicycle being held and framed by tiers of arched galleries. By putting together two theatres they invented the amphitheatre (pl. 112) which was built in an ellipse and used for circus performances. This is a masterpiece of practical planning. The circuses or hippodromes came from the Greek stadium: they were usually made of wood and have left few remains. The *thermae,* one of the Romans' monumental inventions, contained public baths, games-rooms, all kinds of rooms used for the recreation of the body and the mind (promenades, gymnasia, libraries, lecture-rooms). Provided with a central-heating system of hot air which flowed under the floor and between the walls, the bathing-places comprised a *caldarium* (room for hot baths), a *tepidarium* (a room heated with warm air to induce perspiration) and a *frigidarum* (for the cold

107

114 *Pont du Gard, Nîmes*

115 Porta Nigra, Trier

bath). The ruins of the Baths of Caracalla in Rome, with their enormous arches are the most grandiose of the Empire. Anxious, also, to supply their towns with abundant water, the Romans tapped distant springs, conducting the water by means of enormous aqueducts (pl. 114) made of superimposed rows of arches, to water-towers in the city. Domestic architecture consisted of tenements of several stories as well as private villas. These latter combined the old Etruscan with the Greek form of house. Round a court or *atrium* in the middle of which was an open tank or cistern *(impluvium)* were grouped the service quarters, the public rooms, the master's office or *tablinum;* then behind this part, which was of Etruscan origin, came the private quarters which were exactly the same as the Greek house, set round a garden fringed with columned arcades *(peristyle)* (pl. 116, 117).

The Romans had a splendid sense of monumental grandeur, as can be seen from their amphitheatres and aqueducts. They obtained excellent effects from a combination of straight lines, vertical or horizontal (columns and entablatures), and curved lines (arches and vaults). The great height of some of their structures did not favour the adoption of one particular order throughout; so Roman architects made it a rule to superimpose the three orders, the Doric, Ionian and Corinthian, one on the other. From the combination of the Ionic and Corinthian they made a fourth order, the Composite (often called Roman). Except in religious monuments they usually omitted fluting from their columns, leaving them smooth. The shafts, instead of being set up in segments, were usually cut from a marble monolith. The Romans unfortunately indulged a taste for

116 *Peristyle of the House of the Vettii, Pompeii*

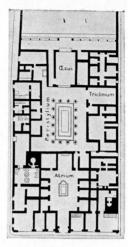

117 *Plan of a Pompeiian House*

the picturesque which diminished the grandeur of their loveliest monuments, and only their later ruin, which stripped them of ornament, was to reveal their honesty and strength of structure.

They made a considerable use of polychromy in their building, combining marbles of different colours which were brought from all over Europe.

Generally speaking they sought effects of luxury and strength, calculated to appeal to the mob's imagination, whereas Greek buildings, intended for a more cultured public, were primarily addressed to the intellect.

118 *Arch of Titus, Rome. Erected A.D. 81 in the Forum Romanum*

119 Architectural Painting, Pompeii. 4th Style

The interiors of Roman houses were covered with paintings showing decorative architectural themes (pl. 119) and arabesques, with panels depicting scenes from mythology.

The Roman contribution to sculpture was less outstanding. They admired the Greek plastic achievement, but did little more than painfully copy it. Augustus' initiative resulted in the creation of an official style, nobly dignified, with conventional drapery effects and formal gestures (pl. 120). The practical Roman mind transformed the pathos of the Hellenistic relief into an historical and narrative genre (Arch of Titus, pl. 121, Trajan's Column). Their most original creation was the portrait which, unlike the Greek portrait, reproduced the model without idealizing him, with an exact physical truthfulness (pl. 122): this was the revenge of the old indigenous stock over the Greek aesthetic. In the minor arts the Romans followed Hellenistic models, and made some fine bronze articles of which many were found intact in the ruins of Pompeii and Herculaneum. Pottery, on the other hand, assumed a purely industrial character.

3. EASTERN RESISTANCE

Alexander had pushed the frontiers of the Greek world as far as the Indus. The dynasties which succeeded him in Iran and Mesopotamia carried on a superficial Hellenism which stifled native art. After the Seleucid kings, the Parthian dynasty of the Arsacids, who described themselves on their coinage as 'Phil-Hellenes', remained attached to Greek culture. But the revolution of the Sassanians (A.D. 227–641) represents a return to the national tradition of Achaemenian Aryanism, based on the restoration of the Mazdakite religion. The Sassanians, conquering the Romans and Byzantines, drove Hellenic civilization back to the coast, at the moment when they themselves were overcome by the Muslims. Turning their back on the Mediterranean, they developed an art which was to be the basis of the invasions of the West by the East in the form of Islamic and Byzantine art.

In the domain of building the achievement of the Sassanians is more or less parallel with that of the Romans, substituting for Greek architecture with its columns and architraves a system of massive brickwork to take the thrust of arches. Inheriting Mesopotamian building methods, they perfected the science of constructing arches, barrel-vaults and domes, using the latter with a daring unsurpassed even by the Romans (the great elliptical barrel-vault of Ctesiphon is 84 1/2 feet across, 123 1/2 feet high, and 156 feet deep, pl. 124). They managed the transition from the square plan to the circular plan of the cupola by means of squinches (arches placed

120 Group of Figures from the Ara Pacis Augustae, Rome. Augustan

diagonally at the internal angles of the square), or large, curvilinear inverted triangles called 'pendentives', and contrived to set the strains of the vaults one against the other. The plans of their palaces (Ctesiphon, Sarvistan, pl. 125, Firuzabad, Taq-e-Eivan) tend to focus round a higher vault, an idea later adopted by the Byzantines. This vault crowns the throne-room or *divan* which is open at one side, an arrangement which

121 *Triumphal Procession with the Spoils of Jerusalem. Arch of Titus, Rome*

122 *Male Portrait. Limestone Head from Praeneste. Berlin*

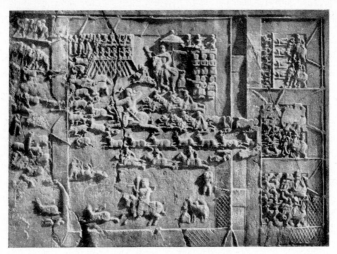

*123 Hunting Scene from the Inner Wall of Taq-i-Bustan. Sassanian.
About A.D. 590–628*

the Muslims followed. Inside, the masses of brick were covered with plates of painted stucco or enamelled terra-cotta in the Achaemenian manner. The Romans likewise covered their walls with inlaid decorations of this kind, but in their case it was used to hide the structural basis and was borrowed from the Greek orders. The monotheistic religion, which had no idols, did not inspire the Sassanians to any great architectural undertakings as was the case in Persia.

Sculpture spread round the walls like a tapestry was a conception foreign to Greek art but was characteristic of the Assyrians and Achaemenians. On the walls of the palaces and rock tombs of Naqsh-i-Rustam or Taq-i-Bustan, warlike or hunting scenes were depicted in tiered rows comparable with the oldest conventions (pl. 123). Although, under Greek influence the relief was more vigorous than among the Assyrians or Persians, the frontal and profile positions inhibited the free expression of volume. Statuary was rare and anti-classical in spirit (pl. 126).

The Sassanians had a considerable influence over Islamic and Byzantine art, and even on Roman art, through their handicrafts (silverwork and textiles) which carried on the Mesopotamian tradition of zoomorphic imagery, whether naturalistic or fantastic, and it was through them that this fund of imagery created by the Sumerians as long ago as the second millennium B.C., was passed on to the Middle Ages.

Recent researches are revealing in upper Mesopotamia, Syria and Palestine, traces of monuments built by pagan communities, either Jews or pre-Islamic Arabs. These show, in the early centuries of our era, a widespread revolt against Hellenism. At Dura-Europos, in the upper Euphrates

124 *Palace of Shapur I (A.D. 242–272), Ctesiphon. (an old view)*

valley, paintings were recently found in a temple dedicated in about A.D. 70 to the Palmyran gods. These show already all the attributes of Byzantine hieratic art (pl. 127). The transition towards early Christian art is demonstrated at Dura-Europos itself, by the paintings of a synagogue and in a Christian chapel of the third century. In Egypt, during the Roman period, panels painted in wax or distemper now replaced the masks of mummies in the sepulchres of Fayum and in the region of Thebes. The evolution of these from the first century B.C. to the fourth century A.D. shows the progressive Orientalization of the Hellenic type (pl. 631).

The spirit of the ancient East persisted in the castles, vaulted in the Sassanian manner and no doubt built by the first Omayyad Caliphs,

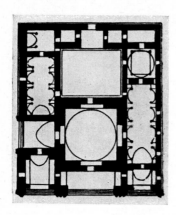

125 *Plan of the Palace at Sarvistan. Sassanian*

*126 Parthian Statue
found at Shami (Tehran)*

*127 Sacrifice to the Palmyran Gods.
Dura-Europos. About A.D. 70*

which have been found in the Syrian desert. One of them, at Mchatta,
had a great continuous frieze running round the lower part of the external walls, reproducing the Iranian theme of animals and birds sporting
among sprigs of vine, of which the early Christians made a Eucharistic
symbol (pl. 269).

IV. EARLIEST FORMS OF CHRISTIAN ART

The decay of the plastic arts of the ancients, which shrank progressively under Oriental influence from the third century A.D. onwards, is one of the most remarkable phenomena in the history of art.

For the first time in the history of world-civilization Greece had given pride of place to all that was *temporal* in human life. The lucid speculation of thinkers, even those of a Plato, projected the light of reason into the dark places of the soul, and the relationship between the soul and the beyond became a matter for pure dialectic and not an article of faith. Once man was delivered from his obsession with the deity, religion gave way to metaphysics.

The religions of the East, which at the end of the ancient world began their onslaught on paganism, reforged the chains of man's submission to God, but by means of initiation they offered the believer a form of participation which united him with the person of a redeeming God. It was by an intuitive and mystical knowledge and no longer a rational form of it, that man was able to cross the gap separating the world of appearances from the beyond. Of all the religions which were struggling between themselves to take over the Empire, Christianity, which triumphed, was the most spiritual: it submitted human destiny to a future life, as was the case with the ancient Egyptians who had some influence on early Christianity.

The pure spirituality which Christianity had inherited from Judaism was to lead its first followers into an aversion from art, which had served the worship of idols only too readily. When the new religion broke new ground and attracted the pagan masses, it had to come to terms with the mind of the illiterate classes who needed images to guide their belief. Having allowed such imagery against its inclination, Christianity had to purge it of that physical emphasis which, ever since the Greeks, had made it a reflection of earthly things. If it was to be no longer an object of worship, but only a means to it, the image was none the less to play a part in the new faith very like the one it had held in the old religions of the East. It was an instrument of theology, the figurative intermediary on which faith leans in order to appreciate the dogma of which the image is only the garment and the representation. While it was an intermediary shorn of that reality which had given it magical power in the ancient religions – though perhaps secretly the layman never stopped believing in that magical property – the image was to enter a new phase by becoming a symbol; and art is a language which translates the truth of dogma into forms, *parlar visibile,* as Dante put it.

All that was foreign to the clear transcription of the symbol was eliminated. Landscape was replaced by a few guiding accessories. Some com-

128 Temptation of Christ. Mosaic in St. Mark's, Venice. 12th c.

positions were reduced to a few forms linked together like words in a statement, reminding us of hieroglyphs (pl. 128).

Images were now unreally suspended as though in flight, against an abstract golden background; the line of the horizon disappeared, together with the earth itself. Events no longer took place on earth or in the sky, but in the abstraction of an ideal universe. The various features in the composition no longer had the relative sizes that would be theirs in concrete reality, but their size was now determined by the idea behind them: as in the early Egyptian and Mesopotamian arts, the principal person in the composition towered over all the rest, who were grouped like dwarfs at his feet. The composition of landscape was treated with the same severity, a mountain becoming a mere mound of sand, or a building no larger than a footstool (pl. 128). A purely moral hierarchy replaced the material order of things.

This entirely spiritual interpretation of objects, according to which temporal existence is a delusion and the only reality is in the timeless, was to destroy the Greek plastic arts just as it destroyed the Greek aesthetic itself. The Greeks must have seen everything from the corporeal point of view, and this gave all their creations, even in philosophy, the pure edges and the clarity of geometrical forms. Their essential concern was the definition of objects and concepts in their proper dimensions and limits, so that we can understand why their plastic creations were as exactly circumscribed as solids in the three dimensions of space, and why sculpture was for them the major art. The Christian aesthetic was to abolish sculpture, reducing forms to an unreal flatness of surface. The half-profile, or three-quarter view so dear to the Greeks, disappeared and gave place to frontality and to the profile (pl. 129–131). Modelling was flattened into calligraphy. The artist deliberately avoided any expression of

120

129 *Head of Achilles (reversed) from a Pompeian Fresco. Naples*
130 *Head of an Angel from a Mosaic in S. Maria Maggiore, Rome. A.D. 352–366*
131 *Head of Theodora from a Mosaic in S. Vitale, Ravenna. 6th c. A.D.*

movement, which would be guilty of imitating life. He fixed his figures in eternal attitudes and gave his compositions the strictest symmetry. The repetition of figures in endless series, so dear to the ancient East (pl. 132, 133) symbolizes that oneness to which the deceptive variety of appearances is reduced in eternity.

While the sense of volume died out, that of perspective which the Greeks had intuitively discovered also vanished, and early Christian art returned to the old mode of representation used in primitive cultures, composition in superimposed layers or rows (pl. 134). To this was added the radiating composition in which all the elements are arranged round a centre (pl. 135). Applied to building methods this radial form gave rise to the central plan which was an outcome of architectural speculation among the Byzantines. On a centred monument the roundness of the cupolas reinforces the idea of gravitation toward a given point, and this became a striking symbol of monotheism (pl. 136).

The whole gamut of primitive conventions now directed against Greek art, plunged the Greco-Roman world back into a type of vision that it had left behind for eight centuries. The eye no longer saw things in an order whose hierarchy was dictated by their true proportions in reality. As in the primitive cultures, everything was now seen for its own sake, in its essence, with the result that the details on a figure were out of proportion, out of scale with the person, who was so to speak 'blasoned' or emblematized by the accessories of his clothing or equipment. The tendency towards series is to be found even in the stylization of draperies and the handling of hair and beards as decorative motifs. Such was the avoidance of the notion of space that very often the perspective was reversed, the figures in the middle-ground being larger than those in the foreground, while the lines of objects converged towards the spectator and not

121

132 Holy Martyrs. Mosaic Frieze in S. Apollinare Nuovo, Ravenna. 6th c. A.D.

towards the background (pl. 137). This aesthetic system reflects a kind of thought which seeks to identify itself with things in their entirety, by an intuitive sense like that of touch; whereas the Greek vision set objects in a perspective comparable with that which the analytic operations of reason impose on ideas.

This conception is so Oriental that the earliest Christian art produced in Rome still knew nothing of it. Without Byzantium it might have seemed that the Classical plastic code was only going to be changed as regards meaning (pl. 130). Quickly developed in Byzantium in the fifth and sixth centuries, the new aesthetic rapidly spread over the entire Mediterranean, then to the still barbarous peoples of the West. The poverty of these latter peoples as regards any artistic tradition made them welcome the Byzan-

133 Bowmen. Frieze in enamelled Brickwork from Susa. 5th c. B.C. Paris

tine example only too greedily, without in the least understanding its lofty implications of dogma. For them, it was only a matter of being given a repertory of forms, which they used much as children repeat parrot-wise the sounds of a foreign language. Obstinately hostile to the portrayal of the human figure, even in this conventional form, for several centuries they pursued the purely imaginative speculations they had inherited from their nomadic ancestors, seeing in Byzantine art no more than a vehicle for those Oriental forms which reminded them of their own origins; and all this at a time when Byzantium itself was undergoing a serious disturbance of conscience.

134 Adam in the Garden of Eden. Ivory Diptych (detail). 4th c. A.D. Florence

A survey of the Western world and the Mediterranean basin in the seventh and eighth centuries would show, indeed, such a complete regression from the Greek plastic arts that the human person and the figure in general tended to disappear from art entirely, being reduced to a purely ornamental expression. Islam, established on the south and eastern fringes of the Mediterranean, imposed in those regions an outlook hostile to images, strictly observing the spirit of the Koran and opposed to the portrayal of anything human or living. In Byzantium a great movement – the iconoclastic crisis – which sprang partly from Islamic influence, tended to forbid the worship of images as being idolatrous, and to suppress the figurative portrayal of holy personages. In the West, the impulse towards ornamentation thrived and encroached on even the few representations of sacred art that were attempted.

135 Last Supper. Miniature from a Syriac Codex 12th c. London

136 *Christ, Angels and Prophets. Mosaic in the Chapel Palatine, Palermo. 12th c.*

However, just when it might be expected that a kind of artistic puritanism was finally about to dominate the world, a simultaneous reaction in East and West restored form and shape to the figure. In the ninth century the Macedonian renaissance in Byzantium and the Carolingian renaissance in the West both aimed at redirecting art towards the spirit of the classical arts. Under this influence the Byzantine hankering after Orientalism was profoundly shaken as it began to long for the harmonious rhythms of ancient Greece. As for Charlemagne, wrapped in his northern mists and far removed from the home of classicism, he only received the classical influence at second-hand, by way of Byzantine art which was fortunate enough to thrive on the very soil on which the ancients had laboured.

The Macedonian and Carolingian revivals, both of them intellectual undertakings brought about by the heads of states, were purely formalistic in character. It is true that they created masterpieces, but a genuine

137 *Abraham and the three Angels. Mosaic in S. Maria Maggiore, Rome. 352–366*

138 *Interior of a Catacomb (Cubiculum with Arcosolium and Loculi), Rome. Early 4th c.*

revival cannot spring from such unspontaneous movements. In eleventh-century France and thirteenth-century Italy, the West, finally emerging from its protracted childhood, was to create a mode of expression as original as Greek art itself.

1. EARLY CHRISTIAN ART IN ROME

The Art of the Catacombs

While in the East some figures, though still pagan, already contained elements of the aesthetic which was to triumph with Christianity, in the West the first Christian art was no more than the last phase of ancient art. The earliest images of the new cult are to be found in the catacombs, underground cemeteries made by the Christians during their secret life in the first three centuries of our era, down in the chalky sub-soil of Rome. In the walls of long passages *(ambulacra)* which were practically sub-terranean towns, the sepulchres *(loculi)* were set in tiers, closed with stone slabs bearing the names of the dead. Occasionally a more imposing tomb cut in the shape of an arch *(arcosolium)* was the resting-place of some notable or martyr, while clearings in the gallery containing *arcosolia* served as funeral chapels *(cubicula)* (pl. 138). The chapels were often decorated with stucco or mural paintings, very fragile because they were executed straight on the unprepared wall, in the manner of the Egyptians or Etruscans. The dominant idea in these decorations was the future life to which the Christian soul was called after shedding its earthly trammels (of which the symbol was the figure of the *orante*), thanks to the Redemption brought by Christ. Subjects taken from the Old and New Testaments were rare and without any historical significance, being used as apologetic

139 Christ and the Apostles. Wall-Painting in the Catacomb of Domitilla, Rome. 4th c.

evidence of divine mercy. For the most part the Christians contented themselves with pagan legends and images to which they gave a new meaning. Thus Aristaeus, the god of gardens, with a lamb on his shoulders, became the Good Shepherd, a symbol of Christ. The amorous shepherds and harvesters of the vine found in the villas of Pompeii end their career by symbolizing Paradise and the Eucharist, respectively. Orpheus charming the wild beasts prefigures Christ, while the pagan myth of Eros and Psyche becomes a symbol of the trials undergone by the human soul before entering heaven. Going even farther in their passion for cryptograms the Christians, in order to portray Christ, his Passion and the Redemption, created a whole system of picture-puzzles – and no doubt the persecutions had something to do with this esotericism. Findings in

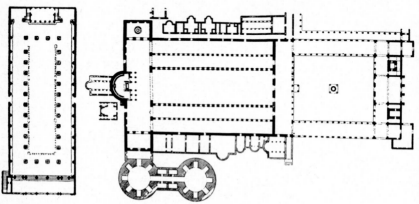

140 Roman Basilica, Pompeii. 1st c. B.C.

141 Plan of Old St Peter's, Rome. Middle of 4th c.

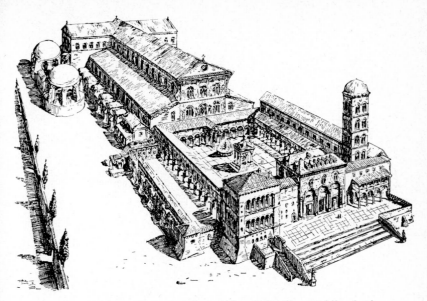

142 St Peter's, Rome. Reconstruction of the old Basilica. Middle of 4th c.

the catacombs also include funerary lamps, and gold-bottomed flasks in which the blood of martyrs was kept. A fine bronze medallion of the second century, from the Domitilla catacombs, shows the oldest portraits of St Peter and St Paul, which set standard types for the Middle Ages.

Art after the Triumph of Christianity

The Basilicas

The early Christians had no interest in forms themselves and were content with the models they borrowed from Hellenistic plastic conventions; all they cared about was the idea behind them. This state of affairs continued until Christianity came out of hiding and became the official religion of the Roman Empire, when it celebrated its victory in an ostentatious way, for which reason the art of the Christian Empire may be called 'triumphal art' (from 313 to the fifth century).

The most noticeable result of this victory was the creation of an architecture to house the new religion. The inconvenience of the Greco-Roman temple as well as its idolatrous associations led the new cult to reject it as a possible form. The temple with its porticos was conceived from the outside, being the house of God to which only priests could have access, whereas the church (*ecclesia,* meaning 'assembly') was a place for the

143 S. Sabina, Rome. 5th c.

meeting of all the faithful, who were called without distinction to participate in the deity. Thus it had to enclose an immense space. The Christians found a ready-made form for this in the ancients' repertory of architectural inventions – the basilica, a long rectangle with nave and aisles, which used to serve as a meeting-place, a tribunal or a closed market (pl. 140). To this they added only a transept or transverse nave, to give it the shape of the cross (pl. 141). The apse, a semicircular or polygonal recess beyond the crossing containing a bench *(presbyterium)*, was reserved for the priests. The altar was at the crossing of the transept and nave, and the ceremonies took place in the main nave, the faithful standing, men to the left and women to the right in the single or sometimes double aisles which at times had a gallery. The church was entered by a narthex in which the catachumens met, and a courtyard surrounded by four colonnades (the atrium), which was the origin of the cloister of the medieval monasteries. In the centre of the atrium stood the *canthare*, a fountain for ablutions which was the origin of our stoup for holy water (pl. 142).

The Roman basilica, like that of the ancients, was timbered over, except for the apse which was given a semi-dome. The pillars separating the nave from the aisles were surmounted by architraves, or more frequently arcades (pl. 143).

144 Marble Figure of Christ, Rome. 4th c. A.D.

Symbolic of the Christian soul, which should be completely turned towards the inner life, the brick-built basilican church appeared from the outside as an unadorned structure. Inside, on the contrary, luxurious adornment was spread everywhere to give the faithful the impression of some supernatural place. The columns were of marble, the lower walls were covered with decorative mosaics in precious marble, to which were often added porphyry, mother-of-pearl, onyx and other rare materials. In the upper parts, above the arcades, on the triumphal arch separating the nave from the transept, and in the apse, were frescoes of scintillating mosaics, showing the main figures in scenes from the Testaments. The altar was surmounted by a canopy in worked gold or marble (ciborium), while the choir was surrounded with an incrusted marble screen (chancel) containing the ambons or pulpits for the reading of the Epistle and Gospel.

The principal basilican churches still standing today are, in Rome, S. Paolo fuori le Mura, built in the fourth century and rebuilt after the fire of 1823 (reconsecrated 1854); S. Lorenzo fuori le Mura (fourth to sixth century); S. Giovanni in Laterano (fourth century, but much restored); S. Maria Maggiore (fourth and fifth centuries); S. Agnese (fourth to seventh century); S. Sabina (pl. 143); S. Maria in Trastevere. The great basilica of St Peter, with a nave and double aisles, built by Constantine, was destroyed during the Renaissance, and is known to us only from old illustrations (pl. 141, 142).

New Plastic Conceptions

The plastic language of triumphal art – the art of the Church triumphant – is the same as that of the final period of ancient art. The spirit of Classical sculpture remained until the fourth and fifth centuries in the sarcophagi, great works in marble, in which from the second century onwards the pagans had themselves buried when the influence of Oriental religions, including Christianity, replaced cremation by interment. The Roman sarcophagi were decorated with Christian scenes, vigorously carved in the round but gradually declining under Oriental influence, which was to triumph in the sixth century. The face of Christ was most often taken from the Greek adolescent type (pl. 144).

The real innovation of triumphal art was the figured mosaic. Used in Hellenistic art in the form of pictures for adorning pavements the mosaic, now set upon walls, showed a host of figures spread over a large surface. The oldest mosaics, in the vault of the circular aisle of S. Costanza (after 337), were marble renderings of the symbolic ornamentation of the catacombs. Those in S. Maria Maggiore (pl. 130, 137) date from the fourth and fifth centuries and form the oldest cycle of evangelical and biblical pictures. They still have traces of the ancient aesthetic – figures shown in three-dimensional space, landscape backgrounds, Greek or Roman dress. But the perspective was already changed; the golden background had not appeared here any more than at S. Pudenziana (fourth century) which is dominated by a bearded Christ based on the Jupiter type. The mosaics of

the Mausoleum of Galla Placidia at Ravenna (fifth century) are still close
to the spirit of antiquity and contrast sharply with those of S. Apollinare
Nuovo and S. Vitale, built in the sixth century at the moment when
Ravenna was part of the Byzantine Empire and in the grip of the Oriental
aesthetic.

2. BYZANTINE ART

Historical Background

It was in the East, in the great Hellenistic cities of Egypt, Asia Minor and
Syria, that the Christian dogma and ritual were shaped before the Church
had actually triumphed, as is proved by the abundance of Greek names in
the new religion's vocabulary (Christ, Christian, angel, Apostle, bishop
(*episcopus*), priest, diocese, synod, church (*ecclesia*), baptism, Eucharist,
etc.). It was thus the Eastern Empire that rose from the split in 395, which
was to be the most active centre of Christian art. Whereas the Western
Empire fell under the onslaughts of the barbarians, the Eastern Empire
survived until the fifteenth century. Byzantium (Constantinople), which
Constantine founded in 327 was to be its centre; but in the fourth, fifth
and sixth centuries, before the Moorish invasions, Christian art flourished
all round the Mediterranean fringe, in Antioch, Syria, Palestine – where
splendid basilicas were built on the holy sites – and at Alexandria and
Ephesus. Generally speaking the coastal cities remained faithful the long-
est to the Hellenistic aesthetic, while under monkish influence the hinterland developed a more Oriental and primitive art which gradually affected the first type. This was the case in Syria and above all in Upper Egypt
(Baouit), where the monks decorated their monasteries with frescoes and

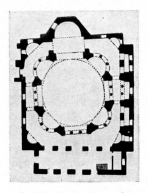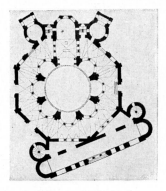

145 *Plan of SS. Sergius and Bacchus, Constantinople. 1st third of 6th c.*
146 *Plan of S. Vitale, Ravenna. 526/534–547*

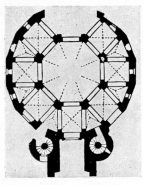

147 *Plan of the Chapel Palatine, Aachen. Late 8th c.*

sculptures full of a primitive vigour already suggestive of Romanesque art (Coptic art, pl. 152).

The period showing the widest extension of the Byzantine Empire and its art was the sixth century, when Justinian retook Africa from the Vandals – setting up many basilicas there – and, from the Goths in Italy, Ravenna (the centrally planned S. Vitale, and the basilica of S. Apollinare Nuovo). In Byzantinum itself Justinian built the churches of the Holy Apostles, SS. Sergius and Bacchus and S. Sophia. After the conquest of part of the Mediterranean by the Arabs, Byzantine art had a phase which is called the iconoclastic crisis. A gust of puritanism, not unlike that of Protestantism later, taxed the excessive image-cult which was widespread in the fifth and sixth centuries, with being idolatrous. In the seventh and eighth centuries, perhaps under the aniconic, anti-image influence of Islam, Byzantine art was reduced to the level of ornamental background. It was reborn in all its splendour from the ninth to eleventh century, with the Macedonian dynasty. The finest monuments were in Greece (Daphni; S. Luke in Phocis); but Byzantium reached into the West, towards Venice (S. Mark's, Venice; churches on Torcello) and, in the twelfth century, to Sicily (mosaics at Palermo, Cefalu, Monreale); and, into the East as far as Russia (S. Sophia, Kiev). In Armenia a prosperous Christian community continued building admirable churches in dressed stone; in Asia Minor monks from Cappadocia evolved a popular art, full of pathos, very different from official Byzantine. In the thirteenth and fourteenth centuries Byzantine art spread into Serbia and Bulgaria; its figurative designs were more economically carried out in paint. The finest specimens are in Greece, at Mistra (Peloponnese), on Mount Athos and in the territory governed by the Serbian Tzars, in Macedonia and Serbia (Oratchanitsa, Stoudenitsa, Nagoritchina, Sopot-

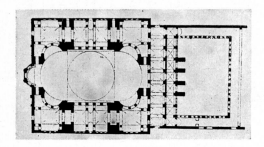

148 *Plan of S. Sophia, Constantinople. 532–537*

chani, pl. 154). Byzantine art endured until our own time in the icons of
Russia, Crete and Mount Athos.

The conversion of Prince Vladimir to the Greek Orthodox faith in 989,
which at the same time called into existence a new Christian province,
directed the artistic activities of the Russian Slavs towards Byzantium.
The peoples of Poland and Bohemia on the other hand, who belonged
to the Roman Catholic Church, continued to develop under the influence
of Western styles.

Architecture

Eastern Christian art in its early stages followed the basilican system, in
the Greek churches (S. Demetrios, Salonica), in Palestine (Bethlehem), as
well as in Syria, Asia (Anatolia), the region round Ravenna, and Africa
(Tunisia). The churches there were all roofed with timber as were the
Roman churches, though one or two in Anatolia had tunnel-vaults. But
the real creation of Byzantine architecture was the vaulted church, centrally-planned. The central plan often consisted of a simple cupola set on
a ring of archways and surrounded by an ambulatory: SS. Sergius and
Bacchus, Constantinople (pl. 145); S. Vitale, Ravenna (pl. 146); St George
of Ezra, Syria. Then, developing the principle of Sassanian buildings the
Byzantines elaborated complex plans in which the domes and tiered
tunnel-vaults buttressed each other and took the strain of a lofty central
cupola (pl. 149).

The central plan was combined with the basilican plan at S. Sophia at
Constantinople, constructed between 532 and 537 by order of Justinian.

149 Isometric drawing of S. Sophia, Constantinople

150 Interior of S. Sophia, Constantinople. 532–537

The architects were the Anatolians Anthemius of Tralles and Isidorus of Miletus (pl. 148–150). Ten thousand men worked on the building which is the most grandiose structure of Byzantine art; every province of the Empire sent its most precious materials for its decoration. A high cupola (reconstructed after collapsing, 558–562) by Isidore the Younger (nephew

151 Byzantine Capital. Gallery
of S. Vitale, Ravenna. 6th c.

152 Coptic Bas-Relief in Sandstone
from Egypt. Probably 4th c. Washington

of Isidore of Miletus) is 170 1/2 feet high against a diameter of 100 feet.
Its pendentives rest on four great arches set on enormous pillars; at the
north and south it is held by two tunnel-vaults and is buttressed at the
east and west by two huge half-domes which in their turn rest on retain-
ing recesses or niches. The building is contained in a rectangle, 250 feet
by 233 feet. It has two galleries. These vast dimensions reflect a taste for
the colossal, at once Roman and Asiatic, in keeping with Justinian's enormous Empire. The Greek spirit predominates in the buildings of the Macedonian period, when, using moderate dimensions, architects sought harmony through pleasing exactness of proportions. They then achieved the
perfect central plan in the form of a Greek cross (i.e. with all four limbs
of equal length) in which four vaults (either barrel, half-domes or

153 Detail of an ivory
Episcopal Throne.
Archbihop's Palace,
Ravenna. 6th c.

cupolas) counterbalance the central dome (S. Sophia, Kiev; St Luke of Stiris, Phocis; various churches in Constantinople; St Mark's, Venice; Holy Apostles, Ani in Armenia). Sometimes the cupolas were set on a high drum or circular wall.

Except in Asia Minor and Armenia, where they built with ashlar or freestone, the Byzantine structure was made of enormous solid masses of brick carrying light domes of the same material. The use of freestone led Anatolia and above all Armenia, like later Romanesque art, to the idea of external decoration related to structural meaning, with niches, close-buttresses, plain brick clamping against rough-cast walls; the Macedonian architects also gave thought to external plastic effects. But in the fifth and sixth centuries the Byzantine building showed only a naked structure from the outside. All the decoration was reserved for inside, where it was not built-in but applied to the walls by way of adornment, in the form of marble facings and mosaics. The worshipper found himself plunged into a supernatural atmosphere by the vastness and lightness of the domes which hardly seemed to touch their pendentives; and the luxury of the setting, the wealth of colour-effects, the glinting of the mosaics, were all calculated to transport the worshipper into another world.

At Novgorod and Vladimir Russian architects, building their churches in the form of the Greek cross, made their own original additions: cupolas were surmounted with drums and bulbous domes, which appear from the twelfth century onwards. In Vladimir several stone churches of the twelfth and thirteenth centuries are decorated on the exterior with carved reliefs which appear to have been inspired by Armenian and Georgian churches.

The Figurative Arts

From the sixth century onwards sculpture shows the rapid reabsorption of a technique which had been the chief concern and the main experimental field of Greek art. Sculpture in the round disappeared entirely, and only a few capitals, marble balustrades and, at Ravenna, one or two sarcophagi were treated with the hand-drill or bore, but no longer with the chisel. At the same time these features were only decorated with ornamental motifs, not worked in relief but laid on in imitation of the coloured effects of mosaic. Deriving from the ancient composite column, the Byzantine capital evolved quickly until by the sixth century it was no more than a down-turned pyramid covered with open tracery (pl. 151). However, the art of relief survived in small articles made out of precious materials such as ivory and gold. Ivory craftsmanship in the fifth and sixth centuries shows a progressive flattening of Greek contours, the immobilizing of attitudes, the schematization of modelling, a tendency which is seen completely evolved in the Throne of Bishop Maximian at Ravenna (sixth century, pl. 153), which came from Alexandria or Con-

*154 Death of the Virgin.
Fresco at Sopotchani
(Jugoslavia). 13th c.*

stantinople. In the Macedonian period a tentative renaissance of the
plastic sense showed itself in ivories.

In the domain of figurative representation, the mosaic was the great
art of the Byzantine period. By the unrealness of its gold backgrounds
and its glittering colours the mosaic gave the Byzantine artist an ideal
medium for his desire to rid the spectator of every naturalistic illusion
and suggest the very presence of the supernatural.

The great creations of S. Vitale and S. Apollinare at Ravenna in their
totality show the full achievement of the new aesthetic. A hieratic concept
of monarchy inspires the mosaics of Justinian and Theodora at S. Vitale.
As in the old Eastern monarchies the *basileus* whose person is consub-
stantial with God has his secular power by divine right, and appears to
his subjects surrounded by the superhuman attributes of royal pomp. The
heavenly court in S. Apollinare Nuovo shows itself to the faithful in all
the ceremonial trappings of the monarch's own court. In the Ravenna
mosaics the Oriental aesthetic had overcome the Grecian: the unmodelled
forms are flattened into the abstract surface of the gold background; the
manifold gestures of life are frozen into a few solemn attitudes; nothing
remains of the natural figures but a few stylized outlines; the three-
quarter view is replaced exclusively by frontal and profile positions;
while the deliberate repetition of gestures and attitudes, the frieze arrangements recalling the enamelled ceramic friezes of the Achaemenians
(pl. 132, 133) and the taste for rigorously symmetrical compositions, suggest in the spectator's mind a return of all the forms in the creation to
some eternal unity (pl. 136). The landscape disappears and a few small
accessories serve to suggest the location of whatever scene is represented.
When the art of mosaic revived in the ninth century, the apologetic spirit
following the iconoclastic crisis imposed a strict iconographic order on

137

155 King David from the Paris
Psalter, Early 10th c. Paris

156 Crucifixion from the Rabula Gospels. Syriac.
About 586. Florence

the distribution of images on church walls. The major works at Kiev
(Ukraine, eleventh century), Greece (Daphne, St Luke at Phocis, end of
eleventh century), St Mark's, Venice (end of eleventh century) and Sicily
(Palermo, Cefalu, Monreale, all twelfth century) show biblical scenes arranged according to the liturgy and surmounted by the colossal, awesome
figure of the *Pantocrator* (Almighty) who is set in the central dome at,
so to speak, the umbilical point of the church, and has something of the
ancient gods in the gravity of his brow (pl. 136). The Oriental conception
of superhuman divinity has triumphed here over that of the Greek god,
represented on a human scale, which survived in triumphal art (pl. 144).
The gospel and biblical scenes are emptied of historical content and have
only a symbolic and liturgical meaning. In the Passion, Christ is always
portrayed indifferent to pain and insult. The modelling, drawing and
arabesque tend to a formal perfection that was to be recaptured by
Cimabue in the Trecento (pl. 184, 185).

The more popular art of the fresco – a cheap substitute for the mosaic –
shows different characteristics. The monks who decorated the cave-
churches of Cappadocia (Asia Minor) from the ninth to the thirteenth
century were the first to try and express the human pathos of the gospel.
This they did with a naïve violence. Strengthened by Western influences
this outlook spread to the Greek painting of Mistra in the fourteenth
century as well as to churches in Serbia, Rumania and Bulgaria. The best
school of fresco-painters was in Jugoslavia (Sopotchani frescoes, thirteenth century, pl. 154).

In Russia at about the same time mosaic gave way to fresco painting,
which was to flourish principally in Novgorod and later in Moscow and
Yaroslavl. From the fourteenth century onwards it gradually became
the practice to cut off the altar-space from the rest of the church by

putting up iconostases, screens to which icons (sacred paintings on wood) were attached in vertical and horizontal rows. By their faithful adherence to earlier models iconographers were to preserve the traditions of Byzantine art for a long time to come.

The various streams to be found in Byzantine art are also reflected in the miniature, the art of book-illustration which began in Egypt in the Hellenistic period. The Alexandrian taste for the picturesque persisted there for a long time thanks to the system of copying prototypes (*Vatican Homer* and *Vatican Virgil*, fourth century, the *Vienna Genesis*, fifth century, *Scroll of Joshua*, sixth century). It took on a new lease of life in the Macedonian period, in the *Theriaca* – a treatise on medicine – of Nicander (eleventh century, Bibliothèque Nationale) and the *Paris Psalter* (tenth century, same library, pl. 155) which astonish us with images that would appear to be contemporary with the frescoes of Pompeii. Side by side with this aristocratic group, a monastic group shows a more religious and more Oriental spirit: this tradition originated in Syriac monasteries in the sixth and seventh centuries, heralding the pathos of the Cappadocian frescoes (*Rabula Gospels*, Florence, pl. 156).

The Slavonic Countries

In the fifteenth century Russian icon-painting became independent, freeing itself from Byzantine influence, a movement which had its parallel in Italy a century earlier. The graceful, delicately refined art of Andrei

157 a Pantocrator from the Pala d'Oro. St Mark's, Venice. Late 11th – Early 12th c.

157 b Rublev. Old Testament Trinity. Moscow. Early 15th c.

158 *Volcian silver Coin. Paris*

159 *Elusate silver Coin. Paris*

Rublev, active in Moscow at the beginning of the fifteenth century, is reminiscent of the neo-Alexandrian style and spiritualized forms of Duccio (Icon of the Holy Trinity from the Trinity-Sergius Monastery, now in the Tretyakov Gallery, Moscow, pl. 157 b). The Novgorod icon-painters manifest the same delight in pictorial narrative as the Lorenzetti brothers of Siena, and they strive for luminous effects in colour. The portable icons painted in the sixteenth century for the Stroganovs, which reproduce the sensitive delicacy of miniature paintings, call to mind the linear elegance and Persian effects of Pisanello. The movement towards Western realism in the seventeenth century marked the end of icon-painting.

The Minor Arts

The Oriental taste for luxury appeared in Byzantium in works of handi-craft made all over the Empire for both local use and export; for the

160 *Eagle-formed Buckle in Gold with Garnets from Cesena, Italy. 6th c. Paris*

161 *Decorative Coursing. Church at Selommes, France. 10th c.*

peoples of the West, not yet skilled as craftsmen, readily gave high prices for them. Thus the treasuries of the Western churches have preserved large numbers of ivories, textiles, carved gems and goldsmiths' work. In the sixth century Syria specialized in the production of large, embossed (repoussé) silverware of ancient derivation, while Byzantium exploited the process of cloisonné enamelling. The finest ensemble of Byzantine craftsmanship in gold in the *Pala d'Oro*, the high altar of St Mark's, Venice (early twelfth century, pl. 157 a), which is lavishly worked with gold, gems, pearls and enamels. The fabrics woven in Coptic Egypt and in Syria, then in Constantinople after the Arab conquest, often took their inspiration

162 *Initial from the Book of Kells. 2nd half of 7th c. Dublin*

from old Persian and Sassanian patterns and served as a means of making Oriental designs known in the West.

3. WESTERN ART IN THE EARLY MIDDLE AGES

Pre-Carolingian

The artistic tradition of the barbarians who settled in the West in the fourth and fifth centuries, had given them little preparation for the complex works of a permanent civilization. Having been accustomed for thousands of years to the few crafts compatible with their nomadic existence (fabrics, articles of finery and equipment), they were now faced with architectural and iconographical needs for which they had to invent everything themselves.

Tribes of the Goths, the most gifted of the barbarian peoples, founded states in Spain (Visigoths) and in Italy (Ostrogoths). They learnt all they could from Rome and Byzantium. The Franks, who settled in Gaul, and the Lombards in northern Italy, imbibed Oriental traditions through the Greeks monks and the Syrian and Jewish merchants who brought them Byzantine and Sassanian merchandise which delighted their luxurious tastes. The influx of these Asiatic peoples revived the ornamental and abstract tendencies which had found expression in Celtic art before being discouraged by the Roman conquest.

141

Any study of early Western art should begin with the minor arts, whose aesthetic dominated even architecture to such a degree that sometimes even the coursing of walls imitated the patterns of the weaver or the silver-smith (pl. 161). The Goths and Franks were to maintain that technique of cloisonné work in gold which was their speciality (pl. 160), both

164 Symbols of the Four Evangelists. Altar-Frontal of the Patriarch Sicuald.
Late 8th c. Cividale

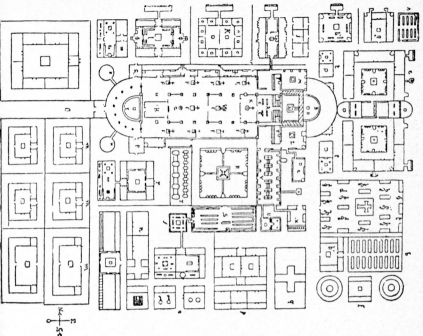

165 'Ideal' Plan of St-Gall. About 820

in lay works (crowns of the Visigoth kings, found at Guarrazar near Toledo) and by adapting it to religious needs (shrines and reliquaries). We know from descriptions written at the time that churches were richly decorated with costly works of this kind.

A supremely monastic art, the illumination, was brought to Gaul by monks from Egypt. The monks used it for embellishing holy books (such as missels and gospels) with a pure decorative impulse which disdained mere realism. The chimerical imagination of the barbarians suggested fantastic forms to them, which they intermingled in a sort of indecipherable ornamental pattern which we call tracery. It was in the work of Irish and English monks in the seventh and eighth centuries that this ornamental medium took the most remarkable forms, in which Celtic, Saxon and Mediterranean influences came together. The oldest of these works, the *Book of Durrow* (Trinity College, Dublin, second half of seventh century, pl. 713), has an obvious relationship to the magnificent trinkets found in the graves of Anglo-Saxon chiefs (treasure-trove of Sutton Hoo, about 650, pl. 48). Mediterranean influence is seen in the *Lindisfarne Gospel* (British Museum, between 698–721), while the admirable *Book of Kells* (Trinity College, Dublin, between 760–820, pl. 162) shows – at least in the miniatures showing the human figure – the influence of such Byzantine works as the *Rabula Gospels* (pl. 156) or *Etchmiadzin Codex*. The *Lichfield Gospel* (Lichfield Cathedral, eighth century) is in a similar style to the *Book of Kells*. The *St Gall Gospel* (Bibliothèque de St-Gall, Switzerland, between 750–760) is considered to be a purely Irish example of a style in which the human figure itself became no more than a part of a rhythmic pattern.

Fourth-century Gaul had a period of building activity which resulted in basilicas of the Roman type, decorated with rich mosaics. The mosaics gave way to frescoes after the barbarian invasions of the fifth century. An offshoot of Roman triumphal art, this form still flourished in the fifth century, to judge from the rotunda-style baptisteries which were used for baptism by immersion, and of which a number of specimens survive in Provence (Marseilles, Fréjus, Aix, Riez, Mélas, Valence). At Ravenna in Italy, Amalasuntha built a domed rotunda (after 530) over the tomb of her father Theodoric, king of the Ostrogoths (pl. 163). This cupola is a monolith, 35 ³/₄ feet in diameter and weighing 300 tons, the last example in the West of the taste for components of colossal dimensions which we noted in the most primitive civilizations. The Visigoth art of Spain, whose capital was then Toledo, has left few remains (S. Miguel de Tarrassa), but some characteristics of this art appear to have persisted in the monuments raised by the Christian kings of the Asturias in the

166 *Chapel Palatine (now Cathedral), Aachen. Late 8th c.*

I Christ the Saviour. Bamberg Apocalypse from Bamberg Cathedral. Munich

167 St Matthew. Minature from the
Ebbo Gospel. Between 816–835.
Epernay

168 Christ. Miniature from the
Godescalc Gospel

ninth century, which also show some Oriental influence (Santullano,
S. Miguel de Liño, S. Cristina de Lena, S. Maria de Naranco).

The narrative sarcophagi of Arles, imitated from the Roman in the
fourth century, show the last traces of ancient plastic traditions in Gaul,
but in a profoundly debased form. Figurative sculpture disappeared in
the fifth century. The workshops of the Pyrenees continued to produce
columns, capitals, sarcophagi and marble plaques for chancels, all in an
exclusively ornamental style. These products of the Pyrenean quarries
were exported to northern Gaul (Jouarre crypt), especially in the seventh
century when there seems to have been considerable artistic activity; but
this industry was killed by the Muslim invasions which ravaged the
whole of southern France in the early eighth century. Sculpture in the
round tended to disappear all over the barbarian area, being replaced by
carved panelling in stone which often imitated the goldsmiths' cloisonné-
work (altars at Cividale in Lombardy, pl. 164).

Carolingian and Ottonian Art

The Carolingian reformation showed the same characteristics in art as
in politics and literature. It tried to react against the anarchy of the
barbarians by a return to the traditions of the Roman Empire. It was in
Classical and Byzantine Italy that Charlemagne sought his models for a
revival of figurative and monumental art. The famous Chapel Palatine
at Aachen (Aix-la-Chapelle) was only a simplified edition of S. Vitale

ASCENSIO SCEMARIÆ

S GALL PANE PORRIGITVRSO

169 Tutilo. *Assumption and Scenes from the Legend of St-Gall.
Ivory Codex Cover. About 900. St-Gall*

170 *All Saints,*
Earls Barton.
Tower about 935

at Ravenna, but enriched with ancient materials taken from Italy (pl. 147, 166). The Carolingian artists eagerly adopted plans for buildings on the principle of the Greek cross (Church of Germigny-des-Prés near Orléans) and they made great use of the 'double-basilica' plan (with two apses and two transepts). The influence of the monks, who were the guardians of the literatures of antiquity and of the principles of civilization, now dominated everything. Monasteries were built all over the Empire, and the 'ideal' plan, dating from the ninth century and preserved at the abbey of St-Gall in Switzerland, shows us, fully formed, the typical medieval lay-out: monastery buildings set round a cloister flanking a church, together with agricultural, industrial, hospital and teaching accommodation, all giving a good idea of the part that monks were playing in both material and spiritual civilization (pl. 165). The most strikingly ornate example of Carolingian architecture left in England is the west tower of All Saints, Earls Barton (pl. 170).

Carolingian art reacted violently against the formlessness of the barbarians and introduced representation once more. It was often nearer to ancient than to Byzantine art, as can be seen from the frescoes in the crypt of St-Germain-d'Auxerre, or those in S. Maria de Castelseprio which

147

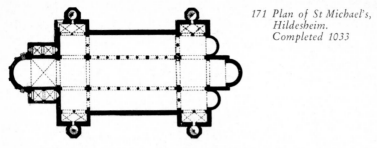

171 *Plan of St Michael's, Hildesheim. Completed 1033*

were rediscovered in Lombardy in 1944. Monastic schools of illumination flourished all over the Empire (at Rheims, Tours, Metz, in France; at Reichenau, St-Gall, Fulda, in Germanic countries). The schools of the East were distinguishable by a romantic, roughish style heralding German Gothic expressionism *(Utrecht Psalter, Ebbo Gospel,* pl. 167, both illuminated at Rheims); while the Tours school *(Bible of Charles the Bald)* or the so-called 'Palace school' which illuminated gospels for the Emperors, sought solemnity of gesture and composition *(Godescalc Gospel* illuminated for Charlemagne, pl. 168, *Gospel of St-Médard,* Soissons).

We know from old descriptions that the churches were embellished with magnificent bronze objects (the so-called *Chair of Dagobert)* but little trace has remained of them. Gold craftsmanship is better represented, these objects sometimes attaining a splendour which was not to be improved on in the Middle Ages (Charlemagne's Treasure at Aachen). The Carolingian artists were able to revive the ancient craft of glyptics, the carving of gems. A renewed feeling for relief came out in ivory

172 *Interior of St Michael's, Hildesheim*

173 *Vuolvinio. Golden Altar in S. Ambrogio, Milan. Late 9th c.*

174 Noli Me Tangere from the Bronze Doors of Hildesheim. Early 11th c.

carving (ivory bindings for gospels, pl. 169) and through the embossed work that was done in gold (*Golden Altar* in S. Ambrogio, Milan. pl. 173, cover of the *Codex Aureus*, Munich).

The Carolingian impulse was checked in Gaul by the anarchy brought about through the Norman invasions in the eleventh century. Meanwhile in Italy and above all in Germany under the prosperous Ottonian dynasty, Carolingian principles persisted into the eleventh century. At Trier and on the Reichenau as well as at Regensburg, Cologne and Fulda, magnificent illuminated manuscripts were produced in a truely Imperial spirit. The Germanic taste for fantasy appears in the ornamental forms although antique motifs are also to be found. However, in the depicting of the human figure, new and highly individual forms of an extra-ordinarily moving expressiveness ran counter to the antique art of the South, which had been the inspiration of Carolingian times. No longer did the artist try to portray biblical events in an illusionistic manner, but instead concentrated on expressing their spiritual significance (*Codex Egberti*, Trier; *Gospel of Otto III, Pericopes of Henry II*, both Staats-bibliothek, Munich; *Bamberg Apocalypse*, colour pl. I; *Hitda Codex*, Darmstadt). While France could now produce nothing better than shapeless reliefs, the plastic sense in Germany expressed itself wonderfully in the eleventh century in the medium of embossed and cast metals (*Golden Altar*, Basle, now in Cluny Museum). Bishop Bernward had two pillars, a chandelier and bronze doors of fine quality made for his cathedral at Hildesheim, which had two transepts, two choirs and two apses (pl. 171, 172, 174), while a little later in about 1060 the craftsman who cast the doors of Augsburg Cathedral, with mythological and biblical scenes, gave them an Alexandrian grace.

175 Carved pillar in Ste-Marie, Souillac. 12th c.

V. THE RISE OF THE WEST

Romanesque and Gothic Art

If any century in Western civilization deserves the name 'Renaissance', then it is the French eleventh century rather than the Italian fifteenth. From the sixth to the tenth century nothing had appeared in the West worth calling a style (we speak of Merovingian or Carolingian 'art', not 'style'). Planting themselves as best they could on the remains of the ancient civilization they had destroyed, and asking Byzantium for lessons which they hardly understood, the barbarians from the sixth to the tenth century never abandoned the tedious ornamental crafts they brought with them from their nomadic past, but failed to fetch from their own darkness that coherent system of constructional methods, architectural, plastic and decorative forms that make a style. But suddenly the veil was torn aside. Architecture in the eleventh century made marvellous strides, a sure sign of a return to building cities. From the basilican church, a building with the unfinished look of a framework covered with temporary

*176/177 Comparison of an Assyrian Cylinder-Seal with a Detail from a Capital
in St-Martin-d'Ainay, Lyon*

roofing, emerged the Romanesque church whose vault, dominating the whole economy of the structure, ensured the unification of all its parts. The monument was no longer a mere inorganic set of walls and roofs providing the necessary closed and covered areas. Like the Greek temple the Romanesque church was an articulated organism, all its parts being unified in their functions and proportions. The bay became the standard measurement for length, the storey for height, bringing new basic units to architectural composition to replace the column and entablature of Greek art. With a rhythm punctuated by the tall shafts, the groin-vaults, and the moulding of string-courses marking the galleries – the entire flow obeys a harmonious regulation of spaces, volumes and surfaces. Moving in a leisurely way from support to archway and from storey to storey, the eye impresses on the mind the perfect unity of all the building's constituent parts, which are given as it were a musical measure by the alternating strong beats of the solid parts and the unaccented beats of the open spaces. This constructional arithmetic which the Greeks had understood intellectually, was reinvented empirically, and in another mode, by the Romanesque artists, who are to be thanked for imposing this notion of order and number on the taste for the indefinite and boundless which the barbarians and the East had in common. After a long eclipse the West emerged victorious from an uneasy struggle for logic which had lasted six hundred years.

All the characteristics of Romanesque art stem from this notion of order. The decoration which had been scattered here and there like tapestry on the walls of Byzantine churches was now confined to the major parts of the building, and to emphasize them it was raised into relief, so that a forgotten technique was now revived – that of sculpture in which the ancient world had expressed its faith in the life of the body. Sculpture is the daughter of architecture, arising from its needs and sharing its spirit. By the powerful articulation of its volumes the Romanesque monument was so to speak modelled spatially.

*Subordination of Sculpture
to Architecture*

178 *Feast at Simon's. Section of a
Tympanum at Neuilly-en-
Donjon. 12th c.*

179 *Last Supper. Tympanum at
Charlieu. 12th c.*

180 *Last Supper. Capital at
Issoire, 12th c.*

Whether it aims at grandeur or harmony – except in the province of
Poitou where it lapsed into the picturesque – Romanesque architecture
was always sober and restrained in composition. In the few parts yielded
to it by the architecture, sculpture, constrained by its narrow frame,
wreathes and writhes with a delirious energy. The seductiveness of Ro-

153

Humanization of the Holy Face

181 Head of Christ. La Madeleine, Vézelay. About 1130
182 Head of a Prophet. About 1160. Senlis
183 Head of Christ. South Porch of Chartres Cathedral. Before 1212

manesque sculpture is due to an analytic view of nature before it was frozen into canons, fixed expressions and attitudes; it is a surge of forms elbowing each other, merging one into the other on arch mouldings, pilasters, tympana, spandrels and capitals (pl. 175). Everything from the very beginnings of mankind came together to enrich this marvellous language in stone: pagan myths and Christian scenes, fragments of antiquity, barbarous ornament, Byzantine, Sassanian, Assyrian and even Sumerian forms, for the old animal symbolism of the cylinder-seals of Sumeria and Elam found its final transformation here (pl. 176, 177). Thus Western man, as he started creating once again after six centuries, began by remembering; but he used all the forms that he remembered from the depths of the past as though they were words, creating a new language with them which he spoke with a wonderful oratorical ease. What we have called 'monsters', those composite creatures which the artist invents out of bits and pieces taken from all the civilizations of the world and to which man himself indulgently lent his own body, did not need to be explained away by St Bernard as having little or no intellectual content. Unlike Byzantine art, Romanesque had no very deep religious bearing, and when the glow of inner life shines through the faces on Chartres Cathedral or at St-Loup-de-Naud, that is because the Gothic genius was wakening there already. This fabulous bestiary is a sign of an orgiastic desire to create forms, gripping man's imagination when it was unleashed after six hundred years of abstinence. In behaving thus the Romanesque architect was spendthrift of his inheritance; freed from the pressure of centuries and millennia the Gothic image-maker was able to see nature with fresh eyes and a virginal imagination.

184 Byzantine Head of Christ.
S. Sophia, Constantinople.
11th c.

185 Cimabue. Head of Christ.
Late 13th c. Washington

Virginal is the term we are tempted to apply to Gothic art. For it is pure creativity. Everything here is new, structure and setting, decoration, inspiration, plasticity. With Greek art, Gothic is the only example in Western civilization of a complete renewal of formal vocabulary through the complete invention of a style. Rome profited from Greece; Byzantium issued from Rome and from the East; Romanesque art was a quadroon product of the East, Byzantium, the barbarian and the antique; Renaissance art and that of modern times borrowed from antiquity its entire architectural and decorative morphology and a great part of its idea of beauty. Gothic art, on the contrary, shook off the burden of well-worn forms which cramped the urge of Romanesque art, and started off from nature. The creative impulse of that admirable twelfth century must have been extraordinarily powerful to inspire such courage in the Gothic artist, filling him with the will to start from scratch at the very moment when all over France Romanesque art was only beginning to flower.

Romanesque art was already a century old and its maturity had hardly lasted thirty years, when the will to create that gave us Gothic art began to stir in the Ile-de-France. The first Gothic cathedrals were erected in competition with the finishing or even the beginnings of the great Romanesque minsters in other provinces, so that critics have jokingly remarked that Gothic art was nothing more than 'Ile-de-France Romanesque'.

The discovery of a new vault, or rather the rational analysis of its properties, allowed Gothic architecture to achieve that Christian dream

155

186 Keep at Loches. 12th c.

which the Byzantine artist had only been able to satisfy by a sort of mirage. Overcoming its weight, the edifice was to soar light and airy, triumphing over matter. The cathedral is a vertical flight just as the Greek temple and the Romanesque church are horizontal in movement. The Romanesque inertia of the surfaces gave way to the vibration of shafts, fenestration, and stained-glass windows, which cause an interplay of lights in a variety of modes comparable with the tones of orchestral instruments. The cathedral is the realization in stone of that symphonic utterance which Germany was to express in pure sound seven hundred years later. In this sense it is the first mature manifestation of the lyrical gift of the North; but in order to take shape it needed the awakening of specifically French genius which was heir to the plastic imagination and the rationalism of the Mediterranean. The cathedral certainly embodies a desire for growth and expansion which causes it to develop organically like a living thing, but it also obeys certain inflecting rhythms, and this development was achieved through a reasoning which, by deduction, exploited a principle to its utmost limits. It was the first appearance of that French logic which later had a sterilizing effect when applied to pure speculation. Here, however, it was marvellously fertile because it was acting on nature itself after having brushed aside everything that went before – just as Cartesian reasoning was to do later in philosophy. Reason governs the Gothic like a queen, not merely creating a system but bringing forth a world; for the cathedral is a manifold world like the universe itself, in which a host of images have their being.

The Western sense of imagery came to life – or to a second life – in Gothic art. If, as M. Emile Mâle has shown, it is true that the image still subserved the idea, it refused to be its slave and lent rather than gave itself. Rejecting the yoke of the Byzantine symbol, the image was no longer a simplified ideogram, but on the contrary it sought to embody some concrete form already in nature. Thirteenth-century France restored Mediterranean anthropomorphism and realism to the West, after it had been temporarily supplanted by Eastern ideomorphism (pl. 181–183). This wonderful evolution, which in its progress takes us from the majestic portals of Chartres to those of Rheims, went through the same phases as Greek sculpture from the sixth to the fifth century B. C. Moreover, from the twelfth century to Claus Sluter, Gothic plastic art followed the same lines as Greek art, from the *korai* of the Acropolis to the *Laocoon;* there could be no better proof of the constants that are to be found in the life of forms as well as in the progress of the Western mind (pl. 698, 710).

The architectural and plastic formulae invented by the Ile-de-France were quickly recognized everywhere, for the logical always imposes itself as obvious. So Europe spoke Gothic as the Mediterranean had spoken Greek. But not all Europe; for Italy refused to absorb the Gothic. After 1250 Italy was working out her own Renaissance without heeding the example of France, and in a different way – not through a revolution but through a renewal of traditions, an 'involution'. Nicola Pisano and Giotto went direct to antiquity for the new inspiration which led them to a sense of nature and of man; at Siena even Byzantine art, with Duccio, was to have its austerity melted into feeling and tenderness. But the overwhelming tyranny of Gothic art came to check this impulse. For a hundred years Italian art was oppressed as though by a foreign occupation. We can understand why the angry men of the Renaissance, in the fourteenth century, denounced that art as *tedesco* (teutonic), a name which was to stick. The Gothic principle acted on the Italian mind like a virus, and when Florence at last shook itself free at the beginning of the fifteenth century, Italian artists had to start from where they had left off in the thirteenth. Donatello's direct precursor was Nicola Pisano, while the innovator Masaccio had, so to speak, to stir the ashes of Giotto.

1. ROMANESQUE ART

Romanesque art was born in France in the second quarter of the eleventh century. Its name was given to it in 1823 by M. de Gerville, by analogy with the romance languages. By 1100 it had emerged from the experimental stage, having already created great buildings, and in the twelfth century it went through a striking development which was reflected in many local variations. It gradually died out as it was ousted by the Gothic style towards the end of the twelfth century. It affected all the countries that had not come under Byzantine influence, but France, Spain and England produced its most characteristic forms. In Italy, where apart from some French influence it was little more than a continuation of primitive Christian art, it was known as 'neo-Latin', while in Germany the Rhenish school was the outcome of Carolingian and Ottonian art.

Architecture

In the eleventh century the demand for works of architecture became heavy, reflecting the changes that were going on in politics and trade. The few civic buildings in stone that have survived are municipal monuments and castles. The latter consist mainly of a large tower or keep, raised on a mound serving as a redoubt or for living in, and surrounded by a wall or enceinte (pl. 186). The finest churches were those of the monasteries, for the Romanesque period was the golden age of monasticism. The monastic communities of Cluny and Cîteaux, both in Burgundy, played a fundamental part in the politics and society of the age – a part which quickly became international.

Although it did not entirely ignore the central plan, Romanesque art gave all its energy to developing the basilican plan. In order to meet the new needs of the faith, the church was considerably extended at the east end: to the simple rounded apse was added a straight part (the choir or chancel, pl. 187) and 'stepped' chapels (Benedictine plan, pl. 188) or chapels lined along the transept (Cistercian plan). In some of the largest and most beautiful constructions, Romanesque art laid down the definitive form for Western churches, by prolonging the aisles of the choir right round the apse (ambulatory) and by making the chapels (apsidal chapels) radiate round this ambulatory (pl. 189). The Western church in the Middle Ages was thus a harmonious combination of the basilican plan with the radiating plan.

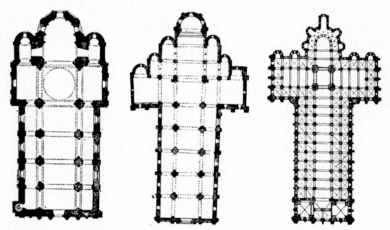

187 Plan of the Abbey Church, Cellefrouin. 12th c.
188 Plan of the Abbey Church, Châteaumeillant. 12th c.
189 Plan of St-Sernin, Toulouse. 12th c.

190 St-Front, Périgueux.
12th c.

191 Aisle of La Madelaine,
Vézelay. 12th c.

Like the Byzantine church, the Romanesque church had all its sections vaulted over. All its characteristics spring from this form of covering. Domes were sometimes used at the crossing, but over the naves, only in a group of south-western churches (Aquitaine school, St-Front at Périgueux, pl. 190); groined cross-vaults (groin-vaults) are usually found only over the aisles (pl. 191). The longitudinal plan led naturally to the use of the barrel- or tunnel-vault (pl. 192); and as this exerts a continuous, non-localized pressure, to take the thrust the architect had to use massive piers, and thick walls pierced with narrow windows. The strain of the nave vault, in the best-planned buildings, was taken by raising the aisle vaults almost to the same height as the nave, thus 'blinding' it as in the Poitou churches (pl. 193). Sometimes, when the nave was very high, it was buttressed by galleries over the aisles (Auvergne school, and large so-called 'Pilgrimage churches'); the purpose of these gallery-vaults was perfectly served by basing them on the quadrant, i.e. making them 'half-tunnels' (pl. 195). The arches and vaults were generally round-headed, though the pointed arch was not unknown.

Byzantine architecture sought broad stretches of surface; in the basilican church the arcades made an unbroken series and nothing intervened to disturb the mural surfaces either inside or outside. The Romanesque church, on the contrary, like the Greek temple, tended to knit independent elements which, taken together, result in the total edifice. These elements are the bay on the horizontal plane and the storey on the vertical. The bays are articulated internally by the use of shafts which, applied to the

159

192 Nave of St-Nazaire, Autun. 12th c.   *193 St-Pierre, Aulnay. 12th c.*

piers, rise up into the vault and are usually prolonged across its surface, as far as the opposite bay, by lateral supporting arches. The applied-shafts allow the eye to measure the edifice longitudinally, whereas moulded projections mark the storey-divisions in the elevation, constituting main horizontal lines which create a perspective-effect (pl. 203).

On Roman, basilican or Byzantine monuments, the decoration was no more than an adornment stuck on the walls with no relation to the structure. The Romanesque architect, always after logic, achieved a close co-ordination of decoration with structure, to which end he reintroduced

194 Archivolt of the Porch. Andrieu. 12th c.

II Madonna and Child. Stained Glass. Chartres Cathedral

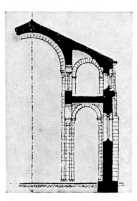

195 *Vertical Section. Issoire.*
12th c.

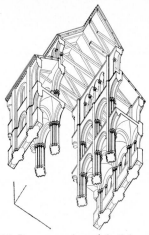

196 *Reconstruction of St-Etienne,*
Caen. Late 11th c.

moulding (pl. 194) – a kind of geometrical sculpture that had become stunted in Byzantine art but which Greek art had recognized as useful – in order to stress the main parts of the building. The Romanesque builders liked effects of strength as well as harmony, but occasionally they were tempted by the picturesque, as at Poitou and Saintonge where they over-burdened their façades with carvings. They had an admirable feeling for the composition of monumental masses by the forward movement of the

197 *Choir. Paray-le-Monial. 12th c.*

198 *Abbey Church, Fontenay.*
12th c.

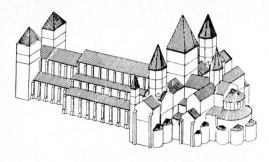

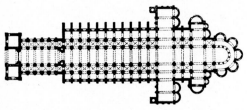

nave inside, the radiating rhythm of apse and chapels at the east end (pl. 197) and the tiered arrangement of the façade at the west. A new element, the belfry or bell-tower, often topped with a pyramidal roof, added a vertical emphasis.

The great variety of these schools of architecture is a sign of feudal separatism. When we reflect that in the twelfth century Gothic art was arising concurrently with the triumph of Romanesque, we must agree with the German historians Dehio and Bezold: 'French architecture in the eleventh and twelfth centuries, with its divergent styles flowering simultaneously, is a phenomenon unparalleled in the whole history of architecture.'

The Norman school was the oldest. Between 1025 and 1070 it was already capable of erecting great structures such as the nave of Mont-St-Michel at Bernay and St-Etienne (l'Abbaye-aux-Hommes, pl. 196) and La Trinité (l'Abbaye-aux-Dames) at Caen. It used galleries, but still timbered the naves to which the thirteenth century would have given pointed cross-vaults. The Normans sought very sober, over-all architectural effects and avoided figure decoration.

The Burgundian school benefited from being the home of the two great congregations of Cluny and Cîteaux. The Cluniac order built great churches, lavishly decorated with sculptures. In reaction the Cistercians built very stark edifices (abbey church of Fontenay, pl. 198). The abbey church at Cluny (rebuilt 1088–1120), no longer standing, was then the largest church in Christendom, with a length of 643$^{1}/_{2}$ feet (pl. 199). The Burgundian church had a very daring structure (the nave of Cluny was

96 ½ feet tall), while in decoration the Burgundians were influenced by Classical architecture (cathedrals of Autun and Langres).

The Provençal school went in for small buildings but gave them very harmonious proportions (St-Trophime at Arles, Montmajour Abbey); of all the schools this one owed most to antiquity (porch of St-Gilles-du-Gard).

The Auvergne churches were powerfully buttressed by means of quadrant-sectioned galleries which darkened the naves, but they have a harsh grandeur about them (Issoire, pl. 195; Notre-Dame-du-Port at Clermont).

The south-west region (Poitou-Saintonge) built churches with narrow aisles almost as tall as the naves and façades covered with profuse decoration (Notre-Dame-la-Grande at Poitiers).

A group of churches without aisles in Languedoc and in the south-west has series of domes over the nave (Cahors, St-Front at Périgueux, pl. 190). The biggest Romanesque buildings belong to an inter-regional type found along the routes used by pilgrims to Compostela (St-Sernin at Toulouse, pl. 189; Figeac, Ste-Foy at Conques, Santiago de Compostela, pl. 203). These churches have double aisles and an ambulatory, suitable for the crowds of pilgrims and already anticipating the Gothic cathedral.

200 Last Judgement. Tympanum in St-Pierre, Moissac. About 1120

Sculpture

It was at the end of the eleventh century, after six centuries of inactivity, that monumental sculpture came to life again. Languedoc and Spain show the oldest specimens. The low-relief figures at St-Sernin, Toulouse, (*Christ, Apostles* and *Angels,* pl. 699) and the cloister of St-Pierre at Moissac *(Apostles)* show a still hesitant modelling imitated from Byzantine ivories. Built about 1120, the main portal at Moissac is evidence of a school fully versed in its medium with its tympanum (pl. 200), depicting the apocalyptic vision of St John (Christ shown between four beasts, the evangelist's symbols, which were to appear frequently in Romanesque art).

It was with a generous and lively touch that Romanesque art reintroduced figures into sculpture, which until then had been inhibited by the preference for abstraction of the barbarians. Yet the art of sculpture was not yet practised for its own sake, but waved and twisted in order to fit its frame, lending itself to purely decorative rhythms (pl. 178–180). The Romanesque artists proved to have unlimited imagination in inventing all kinds of ornamental patterns, in which the human figure was reconciled to elements taken from the vegetable and animal worlds as well as from the fabulous code of the East, for the creation of monsters. A frantic vitality enlivens these figures, in their daemonic agitation. One of the most beautiful decorative features of the Romanesque is the capital. Its structure derives from the composite form of the ancients, which certain schools (Provence) carefully imitated; but generally the capitals depict biblical scenes in the form of monstrous shapes which, set onto the capital, cleverly underline its structure (pl. 201). The finest series of

201 *Figured Capital. St-Benoit-sur-Loire.*
    About 1160

202 *Apocalyptic Christ. Fresco from*
    S. Clemente, Tahull. 12th c. Barcelona

203 Nave of Santiago de
Compostela. 12th c.

204 Nave of Ely Cathedral.
12th c.

capitals is in the nave of Vézelay in Burgundy, and is the most fertile in
picturesque inventiveness.

The great variety of the Romanesque schools of sculpture, reflecting
the different architectural schools, may be classified into two main
groups. Some of them show a canon of very elongated proportions, a flat
and calligraphic modelling of draperies, a hint of convulsion in the
movement, and it has been suggested
that schools of this type were influenced by the art of illumination. An
example is the Languedoc school, the
most developed of all, which excelled
in tympana with large, grouped
compositions (Moissac, pl. 200; Souillac). In the same spirit the Burgundian
school (tympana at Autun and Vézelay) made rather more confused
compositions, more drily stylized. The
Poitou school liked lavish decoration
on the façades and especially round
the portals. Other schools preferred a
system of squat proportions and had
a stronger grasp of relief. The influence
of gold altar-fronts inspired several
segmented tympana in central France
(Ste-Foy at Conques, Carennac). The
full proportions of the Auvergne

205 Transept of Peterborough
Cathedral. 12th c.

165

206 Puerta della Gloria in Santiago de Compostela. 12th c.

school probably owe something to the survival of an aesthetic dating from Gallic low-reliefs; Auvergne is the only Romanesque school to attempt carving in the round, in wooden statues of the Virgin which were often overlaid with metal foil. The Provence school (St-Gilles-du-Gard, St-Trophime at Arles) showed a powerful feeling for relief in its imitation of antique sculpture and Christian sarcophagi, which were preserved in large numbers at Arles.

Painting and the Minor Arts

Romanesque art still had the taste of the preceding centuries for luxurious objects worked in gold. The two main centres of production were in the districts of the Rhine and the Meuse, on the one hand, and Limousin on the other. The Meuse school, influenced by Germanic art, still kept up the Byzantine tradition of cloisonné-enamelling in delicate colours, sometimes derived from Alexandrian colouring (sea-green, lake, azure). The Limousin school practised the craft of chasing metals, which consists of running the enamel paste into grooves cut in a bronze plaque; the colourings, much heavier in this case, (garnet-red, dark blue) originated in the smiths' work of the barbarians.

The same differences in colourings are to be found in the fairly numerous wall-paintings which survive in French churches. The Burgundian school (Berzé-la-Ville) tried to imitate the polychromatic brilliance of the Byzantine mosaic, while the Poitou school (St-Savin) used a palette reduced to red and yellow ochres reminiscent of Oriental hues. In the course of the twelfth century a new contribution was made to the arts of colour in the leaded stained-glass window, an outcome of cloisonné (panelled) metalwork. This developed strikingly in the thirteenth century, though the finest windows which date back to the infancy of this art (west front of Chartres, colour pl. II).

Romanesque Art outside France

Romanesque art took a deep hold all over Europe. The closest national school to the French was the English school, which in a sense was the twin of the Norman school, largely on account of the political union between England and Normandy. Thus English Romanesque is known as the 'Norman style'. The great Norman churches (Ely, pl. 204, Peterborough, pl. 205, Durham, Fountains Abbey, Southwell) have the same

207 Fiesole Cathedral. 11th–13th c.

208 Modena Cathedral. 12th c.

209 Cathedral and Leaning Tower, Pisa. 11th-13th c.

characteristics as those of Normandy. They are enormous structures, having galleries, thick walls and massive piers, tall naves which are generally timbered over, stone vaulting usually being reserved for aisles, and an imposing lantern-tower over the crossing. Certain specifically English features appeared at that time and lasted into the Gothic period, such as the lengthening of the nave, and the decorative arcadings, sometimes of intersecting arches, on the façades. As with the French Norman school, the decoration is almost entirely geometrical, but figures are more frequent than in Normandy. The finest example of this Norman style is the great cathedral of Durham. Durham Cathedral shows a very early use of rib-vaulting, though this does not affect the structure or Romanesque appearance of the building. Rib-vaults were given to the south aisle of the choir in 1096 and to its main bays in 1104, the latter being replaced in 1235. The finest development of the art of illumination came in the tenth and eleventh centuries, when the Winchester school's lavish colour and daring draughtsmanship had an almost baroque quality (*Benedictional of St Aethelwold,* British Museum, about 975–980; formerly Devonshire Collection, Chatsworth).

The Spanish school was related to that of Languedoc. It contributed to the revival of sculpture, and from the end of the eleventh century the workshops at Léon and Compostela showed a precocious tendency towards sculpture in the round. The portal of Silo in Castille and cloister at Ripoll in Catalonia, on the other hand, recall Languedoc carving. The cathedral of Santiago de Compostela in Galicia, the goal of the most

210 Antelami. Deposition. Parma Cathedral. About 1170

famous pilgrimage in the West, belongs to the lineage of the great Cluniac churches (Pilgrimage' churches: St-Sernin at Toulouse, Conques); it has the finest sculptures in Spain on the Goldsmiths' Portal (which have been dated to before 1117) and on the Gloria Portal (pl. 206), finished in 1188 by Maestre Mateo, who brought an already Gothic notion of statuary into Spain. Catalonia had a fine school of Romanesque painting, characterized by a taste for lively glittering colours, particularly red and yellow (manuscripts of the Apocalypse, frescoes in the Pyrenean churches, pl. 202).

Italy persisted in its use of the basilican plan during the entire Romanesque period (pl. 207). In its timbered naves it often used alternating strong and weak piers, practically ignored the ambulatory and for preference placed the bell-towers on either side of the choir. Over bays with this alternate-system, Lombardy shows some precocious examples of rib-vaulting which do not affect the Romanesque appearance (S. Ambrogio, Milan). The finest buildings in Tuscany are the cathedrals of Lucca and Pisa (pl. 209), in Lombardy, S. Abbondio at Como, S. Michele at Pavia, Modena

211 Bronze Door of S. Zeno, Verona (detail). 12th c.

212 Christ healing the Blind Man. S. Angelo in Formis. 11th c.

Cathedral (pl. 208), and in southern Italy the cathedrals of Trani, Bari, Salerno and Ravello. In Sicily the Lombard influence mingled with Norman, Muslim and Byzantine influences (Cefalu Cathedral, abbey of Monreale). As for sculpture, Italy proved hostile to the Romanesque love of metamorphosis and dynamism and remained stubbornly attached to the sculptural outlook of antiquity. The principal works of Romanesque sculpture in Italy are in the Emilia province (Benedetto Antelami, ambo of the duomo (cathedral) of Parma, 1178, pl. 210). Italy continued using bronzework for its cathedral doors (pl. 211). It created monumental liturgic furnishings (pulpits, ambos, chandeliers, choir-screens) in white marble incrusted with coloured marble mosaics; one family, the Cosmati (a name suggestive of Greek origins), became famous for this art from the early twelfth century onwards. This art enjoyed great popularity in Rome, which it had reached from abroad, and was facilitated by the vast stocks of marble to be found in its ancient ruins. In painting Italy remained an apprentice to Byzantium. The fresco now began to develop (pl. 212). In the thirteenth century the Tuscans began painting on panels, taking Byzantine models as a point of departure. The mosaics in Sicily were imbued with the Greek spirit.

Romanesque buildings in Germany are set along the Rhine and the Danube, the most civilized regions of the Germanic countries at that time. The Rhenish school, related to the Lombard, shows the most affinity with the earlier Carolingian art. It made free use of the double-basilican

213 *Abbey Church, Maria-Laach. 12th c.*

plan (cathedrals of Worms, Mainz, Bamberg, Naumburg, abbey church of Maria-Laach, pl. 213), the alternate-system of 'strong' and 'weak' supports (Speyer Cathedral, pl. 215) and there was a marked centralizing tendency at the east end, with the bell-towers hugging the chancel (church of the Apostles, Cologne, pl. 214). The block (cushion) capitals were mediocrely decorated, if at all (pl. 172), the Germans having little sense of the monumental in sculpture; but to make up for this the relief-

214 *Church of the Apostles, Cologne. About 1200*

215 *Speyer Cathedral. 11th c.*

work inclines to statuary, and the tradition brilliantly inaugurated in the Ottonian period found its fulfilment in the prophets round the choir of Bamberg Cathedral (about 1220, pl. 216), one of the strongest assertions of that feeling for pathos which is essentially German.

The Low Countries were attracted by both the Norman and Rhenish influences, most noticeable in Tournai Cathedral.

The Meuse and Rhenish regions show Germanic skill in the metal crafts. Precious objects in brass and bronze, sometimes embellished with enamels, were made at Cologne and round Liége (pl. 217). Between 1107 and 1118 Reiner von Huy made the bronze fonts for St-Barthélémy at Liége, a tradition which was passed on to Gottfried von Huy and Niko- laus von Verdun, whose work was influenced by German expressiveness (reredos at Klosterneuberg, Austria, 1181), while the monk Hugo d'Oig- nies in the early thirteenth century remained more traditional. On the Rhine and the Meuse there was a faster stylistic evolution than in southern Germany; towards 1200 the *Shrine of the Magi* at Cologne and the stucco reliefs of the choir-screen at Halberstadt (pl. 218) show a far more advanced plastic skill than was seen at Bamberg in 1220.

2. GOTHIC ART

The term '*gothique*' is the French equivalent of the expression '*tedesco*', used by the Italians of the Renaissance to decry medieval art. The term has led to regrettable misunderstandings because in reality Gothic was a French creation. It appeared in the Ile-de-France towards 1125 (St-Denis and Sens) and flourished first in that province, while other regions were

217 *Chased enamel
Plaque.
Mosan (Meuse)
School.
12th c. Paris*

still following the Romanesque. Gothic art reached its maturity in the thirteenth century; it quickly spread to England and found its way all over Europe in the thirteenth and fourteenth centuries. Italy was only superficially touched by it and was the first to give it up, when Florence led the way in the early fifteenth century in developing the Renaissance aesthetic. In its belated Flamboyant phase, Gothic art had a strong hold in Northern Europe in the fifteenth century. It persisted in France till about 1530 in religious buildings and in both England and Germany continued in a somewhat debased state until the seventeenth century.

The Creation of Gothic Art in France

The thirteenth century was the great age of Gothic art. The century of St Louis, comparable with the Greek fifth century, saw the first creation in the Middle Ages of a coherent political and social system. Religious dogma and philosophical thought were crystallized in great works of which the most important was St Thomas Aquinas' *Summa Theologica*. The true dogmatic and intellectual centre of Christendom was no longer Rome but the university of Paris, where the Italian St Thomas was teaching. The cathedral was the monumental expression of that demand for order which dominated the fields of fact and thought; it also marks the awakening of the people and a certain secularization of the faith. The intellectual centres now moved from the monasteries to the universities, while the artistic initiative passed from the abbots to the bishops, who were encouraged by a burst of popular enthusiasm. Like the ancient temple, the cathedral was the city's monument, and of all the great monumental forms created by civilizations it best expressed the common effort of a whole society. The gradual expansion of the Gothic style throughout France coincided with that cohesive force which tended to weld the whole territory of ancient Gaul into a strong state centred in the power of the throne.

Architecture

The decisive elements in the new architectural style were the pointed cross-vault with ribs and the flying-buttress.

Invented by the English and the Lombards, but first exploited in all its potentialities by the Ile-de-France architects, the pointed rib-vault is derived from the groin-vault, and its essential property is the concentration of stresses at four points, whereas the Romanesque barrel-vault thrust-down all along the length of the supporting wall (pl. 203, 219). The use of this new vault thus eliminated the carrying function of the walls, which in the thirteenth century were replaced by 'glass screens'. The arches and vaults, being pointed, appeared more slender than the rounded form.

The flying-buttress is a kind of bridge applied to one of the resting-points of the high ogival vaults and passing over the aisle to transmit the thrust of the central structure to a buttress situated beyond the aisle wall (pl. 221). The flying-buttress is in effect a slice cut out of the quadrant-vault which supported the naves of certain Romanesque churches (pl. 195). The equilibrium of the Romanesque church was obtained by

*219 Choir-Vault of
Soissons Cathedral.
Consecrated 1212*

the resistance of continuous walls; but instead of being surrounded by a rampart of walls, the Gothic cathedral, leaning on its light piers and held laterally by its buttresses, could flood the interior with light through its spacious bays (pl. 229, 244).

This result was only achieved in the thirteenth century. The Gothic cathedrals of the twelfth century (Senlis, Laon, Notre-Dame in Paris, pl. 224) had no flying-buttresses, those visible today on Notre-Dame having been added in the thirteenth; the supporting of the central vaults was still ensured by the use of galleries over the aisles. The internal eleva-

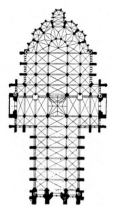

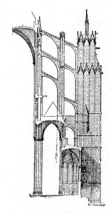

*220 Plan of Amiens Cathedral.
1220*

*221 Vertical Section of the Choir
of Beauvais Cathedral. 1247*

222 *Nave of Laon Cathedral. About 1150*

tion was in four stories: archways or arcades, tribune (gallery), triforium (small circulating gallery), and clerestory with its windows (pl. 222).

The first great cathedral to be built with flying-buttresses and without a tribune was undoubtedly Chartres which was begun in 1194 (pl. 223). It inaugurated the thirteenth-century type of elevation with three stories (including triforium) which was to be followed at once by Rheims (1211; facade, pl. 225) and Amiens (1220).

Gothic art developed extremely rapidly as though with some vital urge to growth. Its evolution took the form of increasing sparsity of walling, increased elevation, the stressing of the verticality of the naves, the proliferation of images.

In 1240 Pierre de Montereau, who was the architect of the nave of St-Denis, further eliminated stone-work by placing windows in the outer wall of the triforium, which was henceforth to be closely associated with the fenestration; the windows were multiplied in the free space left between supports, and were filled with stained or painted glass. The lay-out of these networks of windows and rose-windows has earned Gothic art of the period 1250 to 14000 the name '*gothique rayonnant*' (pl. 229).

A few figures give ample evidence of the increasing height of vaults: Laon (1150), 78 feet; Paris (1163), 114 feet; Chartres (1194), 119 feet; Rheims (1210), 123 1/2 feet; Amiens (1220), 136 1/2 feet; Beauvais (1247), 156 3/4 feet. Beauvais Cathedral marks the end of this craving for height: badly supported by the too spread-out framework, the choir vault which was finished in 1272 collapsed in 1284, and the structure had to be reinforced by doubling the piers.

176

The soaring trend followed the growth of vaults, which resulted in taller and taller arcades ($32^{1}/_{2}$ feet at Paris, $68^{1}/_{4}$ feet at Beauvais). The effect of this was further marked by the emphasizing of the vertical lines, for increasingly slender subsidiary shafts, attached to the piers, rose from the floor to the vault, while the clerestory window mullions prolonged those of the triforium. From 1250 onwards sharp pediments over porches and windows (gables) contributed further to this impression of upward movement (pl. 229).

While the nave was raised and cut, away, the forms clothing its skeleton were multiplied, every one tending to gain its independence and to produce secondary forms. This instinct for growth can be noticed particularly in the increased complexity of mouldings, sills and window tracery.

223 Nave of Chartres Cathedral. 1194

Still kept in a strict hierarchy by the disciplined mentality of the thirteenth century, these forms ended by covering the whole edifice with an unruly vegetation in the Flamboyant style of the fifteenth century.

The Gothic builders perfected mouldings, which were empirically invented by Romanesque art. They created a coherent system of moulding, obeying strict laws. On capitals and decorative string-courses, the fanciful ornamentation of the Romanesque artists (pl. 201) now gave way to supple and living forms based on plant-life (pl. 226). The same instinct for growth animates these floral decorations. On foliage capitals (the final metamorphosis of the Classical composite style) the buds of the twelfth century burst into leaf in about 1220, and after 1250 became branches.

In the thirteenth century the simple Romanesque castle, influenced by the Crusades, became a scientific and formidable structure (Château de Coucy, pl. 227). The plan usually adopted consisted of a rectangular enclosure with a tower at each corner and with the keep in the centre (Philippe-Auguste's plan, Louvre).

The best-preserved of these castles are in the Holy Land, where the Krak des Chevaliers still stands almost intact with its double stone shell. In the fourteenth century a more advanced civilization thought the fortresses of the preceding age much too bleak, and the castle was transformed into a palace (Château de Pierrefonds). The fifteenth century developed the

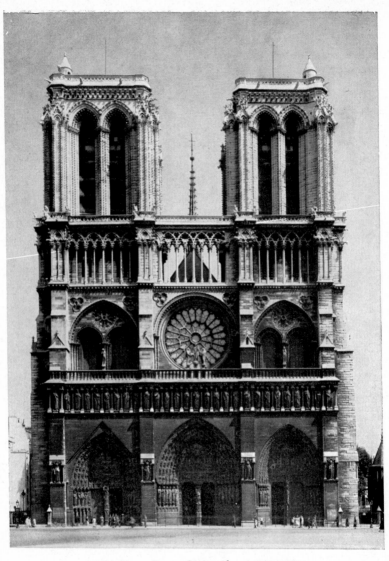

224 Notre-Dame, Paris. About 1200–1235

hôtel or villa, an urban residence suiting the needs of a new social class, the bourgeoisie (Hôtel Jacques-Cœur at Bourges). The Gothic period introduced many new forms of building corresponding with all the activities of a developed society, in the shape of bridges, hospitals, con-

225 *Rheims Cathedral. About 1240–1260*

vents and monasteries, town-halls and municipal buildings, law-courts, markets and the like.

Gothic art was poorer in provincial variants than was the Romanesque. However, in the thirteenth century the different provinces adopted

226 *Foliage Capital from the North Porch of Chartres Cathedral. About 1230*

the forms created in the Ile-de-France, giving them some local flavour. The Champagne school (Rheims Cathedral) was nearest to Ile-de-France classicism. Thanks to a remarkably durable material (Tonnerre stone) the Burgundian school built structures in which the elimination of walls was pushed to its farthest limits (Auxerre Cathedral, Notre-Dame at Dijon, St-Urbain at Troyes). The Norman school made wonderful cathedrals surrounded by fine spires (Bayeux, Coutances, pl. 228, Rouen, Lesieux) and the abbey of Mont-St-Michel which, perched on a rocky island off the north coast, is one of the most lyrical expressions of the Middle Ages. The Normans showed an exceptional lack of aptitude for figure-sculpture. Anjou gave its attention to the decorative possibilities of multi-ribbed vaults (St-Serge at Angers). Gothic art came to the south of France (Midi) as a Nordic import, a whole group of cathedrals designed by Jean Deschamps marking this infiltration (Clermont, Limoges, Narbonne, Toulouse, Rodez). However, the native spirit reacted by creating at the same

227 *Château de Coucy. 13th c. (destroyed 1918)*

228 *East End of Coutances Cathedral. 13th c.*

time a type of church with a nave of very large dimensions and no aisles (Albi Cathedral) which was to be imitated in Spain. Gothic regionalism disappeared in the fourteenth century when architecture was checked by pedantic formulas (St-Ouen at Rouen), but it revived again in the fifteenth century. The Rouen school was the most outstanding exponent of the Flamboyant style, which sprang up under English influence.

229 *Glazed Triforium of Sées Cathedral. Late 13th c.*

230 *Tympanum in the Porch of the Virgin at Notre-Dame, Paris. About 1210–1220*

231 Figures from the Royal Porch of Chartres Cathedral. About 1150

232 Visitation Group on Rheims Cathedral. About 1230

Sculpture

The birth of Gothic sculpture in the Ile-de-France was not much later than that of Romanesque sculpture, since the Royal Porch (Portail Royal) at Chartres was started in about 1140 (pl. 231, 573). Following what was still a Romanesque convention, the figures were raised or flattened to

follow the shape of the column to which they were attached; relief as such was almost non-existent and the modelling of folds mainly calligraphic, but the robes was taken from contemporary clothing and from those stone sheaths sprang heads that were full of personality and life, genuine portraits. The feverishness that twisted the figures at Moissac and Autun was soothed, giving way to calm postures and serene expressions. Sometimes a fleeting smile lit up their faces, and while all over France the Romanesque workshops were making wonderful ornamental fancies, the Ile-de-France sculptors sought a methodical observation of nature and the achievement of harmony. The porches at Senlis (pl. 182), Sens, Laon, and the Porch of St Anne at Notre-Dame (about 1170) are major stages in this growing grasp of relief and truthfulness which recalls astonishingly the transition from the sixth to the fifth century B.C. in Greek sculpture. This rapid advance resulted in the thirteenth century in the almost classical poise of the Porch of the Virgin at Notre-Dame (1210–1220, pl. 230), or the portals and carved porches at Chartres (1200–1240, pl. 231, 701), or the west porch at Amiens (1225–1236, pl. 233). The search for expression is tempered in them by a monumental balance and an idealism which seems to halo the faces with a sympathetic but austere saintliness. If some of these works recall the serene pediments of Olympia, the cathedral of Rheims (west porch, about 1225–1270) is the Parthenon of Gothic sculpture. Its statues are the most perfect works of Gothic plastic art, yet are so close to the supple ease of ancient Greece that critics have even suggested that there was some imitation (*Visitation* group, pl. 232). Facial expressions became more human, optimism was smilingly revealed, but the face lost the lofty spirituality of the previous epoch; worldliness was being introduced in to art through the influence of courtly poetry, *la poésie courtoise* (pl. 234). There is no better demonstration of the progress of humanism than the rapid evolution of the types of Christ and the Virgin. Purely a theological concept in the twelfth century, by the end of the

234 St Modesta on Chartres Cathedral. About 1230

235 Philip the Bold. Memorial Figure in St-Denis. Late 13th c.

thirteenth the Virgin was a tender maternal figure playing with her child. The formidable Christ of the Romanesque tympana was brought down to the piers to welcome the faithful with an evangelical smile at the church door. Under the influence of St Bernard, God was no longer worshipped as the supreme Judge, but the devotion of the faithful was transferred to the New Testament Christ, God become man.

All these works were harmonized with each other, according to the principles of an iconographical programme that required a scholar's knowledge. Byzantine symbolism was a religious symbolism, but that of the thirteenth century had an encyclopaedic character, for it reflected the scholastic philosophy, intent on imposing the logic of thought upon the universe. The cathedral is an immense book which tells the history of the world; Chartres contains no less than 8,000 painted or carved images.

At the end of the thirteenth century the portrait began to appear in recumbents, or funerary statues, whose features are lit up by a smile, a typically French expression (pl. 235).

In sculpture as in architecture the fourteenth century was an academic period. Sculpture became detached from the column or field and approached carving in the round; but the human expression became empty, the modelling conventional and dry, the artist's impotence betraying itself in nervous hesitant poses with the hips unnaturally set (pl. 703). At the end of the century some health was restored to an anaemic art by the vigorous contribution of the Flemish temperament, thanks to Claus Sluter.

The Arts of Colour and the Minor Arts

If the French school of painting was very inferior to the Italian, this is because painting was not the only form of colour-expression in France, as it was across the Alps. Stained-glass windows, illuminated manuscripts

236 Jean Pucelle. Page from the Belleville Breviary. Before 1343. Paris

237 Richard II presented to the Virgin by his Patron Saints. Wilton Diptych. About 1377. London

and tapestries, which were hardly known in Italy, filled cathedrals and princely houses with a fairyland of coloured images. The stained-glass window spread considerably in the thirteenth century in response to the enormous demand from cathedral building-yards. Chartres and Bourges still have their complete sets of windows. This art decayed in the fourteenth century through imitating sculpture, then in the fifteenth under the influence of painting, to achieve only a short lease of life again in the early sixteenth century.

The illumination continued to develop in Paris, which its famous university made the centre of book production. The liturgical works of the preceding period were succeeded by psalters, breviaries and books of hours, all richly adorned for the benefit of the higher social orders, and always executed on vellum. In the thirteenth century illumination was inspired by stained glass (*St Louis Psalter* and *Blanche de Castille Psalter*) while architectural forms also intruded (*St Louis Psalter*). The most elegant works in this art were made in the early fourteenth century in the studio of Jean Pucelle (*Belleville Breviary*, pl. 236). Under Charles V it declined but was to gain fresh vitality from the Flemish contribution at the end of the fourteenth century.

The workshops in which they made both high-warp and low-warp tapestries appeared or are mentioned as being in Paris towards the end of the fourteenth century; the oldest preserved tapestry is the *Angers Apocalypse* (end of the fourteenth century). The Hundred Years War broke up the Parisian workshops, some being moved to Arras where they specialized in tapestries with historical or mythological themes, dense compositions with large numbers of characters. The Touraine workshops, until the early sixteenth century, expressed the poetry of nature in tapestries with a green background.

Painting was less vigorous than in Italy. It remained for a long time overshadowed by tapestries, illumination or stained-glass, and broke free only in the second half of the fourteenth century. The Parisian style then produced some exquisite works, of which only few have been preserved. On the other hand, before Italy, France appears to have developed a lay art which provided the abodes of princes with hunting and fishing scenes, painted in fresco; an example survives in the Ward-Robe Tower at the Papal palace in Avignon (about 1345). The art of portraiture was in the same vein, and seems to have appeared first in France *(Portrait of Jean le Bon,* Louvre).

The minor arts in the Gothic period were under the tyranny of architecture which imposed its forms on furniture as on gold- and silverwork (pl. 238). Sculpture in ivory was very much in favour, and was also inspired by monumental modelling.

The Expansion of Gothic Art

The finest Gothic monuments, after the French, are to be found in England. The English were quick to understand this new style – to whose development they contributed by their very early use of rib-vaulting in

238 *Shrine of St Taurin in St-Taurin, Evreux. 13th c.*

239 Lincoln Cathedral. 12th–14th c.

Durham Cathedral (1096) – and were the only builders to evolve a native form of it in the thirteenth century. The Gothic style was encouraged in England, as in Italy and Germany, by the spread of the Cistercian order. Nothing is more characteristically Gothic than the choir of Canterbury Cathedral, which was built between 1175 and 1184 by the Frenchman William of Sens, who took as his model the cathedral of Sens where Thomas à Beckett had sought refuge. With the exception of Westminster Abbey, which was influenced by the Ile-de-France and Champagne styles and which has an apse with an ambulatory and radiating chapels (chevet), the first phase of English Gothic, known as 'Early English' (Salisbury Cathedral; parts of the cathedrals of Lincoln, pl. 239, Lichfield, York and Wells) is parallel with that of thirteenth century Norman Gothic; but whereas the Norman school increasingly shed its native characteristics as

240 Vault of the Chapter House of Wells Cathedral. 1293–1319

241 *Angel Choir of Lincoln Cathedral. Between 1256–1320*

it evolved, the English school stressed its own local features. English builders had a liking for square east ends with an elevation resembling that of the façade, as at Durham, long naves, double transepts, slender forms (such as sharp grouped lancet windows and extremely slender attached shafts). Salisbury Cathedral (pl. 242, 243) which was begun in 1220 and consecrated in 1258, is perhaps the purest and most elegant example of the first phase.

Towards 1260 there came a sharp division between the development of the Norman and English schools. The Norman school lost its personality and was absorbed into French High Gothic. While French Gothic architecture suddenly came to a standstill in the fourteenth century, England, boldly following its own internal evolution, towards 1280 began creating the Curvilinear or Decorated style, which both anticipated and begot French Flamboyant. This style, so fully achieved in the choir of Lincoln Cathedral (1256–1320, pl. 241), Exeter Cathedral (about 1280) and the nave of York Minster (after 1290) is distinguished by a lavish ornamentation spreading even into the vault (renewed in 1890 at York), with

189

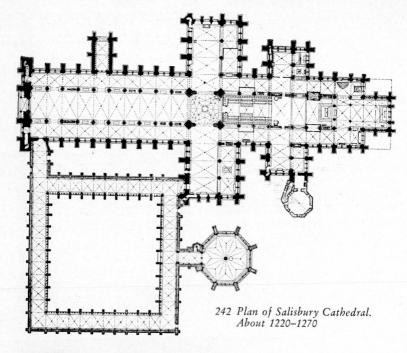

242 *Plan of Salisbury Cathedral.*
About 1220–1270

243 *Interior of Salisbury*
Cathedral.
About 1220–1270

244 William Torel. Tomb of Eleanor of Castille in Westminster Abbey (detail).
1291

245 Freiburg Minster. Tower 13th,
Spire 14th c.

246 East End of Bamberg Cathedral.
Middle of 13th c.

its intermediate ribs and carved bosses and its structure developing away from the simple Gothic cross-vault. The taste for curves and flourishes was further developed in the fourteenth century (Lady Chapel, Ely Cathedral, 1321–1349), while the chapter houses, built on a polygonal plan with a central pillar, are remarkably elegant (pl. 240). At a time

247 Choir of Cologne Cathedral. 1248–1322

248 'Stone Harp' of the West Front of Strassburg Minster. 14th c.

249 Christ before Pilate. Choir-Screen of Naumburg Cathedral (detail). About 1240–1250

250 *Head of the Bamberg Horseman in Bamberg Cathedral. Before 1237*

when all fifteenth-century Europe was indulging in elaborate curves, England rejected them to create its Perpendicular style with all the stress on verticality.

During those three hundred years, parish churches for the most part remained faithful to the simple design inherited from the Saxon period, in which the central tower serves as a massive nucleus for four unequal arms: these churches were often roofed with timber.

In the representational arts, English Gothic is notable, in the same way as in architecture, for its leaning towards elegance. In sculpture this meant the lengthening of forms and a slightly mannered gracefulness (Wells, Winchester, Salisbury, Lincoln, Westminster, pl. 244). Craftsmen of Derbyshire, Yorkshire and Nottinghamshire carved portable sculptures in alabaster during the fourteenth and fifteenth centuries, which they exported all over Northern Europe and France. During the thirteenth and fourteenth centuries the miniature achieved great subtlety of line, and the painting of the period derived from it. The *Wilton Diptych* (National Gallery, London, pl. 237), painted towards 1377, portraying Richard II being presented to the Virgin, is one of the most refined works of the Middle Ages. Historians have attributed it successively to the French, English and Czech schools, but all that is certain is that it was executed at the English court. Towards 1400 the miniature began to return to the International Gothic style (*Beaufort Book of Hours*, 1401–1410).

Gothic art in Germany was, on the contrary, an imported art. The earliest Gothic monuments (Limburg an der Lahn, Maulbronn, Bamberg, pl. 246, Naumburg, choir of Magdeburg) appeared during the first half of the thirteenth century in a region that was still Romanesque. Cologne Cathedral (choir begun 1248, pl. 247) was the first real Gothic building in Germany, but it was inspired by Amiens and Beauvais while the nave of Strassburg (1250–1270) was a replica of that of St Denis. The German churches of the fourteenth century were more original. In their profuse decoration they heralded the Flamboyant without having yet conceived its forms. The buildings were entirely clothed in a sort of vibrating tracery (façade of Strassburg Minster, pl. 248, and of Cologne Cathedral – carried out only in the nineteenth century – openwork spire of Freiburg im Brisgau, pl. 245). In the thirteenth century Westphalia pro-

251 Eckhart and Uta in Naumburg Cathedral. About 1250–1260

duced a type of church with aisles as high as the nave (Hall churches: Minden, Münster, Osnabrück, Paderborn) which was to spread in the fourteenth century to the Baltic, where brick construction was the rule.

The workshops of Rheims were the source of German Gothic sculpture. About 1235 at Bamberg (Franconia) Gothic sculpture replaced the Romanesque without any transitional stage, after the Romanesque had just expressed itself in the outstanding *Apostles* and *Prophets* of the choir screens (pl. 216). Artists who were no doubt trained at the Rheims workshops took inspiration from its elegant forms and gave them a specifically German intensity (*Visitation, Church and Synagogue, Horseman,* pl. 250). Between 1260 and 1273, the cathedral workshops at Naumburg developed an expressionism which foreshadowed the mood of Europe a hundred years ahead and the pathos of Claus Sluter's sculpture (*Christ before Pilate,* pl. 249, *Eckhart and Uta,* pl. 251). The statues of *Church and Synagogue* in Strassburg Cathedral add a touch of Germanic unreality to the elegance of Rheims. At the end of the thirteenth century and the early fourteenth, the *Wise and Foolish Virgins* from the west front of the same cathedral have a rich local touch which saves them from the academicism that is noticeable in the Prophets of the neighbouring portal.

In Spain, the slight artistic traditions of Castille gave a ready welcome to Gothic architecture from the thirteenth century onwards. The cathedrals of Burgos and Toledo were inspired by the Bourges and Coutances types, while León Cathedral reflects the forms of Rheims and Amiens. Catalonia, where there had been a prosperous Romanesque school, proved more cautious and hesitated between the northern French type with aisles and ambulatory, and the southern type with side-chapels but no aisles (Gerona Cathedral). The sculptors' shops at Burgos and León give further evidence of the wide influence of Rheims (pl. 252).

The Resistance to Gothic Art: Italy

Architecture

Italy was the country most hostile to Gothic art. It never made more than a superficial impression, in its southern French form (lower church of St Francis, Assisi, 1229–1236); the mendicant orders who introduced it also followed the austere Cistercian manner. In the late thirteenth and fourteenth centuries a more personal style was developed but proved to be absolutely opposed to the Gothic spirit, in which the decoration is expressive of the structure; embellishments of polychrome marbles, in the Byzantine manner, covered both the outside and inside of brick-built cathedrals (cathedrals of Siena, Florence, Orvieto, pl. 254). The severe town halls (Palazzo Vecchio, Florence, pl. 253, Palazzo Pubblico, Siena) have a certain Romanesque roughness. The Flamboyant style penetrated

253 Palazzo Vecchio, Florence. Ascribed to Arnolfo di Cambio. Begun 1298

254 Façade of Orvieto Cathedral. 14th ç.

century, which amounted to a foreign occupation. In the early fifteenth century the Renaissance had to begin all over again, by first of all driving out the Gothic infection.

Painting

Meanwhile Italy gave the world a new mode of expression in its painting. A national school broke away from Byzantinism towards 1250, under the influence of the new naturalistic and humanistic outlook introduced by St Francis of Assisi. The first tokens of this were at Pisa and Lucca (school of the Berlinghieri, pl. 258). At the end of the century, Florence and Siena took the lead. The sources of Florentine realism are to be found in certain mosaics, rather than in Cimabue (active between 1272–1302) who paid tribute to the theological spirit of Byzantium in some dignified icons (pl. 185). Through Duccio (active 1285–1308/11) of Siena the antique Alexandrian grace preserved by Byzantium began to show some signs of tenderness (his Madonnas and saints), but his Passion scenes express a growing sense of pathos, as in the *Maestà* (Virgin in Majesty) for the Siena Duomo (pl. 259).

257 Giovanni Pisano. Birth of Christ from the Pulpit in S. Andrea, Pistoia. 1298–1301

258 Berlinghieri. St Francis (detail). 1235. Pescia

259 Duccio. Road to Calvary from the Maestà. 1310. Siena

The future of painting lay in another direction. The true Renaissance was clearly affirmed in Rome by Pietro Cavallini (active 1273–1316) who rediscovered Classical dignity (mosaics in S. Maria in Trastevere) frescoes at S. Cecilia in Trastevere). The Florentine Giotto (about 1266 –1337) carried on the efforts of Cavallini and Nicola Pisano, giving Italian painting its main impetus. His principal works are the frescoes of the *Life of St Francis* in the upper church at Assisi (about 1300); those of the *Life of Christ* in the Arena Chapel at Padua (1305, pl. 261, 262); those of the *Legend of St John and St Francis* in S. Croce, Florence (1311

260 Simone Martini. Annunciation. 1333. Florence

261 Giotto. Betrayal (detail). Arena Chapel, Padua. 1305

262 Giotto. Joachim and the Shepherds. Arena Chapel, Padua. 1305

–1317). First and foremost a monumental artist and fresco painter, Giotto sought the truth of natural forms while never losing the Byzantine longing for clarity which subjects the composition of the work to some central idea. But this idea, which in Byzantium was spiritual, became both dramatic and plastic in Giotto. His concise art is a work of the intellect; he sacrificed the accidental to the greatest expressive concentration. He also brought with him that heroic sense of human life and that taste for virile strength which were to inspire Florentine art until the sixteenth century.

The creative effort of Giotto excited such lively admiration in his contemporaries that it resulted in the academic style of the Giotteschi. However, his successors were to temper his greatness with the influence of Sienese tenderness. Such was the case with Bernardo Daddi (active 1317 –1349).

The history of Italian painting in the second half of the fourteenth century shows an eclecticism striving to blend Giottesque precision with the narrative spirit of the Sienese school and the angular style of the Gothic. Taddeo Gaddi (died 1368) who was a direct pupil of Giotto's remained nearest to his sobriety. Andrea Orcagna was also a sculptor, and this can be felt in his work. In the third quarter of the century, Sienese influences took such a hold in Florence that it sometimes becomes difficult to distinguish Sienese from Florentine works.

At Florence, Giotto imposed on nature a dramatic and aesthetic order dictated by his intelligence. Sienese art on the contrary is all sensibility, seeking in reality only what makes the quickest appeal. Under Gothic influence Simone Martini (1283–1344) opposed the supple grace of his Madonnas to the robustness of Giotto; he achieved intense pathos not by a concentration of means but by accumulating tragic effects (*Story of Saint Martin,* frescoes in the lower church of St Francis – S. Francesco – at Assisi; *Annunciation,* Uffizi, 1333, pl. 260).

In the second quarter of the century Siena itself came under Florentine influence. The brothers Pietro and Ambrogio Lorenzetti (died 1348) assimilated the robust Giottesque plastic language while also developing the feeling for the picturesque which was typically Sienese, (*Allegory of Good and Bad Government,* Palazzo Pubblico, Siena, 1337).

Wearied by this sterile struggle between conflicting elements, the fourteenth century ended in Italy, both in painting and sculpture, in a decadence which gave no inkling of the wonderful example of creative energy that Florence was soon to give the world.

VI. ISLAM

Islam, which is too often only mentioned casually in histories, or else used as an introduction to the arts of the Far East, is a civilization of the Western Mediterranean. Springing from the same monotheistic source as Christian civilization, Islam developed in rivalry with the first forms of Christian art in Byzantium and in the West. Profiting from the rich cultural traditions of the Syrian, Egyptian and Iranian countries on which it was grafted, Muslim civilization flourished far sooner than that of the West, which stagnated in a state of barbarism until the twelfth century and was outstripped three hundred years earlier by the Arabs. (In the twelfth century the caliph of Córdoba is said to have owned some several thousand books, while four hundred years later Charles V of France, who was very proud of his library, only had nine hundred.) In every domain of civilization Islam was the first to define the values which were to become those of the Middle Ages: chivalry, courtesy and that noble conduct which Joinville called *prudhommie* (integrity) were moral rules already practised in the East in the ninth century. It was by trusting to the speculations of Arab theologians and philosophers that Christian thought achieved what it did in the twelfth and thirteenth centuries. St Thomas Aquinas only knew Aristotle through the commentaries of Averroes of Córdoba. We also owe our commercial techniques to Muslim civilization (such words as cheque, *douane* and tariff being Arab), as well as arithmetic, algebra, the first rudiments of medicine, mechanics, chemistry, geography and astronomy. The awakening West was to take all it could from this magnificent source of art and science, by way of Spain, Sicily and the great Italian ports.

The earliest Islamic works of art were not so unlike those of the West as they might appear. The decorative spirit of the Muslims is nearer that of the early West than was the sacred imagery of Byzantium. Our understanding of Muslim art has been distorted by the accusation that, in obedience to some prohibition in the Koran, it excluded any image of living things. Nothing of the sort is to be found in the Koran, and only in later texts was the artist warned against the realistic reproduction of living things. But if the Muslims created an ornamental system of geometrical devices which perhaps shows their taste for the abstract speculations of mathematics, in everyday decoration they made lavish use of animal, vegetable, floral and even human forms. However, these forms were never 'represented' for their own sake as in the aesthetic which prevailed in the West from the Gothic onwards; they were freely interpreted so as to make a plastic language of infinite wealth, whose terms all strengthen and enhance each other in a system of exchanges at which the Oriental imagination excels. This style of metaphor gives Muslim literature that dream-like quality which is its peculiar charm (the poets compare animals with flowers, flowers with stones and stars; the wound of a gazelle becomes a 'pied flower' and so on). Indeed, this art is closest to Romanesque formalism (pl. 263). The Romanesque and primitive Muslim imageries both sought their forms in the same Oriental sources – Chaldeo-Assyrian, Sassanian and Persian – which had been enriched by the peoples of the steppes and the ornamental instincts of the barbarians. This stock of imagery, further enlarged by observing nature, resulted in a system of infinitely adaptable metamorphoses which allowed the Islamic aesthetic to last almost to our own time, whereas in the West our equivalent tradition was interrupted by the rise of realism in the thirteenth century.

The profound difference between Romanesque art and that of Islam lies in one particular means of plastic expression; for Romanesque art, originating in sculpture, tended towards carving in the round, whereas Islam reduced every form to a surface and expressed itself in polychromy. For the realistic West sculpture was the fundamental art, while for Islam this was perhaps weaving. Whether it be in stucco, plaster, stone, or open-work marble as in India, Muslim monuments are covered in 'tapestries' of forms which drape them like flowing robes (pl. 265).

Starting from myth, Romanesque art seeks the real. During its long life Islamic art never lost the anti-realist instinct of the early civilizations. This instinct rested on a philosophy which denies the very existence of a world in which the whole chain of causality is in the hands of God. Arab thinkers were the first – in the Mediterranean world at least – to formulate the idea of 'nothingness'. This non-reality of things permits every imaginative fancy to both poet and artist; being embroideries of thought upon appearances they imply no consequences, they are no more than fables and tales. The art of Islam is thus a mirage, a fantasmagoria

263 *Tympanum from a House in Kubatchi (Caucasas), 12th–13th c. Washington*

264 Interior of the Córdoba Mosque. 755

of images woven on the web of nothingness. The forms so abundantly borrowed from nature are never evoked as anything more than the graceful phantoms of a dream. The scarceness of sculpture in the round perfectly illustrates this aloofness from the real; we are told that a thirteenth-century theologian forbade in his home any 'images that cast a shadow'. Three-dimensional sculpture asserts the reality of the space in which it is set; it was to be the chief art in the West and, when painting came to life, its object was to deceive the eye by creating an illusion of three-dimensional space on a plane surface.

When the Crusaders reached the East they found a decaying society. The decline of Muslim sciences coincided with a revival of puritan

265 Court of the Lions of the Alhambra, Granada. 1353–1391

orthodoxy leading to intolerance. Free-thought arose in reaction to this, and the sceptical philosophers, twelfth-century Voltaires, saw religion as a mere drug, an opium used for secular ends to ensure public order. Western Islam – the Magrab – was aware of its decadence; the refined monuments of Seville and Granada are the decadent forms of an art which in its maturity had produced the great Córdoba Mosque (pl. 264). However, the eastern Muslim region was yet to have its true renaissance, thanks to the new ethnic contribution brought by the Turkish and Mongol invasions. The eagerness of these barbarians for culture led to a brilliant renaissance in the arts and letters; they gave fresh youth to the ageing Muslim art, by bringing from the refined China of the Sung dynasty those elements which, acting like a fermentation on the ancient layers of culture in Iran, produced the exquisite flowering of the Persian miniature. The miniature is a perfect reflection of Muslim literature during those Turkish and Mongol periods when, as is to be expected in an advanced civilization, thought was expressed not so much in the sciences or metaphysics as in literature, history, lyric and epic poems. The human figure now predominated, but in the midst of gardens perfumed with flowers and peopled with graceful creatures, it was as intangible as a form seen in a dream (colour pl. III). In the same period, in the first half of the fifteenth century, the miniaturists and certain painters of the West such as Pisanello, were evoking the fleeting images of the declining Middle Ages in their fairy-like, nostalgic creations.

The Turkish and Mongol conquerors had a monumental sense of architecture which raised some imposing works. But perhaps for Muslim

III Prince Humay and Princess Humayun in a Garden. Persian Miniature. Paris

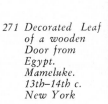

270 Marble Pilaster from the Palace at Medina-az-Zahra (near Córdoba). 936

271 Decorated Leaf of a wooden Door from Egypt. Mameluke. 13th–14th c. New York

palaces, tombs at Delhi, Agra and Lahore). Muslim India proved to have a monumental sense comparable, with that of the West (Taj-Mahal, Agra, tomb of the Empress Mumtaz Mahal, 1630–1647, pl. 273). The innate naturalism of the Hindu soul reappeared in the miniature, which was informed with all the poetry of love and pride. The empire of the Ottoman Turks (1300), which was established at the expense of the Byzantine Empire, apparently hoped to prolong the greatness of Constantinople, after its destruction. After the downfall of Constantinople, now renamed Istanbul, the church of S. Sophia greatly influenced the form of mosques, the tendency now being towards the central plan (mosque of Bayezid by Viheir-ed-Din, 1481–1512; Sulaimaniya Mosque (1550) by Sinan, who built a large number of monuments including the Shah Zasi and Sultan Ahmed Mosques). Decorative art (textiles, carpets, ceramics) increasingly took naturalistic themes from flowers, etc. (tulip, marigold, pomegranate, hyacinth, rose, vine). The art of the Osmanlis (Ottomans) spread throughout their empire to Syria, Egypt, Tunisia and Algeria, to decline entirely in the eighteenth century under Western influence when it was ruined by rococo features.

Architecture

Despite its wide radiation in both time and place, Muslim architecture owed its remarkable unity to a religious faith and an unchanging way of life. Concurrently with the West and Byzantium but over a much greater area, Islam spread vault-construction throughout the world after it had been devised by Mesopotamia and Iran. Although construction with stone materials was almost as much favoured as building in rubble and brick, it was brickwork which dominated all Muslim architecture, resulting in an aesthetic of applied decoration for ornamental effect, rather than a monumental plastic code.

From the very beginning Islam created a type of sancturay – the mosque – adapted to a religion without ritual, but of which the essential activity was communal prayer. In order to shelter the congregation, Islam imitated the long colonnades in the naves of Christian churches, multiplying them to give the impression of infinite numbers, but placing them crosswise and not down the length of the building (pl. 264, 274 a). The classic mosque was composed of four porticoes or *liwan* framing a courtyard or *sahn* in the centre of which stood a fountain for ablutions *(midha)*. The *liwan* standing at the far end of the courtyard and which served as a prayer-chamber *(haram)* consisted of several naves (or aisles), while the far wall or *quibla* pointed perpendicularly in the direction of Mecca, marked by an archway or niche, the *mihrab;* a *minbar* made of wood served as a pulpit. Sometimes a large, deep nave led to the *mihrab,* which was topped with a dome. One or several 'minarets' or belfries were used by the *muezzin* for the call to prayer. These minarets took many different shapes. At first they were strong square towers, then in Mesopotamia they took on the helix form of the Assyrian ziggurats. Persia, from the ninth century, created the standard type of very slender tower, elongated and candle-like, with a balcony at the top. Seljuk Persia in the twelfth century invented a second type of mosque on a cruciform plan, no doubt suggested by the old Sassanian palaces; this had four perpendicular *liwan* in the central court, opening their high wide vaults upon

it. Finally the Ottoman Turks in the sixteenth century gave the mosque a basilican form with a central cupola, inspired by S. Sophia. The mosque-school or *medersa* grouped four sets of buildings round the central courtyard, corresponding with the four orthodox rites taught there (pl. 274 b). The Mongols introduced into Persia a circular mausoleum surmounted by a dome, which the Egyptian Mamelukes combined with the mosque. The design of palaces still followed that of the Assyrian palace divided into two parts, each of them grouped round a courtyard: the *selamlick* for public activities, the *harem* for private life. The audience or throne-room *(diwan)* opened on to one of the sides of the *selamlick.* The dwelling showed nothing but blank walls from the outside, the few openings being sealed by wooden grills called *moucharabieh.* The interior was veneered

272 *Funerary Mosque of Kait-Bey, Cairo. 1472*

214

273 *The Taj-Mahal, Agra. Tomb of Mumtaz Mahal. 1630–1647*

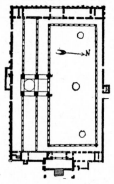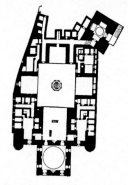

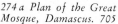

274 a *Plan of the Great Mosque, Damascus. 705*   274 b *Plan of the Great Mosque of Sultan Hassan, Cairo. 1356*

with decorations in stucco or porcelain, while often fountains played here and there for coolness. Long before the Christians, the Muslims, who love flowers, knew that refinement in the art of living, the culture of gardens (gardens of the Generalife, Granada). The finest palaces still standing today are to be found in Spain and India.

The Muslims were very skilful in throwing light arches over wide spans, sometimes also using the sectional method of construction tested by the Sassanians. From the tenth century onwards in Mesopotamia and Spain they were using the rib-vault, two hundred before the builders of the West (pl. 266). They also had astute carpenters who designed complex ceilings with lavish decorations. The Muslim architects, except in a few early Islamic edifices, used the arch in preference to the lintel. Encouraged by their instinct for ornament they gave their archways and vaults all kinds of profiles, both pointed and round: the stilted, the horseshoe, the multifoil, the cusped, the ogee, and the four-centred arches. They sometimes even superimposed arcades (Córdoba Mosque, pl. 264) and intersected the arches.

The structure prepared by the architect had to take a facing of applied decorations which tended to cover all its surface. The constructional elements themselves rapidly became ornamental motifs such as the corner squinch used for the transition from the square plan to the cupola; fragmented and multiplied this feature was transformed into *mukarna* or 'stalactites' which ended by being grafted everywhere: on arches, pendentives, capitals, ceilings, friezes, lintels etc. (pl. 267). The surface decoration, carried out exclusively in arabesque, was done in plaster, stucco, wood, mosaic or, in India, in openwork marble, and in Persia under the influence of the Safavids, in polychrome porcelain which clothed the whole edifice like a robe.

The decorative themes found their source in the foliated scroll-work alive with animals and fruits, common to Hellenistic and Byzantine art (pl. 269, 270). Gradually in both Mesopotamia and Egypt this scroll-work lost all its relief, its design thinned into the purely abstract type of pattern since called 'arabesque'. Arabesque patterns throw up against a dark ground their flat braiding, interlaced in geometrical designs in which the starred polygon plays an essential part (pl. 271). The Muslims also made much of inscriptions of extracts from the Koran in Kufic script.

The Minor Arts

While the peoples of the West were still leading a crude barbarian existence the Muslim princes succeeded in bringing all the refinements of intellectual culture and material luxury to the art of living. They attached great importance to the beauty of everyday things and to the decoration of their houses, and set up workshops in their palaces as well as seeking far and wide for objets d'art and skilled artists. Commercial exchanges became so active between the Muslim countries that the exact origin of old pieces is often hard to trace.

The repugnance shown by the Muslims for representation of living figures hindered sculpture, but in the lay crafts there were none of the limitations that restricted decoration in religious buildings, where the geometrical style alone was allowed. The art of Islam, in a word, maintained into modern times the ancient zoomorphic and phytomorphic (based on plant-forms) decorative style of the East, which it took at firsthand from Iran and Mesopotamia, where it was still flourishing in the Sassanian civilization at the time of the conquest. Thus living forms were suggested only obliquely, through a decorative stylization which stripped them of all reality or representational value. Perhaps the Shiite heresy which at various times took hold of Iran, the crucible of Islamic art, had some indulgence towards this decorative imagery, being at all events less puritanical than was the Sunnite orthodoxy. Varying on both geometrical speculation and the fluid stylization of living forms, the Mohammedans had thus an inexhaustible stock which they exploited to the full. Under Mongol rule from the thirteenth century onwards, Persia showed a bent for human representation which emerged in the highly-developed miniature. In its final phase Muslim art was energized once more by the introduction of naturalistic floral themes which gave a spring-like youthfulness to their ceramics and carpets (pl. 275).

Mohammedan decoration is essentially polychromatic. No doubt weaving was considered as the highest art in Islam. The best tissues in cotton and silk used in the oldest Sassanian decorations are no longer known to us save in fragments, so far as the earliest periods are concerned, which are mostly treasured in Western churches which imported them at great cost for wrapping and preserving holy relics. This art also prospered in the West, especially at Palermo in workshops which the Norman kings of Sicily maintained on a royal scale (pl. 268). The art of rug-making which

277 *Persian Perfume-Brazier.*
Early 13th c. Tehran

278 *Detail of a Baptismal Font.*
Mesopotamian (Mongol
Period). Mid 13th c. Paris

Pieces of pottery have fortunately been recovered in large quantities by digging, or were found concealed in the walls of buildings. The workshops of Mesopotamia (Samarra, Iraq) or Persia (Susa, Rhagae) soon restored to its high place the art of enamelled faïence which had reached such a fine perfection under the Achaemenians. It was they who invented lustred decoration with metallic or mottled sheens, varying from golden yellow to a coppery red, or from brown to green. The best specimens came from the shops at Rhagae, Sultanabad, Gurgan and Rakka in the eleventh, twelfth and thirteenth centuries. Animal and floral decorative imagery they treated with an exquisite fantasy, and they gave little scope to the geometrical style (pl. 276). In the eighteenth century Chinese influence began to filter into Persia, while Asia Minor was to renew its repertory by adding naturalistic floral decoration with a rich range of colour. Lustred decoration spread throughout Islam and in the West resulted in Hispano-Moorish faïence (Malaga, Valencia) which was to survive after the Muslims left Spain (thirteenth to sixteenth century). The working of glass which the Syrians and Egyptians mastered was related to that of faïence and was enriched with enamels, for example in the lamps for mosques.

Mohammedan metalwork began in Mesopotamia, where copper-mines provided the necessary raw material. From the tenth and eleventh centuries the region of Mosul produced bowls, cauldrons and ewers in incised copper or brass. A little later in the twelfth century it began to make brass objects chased with threads of silver, gold or red copper, a technique known as 'damaskeening' (pl. 278). This art subsequently spread to Syria and Egypt. Its patterns are the same as those of pottery. Mixed with pewter, the copper of Mesopotamia gave some fine articles in bronze (fountains, ewers, braziers, mirrors, mosque-lamps, door-panels), the

IV Jan van Eyck. Madonna in her Chamber. Frankfurt

Swiss historian Jacob Burckhardt in 1860 defined the Renaissance as an affirmation of the individual, who now emerged from the anonymous crowd of the Middle Ages. From now on the work of art was strongly marked by its author's imprint, and the creative activity of the intellect in the field of the arts was to be considered as one of the finest in the history of man. The artist was promoted from the status of artisan to become an aristocrat of the mind. Yet the time had not come when great isolated workers, commissioned by the society of their time, were to leave their ivory tower to overwhelm mankind with their messages. Setting a distance between itself and the masses, the art of the Renaissance was exalted by the enthusiasm of an aristocratic class of wealthy patrons and intellectuals. It became a princely activity, and now, more than in earlier periods when it had been swept along by the collective urge of society, it came to depend on patronage. Freed from all spiritual or temporal usefulness, the work of art as it became an 'objet d'art' was to be an end in itself. It was made for a pure act of contemplation to which only an enlightened élite could aspire. The fertility and variety of Italian art of the Quattrocento benefited from the political division of the peninsula into rival principalities which resulted in great competition in all cultural matters. The Medicis of Florence, the Aragons of Naples, the Sforzas of Milan, the Estes of Ferrara, the Gonzagas of Mantua, and the Monte-

283 *Paradise Garden. Cologne School. About 1420. Frankfurt*

284 Konrad Witz. Sabothay and
Benaiah from the Mirror of Salvation
Altarpiece. About 1435. Basle

285 Andrea del
Castagno. Portrait of
Pippo Spano. Florence

feltros of Urbino outbid each other for artists of repute. Works of art, valuable evidence of the greatness of man, were now collected by princes as priceless treasures; the idea of the 'museum', a temple reserved for the cult of the beautiful, belongs to the Renaissance.

The art of the Quattrocento was the most heroic attempt that had been made to bring the world down to the human scale. Whatever in the world cannot be grasped by the senses or the human intelligence, all the infinitude of nature and the yearnings of the soul towards the beyond, whatever can be perceived only by mystical intuition and escapes the pure lucidity of consciousness, all this was rejected from a world ruled by architecture and sculpture whose logic is based on the idea of limitation. The Quattrocento went farther along this humanistic road than the antiquity it thought it was reviving; the notion of 'man the measure of all things' must have been powerfully rooted in the make-up of Mediterranean man, to have been capable of asserting itself so strongly after fourteen hundred years of Christianity in which man had lived bowed under the yoke of God. Faith, the need to accept values which the mind considers as supreme, now gave way to that impulse towards knowledge which drives man to accept only such ideas as can be proved true by reasoning. Rationalism was the true principle of the Italian Renaissance; it dictated its every step in the field of thought and art. Dedicated to the understanding of nature, art became a rational pursuit of the appearances of the external world, but this conquest of the visible found itself checked by a speculative inquiry, no less logically pursued, into the abstract 'laws' of beauty. This contradiction caused a tension resulting in a host of creations of genius, such as mankind had never seen before.

286 Hans Memling. Madonna (detail). 1487. Bruges

287 Perugino. Madonna and Saints (detail). Paris

288 Master of Moulins. Madonna (detail). About 1498. Moulins

Even Greek art never had such a wealth of talent – though it is true that Classical humanism expressed itself in philosophical speculations which Italy had nothing to equal. It was in creations in the plastic field that Renaissance humanism found its most powerful expression, its works of pure thought being overshadowed by the revival of ancient philosophy. Quattrocento Italy is perhaps the most remarkable instance of a civilization developed mainly in plastic terms.

Their sharp minds and eagerness for knowledge fitted the Florentines for the task of presiding over the new civilization. The Medici family, and especially Cosimo who first established its power, has a title to the glory of the early Renaissance, which for a century brought such fame to Florence. The first half of the Quattrocento witnessed the final flowering of the Gothic aesthetic in the northern and central provinces of Lombardy and the Marches. Towards the fourteen-sixties in Venetia (Padua and

Venice) a new centre began to develop values which were alien to the intellectualist aesthetic of the Florentines. Sixteenth-century art sprang from the union of Florence and Venice.

The other European countries did not ignore the Italians' brilliant example, but they first had to soothe their nostalgia for a vanishing enchanted world; and that is why Northern Europe of the fifteenth century produced one of the deepest expressions of the Middle Ages. It was not without some anguish that knowledge began to challenge faith in men's minds. The art of the fifteenth century, which gave such prominence to expressing the pangs of death, is evidence of that tragic debate. It is as though the more Italy exalted man's greatness, the more desperately Northern civilization clung to Christianity and sought to diminish man. Italy itself was not entirely untouched by these passionate debates, as can be seen from the tragic and victorious offensive of the Germanic Flamboyant style against the Ferrarese school. The Renaissance spirit slowly advanced against such trials as these. France remained less aloof from it than any other country, and the keen-minded Jean Fouquet is a lay brother of Fra Angelico. However, the situation looked desperate and there seemed little hope of the North emerging from its tangled forest of belated Gothic when, in about 1480 to 1490, the cloud suddenly broke. As though the word had been passed round, artists of every nationality shook free of the torments of expressionism, and Italy herself threw off the harshness of a style which was intent on truth alone. At Venice, Bellini, in Umbria, Perugino, in Florence, Ghirlandaio, in Flanders, Memling and Gerard David, in Germany, Holbein the Elder and Tilman Riemenschneider and in France, Michel Colombe and the Master of Moulins devoted themselves to a calm vision of harmonious forms. Resistance was overcome, and through the broken dykes Italy was to overflow into the North in a torrent which produced a crisis that was to have enduring after-effects on the artistic development of all Europe.

1. THE RENAISSANCE IN ITALY

Architecture

The great Florentine artists' innovation early in the century was deliberately to cast aside Gothic principles in an attempt to return to the architectural forms which had been developed in Classical antiquity. Since they had never understood the inner form of Gothic architecture they had no qualms in giving up what for them had never been more than a setting for something else. The architect Brunelleschi and the sculptors Donatello and Ghiberti early in the century began studying the remains of ancient Rome, which at that time were still almost intact, and became the leaders in the new reform.

In the field of architectural forms, the Renaissance left behind the complex designs and intricate planes of the Gothic builders, returning to simple compositions with clearly defined volumes and sharp surfaces of which many an example was still to be found in Roman art. The great idea of that time was the central-plan building arranged round a main cupola (or dome), the masterpiece of this type being Bramante's plan for St Peter's, Rome.

Brunelleschi (1377–1446) brought to completion a work begun in the fourteenth centurry, crowning with a mighty dome (344½ feet to the lantern-light) the crossing of S. Maria del Fiore, Florence, which was

289 Florence Cathedral. 'Giotto's Campanile'; Brunelleschi's Dome (1420–1434)

inspired by the Pantheon in Rome. At S. Lorenzo (pl. 294) and S. Spirito he left medieval forms behind and gave his churches all the bright harmony of the old basilicas. The contract for the dome of S. Maria del Fiore was competed for in 1417 and the dome was built between 1420 and 1434 (pl. 289). S. Lorenzo, the Medici family's church, was begun in 1416 and swiftly completed. In this building, as in the Pazzi Chapel of S. Croce (after 1430), Brunelleschi returned to the Classical decorative grammar, with Corinthian columns, entablatures, pediments, fluted pilasters, rosettes, scalloping, garlands, cornices, ovolos, denticulation, and pure semi-circular arches.

It remained for Michelozzo (1391–1472), who was a pupil of Brunelleschi and Donatello, to create the typical Florentine palace (Palazzo Medici-Riccardi), a strong stone cube enlivened with Classical decorations and topped with a monumental cornice. Closed off from the outside world in the manner of the Greek or Roman villa, its interior contains a charming pillared courtyard or *cortile* (pl. 295).

Leon Battista Alberti (1404–1472) had the most speculative mind of his time. His researches resulted in the art of Bramante, and he wrote the first treatise on architecture *(De re aedificatoria);* but he contented himself with intellectual pursuits and most of his designs were carried out by others.

In the Palazzo Ruccellai (1446–1451) Alberti was the first to re-introduce the idea of superimposed orders – Doric, Ionic and Corinthian – followed by the Romans, which he did in the applied decorations of his façade (pl. 292). The basilican church of S. Andrea, Mantua (p.296),

229

290 Palazzo Strozzi, Florence. Begun 1489

which was built after his design at the end of the century is an aisleless building which later inspired Vignola's Gesù in Rome. In the Tempio Malatestiano (S. Francesco) at Rimini (about 1446) his façade is based on the ancient triumphal arch.

One of the finest achievements of the Quattrocento is the great ducal palace constructed at Urbino in the Marches for Federigo da Montefeltro. It was begun in about 1455 and finished about 1480, the work being carried out by the Dalmation Luciano Laurana and later the Sienese Francesco di Giorgio. Decorative sculpture has rarely reached greater delicacy than here. The ducal apartments have several chambers fraught with humanistic meaning: a twin chapel with a Temple of the Muses, a *studiolo* or study decorated with portraits of great men and inlaid-work with symbolic patterns.

The architectural creations of the second half of the century in Florence had not the same genial inventiveness as this. Bernardo Rossellino (1409 –1464), Benedetto da Maiano (1442–1497) who in 1489 began the finest of Florentine palaces (Palazzo Strozzi, pl. 290), Giuliano da Maiano

291 Palazzo Vendramin-Calergi, Venice. Finished about 1509

(1432–1490) and above all Giuliano da Sangallo (1445–1516) all prepared the way for the masterpieces of the great architects of the sixteenth century by their patient researches in matters of detail. At the end of the century the new style developed in Florence spread all over Italy. Lombardy, which had felt the Gothic influence more strongly than any other Italian province, applied it in a diluted form, largely picturesque, in the Certosa, Pavia (pl. 293). Founded in 1396 and built in 1428 by Giovanni Solari, then continued by Giovanni Antonio Amadeo (1447 –1552) the Certosa (Charterhouse) is the most famous example of this new style, and it is a pity that the Italian Renaissance was to be known to Europe by this, rather than by Florentine examples. Pure Gothic lingered on in Naples, which was under the patronage of the Aragon family. Venice passed rather late from the Gothic – which like Milan it had known in its Flamboyant form – to the Renaissance manner, which Antonio Rizzo (died 1498) transformed into a flowery, cheerful style in the tradition of Venetian art. Florentine influence came to the fore with Pietro Lombardo (died 1515), a sculptor and architect who, with a sense of perfection tending to Byzantinism, both built and decorated the marble gem, S. Maria dei Miracoli. In lively contrast with the cold straight masses of the Florentine palace – which derives from the fortress – the spirit of fenestrated architecture which had held sway in Venetia in the Middle Ages appeared once more in the Venetian Renaissance palace, whose first completely developed expression is the Palazzo Vendramin-

231

292 *Alberti (design 1446).*
Palazzo Ruccellai, Florence

293 *Window of the Certosa,*
Pavia. Begun 1473

Calergi (pl. 291) on the Grand Canal, a work designed no doubt by Mauro Coducci (died 1504).

In the first half of the fifteenth century the ferment of the Renaissance is thus seen to have wrought its work in Florence alone, in an Italy which was otherwise overrun by Flamboyant Gothic.

Sculpture

In the portrayal of figures sculpture was now the major art, for sculptors were twenty-five years ahead of painters in the discovery of the new style, the painters always keeping their eye on the sculptors' experiments. The statue was the ideal of the period. No doubt sculpture owed its prominence to the fact that it was an essentially physical art in a period whose main aim was to give their due to the beauty and strength of the human body. It is also privileged by being situated in real space, and all the arts of the Quattrocento were dominated by an urge to master the three dimensions of space either in reality (through sculpture) or in appearance (through painting). Side by side with the shaping of marble the Italians developed bronze statuary, which incidentally they had never allowed to fall into neglect.

Of all the great masters who made their contribution to the new plastic language, only one was not a Florentine. This was Jacopo della Quercia (1374–1438) who came from Siena. With a minimum of modelling he attained from the very start that vigorous sense of the human body which was to haunt the whole century until it was caught again by Michel-

bardy alone, faithful to its Gothic traditions, remained immune, and the declamatory art of Niccolo del Arca (died 1494) and Guido Mazzoni (1450–1518) shows strong traces of Germanic influence.

Painting

It was in the north and, from the end of the Trecento, in Lombardy, that old Italic province of 'long-haired Gaul', that the craze for naturalism first showed itself in the portrayal of animal and floral forms, in the work of such delightful draughtsmen and illuminators as Giovanni de' Grassi. In that northern region of Italy, which continued to be deeply imbued with feudal civilization, the old ideals of chivalry and courtly love which had seduced the medieval imagination flowered once more in the first half of the fifteenth century, when nature became the servant of fantasy. At Verona, Stefano da Zevio (1375–after 1438, pl. 282) and above all Antonio Pisano, called Pisanello (1397–1455), produced the last echoes of the Middle Ages, though Pisanello showed all the feverish curiosity of the Quattrocento in his studies of animals. Pisanello grasped all the living arabesque of animals, the texture of plumage and coat, while paying little attention to anatomical structure, which guided the Florentines in their studies of the human body (pl. 302).

Pisanello's paintings, which are very scarce, consist of little more than a few pictures and the frescoes at Verona of the *Annunciation* in S. Fermo Maggiore, and of *St George rescuing the Princess,* which is treated in legendary fashion, in S. Anastasia (1431). This artist also modelled and cast medallions (pl. 320), and this experience led him to create the profile portrait (*Princess of the House of Este,* Louvre).

This representational lyrism spread through central Italy of the Marches and Umbria, where it met another important stream, the old Sienese style, to produce that exquisite Gentile da Fabriano (1360–1440) whose masterpiece is the *Adoration of the Kings* (Uffizi, Florence, 1423, pl. 303). This princely procession is imbued with all the charm and fantasy of the medieval mind.

Pisanello and Gentile are the Italian exponents of what we might call

301 Antonio Rosselino. Madonna. In S. Croce, Florence. Marble. About 1478

'naturalistic mysticism', a feeling of adoration for the marvels of nature,
which in the Middle Ages they called *mirabilia*. It remained for Florence
to introduce a more scientific naturalism.

It was only towards 1425 that the Florentine school of painting, which
lagged behind sculpture, managed to break its enslavement to a senile
Giottesque tradition which had been only slightly rejuvenated by the
sincerity of the Camaldolese monk Don Lorenzo Monaco (about 1370
–1425?). The founders of the Florentine Renaissance school were Masolino (1383–1447, pl. 304), Fra Angelico and Masaccio. Though Fra Angelico was a Christian painter while Masaccio founded a pagan humanism,
both of them belong to the Renaissance in their plastic outlook. Fra
Angelico was a meeting-point of styles and ideas emerging from the past

304 Masolino. Story of Herod. Fresco at Castiglione Olona. About 1420

but seeking the future, and if he glimpsed a heavenly beatitude he was none the less carried along on the wave of discovery that gripped his generation. With Paolo Uccello he created perspective, and with Masaccio, he mastered modelling, expounding the laws of a harmonious composition in his invention of the *Sacra Conversazione* in which he set the saints in a semi-circle round the Virgin, or in attendance at her Coronation (pl. 305). The serene abstractness of his style makes him an early classical master, half-way between Giotto and Raphael.

A late-comer to painting, Guido di Pietro, called Fra Angelico (died 1455), gradually broke away from Gothic illumination. Entering the Dominican friary at Fiesole in 1407 he decorated the friary of S. Marco in Florence with frescoes after it was founded in 1436 by Cosimo de' Medici for the Florentine Dominicans. He was called to Rome in 1445 by Eugenius IV, where from 1449 to 1450 he painted frescoes showing the stories of St Stephen and St Lawrence in the Chapel of Nicholas V in the Vatican. He had a large output and made great use of his apprentices.

In Fra Angelico's work the human being is still that fragile creature who draws all his strength from God alone. Masaccio (1401–1428) was the first in painting to define the plastic and humanistic ideal of the Renaissance without the slightest hesitation. He died at the age of twenty-seven and left little more than the frescoes of the life of St Peter in the Brancacci Chapel in the Carmine at Florence; but this chapel became a sanctuary for the training of a long line of Italian artists up to Raphael and Michelangelo (pl. 306 a). Masaccio was a forerunner of genius who at one stroke found the target which the Italian school as a whole was to reach only fifty years later. Renewing Giotto's ideal of concentrated strength, he heralded the sixteenth century by his monumental sense of composition that points the way to Raphael, and his broad and powerful

notion of the human body, his heroic and dramatic intensity (pl. 306 b) which only Michelangelo could rival. But his contemporaries went no further than the experimental stage. They were still trying to find the laws of painting which for them was a problem in itself; they were after a definition of spatial laws, that is to say, how to represent the three dimensions of real space on the flat canvas. They found the as yet unformulated rules of linear perspective and, by their use of foreshortening produced results which recall sculpture, whose effects they tried to reproduce by the device of illusionism *(trompe-l'œil)*, or through the cameo. Paolo Uccello (about 1400–1475) brought a naïve passion to these semi-

306 a *Masaccio. Tribute Money (detail)). Fresco in the Carmine, Florence.*
1427–1428

306 b Masaccio. Expulsion. Carmine, Florence. 1427–1428

307 Uccello. Rout of San Romano (detail). London

scientific researches and remained sensitive to the charms of nature. On the contrary the sharp and metallic art of Andrea del Castagno (1390?–1457?) ignored landscape and his world seems to have been one of bronze or marble (pl. 285). He saw everything from the point of view of volume, reducing nature to a pure geometry of his own creation.

The main works of Paolo Uccello are battle-scenes (Paris, London, pl. 307, Florence) and the poorly-preserved frescoes in the Chiostro Verde of S. Maria Novella showing the Deluge.

Andrea del Castagno painted frescoes in a sculptural style for S. Apollonia in Florence (pl. 285).

Meanwhile, the Florentines who followed this generation of pioneers were not on the look-out for new territory to conquer. Painters, sculptors and goldsmiths, Andrea del Verrocchio (1435–1488) or the brothers Piero (1443–1496) and Antonio (1432–1498) Pollaiuolo, still remained obsessed by form in relief. Most of these artists were content with exploiting new discoveries without adding to them. Fra Filippo Lippi (1406–1469, colour pl. V) who was a follower of Fra Angelico, expressed a romantic pathos which anticipates Botticelli. Ghirlandaio (1449–1494) fell into a bourgeois optimism, while Benozzo Gozzoli (1449–1497) undertook a facile second version of the 'poetry' of Gentile da Fabriano. Only Alessio Baldovinetti (1425–1499), thanks to his researches into harmonic composition which were all pursued round a main theme, that of the Virgin and Child, shows early signs of that intellectual view of perfection which, 'scientifically' arrived at, could do nothing more than repeat itself – meaning that of Leonardo da Vinci.

With the Pollaiuolo brothers, Piero di Cosimo (1462–1521) and Sandro Botticelli (1444–1510) the end of the century led to the harshness, oddness and morbidities of mannerism, that 'sickness of styles' which these always suffer at the end of a creative period. The case of Botticelli is

308 Botticelli. Birth of Venus. Florence

typical of the intellectualist frenzy which was then widespread in Florence. This mystic soul, torn between Christianity and paganism, but possessed by the demon of intellect, was condemned to a restless existence. The languishing sadness of his Madonnas, the nostalgia of his portraits, his nervous and troubled style which gives all his compositions a spasmodic rhythm and quickens the edge of his line and the impetuousness of his figures, betrays the deep torment of an art which has reached its

309 Sassetta. Mystic Marriage of St Francis (detail). 1443. Chantilly

310 Cosimo Tura. Pietà. Venice

*311 Piero della Francesca.
Resurrection (detail). Fresco in
the Palazzo Communale,
Sansepolcro*

*312 Piero della Francesca.
The Queen of Sheba adoring
the Holy Wood (detail).
Fresco in S. Francesco, Arezzo.
About 1455–1460*

limits and can only react against its own impotence in a final spasm of genius.

Botticelli was at first a goldsmith, then a pupil of Antonio Pollaiuolo and Filippo Lippi, and became a religious painter (*Madonna of the Magnificat*, Uffizi, Sistine frescoes). Towards 1485 he began painting themes inspired by antiquity (*Primavera* – an allegory of Spring – *Birth of Venus*, pl. 308, both Uffizi); Savonarola's preaching brought him back to Christianity and he returned eagerly to religious painting.

Siena, in its isolated hill-top position, remained a medieval town into the fifteenth century. Sassetta (1392–1450, pl. 309) and his follower Sano di Pietro (1406–1481) had all the candidness and wonderment of the primitives. Matteo di Giovanni (1435–1495), Neroccio (1447–1500), Giovanni di Paolo (1403–1482) and others finished by adapting the learned art of Florence to the outmoded *cantilena* of Siena.

It is outside Florence and in schools to which she had taught independence, that we must seek further signs of the great movement of discovery which animated the Quattrocento. Piero della Francesca (about 1416/20 –1492) inherited something of the keenness for perspective of Paolo Uccello and Castagno, as well as Masaccio's taste for monumental grandeur. He gave his figures a granite consistency and no artist more haughtily expressed the pride of Quattrocento man (pl. 311). Piero della Francesca's chief work is a series of frescoes in S. Francesco, Arezzo, depicting

313 Mantegna. Agony in the Garden. 1459–1460. London

the *Story of the True Cross* (pl. 312). He left also the remarkable portraits of the duke of Urbino, *Federigo da Montefeltro,* and his wife *Battista Sforza* (both Uffizi).

The Florentine view of art was brought to the painters of the north by the Tuscan sculptors, Donatello among them, who came to work in Padua. The intellectualist turn of mind of the Florentines, as it made itself felt in a region where Germanic influences were still active, gave rise to a school of painters in Ferrara who were fired by a quest for the supernatural and whose tense style and fantastic imagination came as a flamboyant intrusion into Italian painting.

The liveliest of these painters was Cosimo Tura (1430–1495, pl. 310), who owed something to Piero della Francesca. Francesco Cossa (1435 – about 1477) was the author of a series of frescoes in the Palazzo Schifanoia at Ferrara. Ercole de' Roberti (died 1496) and Lorenzo Costa (1460–1535) toned down the pitiless style of Tura and Cossa.

The Florentine school died of anaemia through setting all its faith in the intellect and thus failing to appreciate the gifts of the imagination. The intellectualist leaven of Tuscany, however, working on a powerful imagination, produced the greatest painter of the Quattrocento in the Paduan Andrea Mantegna (1431–1506, pl. 313). He added to the spatial

314 Mantegna. St James led to Martyrdom. Fresco in the Eremitani, Padua (destroyed). 1449–1454

315 Carpaccio. Story of St Ursula (detail). 1491–1495. Venice

values of the Florentines what Berenson has called 'tactile values'; not content with the visual appearance of things, he tried to give the illusion of material texture. He pushed the mania for antiquities much farther than the Florentines had done, and achieved in paint Alberti's dream of recreating a vision of the Latin world. He renewed the traditional garments and introduced Roman costumes into art, observing them with all the exactness of an archaeologist.

316 Antonello da Messina. Male Portrait. 1475. Paris

Being a northerner he introduced nature into the abstract Florentine world, while submitting natural forms to the decorous laws of architecture and sculpture. His art was a broad synthesis of the many ideals by which Quattrocento man was lured.

Mantegna's work as it comes down to us is fairly plentiful, but unfortunately the frescoes of the *Life and Martyrdom of St James and St Christopher* in the Church of the Eremitani at Padua (1449–1454, pl. 314), one of the finest achievements of the Renaissance, were completely destroyed by

317 Giovanni Bellini. Transfiguration. About 1480. Naples

bombardment in 1944. Of his great decorative works the *Gonzaga Family* still survives (in the ducal palace at Mantua) as does the series of the *Triumphs of Caesar* (Hampton Court), paintings in tempera which were intended as settings for the theatre in the palace at Mantua.

Venice, which was long a province of Byzantine art, only threw off that influence in the early fifteenth century. Jacopo Bellini (died 1470), with an inquiring mind typical of his century, was the first to sift in his paintings the mingled influences of Byzantinism, Gothicism and the Florentine 'scientific' outlook, which were struggling for possession of the Venetian school in 1430 or thereabouts. It was then that two streams became apparent in Venice, which were to survive until the dawn of the sixteenth century. Gentile Bellini (1429–1507) son of Jacopo, and Vittore Carpaccio (died 1527) a contemporary of Giorgione, both painted works of a picturesque and other-worldly quality which prolong the credulity of a Pisanello, filled with wonderment both at the real and the imaginary. Gentile Bellini, who made a journey to Constantinople in 1479, came under the influence of Eastern art. Carpaccio gave an ear to Gentile's teaching. He had a taste for narrative cycles and spectacular *mises-en-scène* which he executed for various Venetian societies and confraternities (*Story of St Ursula*, 1490–1498, pl. 315; *Lives of St Jerome and St George*, 1502; *Life of the Virgin*, 1504; *Story of St Stephen*, 1511–1520).

Another group of painters cast their eyes towards Padua where Donatello and Mantegna set the plastic inquiries of the new century in opposition to the picturesque spirit of Gothic art. This tradition was carried on by Carlo Crivelli (died 1493), Antonio (died 1476) and Bartolomeo (died 1499) Vivarini, to end in Giovanni Bellini (died 1516). Giovanni was the younger brother of Gentile, and after beginning with Byzantinism

247

318 Signorelli. Fall of the Damned. Fresco in Orvieto Cathedral. 1499–1505

was drawn away from it by Mantegna who became his brother-in-law in 1453. Taking up the oil technique which had been brought to Venice in about 1575 by Antonello da Messina (pl. 316) he softened the harsh sculptural style of Mantegna, insisting much less on the clear outline of his forms than on the transitions that join them together (pl. 317). By turning away from the analytic outlook of the Quattrocento and towards a pursuit of harmony he helped to prepare for the Cinquecento, and Giorgione and Titian learnt a good deal from him.

Meanwhile in a neighbouring province, while Florence was still sunk in its tense struggle to achieve the impossible, the Umbrian Perugino (1446–1524, pl. 287) was working on the same lines as Giovanni Bellini towards those aspects of the harmonic ideal which were to prevail in the sixteenth century; he was one of the teachers of Raphael. Luca Signorelli (about 1450–1523), also of Umbria, was already haunted by those nightmares of terror that obsessed Michelangelo, and his work contained some of the rudiments of the Baroque style. Everything was now ready for a second powerful drive in Italian art.

Of Perugino's work there remain some frescoes (Sistine Chapel, Rome, and the Cambio, Perugio) and numerous religious paintings. His art

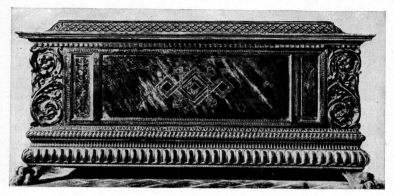

319 Florentine Cassone

declined and became somewhat slack towards the end of the century. Luca Signorelli's best-known works are the frescoes of the *Last Judgment* in Orvieto Cathedral (pl. 318). Another artist, who came from Perugia, Pinturicchio (1454?–1513), was a follower of the facile and picturesque art of Benozzo Gozzoli. His most outstanding work was the decoration of the Borgia Apartments, carried out from 1492 to 1494 for Alexander VI in the Vatican.

The Minor Arts

The minor arts in Italy during the Quattrocento followed the same principles as the major ones. The Italian decorative sense has always been spoiled by the figurative and monumental emphasis given to everything in imitation of architecture and sculpture. Italian artisans from the fifteenth century onwards specialized, in matters of furnishing and jewellery, in pieces composed of many different materials which they put together like carved or painted objects. Their furniture derives from the styles of antiquity, their tables imitating the Roman *cartibulum* and the coffers or *cassoni* the sarcophagi (pl. 319) while their chairs take the X-shape of the chairs used by Roman magistrates. Decorative pottery which was influenced from the outset by Hispano-Moorish faïence, flourished in centres at Gubbio, Deruta, Urbino and Faenza, but it soon took on

320 Pisanello. Portrait-Medal of the Byzantine Emperor Johannes VII Paleologus. About 1447. Florence

249

an historical or narrative bias. The cult of antiquity also had something to do with the revival of the portrait-medal (pl. 320), of which Pisanello was the greatest exponent. Italy was never outstanding in the art of illumination, except in Lombardy where the French influence was felt. The best Italian achievements in this line were tarots or playing-cards. As for engraving, it came from Germany, by way of Venice. The clear-cut works of the Florentines and of Mantegna above all are master-pieces of copper-engraving.

2. LATE GOTHIC AND THE RENAISSANCE IN EUROPE

The Flamboyant Style

While Florence, isolated even from the rest of Italy, was busy throwing off the Middle Ages and developing a monumental art based on Classical models, the rest of Europe was plunged in the excesses of the late Gothic style called 'Flamboyant' because of its sinuous forms (pl. 321).

This style arose in France at the close of the fourteenth century, in the Amiens and Rouen areas. It stemmed from a 'biological' evolution of those Gothic principles which, more rapidly in England than elsewhere,

321 Martin Chambiges. Rose-Window in the South Transept of Sens Cathedral. 1490–1497

had given rise to the English Decorated or Curvilinear style (c. 1280) which inspired the first continental experiments in the Flamboyant. This evolution was modified by the rationalistic outlook of France. The Flamboyant style spread all over Europe, meeting no resistance except in Italy, where none the less it triumphed in Venetia, Lombardy (Milan Cathedral) and the Kingdom of Naples; but it was checked by the Florentine Renaissance. The most obvious forms of this style were perhaps those to be found in Germany and Spain. England gave up its sinuous style just when the rest of Europe was beginning to adopt it, and towards 1350 invented the Perpendicular style, which is typified by an overemphasis on stiff, vertical lines and fan-vaults with intricate

322 Cloister of Gloucester Cathedral. 1351–1377

ribbing (much of Gloucester, pl. 322, and Winchester Cathedrals; York Minster, except for transept; Abbey Church, Bath; Divinity School, Oxford; St George's Chapel, Windsor; Henry VII Chapel, Westminster; King's College Chapel, Cambridge).

The fifteenth century did nothing to modify the Gothic structure. Buildings were now more solidly constructed in spite of the light appearance given by the openwork carving of their decorations whose lavishness overlaid the main divisions of the edifice. All the members of these structures assumed an independent life, multiplying at each other's expense, and their moulding with all its complexities became squarish. The vaults, whose structure became farther and farther removed from the original design of pointed rib-vaulting, were now covered over with a dense network of non-functional, intermediate ribs which took on either a star pattern as in Spain, or a pattern of interlaced branches as in Germany.

The overseers of these works now did their best to surprise the eye by suggesting instability or some feat of skill by means of dropped keystones, 'cork-screw' pillars, whose twisted effect suggests that they are giving way beneath their load. An overall emphasis on the curve, specially noticeable in the tracery of windows, suggests the writhing of flames (pl. 321) which earned the name 'Flamboyant' for a style which, by comparison with the fine, logical clarity of the thirteenth century, gave expression to a tormented and impassioned state of soul. The same anxiety was to take hold of sculpture. This time it was the Netherlander Claus Sluter who created that style imbued with pathos so typical of the fifteenth century.

The Flemish Genius

Flemish genius appeared as a new artistic force in fifteenth-century Europe. If architecture, whose formulae were invented in France, was still alive enough in that country to give birth to a final change of style, yet the Gothic plastic language was failing by the end of the fourteenth century, when it had already exhausted all its potentialities. It was the grafting of Flemish genius which was to restore energy to France and enable it to prolong the Middle Ages until about 1500.

The first Flemish artists including both painters and sculptors (André Beauneveu, the Limbourg brothers) began by enriching the French school with their talent, as they were attracted by the reputation of Paris. The political fortunes of the dukes of Burgundy, which were now favoured by the disasters of the Hundred Years War, allowed the Flemish genius to find its native expression. At the end of the fourteenth century the sculptor Claus Sluter, of Haarlem, was already defining at Dijon the principles of a new art of statuary in which everything was to be governed by emotional expression (Tomb of the dukes of Burgundy, porch and Calvary called the Puits de Moïse (Moses Fountain) at the Chartreuse (Charterhouse) of Champmol, between 1395–1404). Sluter freed the statue from architecture. In his hands it is no longer merely a figure applied on a porch or door, but has all the appearance of coming to life

323 *Claus Slutter. Moses from the Moses Fountain. Former Chartreuse of Champmol, Dijon. 1395–1404*

324 *Limbourg Brothers. March from the Très riches Heures du Duc de Berri. Between 1411–1416. Chantilly*

under the stress of some passionate movement that frames its gestures, distorts the face and makes the draperies swirl (pl. 323). The artist refound the antique theatrical approach to drapery which can amplify both gestures and expressions; he stressed its billows and folds and reliefs, his intense realistic curiosity turning him into a keen observer of individual types and facial expressions. Claus Sluter's genius invented a whole dramatic repertoire of gestures, expressions and models, which was so fraught with the sense of doom that obsessed the fifteenth century, that the whole of Europe adopted it. Strangely enough it was in Flanders that this was to have the least fruitful outcome, and it was from Dijon, where his work was preserved, that Sluter's style spread across Germany and France and into Spain.

Flemish painting emerged from a great international movement which at the close of the fourteenth century, tended to fuse together the Paris school's linearism and the delicacy of Lombard colouring with the naturalism that arose in the North. The brothers Pol, Hennequin and Hermann de Limbourg accomplished a revolution by introducing the landscape copied direct from nature into their painting. At the same time, as they worked for a French prince, they kept close to a traditional genre and expressed themselves through the medium of the miniature (*Très riches Heures du Duc de Berri*, between 1411–1416, pl. 324). The brothers Hubert (died 1426) and Jan (died 1441) van Eyck freed painting from the tyranny of the book and monumental composition, by creating easel-painting. Together they painted the great altarpiece with the *Adoration of the Lamb* for St Bavon, Ghent, which was finished in 1432 (pl. 281).

After his brother's death, Jan van Eyck devoted himself mainly to portraiture. The van Eycks showed themselves against the Middle Ages and
fully committed to the Renaissance spirit by bringing the principle of
integral realism into their art. Casting aside the entire paraphernalia of
medieval conventions, they translated the symbols of the great theological
composition of St Bavon through human characters observed from the
life and against a background of genuine landscapes. At the other extreme
from Byzantine art, this meant a remarkable effort to represent the
supernatural world through the most concrete appearances of the external
world. In his portraits (pl. 326) Jan van Eyck knew how to transfer the
models who posed for him onto the painted panel with a life-like exactness that no other painter has surpassed. The van Eycks achieved spatial
depth at the same time as the Italian Quattrocento painters, but suggested
it by different means, using a diminishing scale of tones according to
distance (colour or aerial perspective). Whereas the Italians made nature
fit their geometrical vision, the van Eycks enveloped everything in a
flood of light and atmosphere. These two painters gave such vital truth
to reality that their pictures fill the spectator with an almost halluci-
natory sense of immediate presence. In order to express such intense
realism the van Eycks used the technique of painting in oils, which they
perfected and established. Since it makes it possible for the painter to
exploit the interplay of successive transparent layers or 'glazes' of colour,
this process enables him to render the texture and other qualities of any
kind of element or object, whether it be cloth, gold, flesh, sky, water or
light itself (colour pl. IV).

Jan van Eyck's was entirely a painter's eye; he saw everything in terms
of its fluid and colour values. He was completely free from the tyranny

325 Rogier van der Weyden. Deposition. Between 1434–1443. Madrid

326 Jan van Eyck. Giovanni Arnolfini and his Wife. 1434. London

327 Dieric Bouts. Last Supper from the Altarpiece in St Peter's, Louvain. 1465–1468

of sculpture which gives the brush the edge of a chisel and which dominated the whole century both in the North and in Italy. But after his death the incisive style was to invade Flemish painting immediately. Rogier van der Weyden (died 1467 at Brussels) did not turn to Sluter's example for the principles of his sculptural manner, but found it in the traditions of the more angular French Gothic which he learned at Tournai, his birthplace, a city which had a prosperous school of monumental (funerary) stonemasons dating from the fourteenth century. Rogier's masterpiece, the *Descent from the Cross* in the Escorial (pl. 325), was conceived as a painted low-relief, the figures projecting their shadows on a background of gold. By comparison with Jan van Eyck, van der Weyden looks back to the medieval outlook, with his sharp-edged linear style, his taste for the ascetic, and his lack of interest in landscape, which are all Gothic features. His outlook on life was entirely Christian in its renouncement and mortification, and it was with intense pathos that he portrayed the sufferings of the Passion.

The art of Jan van Eyck, which was perhaps too far in advance of his time, did not leave a very deep mark on it. Only Petrus Christus (died 1472/73) tried to carry on his style while slightly Italianizing it – there being some evidence that he worked in the peninsula where he knew Antonelle da Messina. It was therefore van der Weyden rather than van Eyck who created the traditional Flemish style. Dieric Bouts, who died at Louvain in 1475, derived pretty closely from van der Weyden, although he engaged in plastic experiments which are not unlike those of his contemporaries in Italy (linear perspective of the *Last Supper* at Louvain,

255

*328 Hugo van der Goes. Adoration from the Portinari Altarpiece. 1473–1475.
Florence*

pl. 327). The same applies to Hugo van der Goes (died 1482) who also
seems to have known Italy (Portinari Altarpiece,Uffizi, pl. 328). After
the work of these men, whose style was tensely set in a sort of exasperation of feeling, fifteenth-century Flemish painting ended by relaxing in
the work of Hans Memling (or Memlinc, died 1494), a painter of Rhenish
origin who settled in Bruges. The symmetry of Memling's compositions,
the suavity he gave to facial expressions, his gentle modelling and elegance
of line, were perfectly fitted to express that ideal of piety and that feeling of bourgeois security which he had in common with Perugino (pl. 286).

Germany

Fifteenth-century Germany shows a very active though confused artistic
production. In keeping with the political division of Germany into minor
states and the tendency towards a municipal, provincial outlook, local
schools abounded and flourished. These schools were centred on the Rhine
and the Danube, spreading into Bavaria, Franconia and Bohemia and as
far as the towns of the Hanseatic League and along the Baltic coast. A
land of extremes, Germany tended equally towards mystic unreality and

V Filippo Lippi. *Adoration in the Forest. Berlin*

329 Marienkirche, Danzig. About 1400–1502

naturalist materialism. The dominant bourgeoisie cared less for the aesthetic quality of a work of art than for its representational values, and expected a work to be didactic, moving and life-like. Mysticism and materialism met in an expressionist crisis which was to remain acute throughout the century.

German architecture lost no time in adopting the Flamboyant style in which it found a vehicle for its own lyrical tendencies. Germany delighted in lavish ornament and openwork decoration, encouraging fantastic vaults with a profusion of decorative ribs, and pierced spires (Ulm, Vienna, Strassburg). The 'hall church' with aisles the same height as the nave which developed in Westphalia in the thirteenth century spread to southern Germany (Liebfrauenkirche, Munich, 1468, choir of St Lawrence, Nuremberg), Austria and Bohemia as well as to the North and along the Baltic as far as Danzig, where there was an outcrop of brick architecture influenced by the English Perpendicular style (town halls of Thorn, Lübeck, Stralsund, Danzig; Marienkirche, Danzig, pl. 329).

Sculpture now made great progress all over Germany, especially in the form of wood-carving which produced huge altarpieces seething with figures and ornamentation. The German plastic principles derived from Sluter, but with more emphasis on expressionism. The enormous output of works was spread over many centres: Nicolas Gerhaert van Leyden (recorded from 1462–1473) at Strassburg and Trier, Hans Multscher

330 *Veit Stoss. Altarpiece of the Virgin in St Mary's, Cracow. 1477–1486*

(about 1400–1476) at Ulm in Swabia, Michael Pacher (about 1435–1498) in the Tyrol, Bernd Notke (about 1440–1509; *St George*, Stockholm 1488) at Lübeck, Veit Stoss at Nuremberg (about 1440–1533). All these workshops, whether in the north or south, showed the same trend towards expressionism (twisting of bodies, convulsive movement of draperies with numerous broken folds), towards a naturalism which led artists to go in search of popular folk-types (Hans Multscher) and even physical deformities (Altarpiece of the Virgin by Veit Stoss, Cracow, 1477–1486, pl. 330), but sometimes also towards a graceful and slightly effeminate mannerism (statues of the Madonna). At the end of the century Italian influence made itself felt through the South and sweetened the harshness of the German style. Adam Krafft (died 1509) of Nuremberg and Tilman Riemenschneider (about 1460–1531, pl. 331) of Würzburg mark the transition from the Gothic to the Renaissance manner.

There was considerable activity in the schools of painting, but is was very mixed in its aims because of the many foreign influences which poured into Germany from every side – the French via the Rhine, the Italian through the Tyrol, the influence of the Burgundian (Dijon) school from the West and South, and the Flemish from the North. In the course of the fourteenth century the clash of Sienese and French contributions gave

331 Riemenschneider. Tomb of the Prince-Bishops of Scherenberg (detail). 1496–1499. Würzburg

332 Master of Wittingau. Agony in the Garden (detail). About 1380–1390. Prague

333 Konrad von Soest. Nativity. About 1420. Dortmund

334 Konrad
Witz.
Christ
walking on
the Waves
from the
Geneva
Altarpiece
(detail).
1444

rise – though with different proportions of each – to the Gothic schools
of painting at Cologne (Clarissan Altarpiece) and in Bohemia (pl. 332). The
influence of the Franco-Flemish miniaturists subsequently gave Germany
a touch of the worldly art of the Limbourg brothers. Early in the fifteenth century Cologne and Westphalia (Konrad von Soest, pl. 333) gave
themselves over to a mystic ideal which was markedly ethereal yet naively
inclined towards a poetic, pastoral charm (pl. 283). This form of art
reached its height about 1430. Its last exponent, Stefan Lochner (between
1405/15–1451) in Cologne, gave it a hint of bourgeois piety.

However, towards 1450 the sculptural style broke into Germany from
the North and South at the same time. In the south, the Burgundian style
resulted in the popular dramatic manner of Hans Multscher (about 1400
–1467) in Cologne, and at Basle, after 1434, the lofty art of Konrad Witz
(about 1400–1446, pl. 284, 334), whose powerful, statuesque density and

335 Martin Schongauer.
Foliage Decoration.
Engraving

336 Michael Pacher. Resurrection of Lazarus from the St Wolfgang Altarpiece (detail). 1471–1481

geometrical vision recall Paolo Uccello and Andrea del Castagno and who archieved a strikingly direct representation of landscape. Meanwhile the Flemish sculptural style represented by Rogier van der Weyden and Dieric Bouts came down the Rhine where it met the Burgundian style and penetrated right into Germany with Hans Pleydenwurf at Nuremberg and Friedrich Herlin at Nordlingen. Cologne imitated this with such success that one might well imagine it as coming into the orbit of Flanders rather than of Germany (Masters of the Life of the Virgin, of the Lyversberg Passion, and of St Severin); the bonds uniting the Rhineland school and Rogier van der Weyden are attested by Memling, who brought back to Bruges a breath of mysticism from Cologne. However, in the last decade of the fifteenth century a national German style was developed in the middle-Rhine and in south Germany (Jan Pollack, Michael Wohlgemuth), springing from the mixture of the Burgundian and Flemish styles, which gave to painting something analogous to what the Flemish style gave to architecture; this was mainly achieved by Martin Schongauer (died 1491). Very much influenced by Rogier van der Weyden, Schongauer's medium was mainly the engraving, a new technique for reproducing drawings which gratified the craft-instinct in German artists, their liking for careful workmanship, their passion for infinitely complex detail (pl. 335). It was only at the very end of the century that Italian influence filtered into the Tyrol, where Michael Pacher (about 1435–1498, pl. 336) was inspired by Mantegna, and reached Augsburg, where the elder Holbein (about 1465–1524) was attracted by the harmonious style of Giovanni Bellini.

France

Of all the countries of Northern Europe, France came closest to the Italian Renaissance. Weakened by the misfortunes of the Hundred Years

261

War, through which she lost the guiding rôle she had hitherto played in European civilization, France gave herself without reserve for a whole century to the excesses of the Flamboyant style in architecture (pl. 337). But the evolution of sculpture shows a progressive detachment from the hard dramatic style of Sluter which, first affecting Burgundy, then descending the Rhone valley, finally made its way into the Midi *(Prophets and Sybils,* choir screen of Albi Cathedral). The setting up of the court on the banks of the Loire gave that region a new importance, and brought to the fore that temperate spirit for which it is renowned. Towards 1460 drapery forms became less rigid, expressionism became milder and the individual character of faces was modified, while artists were now attracted by youth, grace and feminity (pl. 338). Following the demands of the national temperament, pathos was now portrayed more restrainedly, rather by suggesting its inward spiritual meaning, than through its outward, physical and dramatic effects. At the end of the century, after the war with Italy, the native French leaning towards harmony found itself in agreement with the Italian stream, as is shown in the *Entombment* at Solesmes (1496), a masterpiece of French sculpture formerly attributed to Michel Colombe (about 1430–1512).

Taking Europe as a whole, French painting is seen to be, with Italian, the farthest removed from the Gothic outlook. The school of Paris

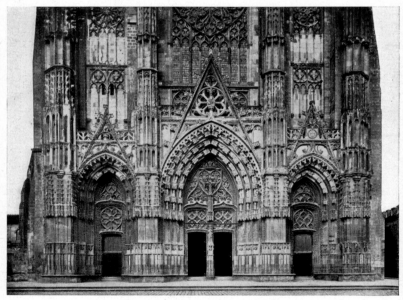

337 *West Front of Tours Cathedral. 15th c.*

338 The Magdalene.
   About 1470. Montluçon

having been dispersed by the Hundred Years War, the new art centres were in the north, on the Loire, and in Provence. The Valenciennes and Amiens painters followed the Flemish style while slightly toning down its harshness. Avignon, which thanks to its position had already become a great cosmopolitan (Franco-Italian) art-centre in the fourteenth century, produced two of the finest works of the period towards 1450, in the *Coronation of the Virgin,* by Enguerrand Quarton (or Charonton), and the *Pietà of Avignon* (pl. 339). The latter painting, one of the highest expressions of mysticism, brings together in an admirable synthesis all the intensity of spiritual passion, a monumental rhythm of composition, and an abstract beauty of sculptural modelling, worthy of a Florentine painter of the Quattrocento. The Italian spirit also moved the unknown master who in about 1460 illuminated the *Livre du cuer d'amours epris,* an allegorical 'novel' by King René (Vienna Library). On the Loire, Jean Fouquet of Tours (died between 1477–1481) – who, incidentally, travelled to Italy in 1445 – eschewed the Gothic spirit in favour of the plastic

263

It might be thought that fifteenth-century Spain came into the orbit of Italy; but on the contrary she refused to do so and her romantic temperament led her to adopt the Flamboyant style. In both sculpture and painting she was dependent on Flemish and German art, which she was to export even into Italy, through the Neapolitan and Sicilian provinces of the house of Aragon.

The Flamboyant style was introduced by the architects of the North. The fifteenth century saw the creation, probably by Flemings, of Seville Cathedral, a splendid structure with nave and double aisles, which was inspired by a regional type of which Barcelona Cathedral set the first example in the fourteenth century; in the sixteenth century the cathedrals of Segovia and Salamanca were to derive from Seville. The architect Hans de Colonia (Hans of Cologne), who was brought to Burgos by a bishop who had been attending the Council of Basle, built at Burgos Cathedral two pierced spires (1442 and 1458)) imitated from those which were designed for Cologne Cathedral. The Burgos workshop produced the first Flamboyant monuments to be found in Spain (Constable's Chapel (1482) in Burgos Cathedral, by Simon de Colonio, son of the Hans already mentioned). Finding a willing soil thanks to the Moorish traditions which were still deeply-rooted in Spain after its liberation, the Flamboyant style now mingled with the Moorish, to create at the time of the Catholic kings the Mudéjar art in which the excess of decoration, taken over from both styles, swarmed over the whole monument. The style of the Catholic kings, sometimes called the 'Isabelline' style, is the first really native expression to be found in Spanish architecture. Enriched with heraldic emblems and Mudéjar features, it is a haughty expression of the triumphant monarchy. The son of an emigrant from Lyons, Juan Güas, built in that style S. Juan de los Reyes at Toledo (1478) and the Infantado Palace at Guadalajara (1480), while Enrique de Egas, the son of an expatriate from Brussels now an overseer at Toledo Cathedral, built the Royal Chapel which

343 *Entrance to the College of S. Gregorio, Valladolid. 1488–1496*

344 Pedro Berruguete. Ordeal by Fire. Madrid

345 Gil Siloé. Annunciation from the Altarpiece at Miraflores. 1499

houses the tombs of the Catholic kings in Granada Cathedral. One of the finest monuments in this style is the College of S. Gregorio at Valladolid (1486, pl. 343), whose author remains unknown; the decoration was made up of floral and vegetable shapes as in Manueline art. During the period of the Catholic kings the lay-out of the different parts of the church took on an original character which was to last until the eighteenth century: the choir *(coro)* was placed in the end bays of the nave,

346 Francisco de Arruda. Tower of Belem (Portugal). 1516

347 *Diogo de Arruda.*
Window in the Chapter-
house of the Convent-Palace
at Tomar

348 *Nuno Gonçalves.*
Benefactors from the St Vincent
Altarpiece. About 1460. Lisbon

west of the crossing, and closed in with high walls full of carvings; east of the crossing the *capilla mayor* ends in a blank wall, with a large decorated altar in front of it *(altar mayor)*. Exquisite grills or screens in ironwork serve to close off the choir, the *capilla mayor* and the chapels.

Spanish sculpture developed in much the same way as architecture, producing enormous decorative backgrounds, liturgical furnishings, gigantic altarpieces alive with figures, stalls *(sillerias)* and choir-screens *(trascoros)*. A great many artists came from Burgundy, France and Germany to work on these; the greatest was a Burgos, Gil de Siloé, no doubt a converted Jew from Flanders or Germany who, working as easily in wood (altarpiece for the Charterhouse at Miraflores, 1496) as in marble (Tombs of John II and Isabella, in the same church, 1489), introduced a strongly Germanic style, graceful in its mannerism and with a marked intensity of feeling, which gave a start to the Castilian school of sculpture (pl. 345).

Painting was based on Flemish models. In Catalonia Luis Dalmau who went to Flanders in 1431, carried out what amounts to a pastiche of van Eyck in 1445, in the Counsellors' Altarpiece in Barcelona. Jacomart Baço, Jaume Huguet, Bartolomé Bermejo, Pablo Vergos, Fernando Gallegos, were all in the same way disciples of the Flemish tradition. Under the Catholic kings, the Castilian artist Pedro Berruguete (died 1503) who worked for a time in Italy, was to free painting from its Flemish bondage by turning decisively towards the Quattrocento outlook (pl. 344). The

Andalusian Alejo Fernandez (died 1543) sweetened Flemish harshness with Italian grace.

Following its great discoveries across the seas, Portugal had a sudden burst of prosperity which in the reign of Don Manuel (1495–1521) showed itself in the rapid strides that were made in art through this ruler's initiative. Portugal then created a style of lyrical exuberance which is unusual in the West, and which reflected the excitement of its great explorers. This is known as the Manueline style. As with the art of the Catholic kings, this style had two phases: the Gothic and the Renaissance. The Manueline style was developed by Boytac in his church at Setúbal and at the monastery at Batalha (about 1509); Diogo de Arruda at the Convent-Palace of the Knights of Christ at Tomar (about 1510, pl. 347); Francisco de Arruda with the Tower of Belem (1516, pl. 346). All these men built the most poetical works in this form of architecture, a kind of naturalistic symphony in stone.

The Spaniard Juan de Castilho was to dry up this creative vein by transposing it into a flat (Plateresque) decorative technique (Monastery of S. Jeronymos at Belem, 1517).

Portuguese painting, like Spanish, was a derivative of Flemish painting. It produced several artists with a sharp eye for realism as well as one of the high-lights in fifteenth-century art, namely the St Vincent Altarpiece (Lisbon Museum, pl. 348). This painting is a portrait-composition of an intense realism suggestive of Jan van Eyck (who visited Portugal in 1428); it was commissioned from Nuno Gonçalves about the year 1460.

VIII. THE RENAISSANCE IN EUROPE
IN THE SIXTEENTH CENTURY

Until the sixteenth century the different artistic civilizations of the West followed smoothly one upon the other, each begetting the next. Even in the fifteenth century the Gothic and Renaissance styles could live peacefully side by side; Milan Cathedral was under completion when that of Florence was begun. But after the sixteenth century Western art was split by the warring forces of ideologies that were mutually exclusive and even by national rivalries . The maturing of new nations, each of which had a personal contribution to make but which all had to vie with the longer-established seats of culture, was to multiply the West's wealth of expression and give rise to three hundred years of creative tension in Europe.

Two personalities represent the hostile ideologies: Erasmus and Luther, the humanist and the prophet, the peacemaker and the revolutionary. Erasmus, whose dream was to introduce the heroes of a Pantheon into Paradise, and who could only see what things have in common between them, did his utmost to rescue the spiritual unity of Europe. For him, there were no differences that reason could fail to reconcile; he considered faith itself as an established truth which like the wisdom of the ancients had already become part of the human heritage, and it might be said that he was not far from confusing revelation with inspiration. As for Luther, the 'God-intoxicated man', against this rule of reason he uttered the protest of the mysticism which he thought humanism had flouted. Faced with this conscious ideal of man turning his life into a cunning balance of the faculties under the guidance of reason alone, and giving the divine, like the human, no more than the share to which it was entitled, Luther brought from the depths of the Middle Ages an image of man in his feebleness, incapable of good without the help of divine grace, and groaning beneath the sinner's fate imposed on him by a terrible God whom he now revived from the rediscovered Old Testament. At the moment when the Church was preparing to make allowances for the dreams of Christian humanism, and while the papacy in Rome was bringing paganism to the baptismal font, Luther drove the Church back into its mysteries.

Even Italy now found itself torn between these two forces. On grounds of intellect in Rome and of sensibility in Venice, Raphael and Titian were defining the laws of a classicism which bases the economy of a work of art on a proper and successful balance of parts one against the other, thus demanding the playing down of individual features, and the sacrifice of any marked expression to the serene impersonality of an ideal beauty. At the same time, Bramante, heir to the long experiments of the Quattrocento, gave his Roman works the exact proportions of the architecture

349 Leonardo. *Last Supper (basis of the composition). S. Maria delle Grazie, Milan*

of antiquity. It was he who brought the central plan (pl. 350–353) to its perfection, as a symbol of harmony, after it had long haunted the Quattrocento. However, this classical idealism was to be immediately compromised by Michelangelo, for if he glorified man's power to the point of making him a superman, it was the better to reveal man's ridiculous weakness when compared with the Almighty; the heroes of the Sistine Chapel are heavy with a strength which they know will never avail them in their struggle with the Infinite. This unbalance gives rise to a despair which torments their bodies and darkens their faces. If Michelangelo was able to keep these extremes of expression in the bounds of his canon of beauty, that was a miracle within his own competence and no other's, but after him there was nothing capable of holding such violence back. Michelangelo gave 'muscles' to architecture as he had done to the human body; he turned his monuments into athletes, before his successors made circus strong-men of them.

In Venice Tintoretto, who was obsessed by Michelangelo, was involved in another drama. The weakness that the painter of the Sistine Chapel had discovered in man by comparison with God, was seen by the decorator of the Scuola di S. Rocco on the cosmic scale. Tintoretto saw this at the very moment when Copernicus was proving that the little earth, which men had believed to be at the centre of things, was no more than a speck in a universe whose bounds were suddenly found to be infinitely remote – yet another sixteenth century principle of contradiction which threw man back into his puniness just when he was priding himself on his self-mastery. Bruegel in Flanders was to settle this conflict by his idea of the 'sovereign peace' of nature. Tintoretto's humanity seems to be at grips with vastness – torrents of darkness, floods of light, whirlpools of space carry the forms twisting and turning in their wake, losing all their

VI Titian. Madonna with the Rabbit (detail). Paris

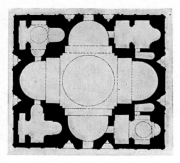

350 Plan of The Holy Apostles, Ani. Before 1031

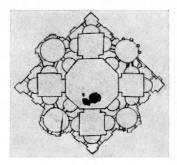

351 Leonardo. Sketch of a centrally-planned Church. Paris

density, torn into shreds by the teeth of shadow and sunshine, gnawed by the infinite.

The search for effects at the expense of harmonious proportions; violence of expression; the breakdown of equilibrium by showing a trance-like movement instead of a state of repose; the quest for the boundless that interferes with the integrity of shapes which are devoured by shadow, light or space – these are only a few features of a new aesthetic which historians have called 'Baroque'.

It was from an obscure interaction between classicism and the Baroque that the crisis called 'Mannerism' emerged in Italy in the second half of the century. Apart from the Venetian school, which kept all its vitality, perhaps because it was the last-comer, all the Italian schools were to suffer from this sickness of styles – a sort of neurosis, a symptom of their inability to define themselves which led the second-rank artists, over-whelmed by the authority of the great masters, into an extravagance of

352 Bramante. Plan for St Peter's, Rome

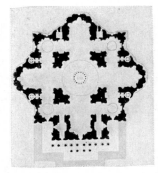

353 Michelangelo. Plan for St Peter's, Rome

354 Crivelli. *Madonna della Candeletta (detail) 1488 (?) Milan*
355 Raphael. *Madonna del Granduca (detail). About 1504. Florence*
356 Michelangelo. *Delphic Sybil. Fresco (detail). 1508–1512. Rome*

gesture and expression, an over-lengthening of proportions, and unnaturally twisted attitudes in the portrayal of figures.

This nervous unbalance was passed from Italy to the rest of Europe. The contact between the Renaissance and Gothic Europe was at first a kind of rapture. Without in the least changing their structure, the schools of the different nations were content to take from abroad an ornamental vocabulary which they used as another embellishment in the Flamboyant manner. Failing to grasp the implications of the pure works being made in Florence they sought models for their Renaissance style in the notorious Certosa of Pavia which, tattooed as it is with arabesques, overlaid with balustrades and candelabra and cupids and insets of every kind, was still not enough to shock men who were quite used to the 'lacework' of their own cathedrals. Such were the sources of the Spanish Plateresque style, as of the Loire castles and the German Renaissance.

At all events, when towards 1530 Rome's prestige imposed its examples of the full Renaissance style, Europe found itself unequal to the occasion, and instead of following the awe-inspiring models of Leonardo, Raphael or Michelangelo, took to the eccentricities of Italian art, that is to say Mannerism, whose contortions followed naturally on the Flamboyant. The crisis resulting from such an upheaval in values could only favour the spread of Mannerism, which thrived at Amsterdam, Leyden, Antwerp, Fontainebleau, Basle, along the Danube and down into Spain and Portugal.

When we consider what a disturbing experience the Italian Renaissance must have been for Europe after being lost for centuries in the maze of Gothic, it is surprising that the crisis was not even worse. But the Gothic style had exhausted all its possibilities and the fertilizing influence of Italian art all over Europe brought fresh sap into its withering branches. One country after another found renewed creative strength and became

Inclining to the picturesque, the architectural works conceived by Raphael (1483–1520) had some connexion with the development of Mannerism. His pupil Giulio Romano (1492–1546) who was also a painter, was even more than Vignola himself the representative of Mannerism in architecture. The Palazzo del Tè at Mantua (pl. 361), which he built from 1524 to 1534, was decorated throughout with his frescoes, and it heralds Baroque architecture.

363 Palladio. Façade of the Redentore, Venice. 1577–1592

In its rivalry with Rome, Venice adopted the new style invented by the eternal city, but overlaid it with lavish decoration. For the Libreria Vecchia di S. Marco, Sansovino (1486–1570) multiplied the pilasters, columns, entablatures, balustrades and statues, so as to contrive a richness of effect nearer to the spirit of painting than to architecture. Andrea Palladio of Vicenza (1508–1580) showed the same taste for splendour in the Basilica at Vicenza (1573) and the Teatro Olimpico in the same town, the latter being finished by his pupil Scamozzi; but in the most original part of his work (villas built in Venetia; church of the Redentore, pl. 363, S. Giorgio, both Venice), on the other hand, he renounced all lyricism in the decorations and sought after a greater classical purity. Of all the artists of the Renaissance he came nearest to the canons of Greek architecture.

In the sixteenth century in Italy, architecture tended to become a theoretical science. Numerous editions of Vitruvius' treatise, enriched with engravings, together with illustrations of Roman monuments, and the treatises of Serlio (1537), Vignola (1562) and Palladio (1570) guaranteed the spreading of the classical manner in architecture throughout Europe.

After the model of the Roman villa, Renaissance Italy created many princely residences in the country. The house or *casino* stands above a set of terraces embellished with yew trees, flowerbeds, pools and fountains, statues and 'rustic' buildings. The most famous of these, the Villa d'Este (1549) was designed by Pirro Ligorio (died about 1580) for the Cardinal Ippolito d'Este (pl. 362).

The aesthetic of the High Renaissance was worked out in the first third of the century by a few great artists. The oldest of them, Leonardo da Vinci, born in 1452, still belongs to the Quattrocento by virtue of his inquiring mind and scientific genius. Born within a few years of each other, Raphael, Michelangelo, Giorgione and Titian were all of the same generation, but Giorgione and Raphael died relatively young while the careers of Michelangelo and Titian stretched late into the century. Born in 1494, Correggio belongs to the following generation, but had already given his full measure before his death in 1534; and by his genius for innovation he must be considered as one of the leaders of the Cinquecento. Even in his lifetime each of these great masters founded a school of his own, which prolonged his art even in degrading it, until the last quarter of the century when the art of the Counter-Reformation began to appear.

Leonardo da Vinci (1452–1519) served his apprenticeship in Florence, in Verrocchio's studio; he then worked in Florence and Milan. Called to France in 1516 by Francis I he died there, at Amboise. Leonardo painted very few works, which unfortunately have badly deteriorated owing to his technical researches into the chemistry of colours (*Madonna of the Rocks,* Louvre, 1483, pl. 364; *Last Supper,* S. Maria delle Grazie, Milan, 1495–1497, pl. 349; *Virgin and Child with St Anne,* 1501; *Gioconda* or *Mona Lisa,* Louvre, 1503–1506). He completed the researches of the fifteenth century into the human body, but he was intent on adding to it his discoveries in the realm of psychology. The *Last Supper* is a systematic study of shades of expression which are inflected according to the individual, while in the *Mona Lisa* he tried to convey the mystery of the inner life. Abandoning the sharp outlines of the sculptor-painters of the Quattrocento, which are still noticeable in the *Madonna of the Rocks,* he rendered the luminous, fluid vibrations of atmosphere and the softness of flesh by veiling the modelling through a chiaroscuro technique called *sfumato*. He embodied the Renaissance conception of the 'universal man'. His scientific treatises, which remained unpublished during his life-time, his host of drawings, all show a thirst for knowledge in all its fields – astronomy, the physical and natural sciences, biology, mechanics, hydraulics, aviation, chemistry and the like. However, he made painting, which is a reflection of nature, into the supreme creative art, and indeed the very end of both the sciences and the arts.

Raffaelo Sanzio, or 'Raphael' (1483–1520), gave a definitive form to the ideal of harmony towards which Italian art had been moving for two hundred years. Born at Urbino, in a remote province, he was a pupil of Perugino, under whose guidance he made his earliest works (*Marriage of the Virgin* or *Sposalizio,* Milan, 1504). It was Florence, where he spent the years 1504 to 1508, that brought him intellectual freedom. There he

364 Leonardo. Madonna of the Rocks. 1507–1508. Paris

365 Raphael. Disputà. Fresco in the Stanza della Segnatura. Vatican, Rome.
1508–1511

developed his type of Madonna with the pure oval face, impersonal and idealized as the faces of antique statues (pl. 366, *Madonna del Granducca*, pl. 355). From 1508 to 1511 he was painting for Julius II, undertaking a series of frescoes in the *stanze* (chambers) and particularly the Stanza della Segnatura in the Vatican (*School of Athens* or *Philosophy; Parnassus* or *Poetry; Glorification of the Holy Sacrament – Disputà – or Religion*, pl. 365; and three scenes together representing *The Law*). Enlivened by intellectual inspiration, Raphael's idealism here achieved an admirable monumental fullness; the happy combination of an artistic temperament with the thought of his age produced in the Stanza della Segnatura one of those major works in which form is the more sublime because of the idea it contains. His portraits (*Baldassare Castiglione*, Louvre, *La Donna Velata*, Palazzo Pitti, Florence) express the humanistic ideal of a calm existence, certainty and self-possession. He was less successful in his religious works, for a systematic idealizing of figures results in a kind of devotional art which is banal, cold and insipid and which unfortunately was to be favoured by the lords of the church for three hundred years (*Sistine Madonna*, Dresden, *Madonna di Foligno* and *Transfiguration*, both Vatican, *Holy Family*, Louvre). In the other frescoes he painted in the Vatican Stanze (*Fire in the Borgo, Miracle of Bolsana* and *Heliodorus driven from the Temple*, 1511–1514) Raphael, who was easily influenced, showed himself to be somewhat disturbed by

366 Raphael. Study for a Madonna.
Drawing. Vienna

367 Giovanni da Udine (after Raphael).
Grottesche in the Vatican Loggias,
Rome

the power of Michelangelo and by Venetian colouring. His last monumental work, partly carried out by his pupils, was the *Story of Cupid
and Psyche* in the Villa Farnesina, in which he invented the mythological
models of the modern age. The Loggias of the Vatican, on which work
was begun under Raphael's direction, were finished by his pupils. There
the biblical scenes are set in a background by Giovanni da Udine (1494
–1561) suggested by ancient ornaments recently unearthed in the Baths
(grottae) of Titus and which for this reason were known as *grottesche*
(pl. 367). This arabesque form of ornamentation was to be copied all over
Europe. We also owe to Raphael the cartoons for the tapestry series of
the *Acts of the Apostles* which were woven at Brussels.

Michelangelo Buonarroti (1475–1564), who came from Caprese in
Tuscany, was the most Florentine in spirit of all the artists of the sixteenth century. His outlook was that of the sculptor-painters of the
Quattrocento who were concerned only with relief, and even his painting
is a transposition of volumes on to a surface. He carried to the point of
frenzy that lust for strength which had obsessed the painters of the
preceding age but, being profoundly Christian, he opposed to human
strength the power of God which thwarts it and makes it of no avail.
This painful strife, man's struggle against an evil destiny, the fury of a
Prometheus against the chains he can never unloose, gives his art a dramatic intensity which is in violent contrast with the humanistic ideal of
harmony embodied in Raphael. The gigantic and uneasy *David* in marble
(Accademia, Florence), which is 16 ¼ feet tall and which he carved in
1502 to 1504, and his earliest paintings (*Holy Family* in the Uffizi) are
still faithful to the Quattrocento principles which he imbibed in the studio

*368 Michelangelo. Creation of the Plants and the Sun and Moon.
Fresco in the Sistine Chapel, Rome. 1508–1512*

of Bertoldo, a pupil of Donatello's, while he was learning the art of painting from Ghirlandaio. Called to Rome, he revealed his genius to an amazed world in the frescoes of the Sistine Chapel (between 1508–1512), where he painted scenes from the Old Testament, prophets and sibyls (pl. 356) in an artificial architectural setting on which he posed sham 'statues' of adolescents, the *ignudi* (pl. 368). His herculean idea of the human body derived from ancient statuary of the Hellenistic period which had then recently been unearthed in Rome (*Laocoon, Belvedere Torso*). His sculptures, which he conceived in colossal terms, all remained unfinished. The Tomb of Julius II was incomplete except for the *Captives* (Louvre, pl. 369, and Accademia, Florence), which in any case he left unfinished, and the overpowering *Moses* whose whole figure is inspired by the breath of divine anger. He worked from 1523 to 1534 on the Tombs of Giuliano and Lorenzo de' Medici in S. Lorenzo, Florence; there his desperate soul is reflected in the allegorical figures on the tombs (*Day, Night, Dawn, Dusk*) and the *Virgin* of the Medici Chapel, in which the titanic bodies swoon in the distress of conquered heroes. His most violent work is the fresco of the *Last Judgment* in the Sistine Chapel (1535–1541) in which a gigantic Christ is shown striking down mankind – a gesture which, in the mind of a great republican and Christian artist who was a follower of Savonarola, was perhaps aimed at the papacy. In this

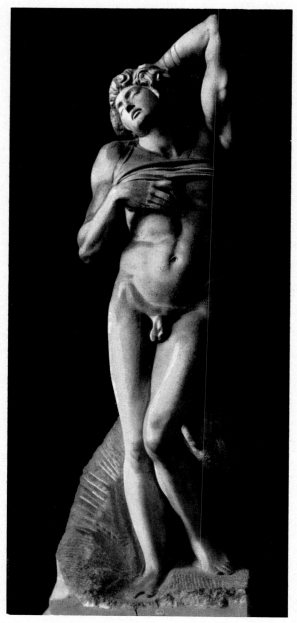

369 Michelangelo. Dying Captive for the Tomb of Julius II. 1513–1516. Paris

370 Giorgione. The Tempest. Early 16th c. Venice

work the balance which Michelangelo had so far maintained in the Sistine Chapel between beauty and expressionism was upset in favour of the dramatic, and it is already a Baroque work.

Being by nature – unlike Florence – more given to enjoyment than to knowledge, Venice created an art more expressive of sensibility than of intellect. The Venetian artists therefore addressed the senses rather than the mind, and their magic colour suggests the material presence of the world. Three artists worked out, in Bellini's studio, the Venetian art of the Seicento: Giorgione, Titian and Palma Vecchio.

Giorgio da Castelfranco, called Giorgione (1477–1511), plunged man into the very heart of nature, which gave the Florence-trained artists

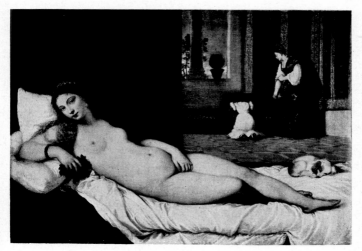

371 Titian. The Venus of Urbino. About 1538. Forence

no more than the elements of a setting thrown into the distance like a back-cloth. The Venetian picture, on the contrary, was to be essentially based on landscape (pl. 370), and even if its distinct forms were not represented, nature was always in evidence in the warm light playing subtly on faces, flesh and draperies, and in the atmosphere enveloping everything. Giorgione founded the principles of modern painting – so-called 'symphonic' painting in which the colours, like orchestral sounds, acted on each other and were no longer flatly applied inside the outlines of the drawing according to the principles of local colour which Raphael so scrupulously observed.

Tiziano Vecellio, or 'Titian' (1477/78 or 89/90–1576), lived to a great age. In Venice he became 'regent' of the arts (pl. 696), but also worked for Alfonso d'Este, duke of Ferrara (*Bacchanals*, Prado and Louvre, *Venus of Urbino*, Uffizi, pl. 371), for the margrave of Mantua (*Entombment*, Louvre), and for Paul III who summoned him to Rome in 1545. His genius earned him the patronage of the Emperor Charles V, who made him a count palatine and called him to Augsburg several times, notably in 1548 when he painted *Charles V at the Battle of Mühlberg* (Prado). After the emperor's death, Philip II kept him in favour and for him the artist made several pictures, among them *Jupiter and Antiope* (Louvre).

Titian was the expression, in the sensuous Venetian mode, of the ideal of harmony and certainty of which Raphael's art was the intellectual form (colour pl. VI). He interpreted the epicurean temperament of Venice, but with a fullness of health which completely purified it, and had a poetry by turns pathetic and meditative, which makes him one

372 Palma Vecchio. Portrait of an unknow Woman. Milan

of the most profound painters of the soul. His work is a vast encyclopaedia of human feelings in which the pagan dream of the golden age, the Christian mysteries, the delights of love, the ritual of death, the splendours of light and all the beauty of nature come together. He is the first of the 'universal' painters whose works are a microcosm of the world.

Palma Vecchio (1480–about 1528) is related to Titian, but his work has more sensual overtones (pl. 372).

In the Venetian orbit a painter from Cremona, Giovanni Antonio Licinio, called Pordenone (1483–1539), a forerunner of genius, was creating the Baroque at the very moment when Titian was developing his serene classicism. He foreshadowed the art of Tintoretto, even of Caravaggio, and prepared the way for Parmigianino (frescoes for the cathedrals of Cremona, 1520–1523, and Spilimbergo, 1524).

At Parma, Antonio Allegri, called Correggio (1494–1534), brought into being an art of sentimental voluptuousness which owed something to Florentine scientific draughtsmanship, as well as to Leonardo's delicacy and the sensuality of the Venetian school. His mannered feminine type (*Mystic Marriage of St Catherine*, Louvre, 1519); his fluid compositions (*Madonna with St Sebastian*, Dresden, about 1525, pl. 373); his expressions of rapture and ecstasy; his dome decorations in sharply-receding upward perspective with violent foreshortening of the figures – the first known to painting (S. Giovanni, Parma, 1520, Parma Cathedral, 1530) – make him, with Michelangelo, one of the founders of Baroque art.

The example given by these great innovators had a paralysing effect on their contemporaries and successors, which showed itself in their retreat into a lackadaisical conformity or else that exacerbation of style known as Mannerism. Every great master left behind him a trail of imitators grouped into a school. At Milan, Ambrogio de Predis (1430–1520), Marco d'Oggiono (1470–1540), Cesare da Sesto (1477–1523) Boltraffio (1467–1516) and Bernardino Luini (about 1480–1532) all vulgarized and diluted the art of Leonardo; Sodoma (1477–1549), who worked at Siena, added a disquieting sensuality to Leonordo's charm; the ar

VII Mathias Grünewald. Crucifixion. Karlsruhe

373 Correggio. Madonna with St Sebastian. About 1525. Dresden

374 *Bronzino. Lucrezia Panciatichi.*
About 1540. Florence

375 *Parmigianino. Madonna with*
Angels. Florence

of Fra Bartolommeo (1475–1517) and Mariotto Albertinelli (1474–1515) offers an empty comparison with Raphael; the cold exactness of Andrea del Sarto (1486–1531) makes him perhaps the most abstract of them all. Deriving from Michelangelo, Corregio, and Andrea del Sarto, a number of painters working at Florence and Parma and who are often called the

376 *Giambologna. Venus.*
Florence

Mannerists represent the first Baroque generation. They are all typified by a deliberate cult of distortion through which they tried to give the fullest expression to their figures. Their portraits, with stilted poses and staring eyes, have a strangeness about them which in Bronzino (Florence, 1502–1572, pl. 374) reaches an almost hypnotic tension. At Parma, Parmigiano (1504–1540, pl. 375) refined Corregio's feminine type, lengthening limbs and body to make it more gracefully fluid; Primaticcio (1504–1570, pl. 379) was to introduce this type into France. In Florence, Andrea del Sarto's pupils prove into what decay the oldest Italian school had fallen: Pontormo (1494 –1555) lengthened his forms beyond all reason and painted strange compositions in which the classicism of this school was

377 Tintoretto. Last Supper (detail). Venice

oddly abused; il Rosso (1494–1540) who was called to France in 1531, accentuated the pathos of Michelangelo by dramatic gesture. In Rome and Mantua, Giulio Romano (1492–1546), who was a kind of studio-overseer for Raphael, tried to continue his master's art by adding a touch of Michelangelesque over-emphasis. His style had an enormous influence all over Europe. Sebastiano del Piombo (1485–1547), who came from Venice to Rome in about 1509, was also led away by this grandiose but dangerous example.

Were it not for Michelangelo, it might be said that the sixteenth century saw the decline of Italian sculpture, which had been so rich in the Quattrocento. In Padua, the bronze worker Andrea Riccio (1470–1532) carried on the tradition of Donatello; in Venice the emigrant Florentine Jacopo Sansovino imitated antique statues to the point of pastiche. Michelangelo's example overwhelmed such artists as Baccio Bandinelli (1493–1560), Guglielmo della Porta (about 1510–1577) and Bartolommeo Ammanati (1511–1592). Other artists of the Florentine school such as the Frenchman Giovanni da Bologna, or Giambologna (1524–1608, pl. 376), and the bronze- and gold-worker Benvenuto Cellini (1500–1571, pl. 413) brought the Mannerist style into sculpture.

The Venetian school, the latest comer in the history of painting, was the only school in Italy to ignore the Mannerist crisis. With its energy still unspoiled it produced some great masters in the second half of the century. Paolo Caliari, called Veronese (1528–1588), came originally from Verona and was a talented decorator. He painted immense canvases, which he arranged as dazzling stage-settings in the midst of splendid

*378 Veronese. The Venetian Republic.
Ceiling in the Doge's Palace, Venice.
After 1577*

works of architecture (*Marriage at Cana*, Louvre, ceilings of the Doge's Palace, Venice, pl. 378). His gay colouring, silvery and musical, expresses all the generosity of the senses and the taste for material luxury for which Venice is noted. Jacopo Robusti, called Tintoretto (1512?–1594), was one of the creators of Baroque art. A pupil of Titian, his eyes were opened by Michelangelo's works in Rome. His tormented genius and creative frenzy poured themselves out on a vast scale in his huge compositions (*Last Judgement* in S. Maria dell'Orto, scenes from the Old and New Testament in the Scuola di S. Rocco, decorations in the Doge's Palace where he painted the biggest painting in the world, the *Paradise*, which is 2153 square feet in area). Tintoretto toned down Venetian colouring in order to render subtler shades of pathos; he was haunted by the notion of space and showed man swept away in a sort of cosmic drama (pl. 377). In the town of Bassano, the Bassani painted with a rustic feeling close to the Flemish style, not often found in Italy.

Several north Italian towns came directly under the influence of Venice. At Bergamo, Lorenzo Lotto (1480–1556) was one of the few Mannerists of the north. Giovanni Battista Moroni (1525–1578) was a remarkable portrait-artist who was as strictly objective as a Holbein. At Brescia, Moretto (1498–1554) and Savoldo (about 1480 – after 1548), both influenced by Giorgione's chiaroscuro, herald some of the experiments to be made in the seventeenth century. Dosso Dossi (about 1479–1542) at Ferrara, gave further evidence in his work of that taste for the unusual which is common to Ferrarese painting; this he did in a manner deriving from Giorgione.

2. THE SPREAD OF THE RENAISSANCE IN EUROPE

France

The early French Renaissance, on which Italian influence was not very deep, developed mainly in the region of the Loire. Decorative features taken from Milanese art – arabesques, putti, candelabra, medallions and lustres – were added to Gothic elements in the châteaux built for Louis XII or his ministers at Blois, Amboise, Chaumont and Gaillon (near Rouen). In the châteaux dating from the first half of Francis I's reign (Blois, Chambord, Azay-le-Rideau, Chenonceau) an Italianate decoration was still often superficially applied on buildings planned and constructed on traditional French lines. This composite style died out towards 1530, a time when a complete assimilation was achieved, particularly in the region of Paris. In 1528 Francis I decided to make Fontainebleau a centre of Italian art. When it came to decorating the rooms and galleries of his new palace, he invited artists from abroad – Primaticcio, Rosso and Nicolò dell'Abbate – to do the work. There he amassed his first items for a collection of antiques, and masterpieces of the great Italian artists – the beginning of the Louvre museum. The rather awkward external architecture of the palace was designed by Gilles le Breton, and was very much in the spirit of the preceding generation; but Rosso and Primaticcio (pl. 379) gave the interior a stucco and painted decoration rich in figures. This style, as yet unknown to Italy, was the first instance of Baroque decorations and had great influence all over Europe (1533–1544). It was not to appear in Italy until about 1550 (Palazzo Spada, Rome).

However, the arrival of two Italian architects (Vignola and Serlio), who were invited to France in 1541, must have helped the French to

379 Primaticcio. Stucco Figures at Fontaine-bleau

380 *Lescot and Goujon. Square Court of the Louvre, Paris. Begun 1547*

throw off their outmoded traditions. In Henry II's reign the antique style was elegantly applied by three great artists, Pierre Lescot, Philibert Delorme and Jean Goujon. Pierre Lescot (about 1510–1578) superimposed the three Greek orders in his reconstruction of the Louvre (1547, pl. 380). Philibert Delorme or de l'Orme (about 1510–1570), almost all of whose works have been destroyed (Tuileries) or interfered with (Château d'Anet), further stressed the French trend towards classical purity by way of a reaction against the decorative style introduced by the Italians (pl. 381); but over-lavish decoration was to return to favour during the reign of Henry IV. As for church architecture, it was only towards 1530 that it accepted Italianate decoration, applied to entirely Gothic structures. This state of affairs continued into the seventeenth century (St-Eustache, Paris).

Meanwhile the builder's craft was beginning to free itself from the empirical approach of the medieval master-mason, to become the architect's science. Following the Italian example the French now published treatises on architecture. In 1547 Jean Goujon prefaced a French translation of Vitruvius, issued by Jean Martin, with what was no less than a manifesto in favour of the creative architect. Philibert Delorme, who published a dissertation on architecture in 1567 as well as various technical works, wanted the architect to become a 'universal man', versed in all kinds of learning and philosophy. Jean Bullant also published a treatise in 1564. Very soon French classical monuments themselves began to be quoted as examples and models, and Jacques Androuet du Cerceau issued his *Plus Excellens Bastimens de France* between 1576 and 1579.

In the first half of the century sculpture followed the restful style of the preceding century, tinged with Italian influence. The Tomb of

381 Philibert Delorme. Tomb of Francis I
in St-Denis. Finished 1558

382 Jean Goujon. Nymphs.
Reliefs from the Fontaine
des Innocents. 1546. Paris

Francis II, duke of Brittany, at Nantes, carved by Michel Colombe
and based on a design by Jean Perréal, and that of Louis XII at St
Denis, finished by the Italian Giovanni Giusti in 1531, were both in
the traditional manner, but the Tomb of Francis I, which was finished
by Philibert Delorme at St-Denis in 1558, and embellished with
sculptures by Pierre Bontemps, was a triumphal arch (pl. 381). Equally
classical was the Tomb of Henry II executed by Primaticcio between
1564 and 1570. Jean Goujon (rood screen of Germain-l'Auxerrois,
Louvre, 1544; bas-reliefs in the Palais du Louvre, 1549–1562; *Fontaine
des Innocents,* Paris, 1546, pl. 382) imposed a classical discipline on
Rosso's art and created a fluidly elegant style unmatched in Italy.
Germain Pilon (1534–1590) added a realistic touch to it, while Ligier
Richier (died 1567), a Lorrain artist, pursued the dramatic Gothic strain
with a certain bombast (*Entombment* in St-Etienne, St-Mihiel).

The art of Jean Bourdichon (died about 1521), who worked under
Louis XII is neither illumination nor is it exactly painting, but it is
evidence of the Gothic decline. France had to turn to foreign artists, but
these were all deeply influenced by French society. In the many
ensembles they painted, notably at Fontainebleau, both Rosso (who came
in 1531) and Primaticcio (from 1532 onwards) developed an art which
was Italianate in style but in which the mythological amorous themes,
the lyricism of the huntsman and the forest, the feminine atmosphere,
all express certain characteristics which were to endure in French art
over the centuries. Their contact with French life helped these artists

383 Jean Clouet. Portrait-Drawing.
About 1535. Chantilly

384 François Clouet. Lady in her
Bath. Washington

to cast off the restlessness of Italian Mannerism and replace it by a calm and temperate style, fluid and supple, a style known as that of the 'Fontainebleau school' which was to be imitated, sometimes most awkwardly, by anonymous native artists, as it was by Jean Cousin and his son of the same name.

France evolved its own idea of portraiture, the psychological portrait centred on the face itself, in which the features which best reveal the dominant qualities of character are most fully brought out. Here again France had to call in foreign artists, to wit Jean Clouet, a native of Antwerp (settled in Tours 1521, died 1540) whose art was carried on by his son François Clouet who was born in France (died 1572) and Corneille de Lyon, a native of the Hague. The Clouets showed a preference for portraits drawn in chalks of three colours: black, white and red. Jean Clouet's art consists of a deep psychological penetration; his drawings, which were swiftly executed sketches with vigorous hatching running across them, show something of his creative impatience (pl. 383). The Italianate art of François Clouet is less acute in its vision, and is more suave; he was at his best in female portraiture (pl. 384). A number of artists carried this tradition of drawn portraits into the seventeenth century, among them Pierre Quesnel and his two sons (François who died in 1619 and Nicolas), the Dumonstier family (Pierre, Etienne and Daniel, the latter dying in 1646), and Pierre Lagneau.

The Wars of Religion resulted in a decadence which Henry IV tried to arrest. The second Fontainebleau school with Ambroise Dubois of Antwerp (1543–1614), Toussaint Dubreuil (about 1561–1603) and Martin Freminet (1567–1619) introduced Romanism into France, but in the form of Antwerp Mannerism.

The Italian style filtered into the Low Countries by way of early French Renaissance art (Palais de Justice, Malines; Palais des Princes Evêques, Liége, 1526–1533; Greffe du Franc, Bruges, 1535). More direct importation took place after 1550, particularly under the influence of Cornelis Floris (Town Hall, Antwerp, pl. 385; rood screen of Tournai Cathedral, 1572; Hôtel Plantin, Antwerp, 1576), while the Antwerp publisher Pieter Coek van Aelst published treatises on architecture by Serlio, Vignola, Palladio and Vitruvius. In the second half of the century architecture tended towards an ornamental style and the picturesque. Hans Vredeman de Vries (1527–1604) engraved and published several works on ornamentation and a treatise of architecture in French after Vitruvius, works which became sources of European Baroque art.

Flemish sculpture passed even more directly from the Flamboyant to the Baroque style than did architecture, and missed out the classical transitional stage at which France after Italy remained arrested. The fusing of the two styles had already occurred in the architectural and sculptural ensemble built at Brou in France by Margaret of Austria in 1522 to 1532. In the second half of the century Cornelis Floris at Antwerp and Jacques du Broeucq in Wallonia learnt much from the Mannerists as well as from Michelangelo.

Painting remained the major art in the Low Countries, as in the earlier period. Italian influence was soon apparent in the admiration for Leonardo which affected Jacob Cornelisz (about 1470–1533) at Amsterdam, Joos van Cleve at Antwerp (about 1485–1540/41) and Quentin Massys of the same town (about 1466–1530) whose *Relations of the Holy Family* of 1509 was already marked by the gracefulness of Leonardo (pl. 386). Jan Gossaert, called Mabuse (about 1470–1533), of

385 *Cornelis Floris. Antwerp Town Hall. 1561*

386 *Quentin Massys.*
Relations of the Holy
Family. 1509. Brussels

Maubeuge had a sculptural vision of the world deriving from Mantegna though corrected by Michelangelo. The imaginary world of Hieronymus Bosch (about 1460–1516), haunted by all the medieval terrors of hell, was untouched by Italian influence but his very modern sense and treatment of colour forestalled Venetian painting (pl. 387). Lucas van Leyden (1494–1533) was influenced by Germany and shows early signs of Mannerist anxiety. In the second half of the century Antwerp in Flanders and Utrecht and Haarlem in Holland tended to become the chief centres of artistic activity. Neo-Roman influence brought with it the Mannerism which from now on was to throw Northern painting off its balance. The Flemish school quickly degenerated with Frans Floris (1516–1570), with his unconvincing imitations of Michelangelo, and Bernard van Orley (about 1492–1542) who hid his lack of inspiration under a hotch-potch of Raphael, Giulio Romano, Michelangelo, Mabuse and Dürer. Dutch Mannerism was more original in its agitation. Jan van Scorel (1495 –1562) and the unbridled Maerten van Heemskeerk (1498–1574, pl. 389) were the Northern painters who followed Rome most closely. Anthonis Mor or Antonio Moro (1517–1576/77) of Utrecht, made energetic and concentrated portraits which recall those of Bronzino (pl. 388).

However, in the second half of the century one great artist stood immune from the Mannerist crisis and rediscovered the true tradition of Northern painting, that is to say the lyrical portrayal of nature. The longing for universality which had already moved Joachim Patinir (about 1480–1524) led Pieter Bruegel (Breughel etc.) the Elder (about 1525–1569) towards an admirable cosmic synthesis in those panoramic

298

387 Hieronymus Bosch. Temptation of St Anthony. Madrid

landscapes in which we feel the throbbing of the great manifold creation (pl. 390); but he associated human existence with that organic life. To the painter of social manners that Bruegel fundamentally was, human exist- ence seemed to be governed by the primary instincts, which are closely

*388 Antonio Moro. Cardinal
Granvelle's Dwarf. Paris*

*389 Maerten van Heemskeerk. Chris
crowned with Thorns. 1532. Ghent*

related to the forces of nature. Although he travelled south of the Alp
in 1552 to 1553, Bruegel took no more than his intellectual disciplin
from Italy, and his style, stemming from that of Bosch, is one of th
most original native expressions of the Nordic genius.

390 Pieter Bruegel. Return of the Herd. About 1560. Vienna

The elements of the Renaissance style did not reach German architecture before the second half of the sixteenth century. Southern Germany (Augsburg and Nuremberg) received its Italian influences at first hand, whereas the whole north and the middle Rhine depended on the Renaissance style as developed in Flanders. This Flemish influence spread right along the Baltic which was still following its tradition of building in brick and stone, and Danzig itself was built by Flemish architects. The group of buildings composing Heidelberg Castle (1556–1609) owed much to the rich fund of decorative features created in Antwerp and popularized by engravers. The items taken from the new style were treated as additions only, applied in the manner of Flamboyant Gothic on a fenestrated structure which was entirely medieval in spirit. This style, more Baroque than Renaissance, was to survive right through the seventeenth century. By the end of the sixteenth a new feeling for the disposition of spaces and solids began to be apparent in architecture (St Michael, Munich, 1583–1597; Town Hall, Augsburg, 1615, pl. 391).

There are two names which sum up the two stages of the Renaissance in German sculpture. Tilman Riemenschneider (1468–1531) of Würzburg was the last of a long line of sculptors of Gothic altarpieces, whose expressionist style became calmer towards 1520. Peter Vischer of Nuremberg (about 1460–1529) who revived the technique of casting in bronze, was much earlier in welcoming the Italian plastic code which he probably knew through the works of the Venetian sculptor Sansovino (*St Sebald's Shrine*, Nuremberg, 1507; figures on the Tomb of Maximilian, Innsbruck, pl. 392). Vischer's style was carried on by his descendants at Nuremberg.

But is was mainly in the arts of drawing, painting and engraving that the German temperament was most spontaneously expressed. The history of German painting, which had its golden age in the sixteenth century, was cut across by a clash between the Italian style and the native bent for expressionism which however had but slight difficulty in overcoming the Southern invasion. The aesthetic of Bellini's school was adopted at Augsburg by Hans Holbein the Elder (about 1460–1520) and Hans Burgkmair (1472–1553). But at the same moment the Danube school witnessed

391 Elias Holl. Augsburg Town Hall.
1615–1620

392 Peter Vischer the Elder. King
Theodoric from the Tomb of
Maximilian. 1513. Innsbruck

393 Albrecht Altdorfer. The Battle of
Alexander (detail). 1529. Munich

a flowering of German expressionism and the involved forms of the
belated Gothic infused with Mannerism in Lucas Cranach (1472–1553),
Luther's friend, who introduced mythological nudes into German art
(pl. 395), and more especially Albrecht Altdorfer (about 1480–1538)
who in his lively landscapes (*The Battle of Alexander,* 1529, pl. 393) gave
his answer of grandiose, cosmic expression to the appeal for universality
which a little later was to haunt Bruegel. Matthias Grünewald (about
1470/80–about 1528), who worked in the middle Rhine and Alsace, was
the most remote of all these artists from the Renaissance outlook. In one
of the most tormented styles known to painting, he interpreted the
anguished ecstasies and visionary sufferings of the Rhenish mystics of the
Middle Ages (Isenheim Altarpiece, Colmar, 1510–1519, pl. 398; *Crucifixion,* Karlsruhe, colour pl. VII); he was the greatest German colourist.
In Alsace, Hans Baldung Grien (1484/85–1545) imitated his style but
made it more complacent. In Switzerland, the struggle between Gothic
and Renaissance resulted in a Mannerist crisis which is expressed in the
extravagance and fantasy of Hans Leu (about 1490–1531), Nicolas Manuel Deutsch (1488–1530) and Urs Graf about 1485–1527/28, pl. 394),
who painted soldiers.

302

394 *Urs Graf. Foot-Soldier.*
Drawing. 1523. Basle

395 *Lucas Cranach. Venus.*
Frankfurt

However, two great painters in Germany were to throw themselves fully into the Renaissance aesthetic: Albrecht Dürer and Hans Holbein the Younger. Albrecht Dürer (1471–1528) was the son of a goldsmith in the city of Nuremberg, one of the shrines of Germanic civilization,

396 *Dürer. St John and St Peter. 1526. Munich*
397 *Dürer. Melancolia. Engraving. 1514*

which was to remain the centre of his activities although in his eagerness to know more about European art he visited a number of foreign countries. In the course of one of these educational trips across Germany from 1490 to 1494 he came across the Germano-Flemish tradition of Schongauer at Colmar and studied the technique of copper engraving. A voyage to Italy from 1494 to 1495 revealed the art of Mantegna and Bellini to him, and he returned there from 1505 to 1507. From 1520 to 1521 he travelled in the Low Countries where he studied Flemish painting and met Erasmus. Like Leonardo he was insatiably curious about every aspect of the world and wrote several aesthetic and technical treatises, in particular on the proportions of the human body (pl. 357). The Paumgartner Altarpiece (about 1500) was still Gothic in spirit, but the influence of Bellini goes deep in his *Festival of the Rose-Garlands* (Prague, 1506),*Adoration of the Trinity* (Vienna, 1511) and above all the *Four Apostles* (Munich, 1526, pl. 396) which is his masterpiece. Wood or copper engraving and drawing were the media in which Dürer wrestled most notably with the German temperament (*Apocalypse*, 1498; *Great Passion*, 1498 and 1510; *Life of the Virgin*, 1504–1511). In his hundreds

398 Grünewald. Angel Concert and Madonna from the Isenheim Altarpiece. About 1512–1516. Colmar

ÆTATIS · SVE · 88 ·

VIII Hans Holbein the Younger. Dr John Chambers. Vienna

of engraved plates and drawings he poured all his genius into an analitical enthusiasm for the forms of nature which was unrivalled outside Leonardo. Freed from the restrictions of harmony that the set himself in his paintings, he returned spontaneously to the tortured, graphic technique of the late Gothic which he had inherited from Schongauer. Out of the conflict between Germanic pantheism and Renaissance idealism, this great mind seems to have shaped a pessimistic philosophy which found an outlet in several of his engravings: *Nemesis* (1503), *The Knight, Death and the Devil* (1513) and *Melancholia* (1514, pl. 397), a symbol of the vanity of the science and works of mankind.

399 *Holbein. Dorothea Meyer. Drawing. 1526. Basle*

A son of Holbein the Elder, Hans Holbein the Younger (1497–1543) left Augsburg for Basle in 1515. He travelled into Lombardy and crossed France; then, driven out of Basle by the Reformation troubles, he sought refuge in England which he reached by way of Flanders. Once in England, he became court portraitist to Henry VIII. A friend of Erasmus, Holbein soon devoted himself entirely to portraiture, and is the most fully European of Renaissance painters. He made a synthesis of all the influences that impinged on him in the course of his wanderings – the Italian sense of harmony and unity, the Flemish painter's objectivity, the German's sharp sense of analysis (colour pl. VIII). Perhaps he has given us the most moving images of the humanists and princes of Northern Europe. As with the Clouets, this psychologist liked to draw portraits (pl. 399); his engraved works are less spontaneous.

Spain

The Renaissance was introduced into Spain at the end of the period of the Catholic kings, by rather piecemeal importations into a land given over to the excesses of the Isabelline style. The powerful Mendoza family seems to have played an important part in this new fashion, for it is to be noted that its name is associated with the first monuments in which the new style made its appearance (College of S. Cruz, at Valla-

dolid, by Lorenzo Vázquez, 1489; Palace of the dukes of Medinaceli, Cogolludo, before 1501; Hospital of S. Cruz, Toledo; Infantado Palace, Guadalajara). Enrique de Egas (died 1532) who also worked in the Gothic style, built the Renaissance-style Royal Hospital at Compostela (1501) and the Hospital of S. Cruz at Toledo (before 1514). In these buildings the Milanese ornamental features were applied on the monument regardless of any architectonic or decorative rhythm, entirely as facings, in keeping with the traditional outlook of the peninsula which had been imbibed through Moorish art; this art has earned itself the name 'Plateresque' on account of its resemblance to silverwork *(platería)*. In creating new decorative patterns based on the arabesque and on chimaeras brought from Italy, the Plateresque artists showed an inexhaustible fund of formal inventiveness which can be compared with that of Romanesque art; the Spanish gift for sculpture was now unleashed, but it was completely undisciplined and it hampered architecture. Castille was the purest centre of Plateresque which followed naturally on Flamboyant. Salamanca, the seat of the great Spanish university, was decked all over with monuments in this style; the anonymous façade of the university (1516–1529), in the form of an altarpiece, is in the same spirit as, though a different style from, that of the College of S. Gregorio at Valladolid (pl. 343).

Andalusia, which had no Gothic tradition and whose prim landscape was suggestive of decorum, was the centre of the purest reaction against the anarchy of the Plateresque; this was due to Diego de Siloé, the son of the Gothic sculptor Gil de Siloé, who built Granada Cathedral (planned 1528) in the Corinthian style but with an uneasiness of spirit which shows an incomplete assimilation; the cathedral of Granada was to be the origin of other Andalusian cathedrals at Málaga, Baeza and Jaén. Jaén Cathedral (planned 1533) by Vandaelvira, with its quadrangular plan without an ambulatory and its pleasing proportions, shows a marked progress towards understanding classical architecture. In

Andalusia the Plateresque decoration instinctively tends towards statuary (pl. 401).

The Habsburg dynasty gave its support to this influx of classicism against the trends of the native tradition. In 1526 Charles V invited Pedro Machuca to draw up plans for the Alhambra at Granada which was to be an immense palace in pure Roman style but which remained unfinished after a century's labour. Even more radical was Philip II's initiative; he allied himself with the Counter-Reformation, reacting against the medieval imagination and preaching austere rationalism to Christendom. To counter the ornamental

401 Façade of S. Salvador, Ubeda (detail). Finished 1556

mildness of Plateresque, Philip, having set up his court at Madrid, between 1561 and 1584 built a combined palace and monastery on the Escorial: this was designed in a classical, unadorned style *(estilo desornamentado)* which has been called the 'Herreran' style after the name of the architect. In a rectangle 715 by 520 feet, fourteen courtyards were laid out symmetrically round a cupola; the pointed roofs, an unusual feature for the Spanish climate, recalled the Flemish style in the same way as the Alcazar at Toledo. This monument – at once a monastery, palace, seminary, hospital, university, library, museum and tomb – is a sort of lay Imperial Vatican and one of the most ambitious expressions of monarchism, typical of the Hapsburg belief in the divine right of kings (pl. 400, 422).

Herrera also planned an imposing structure which unfortunately remained unfinished, Valladolid Cathedral, in the same unadorned style as the Escorial. The Jesuit Bartolomé Bustamente in 1565 set up the hospital of S. Juan de Afuera, Toledo, in the style of Bramante. The Herreran style prevailed in Spain for the first half of the seventeenth century, being increasingly opposed by the Baroque invasion.

Spanish sculpture in the sixteenth century produced some great works which derive from the belated influence of Donatello and the contemporary influence of Michelangelo, both of which were brought into Spain by such Italian artists as Domenico Fancelli, Jacobo Fiorentino, called Indaco, or Pietro Torrigiano (died 1528) a fellow pupil of Michelangelo who came to Seville in 1528 after working in England. Spaniards educated in Italy also brought back the new style, for instance Alonso Berruguete of Valladolid (1486/90–1561), son of the painter of that name,

402 *Alonso Berruguete. Abraham from the St Benedict Altarpiece (detail). 1526–1532. Valladolid.*

403 *El Greco. Burial of Count Orgaz. In S. Tomé, Toledo (detail). 1586*

who was a pupil of Michelangelo (wooden altarpiece for S. Benito Valladolid Museum, 1526–1532; alabaster sculptures on the choir-stall of Toledo Cathedral, 1539). The Castilian tradition of pathos, mingled with Michelangelo's torment, made Berruguete one of the earliest representatives of European Mannerism. His style, anticipating El Greco's by fifty years, may be compared with the latter's for its impassioned restlessness, the writhing attitudes and lengthened proportions of his figures, the feverish agitation of bodies, whose souls seem to be bursting from them as though thrust out of the flesh by some ungovernable tension (pl. 402). The French artist Juan de Juni (died 1577) seems to have been trained in the school of the Milanese sculptors Guido Mazzoni and Niccolò dell'Arca; he added a pathetic realism and a violent expressionism to Berruguete's frenzy, both of which are alien to the native tradition of his homeland (pl. 709). Reacting against this romanticism, Philip II in 1579 summoned from Milan Pompeo Leoni, a bronze sculptor who had a haughty and impressive style inspired by Donatello, in which he cast for the Escorial the fifteen statues of the *capilla mayor* (1592–1590) the five figures for the Tomb of Charles V (1597) and yet another five for the Tomb of Philip II (1598).

Spanish painting in the sixteenth century was still almost entirely in the hands of foreigners. Ferdinand Sturm of Zeland (at Seville 1539) and Peeter de Campeneer of Brussels (at Seville 1537) brought Flemish Mannerism with them; Luis de Morales (died 1586) shows the influence of Quentin Massys in his religious images; the Dutchman Anthonis Mor whose name was given the Spanish form 'Antonio Moro', became the official court portraitist and founded a tradition which was taken up by the Portuguese Sanchez Coello (1515?–1590) and the Spaniard Pantoja de la Cruz (1551–1610). Scorning the Spanish painters, Philip II brought from Italy the Genoese Luca Cambiaso in 1583, the Florentine

404 *El Greco. Resurrection. About 1595. Madrid*

Federico Zuccaro, 1586 and the Bolognese Pellegrino Tibaldi (1588) to work on the Escorial decorations.

However, a great painter was to become the very incarnation of the deep Spanish soul: Domenikos Theotokopoulos, called El Greco (1547 –1614), was born on the isle of Crete; he was trained at Venice under Tintoretto and the Bassani, and in 1577 we find him established in Toledo which was then the shrine of the mystery and chivalry of old Spain. It was there that he painted his masterpiece, the *Burial of Count Orgaz* (pl. 403). Greco's aesthetic, with its exaggerated lengthening of figures, convulsive attitudes, dark and sulphurous tones, is a striking aspect of the Mannerist frenzy which was spreading all over Europe at the end of the sixteenth century; but this anti-naturalistic formalism became, in his work, a sublime means of expressing the crises of ecstasy and torments of asceticism which at the same date St John of the Cross and St Theresa of Avila were also experiencing in Castille (pl. 404). El Greco was the founder of native Spanish painting for which nothing counts but the inner life (colour pl. IX). And yet his manner was to have but slight influence on the plastic development of the school. His studio-followers were to continue his pious imagery for a while. Luis Tristan (1586–1640) was the only pupil of his who managed to keep something of his master's outlook in the new realistic style adopted in the seventeenth century under the influence of Caravaggio.

In Portugal, the Spanish architect Juan de Castilho dried up the creative vein of the Manueline style by giving it an Italianate setting (Convent of S. Jeronymos, Belem, 1517). This Milanese vocabulary was perhaps introduced by French sculptors originating in Rouen: Nicolas Chantereine, whose mind had also a Burgundian cast, and more especially Jean de Rouen. The cloister of the Convent-Palace of the Knights of Christ was begun in 1558 at Tomar by Diogo de Torralva, in a style derived from Serlio. Earlier than Spain and perhaps more spontaneously, Portugal, which had been hostile to Gothic, readily imbibed the classical experiment and was less close to Lombard art than to that of the Florentine High Renaissance and the severity of Bramante (centrally-planned buildings of Don Jesus de Valverde at Mitra, near Evora; Nossa Senhora da Conceição at Tomar; palace church of Salvatorre de Magos). Towards 1440 to 1450 and thus before Herrera, Diogo de Torralva, of Spanish origin, planned the auster Capela Mor des Jeronymos at Bélem. Alfonso Alvares in the cathedrals of Leiria (1550) and Portalegre (1556) and perhaps the Jesuit church at Evora (1567) carried on that classical spirit which was further strengthened by the arrival in Lisbon of the Italian Filippo Terzi (S. Vicente de Fora, planned 1582).

England was the last country into which the Renaissance style penetrated, and there it met with the greatest opposition. A timid Italian
influence at first resulted in no more than a slight modification of the
Perpendicular Gothic style into the new Tudor style, typified by the
use of flattened, four-centred arches. Following on the Reformation,
there was great activity all over England in the sixteenth century, in the
erection of public buildings, university colleges, and country houses, as
well as halls with superb carved woodwork. The interior decoration was
sometimes more Italianate than the façades (Hampton Court). In the
Elizabethan period the mingled influences of Italy, Germany, Flanders
and France brought in mainly by printed books, gave rise to a new style
or rather a new composite approach to decoration. The decorated part
of the building was frequently a large porchway (pl. 405) with superimposed orders. This style survived into the seventeenth century. Sculpture
showed the same eclecticism, borrowing features from neighbouring
countries. Henry VIII employed such Italians as Guido Mazzoni and
Pietro Torrigiano. Torrigiano made the Tombs of Henry VII and Elizabeth of York in Westminster Abbey (1512–1518). Painting, almost
entirely confined to por-
traiture, owed much to
foreign masters who were
attracted to England by the
glamour of the court, such
as the German Holbein and
the Fleming Anthonis Mor
(Antonio Moro). The Elizabethan period saw the be-
ginning of a native style in
portraiture, represented by
anonymous masters and
miniaturists like Nicholas
Hilliard (traceable from
1560 to his death in 1619,
pl. 407) or Isaac Oliver who
was of French origin (about
1565/67–1617). The Fleming
Hans Eworth (died 1574),
who came to England to-
wards 1545, subjected Holbein's realism to the contemporary International
Mannerism (pl. 406).

405 Porchway of Kirby Hall, Northants.
1572

406 Hans Eworth. Sir John Luttrell. 1550.
     Private Collection

407 Nicholas Hilliard. Young Man among
     Rose-Bushes. About 1590. London

The Slavonic Countries

After the end of the fifteenth century the art of the Renaissance penetrated also into Russia. This was due to the enterprise of Ivan III,
autocrat of Moscow, who had married an Italian educated Greek princess
Zoë Palaeologus. He employed Italian architects to reconstruct the

408 Cathedral
     of
     St Michael
     the
     Archangel
     in the
     Kremlin,
     Moscow.
     1505–1509

Kremlin, upon the highest point in Moscow, as a city for himself and his court. The Bolognese Aristoteles Fioravanti, architect of the cathedral of the Dormition (1474–1479), and the Milanese Alevisio Novi, who built the cathedral of St Michael the Archangel (1505–1509, pl. 408), while working in accordance with the traditional orthodox plan, both used Italian decorative elements.

These are even more pronounced in the Faceted Palace (Granovitaya Palata) built between 1487 and 1491 by Marco Ruffo and Pietro Antonio Solario. The same two architects also built a brick wall round the Kremlin modelled on the Castello Sforzesco in Milan. This lead from the court was, however, not to be followed for many years. In the sixteenth century a completely independent type of church architecture, which owed much to native building in wood, grew up in the region of Moscow. It was characterized by tall pyramidal or 'tent' roofs, the most significant church of this type being that of St Basil the Blessed, dedicated to the Protection and Intercession of the Virgin (pl. 409). Of the secular buildings, mostly in wood, nothing now remains.

In Poland it was a marriage, too, that stimulated interest in the Italian arts. King Sigismund I, husband of Bona Sforza, built a magnificent Renaissance castle (pl. 410) on the Wawel, the highest point in the capital of Cracow, employing two Italian architects, Francesco della Lora and Bartolomeo Berecci. His tomb is also the work of Italian

409 Cathedral of St Basil, Moscow. 1555–1560

410 Courtyard of the Royal Castle (Zamek Królewski), Cracow. Begun 1507

*411 Kazmierz Dolny. Town House.
About 1635*

artists. Giovanni Maria Padovano gave the Draper's Hall in Cracow, at the time of its rebuilding, a richly moulded attic, a feature that was to remain characteristic of Polish architecture until the seventeenth century. During the first half of that century there developed, in some districts of Poland, a bold and exuberant architecture; the buildings it produced are remarkable as examples of the Mannerism that was gaining ground in Central and Northern Europe as a result of the ornamental influence of the Low Countries in the sixteenth century (pl. 411).

3. THE MINOR ARTS

The minor arts in the Renaissance period increasingly imitated the forms of the major arts of architecture, sculpture and painting. The chief item of furniture invented in Italy in the late fifteenth century was the so-called 'cabinet', usually a cupboard in two stages, which was for holding manuscripts and valuables. This article of furniture was made all over Europe in the second half of the sixteenth century. It was generally decorated with sculptural features, caryatids, terminals, garnished colums, carved studs and panels, – taken from printed works showing the devices used by Italian and Flemish ornamental sculptors. The fronts of these cupboards were often treated in the same way as the façades of buildings, with blind windows, pediments, and columns (pl. 412 a). The Italians specialized in cabinets with coloured inlay in wood, the inside often containing perspectives recalling theatrical settings. In Northern Europe, after the Milanese-style decoration with its flat-relief and candelabra, medallions and putti, in the second half of the century they introduced decorations in the round. Northern Europe created other items of furniture such as the twin-sectioned cupboard and two-staged 'buffet' which replaced the medieval sideboard. Walnut, which is of a closer grain than oak, was now preferred to oak which had been exclusively used in the Middle Ages (pl. 412 b); in France the most refined work was produced in the Ile-de-France region, but that of Dijon and Lyons had more life in it.

Ornamental ceramics flourished in such centres as Faenza, Caffagiolo,

*412 a French Cabinet. 2nd half
of 16th c. Paris*

*412 b Hessian Cupboard.
1604. Cassel*

Gubbio (pl. 415) and above all Urbino, which came to the fore in 1500;
all Europe hastened to imitate Italian faïence and in France Bernard
Palissy (died 1590) went farther by making ceramics with naturalistic
reliefs. Florence produced luxurious jewellery, mounted pieces set with
enamels and precious stones on which the Mannerist taste imposed its
finicking network of shapes; Benvenuto Cellini was the most famous
artist in this genre (pl. 413). The Venetian workshops showed great virtuosity in glass-work, embellishing it with filigree, reliefs, gold bases,
crackles, and the like.

Stained-glass and enamelling, which had been the glory of medieval
France, now succumbed to painting. The technique of monumental
leaded-glass which the Le Prince family of Beauvais handled so brilliantly
under Francis I was carried on with less originality till the end of the

*413 Cellini. Amphitrite
and Neptune.
Vienna
Gold Salt-Cellar*

414 Jean II Pénicaud. Calvary Battle. Enamel. Paris

century, but under Henry II the stained-glass window tended to become a painting on glass (Ste-Chapelle, Vincennes), merely another form of picture. Jean Cousin and Robert Pinaigrier designed cartoons of this type. Germany and Switzerland excelled in making miniature medallion-pictures which were fitted into the windows of private houses and which imitated enamels. Enamelwork, indeed, also abandoned the *champlevé* technique (chasing) and was handled as no more than straightforward picture-painting on copper with colours that could be fired; the main centres of production were still at Limoges (workshops of Leonard Limousin and the Pénicaud family, pl. 414). As for their compositions, the craftsmen in glass, enamel and wood tended to make no more than unadorned copies of the numerous German engravings which were circulating in Europe, and particularly those of Dürer.

The tapestry workshops in Brussels were now outstripping those of France. Their tapestries lost their essential character to become no more than a direct reflection of paintings and the two most famous sets woven at Brussels were the series of *Acts of the Apostels* (the *Vaticans Tapestries*), carried out between 1515 and 1519 after cartoons commissioned from Raphael by Leo X, and scenes of *Maximilian out Hunting*, after cartoons by Bernard van Orley. Between 1530 and 1535 Francis I ordered Primaticcio to set up a factory at Fontainebleau, where more respect was shown for the decorative element in tapestry.

415 Maestro Giorgio. Gubbio Faïence. 1528. Private Collection

IX. THE BAROQUE PERIOD

Rightly or wrongly, two words are always associated with the seventeenth and eighteenth centuries: 'baroque' and 'rococo'. Whether it comes from the Spanish *barrueco* (Portuguese *barroco)* a term from gemmology meaning an irregular pearl, or from *baroco,* a scholastic syllogism, or what is less likely from an Indian word, the term 'baroque' was synonymous with extravagance and bad taste for the neo-Classical critics who used it early in the nineteenth century. The epithet 'rococo' has the advantage of being older, but its reputation is no better; it was used by the engraver Cochin in 1755 to mock the fanciful forms of the Louis XV style. The two terms have now lost their former pejorative meaning. Baroque is even praised by contemporary aestheticians, who have extended it to cover an artistic attitude which they oppose to classicism, and of which seventeenth century art is only one aspect. As for the rococo, we can now find some pleasure in it, since we are no longer under the dogmatic tyranny of neo-Classicism.

No doubt in their strict sense these expressions are worth no more than most historical labels. 'Renaissance' is no more apt, while 'Gothic' is absurd. If we are to grasp the general implication of a form of art which gave Europe its specific character, we might say that, coming after the instinct for free inquiry that marked the sixteenth century, it was essentially a *formalism.* It matters little whether this formalism was classical or baroque. The seventeenth century had, so to speak, two liturgies, one of them classical in tendency and the other baroque. But whether they insisted on a curved line or a straight one, the dogmas are similar in that they both tended to give a representation of existence as seen by the intellect; for seventeenth-century man saw everything, and his own life first and foremost, as a kind of show. An awareness of human dignity gave rise to that philosophy of *'éminence'* which makes the whole universe a stage, sumptuously set for the king, the lord of creation. Louis XIV thought himself the royal incarnation of this hero. Antwerp in the seventeenth century shows us another, more modest model of this, but one which is no less significant. Something of an aristocrat, an artist of genius, a good Christian, but with an epicurean delight in the fleshly and spiritual joys of existence, Rubens is one of the highest expressions of the humanism which inherited from the Renaissance all the indulgence towards human nature so eagerly preached by the Jesuits.

The opera, which was the essential creation of these two centuries stretching from 1600 to 1800, is difficult for us to judge today. But those fairy-like displays, operas fixed for ever in stone and paint, stucco, marble and gold, are still there before our eyes. Two stage-settings were

Kingly Majesty

416 Hendrijk Pot. Charles I (detail). 1632. Paris
417 Sir Anthony van Dyck. Charles I (detail). 1635. Paris
418 Hyacinthe Rigaud. Louis XIV (detail). 1701. Paris

provided for God and the king – the two rulers most honoured by the *Grand Siècle;* these were the church and the palace – one might say God's palace and the king's temple.

In order to understand the poetry of the baroque one must have seen Mass being celebrated at St Peter's or any Jesuit church in Europe. Thanks to the grace of the liturgy, in the perfumed mist of incense and organ-music one sees no longer a mere world of marble and paint, a human world, but a great composition in which the movements of the painted figures and the ritual of the priests combine in a grand symphony. The solemn cadence of the incense-bearers vibrates from column to column, and the preacher's eloquence replies from the pulpit to the urgent apologetics of the apostles and martyrs whose effigies adorn the columns. In the depths of the chancel some apparition seems to be stirring in the lights of the high-altar, while clouds of incense, rising into the vaults, mingle with pale clouds of marble in which groups of angels spread their wings. And instead of the drab uniform we wear today, we must imagine the rich medley of colours from the theatrical costumes men wore in those times. The Catholic church, which from time immemorial has known how to stimulate fervour in the faithful by appealing to their senses, offered the Christian of the Counter-Reformation an accessible image of the beyond – an operatic spectacle.

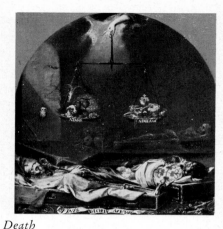

Death

419 Georges de La Tour.
The Magdalene. Paris

420 Valdés Leal. Finis Gloriae Mundi.
About 1671. Seville

Differences of ritual gave rise to different emphases in the churches of the Baroque period and style. In spite of its underlying exuberance, the Italian Baroque always observed the norms of architecture, for the architecture lent itself to this *riforzando,* this *crescendo,* those thousand modulations and mimicries that are needed in order to contrive a spectacular effect. The Spanish Churrigueresque (named after the Churriguerra family) smothered architecture in adornment, so that Spain returned to the woeful excess of ornament she had long imbibed from Moorish influences; in no other country was the thirst for images to be taken so far; no stage-set was ever more thoroughly worked out than a *capilla mayor.* The Austrian Rococo, like the Swabian and Bavarian, was like frozen music with its thousands of chords and deep reverberations; those palace halls and monastery-churches gave birth to the harmonies of Mozart. Flemish Baroque flowed into painting; Rubens gave Southern formalism the rich lifeblood of colour that he inherited from van Eyck.

Just as there were several religious liturgies, so there were different modes of courtly ritual. The Escorial and Versailles rivalled each other in pride and dignity. In the solitude of Guadarrama, Philip II made himself an immense structure in naked stone so that no worldly appearance could intrude on the sublime intimacy between God and his earthly representative, who was king by divine right. More profane, a hundred years later, Louis XIV called on Olympus and not heaven to celebrate his glory. And the grand opera of Versailles laid on a permanent show of a kind of allegorical sun-worship. Here all external appearances were invited to take part in the display – water, sky, trees, marble and gold,

real and imitation nature. Philip II found only one imitator, Joâo V, who in the eighteenth century built the monastery-palace of Mafra in Portugal; all eighteenth-century Europe copied Versailles when French taste was reacting against it. The French were tired of display, and if they left the court it was in favour of the city. Then private life came to the fore, and a domestic ritual came into being to replace that of the court. All eighteenth-century thought expressed itself in the confidential tones of drawing-room exchanges, the drawing-room and salon being its miniature theatre. When 'sentiment' became fashionable, then they made a melodrama out of it. Last of all came the love of nature which called forth a new kind of show, that of the 'natural'. Rocks and cornflowers, streams and windmills, cottages and marble temples filled the stage. Every day, Marie-Antoinette came and played her walking-on part, till such time as the theatre was temporarily closed, threatened by the invasion of real drama.

Yet again Italy gave Europe an aesthetic on which it lived for two hundred years. For Italy, the Baroque was not a point of departure, but on the contrary the supreme effort of a school weakened by a long period of fertility, which was now attempting to recuperate by gathering its forces into a doctrine, and reaping the harvest of its past in the most rational manner possible. By draining the essentials off the wealth of Italian art the Carracci toned down features which were too exclusively local, and by giving their cunning mixture the impersonality of a logical system, they enabled the gains of the sixteenth century to be passed on to other schools. As for Caravaggio, he came just at the right time to give new life to painting, by infusing some naturalism into it after it had been sapped by Renaissance idealism. This great figure paved the way for Zurbarán, Georges de La Tour, the Le Nain brothers, Velázquez, Rembrandt and even for Vermeer – in short all those who refused to yield to the passing fashions of the century and probed deeper into the mystery of human nature. In the face of so many actors and light-weights, these few individuals rediscovered the greatness of authentic man.

421 J.-B. Pigalle. Tomb of the Maréchal de Saxe in St Thomas', Strassburg. 1756–1777

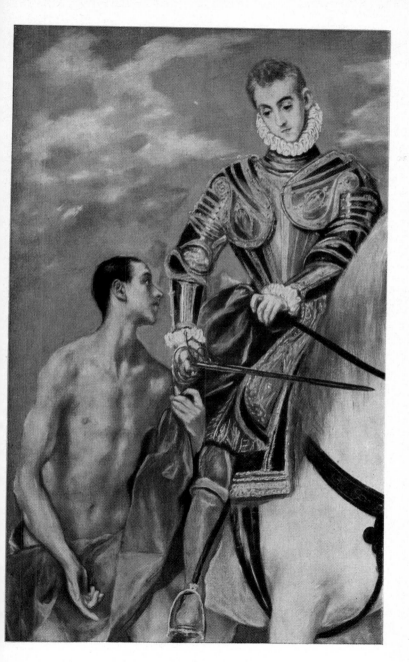

IX El Greco. *St Martin and the Beggar (detail). Philadelphia*

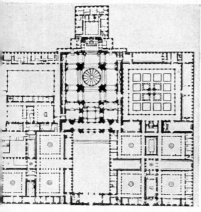

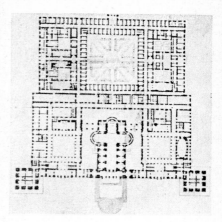

*22 Juan Bautista de Toledo (1561) and
Juan de Herrera. Plan of the Escorial*

*423 Ludovice. Plan of the
Monastery-Palace,
Mafra (Portugal). 1717*

Despite the Protestant dissidence, Baroque art was the most harmonious moment in the 'concert' of Europe. In a great upsurge of enthusiasm, all the peoples who had by now reached their full maturity brought their contribution to a common task. They exchanged their doctrines and talents; French and Italian specialists swarmed over Europe, Flemings and Dutchmen came to work in Paris, while the whole world met in Rome, where the two greatest French painters of the seventeenth century became Romans by adoption.

Europe was divided into two camps as regards the dominant aesthetic. Spain, the Germanic countries, and Flanders eagerly embraced an aesthetic which so thoroughly suited their native instinct. Behind this showy curtain Germany, deeply afflicted by the Thirty Years War, contrived to hide its real decline, to revive again in the eighteenth century. Spain, where only the Church had any rights to speak of, found a marvellous means of governing souls in this apologetic imagery. Rubens quickened the Baroque orchestration by giving it that vital energy which enables forms to generate each other in an unbroken rhythm. He created a new pictorial technique, and in the eighteenth century both the French and English schools were to be enriched by it.

It was natural for the Protestant countries to reject this glorifying art. Holland, which had no external worship to offer God or king, turned towards man and nature; in the seventeenth century it was the only country to see reality as something more than a spectacle or show. England created a great school of architecture, her restraint in expression, fundamental to her insular temper, leading her from 1630 onwards to adopt those principles which were to lead all Europe a hundred years

424 *L. Bruant
(1671) and
J. H. Mans-
art (1677).
Hôtel des
Invalides,
Paris
(general
view)*

later towards neo-Classicism. As for France, her attitude was most complex. It cannot be said that she completely refused the Baroque, since
Europe owes her the whole setting of royal ceremonial as well as the
civilized background of an 'art of living'. But the true vocation of
French art was to provide, in both painting and architecture, the most
perfect definition of that classicism whose rules had been laid down by
Raphael, Titian and Bramante and which had been stifled by the over-
growth of Baroque. France's decorators brought her share to European
Baroque art, while her architects and her greatest painters continued and
completed the work of the Renaissance. Watteau perhaps owed Rubens
less than has been suggested; he profited from Rubens' technique but
his poetic expression is related to Titian's and above all Giorgione's.

The unity of the European movement is demonstrated in the great
international drive which in about 1670 led all the schools towards a
second Classical revival, this time based on Etruscan and Greek sources.
Antiquaries from every country shared in the excavation of pre-Roman
art, the great archaeological centres being at Florence, Naples and Rome.
France sent the Comte de Caylus; Germany its famous Winckelmann
who in 1664 wrote the first *History of Ancient Art* – the *Geschichte der
Kunst des Altertums.* The Frenchman Clérisseau and the Englishman
Robert Adam worked side by side on the ruins of the Palace of Dio-
cletian at Spalato. If it is true that France, thanks to an internal re-

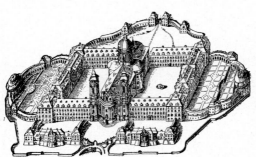

425 *Project for the Weingarten Monastery
(general view). 1723*

volution, reached the principles of the so-called 'Louis XVI' style at the same time as England, nobody can deny England the first place in the conception of a certain architectural purism – in her 'Palladianism', amounting to a neo-Classicism – that was not to affected French art until the last years of the *Ancien Régime*.

This style contains the germs of the 'Spartan' art of the Revolution and the Empire period, which was to put an end to the ostentation and preciousness of the *Ancien Régime*. Involved in his own tragedy, man no longer set himself up as a stage-show for his own amusement.

1. BAROQUE EUROPE

Italy

Architecture and Sculpture

Deriving from Michelangelo, Italian Baroque architecture sought to astonish by the powerful and magnificent effects obtained by emphasized volumes and heavy decoration; but however much it was overladen, architecture never allowed itself to become throttled by ornament as was the case in Spain, and the relationship of mass to mass was always energetically asserted. The original creation of this style was a new type of church. The prototype was the one which was carried out for the Jesuits according to Vignola's plans from 1568 to 1577, the Gesù (church of Jesus) in Rome. Inspired by the Languedoc Gothic church-style, which had found its way into Spain whence the Jesuits brought

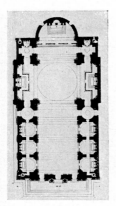

426/427 The Gesù, Rome. Plan by Vignola (1567), Façade by Vignola and Giacomo della Porta (1568–1577)

it to Rome, this structure shows the final triumph of the simple basilican plan, without an ambulatory and with a nave, fringed with small chapels instead of aisles, and with its crossing crowned by a cupola (pl. 426). The barrel-vault over the nave, pierced with lunettes (round windows) is supported by enormous piers without the help of buttresses; the series of bays is boldly marked by great Corinthian pillars and pilasters which rise from the floor into the vaults; designed by Giacomo della Porta (1539–1602), a pedimented façade whose upper part is linked to the lower by projecting scrolls closes the nave (pl. 427). This type of church was built at first in a sober style for from 1580 to about 1625 Counter-Reformation art, influenced by Protestantism, showed something of the Church's concern for austerity. Examples of this are now hard to find, since these churches were overlaid with rich decorations in the following period, but we might give Montepulciano Cathedral (1570) by Ammanati and S. Maria degli Angeli at Assisi (1569, pl. 428) by Alessi. In the same spirit Carlo Maderna (1556–1629) added a nave to Michelangelo's St Peter's and gave it a façade (1606–1626). But Urban VIII's pontificate (1623–1644) was the point of departure for a fashionable splendour, and for the second time Rome saw the revival of a 'triumphal' art, a symbol of the Church's victory. It was in 1629 that the pope gave Giovanni Lorenzo Bernini (1598–1680) the task of furnishing and decorating St Peters, an undertaking which was continued under Innocent X (1644–1655) and Alexander VII (1655–1667). This artist buried the purity of Michelangelo's and Maderna's work under a coating of marble facings, bronzes, stucco and gilt (1647–1633), filling the church with outsize statues and colossal furnishings: *Baldacchino* (canopy), 1624–1633, *Chair of St Peter,* 1656–1665. At the same time he built a great circular piazza surrounded by a double colonnade (1656–1673). The Roman churches already built were now covered with a similar garb; others were built in this style in Rome (pl. 429) and all over Italy (pl. 430) to a great variety of plans – central, elliptical, or in the form of a Latin cross; their vaults opened on celestial visions, apparitions in stucco or painting whose upward perspective was stressed by cunning foreshortening (Gesù and St Ignazio). The pompous palaces built by the Roman nobility were larded with similar adornments; in the Roman Campagna at Frascati, the nobles and prelates built villas in the midst of geometrically laid-out gardens in which fountains played. Apart from Bernini, to whom we also owe the church of S. Andrea del Quirinale (1678) the principal architects in Rome were: Girolamo Rainaldi (1570–1653); Pietro da Cortona (1596–1669), author of the pure cupola of S. Carlo al Corso and of S. Maria della Pace (1655), and above all Francesco Borromini (1599–1667), author of S. Carlo alle Quattro Fontane (1640, pl. 431) and of S. Agnese (1645) which heralds the Rococo in its use of waving curves. In Venice, Baldassarre Longhena (1604–1682) raised the fine cupola of the Salute (1631–1656, pl. 430) as well as the Palazzo Pesaro and Palazzo Rezzonico (1679 and

324

428 S. Maria
    degli Angeli,
    Assisi.
    Begun 1569

429 S. Ignazio,
    Rome. 1626

1680) which have all the traditional Venetian splendour. At Genoa,
Naples, Milan and in the south (Lecce), architecture became Baroque
very early with the increasingly daring use of curves, a tendency which
appeared in Rome with Borromini and was accentuated at Turin with
Guarini (1624–1638) in his Palazzo Carignano (1689). Eighteenth-cen-
tury Rome was rarely to fall into the excesses of Rococo in architecture
(Palazzo del Grillo), but remained faithful to the imposing effects of
the Baroque style (Luigi Vanvitelli, 1700–1773). Certain artists such as
Filippo Iuvara (1685–1735) showed an early tendency towards neo-
Classicism (Basilica della Superga, Turin, 1706–1720, Palazzo Madama,
1718). At the end of the century the archaeological trend advocated by
Winckelmann led to a pastiche of ancient Roman architecture (Museo
Pio-Clementino built at the Vatican by Simonetti). Meanwhile Rococo

430 Baldassare Longhena. S. Maria della Salute, Venice. 1631–1656

431 Borromini. S. Carlo alle Quattro Fontane, Rome. 1640

invaded internal decoration and furnishing in Genoa, Naples and above all Venice. Naples felt the influence of the Spanish Churrigueresque.

Italian sculpture in the seventeenth century was entirely overshadowed by Bernini who, under Urban VII and Alexander VII, found himself entrusted with the dictatorship over the arts that Michelangelo had ex-

432 Bernini. Ecstasy of St Theresa. In S. Maria della Vittorio, Rome. 1646

ercised in the century before. All Bernini's plastic outlook was governed by a quest for movement and expression. The violence of the passions and of human ecstasy was rendered by the physical disorder it provokes; the swooning attitudes of the saints (*St Theresa*, 1646, pl. 432; *Blessed Lodovica Albertoni*; *St Bibiana*) are a theatrical expression of the sensual but devout mysticism which was to take hold of the faithful in the seventeenth century and result in excesses which were condemned by the Church. Bernini also created a type of tomb (Tomb of Urban VIII, 1642, Tomb of Alexander VII, 1672) which is like a stage setting for death, symbolized by a skeleton. By dint of exaggerating the inflections of his modelling, by the use of coloured marbles, and through the fluidity of his figures' attitudes, the sculptor sought to vie with painting – a tendency which was further emphasized in the seventeenth century, when the Neapolitans (Conradini, Sammartino, Queirolo) were to outdo each other in a virtuosity which was in the worst of taste.

Painting

Weakened by three hundred years of creativity unparalleled in history, Italian painting by the end of the sixteenth century, after the Mannerist crisis, had reached a state of decline of which perhaps the Florentine school shows the most lamentable examples with Vasari, Salviati, Zuccaro, Allori. Reacting against this decadence, three painters of the Carracci family – two brothers, Annibale and Luigi, with their cousin Agostino – founded an academy in 1595. This amounted to a school of fine arts which aimed at a return to the traditional rules of art by teaching the methods of the great masters, taking from Raphael, Titian, Michelangelo and Correggio those qualities in which each of them excelled. The Carracci thus created a kind of plastic 'rhetoric' which they applied as freely to devotional painting as to mythological subjects. The ceiling of the Palazzo Farnese (1594), inspired by both Michelangelo and Raphael, was to have an enormous influence all over Europe (pl. 433). A host of pupils of that school filled the churches and palaces of Rome with enormous displays, both pious and pagan: Guido Reni (1575–1642); Francesco Albani (1578–1660); Carlo Dolci (1616–1686); Giovanni Lanfranco (1582–1647); Andrea Pozzo (1642–1709), who specialized in ceiling-decoration; and Dominichino (1582–1641). Guercino (1590–1666)

433 Anibale Carracci. Diana and Endymion. Fresco. Ceiling in the Palazzo Farnese, Rome. 1594

*434 Guercino. Burial of
St Petronilla. 1621. Rome*

*435 Caravaggio. Entombment.
1602–1604. Rome*

was the only painter of this school with any imagination and he understood that the truth was to be found elsewhere, in Caravaggio (pl. 434).

While the Carracci, by a clever but unoriginal reform were consolidating the failing Italian school and guaranteeing it an almost official rôle in Europe, a painter of genius was carrying out a revolution which contained the germ of almost everything of any stature in seventeenth-century painting. Understanding that the Italian school was worn out by three hundred years of intellectualism, Michelangelo Merisi da Caravaggio (about 1565–1610) forced Italian and the whole of European art to take a dose of naturalism. In a country where nothing was being painted but Venuses and Madonnas, he took the humblest types of Roman men and women as his models for saints and heroes *(Calling of St Matthew,* pl. 436, and other paintings in S. Luigi dei Francesi and S. Maria del Popolo; *Death of the Virgin,* Louvre; *Entombment of Christ,* Vatican, pl. 435). By the impressive simplicity of his composition, the violent contrast of lights and shadows which he obtained from oblique lighting, he brought back a powerful frankness of volumes to Italian painting, and led the whole school back to its plastic traditions which since Giotto had always implied a sculptural conception of form.

All that was really worth-while in Italian painting owed something, however little, to Caravaggio. In Rome a whole cosmopolitan school

328

436 Caravaggio. Calling of St Matthew. In S. Luigi dei Francesi, Rome

exploited his chiaroscuro effects and his popular lyricism. Beside Orazio Gentileschi (1563–1646) we find a French painter, Valentin de Boulogne (1591–1634), and Dutchmen from Utrecht, Dirk van Baburen (1590 –1623), Hendrick Ter Brugghen (1588–1629) and Gerard van Honthorst (1590–1656) whose nocturnal paintings earned him the nickname 'Gherardo delle Notti'; we also know from the German Joachim von Sandrart (1606–1688) that there was a German colony at the same time. These foreigners were to spread Caravaggio's style all over Europe.

The Italian provinces, which had been the least touched by academicism, were particularly warm in hailing the Caravaggesque. Caravaggio found a spiritual disciple in Naples, in Caracciolo (1570?–1637) while the Spaniard Jusepe de Ribera (1590–1653) took his reforms back with him to Spain. In Milan, Daniele Crespi (1592–1630) had his own romantic manner which he drew from various sources, while at Bergamo Evaristo Baschenis (1617–1677) composed still-lifes with musical instruments, which he painted in chiaroscuro.

437 *Bernardo Strozzi. The Three Fates.*
Milan

438 *Alessandro Magnasco.*
The Synagogue (detail).
Seitenstetten (Austria)

The most eclectic school of all was at Genoa, which profited from Rubens and van Dyck who both spent a time there. Bernardo Strozzi (1581–1644) heralds Goya, through his violent satirical style and daring technique (pl. 437).

In the eighteenth century the Italian school as a whole stood aside from the European movement, and the French school took the lead. With the exception of Venice, Italy was producing sound but not outstanding painters: Naples had Solimena and Luca Giordano; Milan, Giuseppe Maria Crespi (1665–1747). However, in Rome Giovanni Paolo Pannini (1691–1764) invented a speciality which enjoyed a spectacular success – the painting of ruins. In Genoa the genre-painting of Alessandro Magnasco (1681–1747, pl. 438) heralded Goya's romanticism. Meanwhile

439 *Guardi.*
Drawing.
Paris

440 Giambattista Tiepolo. Marriage of Barbarossa. Fresco in the Residenz,
Würzburg. 1751–1752

the Venetian school, the youngest of all, was still lively enough to
provide the swan-song of Italian painting, which it did in a great
apotheosis of light, colour and splendour. Its painters all portrayed the
beauties of Venice and the decadent and sensual charm of its civilization.
Venice had its portraitists, Vittore Ghislandi (1666–1743) and Alessandro Longhi (1733–1813), a notable genre-painter, Pietro Longhi (1702
–1785), and its landscape-painters, Canaletto (1697–1768) and Francesco
Guardi (1712–1793, pl. 439) who exalted the beauty of its light, its palaces
and canals. It had great decorators such as Piazzetta (1682–1754) and
above all Giambattista Tiepolo (1693–1770), who rivalled Veronese and
who was the most versatile of Italian ceiling-painters, skilled in the art
of setting angels and gods in the radiant glow of limitless spaces, whether
on the curves of a cupola or the flat surfaces of walls. His art had a
strong influence in Central Europe and Germany, where he was invited
to come and paint (Residenz, Würzburg. pl. 440).

Flanders adopted Baroque architecture with the same eagerness as she had welcomed Flamboyant Gothic in the fifteenth century. The transition from Flamboyant to Baroque was made smoothly and gradually thanks to the activities of the ornamental decorators of Antwerp, through whom it came. Without understanding its architectural import, the Flemings saw the Baroque only in terms of ornament, and they applied Baroque decoration to the Gothic framework of their buildings, just as previously they had applied Flamboyant patterns. Their houses thus remained, as in the Middle Ages, a façade pierced all over with windows, just as, despite the efforts of the Jesuits to introduce new forms, the type of church with a nave and two aisles lingered on, while sometimes even medieval elevations were favoured. The extraordinarily lavish decoration, which was often gilded to give it relief, even on the outside of the building, was hung on the wall like a picture, without being built into the structure; Baroque curves on the gables of houses, ousting those of the Flamboyant style, introduced many new ornamental patterns. Now the churches were filled with heavy, symbolical wooden furnishings (pulpits and confessionals etc.). Sculpture was mediocre (Duquesnoy, Lucas Faidherbe, Jean Delcour), which is not surprising since the Flemish genius all flows into painting. The Grand' Place in Brussels, built after 1696 (pl. 441) and the church of St Charles-Borromeus at Antwerp (1615–1621) and Rubens' house at Antwerp are masterpieces of Flemish Baroque architecture.

441 Houses on the Grand' Place, Brussels. 1694–1697

Flemish painting did not escape the crisis of depression which upset all Europe at the end of the sixteenth century. After the waves of Italian influence, which in its various forms – Lombard, Roman, Mannerist – had seemed like a series of nervous shocks, the Antwerp school seemed to have worked itself out. However, at the very close of the century several artists, Abraham Jansens (1575–1632), Adam van Noort (1562–1641) and Otto Veenius or van Veen (1556–1629) at last managed to make the Italian plastic code their own and made Ru-

442 Rubens. Descent from the Cross.
In Antwerp Cathedral. 1611–1614

443 Rubens. Rape of the Daughters of
Leucippus. About 1618. Munich

bens' development possible. After he left the studios of van Noort and van Veen, Peter Paul Rubens (1577–1640) completed his training from 1600 to 1608 in Italy, where he absorbed the lessons of the Venetians, of Michelangelo, the Bolognese school and Caravaggio. On his return he painted his first two masterpieces, the *Elevation of the Cross* (about 1610) and the *Descent from the Cross* (1611–1614, pl. 442) for Antwerp Cathedral. He soon made Antwerp one of the main centres of European art and commissions came from every side. His output, organized on workshop lines with the use of assistants, was the most fertile in the history of painting. Between 1621 and 1625 he carried out his greatest monumental work, the *Life of Maria de' Medici*, now in the Louvre. After being four years a widower, he married in 1630 Helena Fourment, a sixteen-year-old girl, after which his art had a gentler and more intimate note. He then retired to the country, and in smaller canvases in which landscape held an increasingly important place, he expressed his spiritual vision of universal life. Rubens' work is the greatest world of forms ever created by a painter. The energy of life pervades every shape and gives a dynamic quality to gesture and expression; any picture by Rubens is a series of interrelated movements, spiralling or passing obliquely through space (pl. 443, 697) and its impetus seems to pass beyond the limits of the frame. It is the archetype of baroque, or 'fleeting', open composition which gives a brief glimpse of the perpetual motion of the life of the universe. All his forms seem to be bathed in a mellow fluid, thanks to the wonderful means of

444 Frans Snyders. Still-Life. Brussels

expression he created in his transparent handling of paint, which allows the laying of glaze upon glaze, a technique taken over from van Eyck which was lost after Rubens.

The Flemish school in the seventeenth century gives a remarkable example of solidarity and singleness of purpose. In the sixteenth century Flemish painters had aimed at investigating the forms of nature, and artists had specialized in histories, landscapes, still-lifes, genre or anecdotal paintings. This division of labour gave them great skill in their special line, until in the seventeenth century they began to come to each other's help. Rubens' workshop was the most outstanding example of this artistic co-operation.

445 Jan Bruegel the Elder. The Earth or The Earthly Paradise (detail). Paris

The apparent complexity of the Flemish school may be reduced to two main streams which actually meet in Rubens. One of them derives from the heroic and statuesque vision of the Italians and tends to bring its monumental forms into the foreground and middle distance, thus reducing the architectural framework or the landscape to no more than a setting or decoration. This is properly speaking the 'modern' stream. Started by van Noort and van Veen, Rubens became its focal point. Jordaens and van Dyck derive from it, as well as the host of artists who came under Rubens' influence; the bevy of historical painters, Erasmus

446 Brouwer. Drinking Scene. Amsterdam

Quellin, Gaspard de Crayer, van Thulden, van Diepenbeeck, Cornelis de Vos; the animal-painters, Snyders (pl. 444), Fyt and Paul de Vos. In landscape, the trend is seen in a decorative view of nature, scenes being laid out in broad masses harmoniously balanced one against the other; this style, deriving from Paul Bril, is represented by Jaques d'Arthois, Lucas van Uden, Wildens and later Huysmans. Jacob Jordaens (1593 –1678) who was more deeply influenced by Caravaggio and Bolognese formalism, further emphasized the plebian element in Rubens but his heavy, brownish colouring owes nothing to the Antwerp master. This is not true of Anthony van Dyck (1599–1641), perhaps a pupil of Rubens and for some years one of his closest collaborators. He worked in Genoa and Rome, where he was profoundly influenced by Titian and he ended by specializing in portraiture. After emigrating to London in 1632 he became Charles I's favourite painter and, taking the English gentry as his models, he was able to satisfy his tastes for aristocratic postures, and refined, decadent expressions (pl. 417).

The second stream of Flemish painting is a direct continuation of the 'microcosmic' vision of the sixteenth century, in which the human or animal figure is reduced in scale against a vast universal setting. The first stream we mentioned sprang from heroic humanism in the Italian manner, but the second continued the satirical vein of the sixteenth century. Jan ('Velvet') Bruegel the Elder (1568–1625) who inherited it from his father is the centre of this group (pl. 445). David Teniers (1610 –1690) belongs to the same tradition, with Sebastian Vrancx, Snayers, David Vinckeboons, Gonzales Coques, van der Meulen. Adriaen Brouwer (1605/06–1638) gained experience in Frans Hals' studio at Haarlem which helped him to find a freer and less literal manner than that of

Teniers (pl. 446). The composite landscape, seen from a height, which began with Patinir and Pieter Bruegel the Elder, found lively exponents in Valkenborch, Velvet Bruegel, Joos de Momper and others. Roelandt Savery and Tobias Verhaecht carried on the fanciful type of landscape. Flemish painting is so rich that these two main streams left a number of isolated streams untouched. Painters in Bruges and Brussels, within easy reach of Antwerp, paid no heed to Rubens and sprang more directly from the Roman school. In landscape Jan Siberechts of Antwerp (1625 –1703) had close affinities with the rustic realism of Le Nain. This marvellous movement lasted for three-quarters of a century, but after 1680 the school collapsed and nothing remained but a few provincial artists.

Spain

Architecture

In the course of the seventeenth century Spain showed a slow recovery of the native temper as against the stark architectural style invented by Juan de Herrera (died 1597) in the Escorial, which led ultimately to the cold and narrow work of the Pilar at Saragossa, begun in 1681 by Juan Herrera el Mozo. At the same time the Jesuits' policy of power and pomp could not remain satisfied for long with such severe externals. They built, on the Roman plan of the Gesù, vast churches in which the classical canon can be seen debased in a grandiloquent setting: the Clerecia in Salámanca, begun in 1617 after plans by Juan Gomez de Moɪa; S. Isidro el Real in Madrid, begun in 1622 by two lay brothers of the Jesuit order, Sanchez and Juan Bautista; S. Juan Bautista in Toledo, by the latter brother, Juan Bautista. In the second half of the century the Baroque style developed in the great, heavily ornamented altars, laden with pictures and sculptures. For the most part the decoration was borrowed from the provisional settings used in theatres or festivals, while the capitals crowned enormous twisted columns decked with imitation vines (symbolizing the Eucharist), a form of decoration imitated from that of an antique column, which was preserved in St Peter's in Rome, and which was then thought to have originated in the Temple of Solomon, hence the name 'Solomon pillar' given to such supports. This kind of decoration, which also spread to Portugal (pl. 457), finished by passing from wood to stone and thus became architectural.

It was at the close of the seventeenth century that Spain invented its personal version of the Baroque, which is rather abusively called the 'Churrigueresque' style after a family of artists founded by José de Churriguera (1655–1725). Churrigueresque amounted to a disintegration of architecture which was devoured by ornamentation – garlands, fruit, flowers, festoons, mouldings, cartouches, medallions, Solomon pillars,

X Rembrandt Harmensz. van Rijn. Self-Portrait. Vienna

447 Ignacio Vergara. Portal of the Palace of the Marqués de Dos Aguas, Valencia. 1740–1744

448 Fernando de Casas y Novoa. Façade of Santiago de Compostela. 1738–1750

imitation draperies, and, to crown it all, a maze of scroll-work twisting this way and that like a tapestry over the façades or covering the altars, much as the arabesque forms of the Plateresque had done formerly. In 1693 José de Churriguera designed the colossal high altar of S. Esteban at Salamanca, the town where he and his brothers, cousins and sons worked together (towers of the Clerecia, Plaza mayor). Parallel to the Castilian Baroque of the Churriguera, the Figueroa family developed in Seville a still more exuberant variation of the style, which was to have a greater influence on the art of Spanish America than was the Churriguesque. In Madrid, Pedro Ribera (1722–1790) began replanning the city and decorated it with costly monuments (Hospicio Provincial). The most extraordinary work of Spanish Baroque is the *Transparente* (stained-glass window) in Toledo Cathedral, by Narciso Tomé; this vast composition of marble, painting, gold and light, inspired by the operatic scenario, so completely suited the national temperament that in 1732 its dedication was greeted with splendid festivals and its praises were sung in a poem in Latin. Eastern Spain and Andalusia gave themselves up to the greatest excesses of Baroque, in which architecture became swamped in ornament: sacristy of the Cartuja (Charterhouse), Granada (1727 –1764); Palace of the Marqués de Dos Aguas, Valencia (pl. 447); choir of Córdoba Cathedral (1748–1757) by Pedro Duque Cornejo. At Compostela, on the contrary, ornament was held in check by the great rhythms of the architecture; the old Romanesque cathedral, piously preserved, is as though sunk in a setting of wrought stone. After 1680

337

Domingo Antonio de Andrade built the imposing Clock Tower; Fernando de Casas y Novoa designed the west façade, the *Obradoiro* (1738–1750, pl. 448), a lofty resplendent monstrance in stone, whose heavenward movement recalls that of Gothic façades.

Just as the Hapsburgs had led the onslaught on the national Plateresque art, so another foreign dynasty, the Bourbons, was to revolt against Churrigueresque. The royal houses, Aranjuez (1715–1752), la Granja (1721–1725), the Royal Palace in Madrid (1738–1764), were all built on the model of Versailles by Italian or French architects. In the reign of Charles III, the S. Fernando Academy founded in 1752, which was given the power of judging and condemning new buildings, very soon appeared intent on putting an end to Churrigueresque; the expulsion of the Jesuits in 1767 was a further step towards the neo-Classical purge. Religious architecture, completely sterilized, lost its poetry; Ventura Rodríguez, following the precepts of Vitruvius, rebuilt S. Francisco el Grande in Madrid in an academic style inspired by St Peter's, Rome. At the end of the century Juan de Villanueva (1739–1811) introduced a new, more graceful style in the neo-Palladian spirit.

Sculpture

Spanish sculpture in the seventeenth and eighteenth centuries, which was entirely given over to religious images, pushed the art of *trompel'œil* realism farther than any other school has done. Wooden statues were painted in life-like colours, and were sometimes jointed dummies covered with luxurious clothes and jewels. The statues' eyes were of enamel or agate set in the sockets, and they had real hair, eyelashes and eyebrows. Certain statues, grouped in tableaux, were borne in procession on Good Friday *(los pasos)*. In the eighteenth century, the output was in the hands of two schools, those of Valladolid and Seville. At Valladolid Gregorio Hernandez (1576–1636, pl. 449) was responsible for the transition from Mannerism to Baroque, by changing the feverishness of

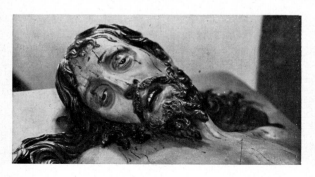

449 *Gregorio Hernandez. Dead Christ (detail). Valladolid*

Martinez Montañes. St John Baptist on the High Altar of antiponce (near Seville). 1609

451 Ribera. Martyrdom of St Bartholomew. 1630 or 1639

Berruguete and Juan de Juni into a formalism full of pathos; the attitudes were always violent, both in the pangs of suffering and the raptures of ecstasy. The art of Martinez Montañes (1568–1649) at Seville was graver and more inward, and his works are one of the highest expressions of religious feeling in the seventeenth century (high altar of Santiponce, 1609, pl. 450). At Granada, Pedro de Mena (1628–1688) sculpted classical types of devotional imagery, while Alonso Cano (1601–1667) developed that austere art towards the rendering of womanly gracefulness which was to become the tradition in Granada in the eighteenth century (José Risueno, died 1721). When it was dying out, the art of coloured sculpture was stimulated for the last time at the hands of the Salzillo family, who brought to Murcia the mannered and affected art of the Neapolitan carvers of cribs, with their large groups of characters *(preseppe)*.

Painting

In a country where the Inquisition was all-powerful, painting was practically a church monopoly. Court paintings were just tolerated, but mythological painting hardly existed, and landscape not at all. It was in the south and east, which looked to Italy for inspiration, and chiefly at Valencia and Seville, that the devotional painting developed. Francisco Ribalta (1551/55–1628), a Valencian painter, brought the model for this

452 Zurbarán. St Hugh of Grenoble visiting the Refectory. Seville

form from Italy. It was also from Valencia that Jusepe de Ribera (1588–1652) left for Naples in 1616, where he made his career. Indeed he was Caravaggio's most ardent disciple, using his chiaroscuro still more violently; but his Spanish harshness of temperament led him to seek his models in the dregs of society, and in his scenes of martyrdom he seemed to delight in painting the human body under torture (pl. 451). The two facets of the Spanish Christian soul were expressed in Seville by two famous painters, Zurbarán and Murillo. Francisco de Zurbarán (1598–1664), who has been called the 'monk-painter', was a mystic who lived his daily life on a supernatural plane; but like medieval man he could think of the supernatural only in terms of the concrete (pl. 452). Of all artists he was perhaps the one who best portrayed that Spanish humanism for which the truth is only to be found by confronting the self with

453 Murillo. Virgin and St Anne (detail). After 1674. Madrid

454 Velázquez. Pablo de Valladolid. About 1633. Madrid

455 Velázquez. Las Meninas (The Maids of Honour). 1656. Madrid

God, and which allows the external world no reality whatever. His sculptural forms, so aggressively carved, and as it were hewn out of darkness, seem to rise from the void under the eye of the God to whom they owe their existence. On the other hand it was the homely, sensual piety of Andalusia which inspired Bartolomé Esteban Murillo (1617 –1682), the painter of the Virgin, and the only Spanish artist besides Velázquez who seems to have been touched by feminine charm (pl. 453). His sweet and somewhat sugary art goes back to Raphael and Correggio. Another Sevillian, Juan de Valdès Leal (1630–1691) showed a taste for theatrical settings which led him away from the native bent for realism,

456 *Goya. The nude Maja. About 1797–1798. Madrid*

and this gives him affinities rather with the visionary tradition of El Greco; he was a kind of belated Mannerist (pl. 420).

Diego Velázquez (1590–1660) was trained in Seville and the first phase of his work had the harsh realism of that school; he painted still-lifes with kitchen themes *(bodegones)*, and devotional pictures. He never lost the Christian view of the blemish in human nature, which led him to take idiots and weaklings as his models, and had a satirical approach to mythology which he mocked in trivial forms such as *Los Borrachos (The Drinkers)*, or *Vulcan's Forge*. He was appointed as chief painter to the royal family in 1623, and in the following year he went to Italy where he came in contact with Venetian painting, which helped him to put off his early Caravaggesque manner. In 1649 he made a second voyage to Italy. Abandoning the sharp sculptural modelling of that school, he no longer tried to show the individuality of forms by means of clear outline, and painted in bright patches of impasto which show delicate tinges of light flowing across flesh and materials. As the official court painter, he occasionally painted groups in movement such as *Las Lanzas (The Surrender of Breda)*, or *Las Meninas (The Maids of Honour*, pl. 455), or *Las Hilanderas (The Tapestry-Weavers)*. Late in life he also painted the first female nude of Spanish art (colour pl. XI). His single portraits, in which the models are shown almost without accessories, are in the tradition of Sanchez Coello and Pantoja de la Cruz. The figure is like a vision emerging from a haze, and sometimes the ground beneath its feet is indistinguishable from the background (pl. 454). No painter ever went farther towards expressing the hopeless mystery of human solitude with regard to the world in which he lives, that has always tormented the Spanish mind.

Juan Bautista del Mazo (about 1612?–1667) and Juan Carreño de Miranda (1614–1685) brought Velázquez's art down to a popular level.

After him, the Spanish school had no life left in it. In the eighteenth century, the Spanish princes had to call in French and Italian painters. However, the school had a final flash of genius in Francisco José de Goya y Lucientes (1746–1828) whose visionary art is a desperate satire on human nature as well as on Spanish society; he outlived the Baroque period and forestalled the French Romantic movement by a generation (pl. 456).

Portugal

Less gifted than Spain in both painting and sculpture, Portugal in the seventeenth and eighteenth centuries achieved its best work in architecture. Unlike what might be expected, the latter owed little to the neighbouring example of Spain. Portugal developed a type of church of its own, with a compact lay-out, tending to be contained in one quadrangle, having no dome, and with all the annexes, sacristies and consistories harmoniously fitting into the whole, giving a pleasing impression of unity. The same classical simplicity was shown in public buildings, in which ornaments were harmoniously, even harmonically spread over the naked walls, in such a way as to avoid any impression of overloading.

The seventeenth century saw the erection of fine religious buildings in a Doric style and with a monastic simplicity, which carry on the austerity of the Counter-Reformation: Jesuit church, Coimbra (1598); Jesuit church of S. Lourenço dos Grilos, Oporto (1614); S. Bento da Vitoria, Oporto (1614); S. Clara Nova, Coimbra, by João Turriano (1648). The Baroque spirit appeared in the north under Spanish influence in about 1680 (churches at Braga). In the eighteenth century, on the king's initiative a renewed Italian influence brought fresh life into the Portuguese school and helped it to find its original vein. King João V (1706–1750), whose fortunes were improved by gold brought from Brazil, had an architect of German origin, Ludovice, to build the enormous monastery-palace at Mafra (1713–1735, pl. 423) whose plan was based on the Escorial but which was Baroque in its architectural excesses. The art of Lisbon and of the south (Alentejo) remained nearest to the neo-Roman spirit of Mafra. Another foreign contribution, thanks to the Sienese artist Nicolo Nasoni, was to strengthen the north's natural taste for the Baroque by creating a decorator's style at Oporto which was full of energy and splendour (S. Pedro dos Clerigos, begun 1732; bell-tower, 1748). On the basis of these elements which were further enriched by Chinese influences, Minho-Douro (archbishopric of Braga) during the reign of Dom José (1750–1777) developed a Baroque art with a dynamic power and naturalistic verve which recalls Manueline art; this movement was arrested towards 1780 by the neo-Classicism of Cruz Amarante which was favoured by English influence. Meanwhile Lisbon was preparing a harmonious fusion of the various regional tendencies in Portugal

343

457 'Solomon Pillar'
from the High Altar
of S. Bento, Oporto.
About 1705

458 Gilt-encrusted Interior of S. Francisco, Oporto. Gothic. 17th–18th c.

which led to an elegant art in which the Baroque decoration was governed by the structure of the building: Queluz Castle (1758–1790); basilican church of the Estrela at Lisbon (1779–1790), by Mateus Vicente.

However lavish the decoration in Portugal, and even in the most lyrical works of Minho-Douro, its distribution always followed rhythmic principles which recall monuments that were being erected in the same period in Austria and Bavaria, whereas Spanish architecture was more intent on astonishing than pleasing by its deliberate disproportions. The same is true of the internal decoration, consisting of gilded woodwork which sometimes covered the whole elevation up to the vaults themselves. Unlike the Spanish churches in which altarpieces were devised to show off sculptures, the Portuguese ensembles obey a purely decorative rhythm which reduces the host of ornaments to a pattern. The finest examples of this art of *entalhadores* are to be found at Oporto: S. Bento (pl. 457) and S. Francisco (pl. 458).

Portugal gave a great impetus to the art of enamelled faïence which it learnt from the Mudéjar workshops in the sixteenth century. At first polychromatic, these ceramics tended to be made in a blue tone only, whence the name *azulejos*. The patterns were entirely decorative in the seventeenth century *(azulejos de tapete)* and became representational in the eighteenth, when they were influenced by Delft china. Whole cycles of pious or profane images were painted in this way, many of them being copies of engravings from the Antwerp school.

From the sixteenth century onwards an immense field of expansion was opened to Western art as a result of the conquest of America by the Spanish and Portuguese. The conversion of the natives gave an unlimited scope to religious art. The Jesuits marked the stages of their missionary zeal with huge monumental buildings, while the different religious orders vied with each other in their plans for new undertakings, and the last generation of cathedrals rose on American soil. Mexico Cathedral (1573 –1656) one of the biggest structures in Christendom, derives from the classical plan of the Andalusian cathedral of Jaén; the same plan was to be followed in the cathedrals of Puebla, Mérida, Guadalajara, and Oaxaca in Mexico, Cusco and Lima in Peru, and Bogotá in Columbia. Transplanted to New Spain, the Churrigueresque style gave rise in that tropical climate to a wild profusion of forms not unlike that of Hindu architecture in the Middle Ages (pl. 459). In Mexico and Bolivia especially, Indian labour gave the imported style a plastic flavour reminiscent of the old pre-Columbian arts. Mexico had a school of painters who were successful in imitating Sevillian painting; everywhere else both painting and sculpture show a spontaneous revival of artistic conventions that reach back to the primitives.

The awakening came later in Brazil, where it only began towards the end of the sixteenth century. In those still uncivilized parts the lack of any native artistic tradition favoured the planting and growth of an art which was able to continue that of the homeland in an original manner. However, by the eighteenth century the colony's level of civilization al-

459 The Sagrario Metropolitano adjoining Mexico Cathedral. 18th c.

460 Aleijadinho. Isaiah from the Bom Jesus. Congonhas do Campo (Brasil). About 1800

lowed it to establish its own artistic schools, capable of inventing their own forms, especially in a region which was thriving since the discovery of gold there, and where the town of Ouro Preto was built; there, at the end of the eighteenth century the son of a Portuguese architect and a black slave, Antonio Francisco Lisboa, called o Aleijadinho (the little invalid) (1730–1814), produced one of the most remarkable expressions of the Baroque style. Does the presence of negro craftsmen explain entirely that aptitude for sculptural form which reached a higher level in Brazil than in the homeland itself? At all events that tendency resulted in the genius of Aleijadinho's work, which brought a great lyrical breath and a primitive energy into the Baroque, which by then was languishing in Europe as a result of formalism and virtuosity (*Prophets,* Congonhas do Campo, 1800, pl. 460).

Central Europe

While Western Europe was resisting the Southern Baroque aesthetic, the style was finding favourable soil in Central Europe and spreading into the Slav and Scandinavian countries.

In the Germanic countries the sharp succession of the Baroque and a belated Renaissance style at the end of the seventeenth century, was encouraged by the break in their traditions which was caused by the Thirty Years War (1618–1648). While the Renaissance style for them had meant no more than applying 'modern' ornament on a Gothic structure, the German artists, educated first by the Italians then the French, were very quick in absorbing the Mediterranean Baroque outlook which sees a monument as a powerfully modelled composition of volumes. The projection of masses was energetically stressed, while all the items of secondary modelling – cornices, pediments, capitals, vertical divisions – were brought into strong relief thanks to a variety of ornaments which were closer to statuary itself than to low-relief. The column and the telamon (male supporting figure) played a fundamental part, while the bell-towers ended in a bulbous crown which no doubt derived from Russian art. After about 1730 the Baroque style evolved into Rococo: overlaying and *rocaille* (decoration based originally on rock- and shell-forms) increased. The ornamentation became asymmetrical and all the features merged into a symphony in space, owing to the rhythmical movement of curves and counter-curves. Two great streams met in this melting-pot of the Baroque. The first Italian stream triumphed in the religious architecture which saw a wonderful revival in Austria, Bavaria, Franconia and Poland. Introduced early on by the Jesuits, the new 'triumphal' style was welcomed with enthusiasm. Round Vienna, in Bavaria and in Swabia great convents and monasteries were built more or less on the Escorial plan (centred on a church, pl. 422) but with a frenzy

461 Daniel Pöppelmann. Pavilion of the Zwinger, Dresden. 1711–1722

of ornamentation in the two main centres of display, the library and the church. Coming from the West after about 1720, the French influence brought the charm of French taste and the example of Versailles, which was regarded by great and small German princes as the supreme model of court art. But no sooner was the French style brought into Germany

*462. Johann Michael Fischer. Interior of the Benedictine Church, Ottobeuren.
1737–1766*

than it had to join the Italian Baroque and became Rococo. French
influence remained the stronger – thought it was profoundly changed
by German lyricism – in the decoration of private and civic buildings.
The general lay-out of palaces and gardens was based on French models
(Versailles, Trianon, Marly); but the decoration was specifically German
in its *rocaille* and its telamones. While Austria remained closer to the
Italian Baroque, the Rococo triumphed in Saxony, Prussia, Franconia
and in the Rhineland. Austria was very early initiated by the Italians
and produced some great architects: Johann Bernhard Fischer von Erlach
(1656–1723), the author of Prince Eugene's Winter-Palace (1703), the

463 Johann Balthazar Neumann. Staircase of the Residenz, Würzburg. 1737–1744

church of St Charles Borromeus in Vienna (1717) and the design for the palace of Schönbrunn (1694); Lukas von Hildebrandt (1668–1745) who built the Belvedere Palace in Vienna, together with its gardens (1693 –1724); and Jakob Prandtauer (1660–1726) who made one of the finest Baroque pieces in Europe, the monastery at Melk on the Danube.

In Saxony from 1711 to 1722 Daniel Pöppelmann (1662–1736), who visited Versailles and Rome, built the most Baroque monument in all Germany, the Zwinger at Dresden (1711–1722, pl. 461); this building, damaged in the second World War but now reconstructed, is like an immense open-air theatre. In Bavaria and Swabia the Asam Brothers, the Thumb and Beer families, the Zimmermann brothers, and Johann Michael Fischer (1692–1766) built churches and monasteries inspired by Austrian art (pl. 462), while at the court at Munich where the Frenchman Cuvilliés (1695–1768) was working they followed Parisian models or that of Versailles. The finest and most princely residence in Germany was the Bishop's Palace (Residenz) at Würzburg, in Franconia, built between 1719 and 1744 by Johann Balthazar Neumann (1687–1753), and in which Tiepolo painted his masterpiece on the ceiling of the staircase (pl. 463) between 1750 and 1753. Magnificent staircases were a speciality with this architect, who also built one of the finest churches in Germany, the Vierzehnheiligen in Franconia, as well as Schloss Brühl in the Rhineland. The Royal Palace, Berlin, which was inspired by the Palazzo Madama in Rome, and of which several of the buildings were erected by Andreas Schlüter (about 1660–1714) from 1698 onwards, is the only great monument in the Italian manner. Near Berlin, at Potsdam, Frederick the Great emulated Louis XIV in building a royal city. The eclectic von Knobelsdorff (1699–1753) remodelled the Stadtschloss at Potsdam in a very sober neo-Palladian style (1744) and designed Sanssouci and its gardens (1744), a fine example of Rococo.

464 *Egid Quirin Asam. Assumption from the High Altar at Rohr. About 1717–1722*

In the Germanic countries, sculpture remained entirely decorative; it was the most tormented in Europe and had something of the broken style of late Gothic work. In Georg Raphael Donner (1693–1741), however, the Baroque forms are restrained by a certain classical tendency. The religious sculptors went in for what amounted to theatrical settings with their sculpted groups (Egid Quirin Asam, 1692–1750, pl. 464), while the stucco-workers of southern Germany showed great virtuosity (pl. 465). Meanwhile, French influence helped Andreas Schlüter with his *Great Elector of Brandenburg*, inspired by Girardon's *Louis XIV*. Decorative painting suggests Tie-

*465 J. M. Feichtmayr and F. J. Spiegler. Stucco-Work and Ceiling Fresco. 1749.
Zwiefalten*

polo's teaching in the work of Franz Maulpertsch (1724–1796) at Vienna,
and Cosmas Damian Asam (1689–1739) at Munich; the Frenchman
Antoine Pesne (1683–1757) introduced Berlin to the court-portrait in the
French manner, as taken up by Daniel Chodowiecki (1748–1801).

466 Raphael Mengs. Parnassus. Ceiling in the Villa Albani, Rome. 1761.

The neo-Classical reformation was late in reaching German architecture (Friedrich Wilhelm von Ermannsdorf, 1736–1800; Simon Louis du Ry, 1726–1799). In 1790 K. Gotthard Langhans (1732–1808) brought in the archaeological style with the Brandenburg Gate at Berlin, inspired by the Propylaea in Athens. Germany made an early contribution to the international colony of Roman antiquaries, notably the theorist Winckelmann (1717–1768), who arrived in Rome in 1755 and published his *Reflections on the Imitation of Greek Works* in the same year, then his *History of Ancient Art* in 1764, in which he advocated a slavish copying of Classical art, an aesthetic outlook which was applied in painting by his countryman Raphael Mengs (1728–1779, pl. 466).

The Slavonic Countries

Seventeenth-century Russian architecture retained its national characteristics; but in spite of the strict edicts of the Orthodox Church, which was opposed to any artistic progress, styles developed and, during the second half of the century, Western influences began to infiltrate.

The Baroque decoration grafted on to the tent-roofed churches – which gradually developed into churches with spires – resulted in a richly ornate style not unlike that found in Mexico at the same time (church of the Virgin of the Sign, Dubrovitsi, 1690–1704, church of the Intercession of the Virgin at Fili, 1693, pl. 467). Thus, even before the reign of Peter the Great, Russia participated in this phase of European Baroque; iconostases, which in Russian churches played the same decorative role as altar-screens in Spain, were lavishly ornamented with gold, acanthus leaves and Solomon pillars. At the same time Russia played her part in the great revival of monastic architecture which was taking place

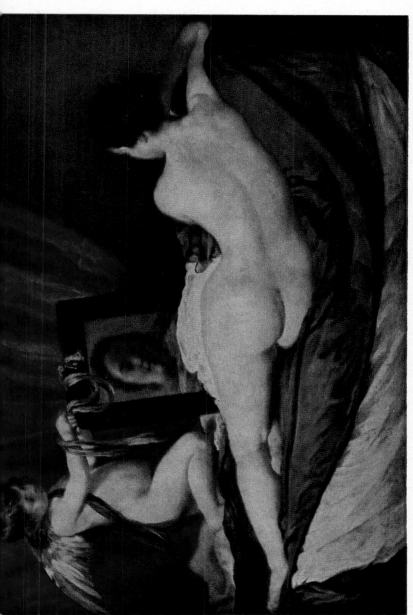

XI *Diego Velázquez. The Toilet of Venus (The Rokeby Venus). London*

467 *Church of the Intercession of the Virgin, Fili. 1693*

all over Europe, particularly in the central part and in southern Germany; here, too, refectories became showpieces, extravagantly decorated (Novodevichi Convent, Zagorsk and Ssimonov near Moscow).

Peter the Great cut short this flowering of Russian architecture, however, when, in 1703, he founded St Petersburg (Leningrad) near the mouth of the Neva; he intended to have the city built by foreign architects, on European lines. To begin with it was to be modelled on Amsterdam; then, in 1717, the Frenchman Le Blond worked out a plan in the manner of Versailles, and finally the Empress Elizabeth (1741–1762) gave reality to the city of Peter's dreams. The Italian architect Bartolommeo Rastrelli (1700–1770) introduced a Baroque style strongly

468 *Bartolommeo Rastrelli. Winter Palace, Leningrad. 1754–1762*

469 *Ivan Yegorovich Starov. Catherine Hall in the Tauride Palace, Leningrad. 1783*

470 Bartolommeo Rastrelli. Banqueting Hall of the Great Palace, Tsarskoe Selo

permeated with German Rococo elements: Winter Palace (1754–1762, pl. 468), Smolny Convent (1748–1753), and the Great Palace at Tsarskoe Selo (the present Pushkin Palace). Buildings of stuccoed brick were painted blue, red, green or yellow. The interior of the Great Palace at Tsarskoe Selo, lavishly decorated with gilded wood, marble, mother-of-pearl and amber (pl. 470) made this into one of the most sumptuous residences in Europe. Catherine II (1762–1796), however, whose tastes were strongly inclined towards France, rejected the Baroque and encouraged instead the neo-Classicism that was supported by the Academy of Fine Arts founded in 1758.

This was the style followed by the Frenchman Vallin de la Mothe (Academy of Fine Arts, 1765–1772; first Hermitage, 1765–1768) and the Italian Antonio Rinaldi (Marble Palace; Palace at Gatchina, 1766–1781). Charles Cameron from Scotland (apartments for Catherine, colonnade and Agate Pavilion at Tsarskoe Selo; country house at Pavlovsk) and Giacomo Quarenghi from Italy (Palace for Alexander I at Tsarskoe Selo; Hermitage Theatre) introduced the Pompeian style and formal elegance of Palladio which the Russian architect Starov (Tauride Palace, 1783–1788, pl. 469) was soon to master completely. In the field of painting, the work of the society portrait painter Dmitri Levitski (1735–1822) was inspired by the French artist Toqué. Sculpture was represented by the huge equestrian statue of Peter I, commissioned by

471 Lazienki
   Palace,
   Warsaw.
   1784–1788

Catherine from the Frenchman Falconet and one of the finest royal monuments of the *Ancien Régime* (1766–1782).

In contrast to Russia, Poland, traditionally subject to Western influences continued after the sixteenth century to participate in all modern stylistic developments. The palace at Wilanów, built by John Sobieski at the end of the seventeenth century, is Baroque in inspiration and the Saxon dynasty, which gave Poland two kings, encouraged this tendency by introducing Dresden Rococo. The architectural splendours of Dresden and Warsaw are depicted by the Venetian painter Bernardo Bellotto (1720–1780), a nephew of Canaletto. Stanislas Poniatowski (1764–1795), Poland's last king, who was educated in France, supported the neo-Classical reaction against the Baroque. He employed the Italian Dominico Merlini (1730–1797), who restored the royal palace using Classical forms in the Palladian manner for the interior as well as for his residential buildings and palaces (Lazienki Palace near Warsaw, pl. 471).

In Russia, as in Poland, great variety was introduced into the planning of parks and it was not unusual to find a pavillon in the Classical style set among the undulating landscape of an English garden (Pavlosk near Leningrad; Arcadia in Poland).

2. THE RESISTANCE TO BAROQUE

Holland

After the political truce in 1609, the seven northern provinces of the Low Countries (to which one of them, Holland, had given its name) found themselves cut off from the twelve provinces of the south. To a

Europe which was monarchical, Catholic and theocratic, the United Provinces were to give a precocious example of a lay democracy based on a bourgeois society almost free of class distinctions. This completely upset the conditions on which artistic production depended all over Europe and resulted in fewer civil and religious undertakings on any large scale, the slowing down of religious inspiration, the almost complete suppression of mythological images which had no interest for the Amsterdam and Haarlem merchant. Reduced to circumstances which had so little encouragement to offer the artist, that small country which held out against all the large European states one after the other, contrived for over sixty years to produce an admirable art, by making the best of the one resource left to it, which was realism.

Dutch architectures has never been given the place it deserves in the history of art. Almost entirely confined to domestic needs, it produced only small buildings, but they are in exquisite taste (pl. 472). From the beginning of the seventeenth century Holland was the only country to reject Baroque rhetoric, and by 1650 it discovered a very pure architecture founded on good proportions, which, after it was interpreted by the English, helped to form the neo-Classical style. Dutch construction in brick was relieved only by a few stone mouldings to emphasize doorways, windows or cornices; occasionally on more important houses broad flat pilasters were set right up the wall. The few religious buildings of the period were also of simple design. Sculpture was so little practised that foreign artists were called in for the few sculptured works (tombs) of any importance.

Painting was therefore the supreme form of artistic expression in Holland. The fluid and mellow quality of the light, which is one of the beauties of the great sea-girt plain, gave the Dutch – like the Venetians – a discerning eye for pure tonality and colour. The bourgeois, positivistic society favoured an art of acute observation which tended to become a faithful mirror of its own existence. Paintings were small, of a size intended for the private house. In order to go about their great naturalistic inquiry the Dutch artists – even more than the Flemings – became specialists of one kind or another: painters of still-lifes or animals, painters of domestics scenes, church-architecture or landscape, the latter being of several

472 Jacob van Campen (design). The Mauritshuis at The Hague 1643–1644

356

473 Pieter Claesz.
Still-Life.
The Hague

subsidiary kinds: marine painting, pastorals, urban scenes, animated landscapes with figures, and ruins.

The wealth of talents that thrived almost as an industry in Holland, makes it difficult to classify them satisfactorily. The local schools were not strongly marked and there were constant exchanges going on between them, while distinction according to subjects, which is often used, is too superficial. But perhaps in the same way as with Flanders we may follow two main streams, of which the first was thoroughly Nordic, while the second shows the Northern analytical temperament blending with the synthetic outlook brought from Italy.

For the most part Dutch painting springs from the analytical vision discovered by van Eyck, which makes, so to speak, a careful check of objects, accounting for one after another within a select and deliberately

474 Ter Borch. Soldier and Woman
(Le Galant Militaire). Paris

475 Saenredam. Church Interior.
Boston

476 Hals. Banquet of the Officers of the Archers of St George. 1616. Harlem

limited field of observation; the painter's task is confined to a faithful visual record with little or no interpretation. Other painters, thanks to their inspiration, their experiments in composition and the life-size scale of their figures, are related more to the main current of European art, and particularly by the link with 'Romanism'. The two streams mentioned above may be distinguished in all the genres. Thus the still-life painters of the Utrecht school, Roelandt Savery, Abraham Boschaert, Simons, Abraham Mignon, Jan Davidsz. de Heem (1601–1683) continued the analytical, monographic vision of the North, painting each object as though it made the whole picture. Others, Pieter Claesz. (1591–1661, pl. 473), Willem Heda (1594–1680/82), Willem Kalff (1622–1693) arranged objects into subtle compositions in such a way as to contrive a picture out of them; they preferred the pictorial quality of things to a strictly

477 Jacob van Ruisdael. Windmill at Wijk-bij-Duurstade. Amsterdam

478 Hals. Wilhelm van Heydhuysen. 1637. Brussels

impersonal representation of them. The compositions of such an animal-painter as Paulus Potter (1624–1642) sometimes aspired to the monumental, while certain paintings by Melchior d'Hondecoeter are purely analytical. The monographic vision was particularly the field of the minor masters of genre-painting, which in its wide range of subjects covered the whole social life of Holland (popular realism of Jan Steen, Adriaen and Isaack van Ostade, Quiringh Brekelenkam, Judith Leyster, Jacob Duck, etc.; genteel realism of Gerhard Ter Borch (1617–1681, pl. 474), Gabriel Metsu, Gerard Dou, Pieter de Hooch, etc.). This indoor-paint-

479 Rembrandt. Wash-Drawing.
London

480 Rembrandt. Jan Six.
About 1654. Amsterdam

ing admirably suited the patient enumeration of forms and objects. The portraitists differ according to the degree of skill with which they set figures in a given space or framework; most of the painters of group-portraits (for confraternities, councils and guilds), a type of picture often found in the Dutch school, often had trouble in grouping all their worthies into one composition. A Jan de Bray or a Bartholomeus van der Helst found it hard to show a number of people round a table in a natural, lifelike manner, whereas Frans Hals or Rembrandt solved the same problem with ease (pl. 476). The greatest of the landscape painters, Salomon van Ruysdael (1600–1670), Jacob van Ruisdael (1628/29–1682, pl. 477), Jan van Goyen and Philips Koninck, owe their superiority to the art with which they composed their pictures with unified designs and well-balanced values, whereas Meindert Hobbema merely accumulated observed details one after another. The Italianate painters (Jan Asselijn, Cornelis van Poelenburgh, Nicolaes Berchem) followed without any thought of variation, the types of landscape-composition they had brought back with them from Rome. Others specialized in town-scenes (Gerrit Adriaensz. Berckheyde, Jan van der Heyden). Of those who painted only churches, Pieter Saenredam (1597–1665) had a fine sense of light (pl. 475).

Holland did not remain cut off from European art. Italian influence was brought in by the 'Romanist' painters who lived in Rome and who almost all belonged to the Utrecht school. These were Pieter Lastman, Abraham Bloemaert, Gerhard van Honthorst, Hendrik Ter Brugghen (1588–1629), Theodor van Baburen. They kept the Caravagesque method of showing volumes by oblique lighting, the art of making compositions with a number of figures, and a taste for rather vulgar realism in scenes taken from low-life such as drinkers, card-players, cabaret musicians, gambling dens and guard-rooms. Both Frans Hals and Rembrandt were produced by this movement. Frans Hals took from it his partiality for shady and 'tough' haunts, while Rembrandt gained a sense of historical painting and of monumental composition. They both broke up the 'monographic' and objective composition of Dutch painting and their

481 Rembrandt. Pilgrims of Emmaus. 1648. Paris

handling of paint was untraditional. Frans Hals (1580–1666), both as a portraitist and as the recorder of Haarlem society, handled his paint with bravure; his brush – the movements of which can be seen on the canvas – seems to obey an eager improvisation, and the artist gave more attention to paint effects than to a lifelike imitation of the model (pl. 478).

Rembrandt Harmensz. van Rijn (1606–1669) is the greatest Dutch painter; his considerable body of work contains a world of its own like that of Titian and Rubens. Rembrandt came to Amsterdam in 1631, where he spent the rest of his life. Beginning with an art which still respected all the bourgeois conventions of his age, he achieved wealth and success; but as the circumstances of his life impelled him more and more to obey some inner compulsion instead of trying to please the public, his popularity declined until in 1656 a court-order made him sell all his belongings. He passed his last years in poverty and in a state of extraordinary spiritual tension and gave himself increasingly to painting works inspired by the Bible, through which he expressed the radiant love and peace within him (pl. 481). Three pictures serve to sum up his career as a painter. *The Anatomy Lesson of Professor Tulp* (1632) was still a collection of lifelike portraits, painted with a painstaking and objective brush. In *The Night Watch* (1642) the artist treated his models – to their dissatisfaction, as events proved – as no more than accessory figures in the scenario of a great spectacle, of which the latent theme is an impassioned struggle between light and darkness; he neglected external reality

482 *Vermeer. Lady at the Virginals with a Gentleman listening. About 1660.*
Windsor

for the poetry of his subject and beauty of effect. In *The Syndics of the
Cloth Hall* (1661) the characters' physical reality was dimmed, and the
eloquent intensity of their souls makes the members of the syndicate
more like a group of philosophers. Rembrandt's brush, ever more urgent
and inspired, makes no more than passing references to the external
meaning of things, and with great smudges of darkness the artist combines his brownish local colouring that lights up in sudden stretches of
impasto (pl. 480). His drawings, also, convey the overflowing of a creative
imagination (pl. 479). Rembrandt's psychological and pictorial development is nowhere better seen than in the extraordinary collection of over

sixty self-portraits – feverish probings into his own soul; towards the end of his life they became moving revelations of human suffering (colour pl. X).

Jan Vermeer of Delft (1632–1675) combined the two great traditions of Dutch painting in his work. This 'intimist' for whom the whole universe could be contained in a bare room animated by one or two figures, belongs to the van Eyck line by virtue of his intense objectivity which gives a kind of magical presence to reality (pl. 482). But it was from the Italians that he inherited his strict science of composition whose hidden geometry can only be detected in his apparently 'natural' scenes after careful analysis; it was to the remote but widespread influence of Caravaggio that he owed the art of rounding his volumes by the device of lateral lighting. He was very Dutch in his sense of that poetry of light which gives things their shapes and colours and very existence. He belonged fully to that 'philosophical' century in which a few painters, notably Rembrandt, Velázquez, Zurbarán, Georges de La Tour and himself, saw human beings as the transcendental presence of a soul.

The Dutch school declined at the end of the seventeenth century as a result of the fashionable French and English influences which thwarted the native realistic tradition. The portraitists Caspar Netscher (1639 –1684) and van Mieris (1636–1681) were influenced by court-portraits, the still-life began to imitate the French floral painters, and in the eighteenth century Cornelis Troost (1697–1750) imitated the society art of the Regency and Louis XV, as well as showing English influence. The school of Gerard Dou was prolonged by several painters until after 1750.

Britain

Architecture

Passing without a well-defined transitional style from Gothic to the classical style, England scarcely felt – and then only very late – the indecisions of the Mannerist crisis which marked the Renaissance in other Nordic countries. Scarcely had a few 'antique' decorations been used in Elizabethan mansions, when at the beginning of the seventeenth century the architect Inigo Jones (1573–1652) brought back his passion for Palladio, after a journey in Italy. He designed the Banqueting-House in Whitehall (1619–1622) in a very pure style, and urged the utmost simplicity in the façades of ordinary dwelling-houses. After the Restoration (1660) Sir Christopher Wren was asked to plan the rebuilding of London after its destruction in the Great Fire of 1666. He rebuilt St Paul's Cathedral (pl. 484) in a Roman style imitated from St Peter's, Rome, with a dome deriving from the design Bramante had intended for St Peter's; this building was to have great influence in France and America in the eigh-

*483 Robert Adam. Portico at Osterley Park.
1761*

teenth century. A large number of churches were built in London after Wren's designs. Dutch influences affected domestic architecture, which was very plain, brick-built with very simply moulded sash-windows, the only ornament being a doorway of elegantly classical style. Several instances of restrained Baroque were created by two architects who had worked with Wren, Nicholas Hawksmoor (1661 –1736) and John Vanbrugh (1664–1726) who built two colossal mansions, Blenheim Palace (Woodstock, 1705–1724) and Castle Howard (1699–1712). In the Georgian period (1714–1760) renewed speculation about architecture led to a revival of Inigo Jones' Palladian style; a *de luxe* edition of Palladio's treatise, annotated by Jones, was published in 1715. Such was

484 Wren. St Paul's Cathedral, London. 1675–1710

the vogue of architecture that even the aristocrasy turned its hand to it. Palladianism was to become the national style in Great Britain. William Kent (1684–1748) was the moving spirit in the period; he introduced the Anglo-Chinese garden about 1720, with an irregular lay-out, and here and there a Palladian, Gothic or Chinese pavillon. Palladian structures and Anglo-Chinese gardens were not long in crossing the channel and became popular in France. Bath, the fashionable spa, built by John Wood and his son of the same name, became a sort of English Vicenza. A new phase began in 1758, when Robert Adam (1728–1792) returned from a voyage to Pompeii and Spalato to introduce features of a neo-Hellenic style (pl. 483), exquisitely elegant, which influenced both façades and internal decoration (pl. 517) in which the artist introduced arabesques, and which was to be imitated in the French Directoire style. English architecture shows a remarkable continuity in its pursuit of a very pure classical manner, in which ornament is only used to bring out the proportions. It is not the smallest of English paradoxes, that in spite of that evolution, the Gothic style should have persisted in the seventeenth and even eighteenth centuries in university buildings (Christ Church College, Oxford, seventeenth century) and some country-houses (Strawberry Hill, Twickenham, 1748; Fonthill, 1795).

Painting

English painting of this period derived from the Flemish; it was founded by van Dyck who came to London in 1632, and by his best disciple, Sir Peter Lely (1618–1680), who was of Dutch origin. To this far-reaching source further Dutch influences were added in the course of the century, and above all some desire to emulate the *galant,* refined art of Watteau whose manner was revealed to London by Philippe Mercier and the engraver Gravelot. Gravelot in particular helped Hogarth to find his own style, and guided Gainsborough in his early period. William Hogarth (1697–1764) perhaps owed something of his verve and broadness of style to Sir James Thornhill (1676–1734), his employer, whose daughter Hogarth married and who was the only native-born painter of Baroque decorations in England. Influenced by the theatre, Hogarth painted series of paintings which follow one another like the chapters of a novel, and with a moralising tendency: *The Rake's Progress* (1735); *The Harlot's Progress* (1738); *Marriage à la Mode* (1745, pl. 485); he found more freedom in the magnificent figures which he brought out boldly with a rich and lively brush *(The Shrimp-Girl, Garrick).* In the Georgian period painting was mostly devoted to portraiture. Sir Joshua Reynolds (1723–1791), who became the first president of the Royal Academy in 1768, fixed the characteristics of the English portrait: sulky feminine portraits with a touch of sentimentality *(Nelly O'Brien,* pl. 486, *Kitty Fisher, Countess Spencer);* masculine portraits which, in spite of an affected

485 Hogarth. The Marriage Contract from Marriage à la Mode. 1745

casualness, bring out fully British personal pride and character *(Colonel Saint Leger, Lord Heathfield, Earl of Eglinton)*. Very much of a theorist and the author of *Discourses on Painting*, Reynolds tried to wrest their secrets from the great masters, Raphael, Correggio, Rubens, Rembrandt, Titian. His rival Thomas Gainsborough (1727–1788, colour pl. XII) was more spontaneous. Gainsborough had a taste for landscape, and coming into fashion as a portrait-painter he still kept that sense of naturalness which he had gained in his contact with the countryside. His art, which is sentimental, like Watteau's by which it was influenced, is a poetic expression of aristocratic elegance *(The Blue Boy, The Morning Walk, Mr and Mrs Robert Andrews)* and of the melancholy, dreamy feminine soul *(Perdita, Mrs Sheridan, Miss Margaret Gainsborough,* pl. 488). He turned the portrait into a mood attuned to some evocation of nature. Allan Ramsay (1713–1784), of Scottish origin and influenced by Quentin de la Tour, Perroneau and Nattier, painted portraits of great natural delicacy. Sir Henry Raeburn (1756–1823) remained in Edinburgh, where he confined himself to painting the robust health, military swagger and red cheeks of Scottish society (pl. 487). John Hoppner (1759–1710), of German origin, and George Romney (1734–1802), who spent two years in Italy, both introduced a neo-Classical coldness into the portrait, a manner which Sir Thomas Lawrence (1769–1830), who painted for all the

366

486 Reynolds. Nelly O'Brien. 1763. London

courts in Europe, brought to icy perfection. The Anglo-Saxons were also responsible for neo-Classicism in historical painting; it was in Rome, under the influence of the archaeologist Winckelmann, and then in London, that between 1763 and 1775 Gavin Hamilton (1730–1797) and the American-born Benjamin West (1738–1820) recreated historical painting, more than a decade before the French painter David, who did not forget their example. Here again, as in architecture, England gave the lead to France.

488 Gainsborough. Miss
Margaret Gainsborough
(detail). London

487 Raeburn. Colonel Alastair Macdonnell of Glengarry. Edinburgh

Though they lacked the prestige of portraiture, which brings fame and fortune to its exponents, the other types of painting were also practised by the English school. Gainsborough's landscapes, which were inspired by the Dutch, Rubens and Watteau, would be enough to make his reputation.

489 Richard Wilson. A Ruined Arch at Kew. 1761–1762. Private Collection

XII Thomas Gainsborough. The Artist's Daughters (detail). London

490 George Stubbs. Lord and Lady Melbourne with Sir Ralph Milbanke and Mr. John Milbanke. 1770. Private Collection

The refined Richard Wilson (1714–1782), who was in Italy from about 1750 to 1756 where he met Joseph Vernet, interpreted the mountains of his native Wales through the honeyed light of Claude Lorrain whom he greatly admired, as did many of his contemporaries (pl. 489). George Stubbs (1724–1806) painted conversation-pieces, portraits, horse-portraits, animals and rural scenes with a cool, clear honesty (pl. 490). Born in Regensburg, the cosmopolitan Johann Zoffany (1733–1810), an anecdotal painter neo-Classical in style, is often classed with the English school because of the long periods he spent in London. Imported from Holland, the caricature developed in England in the eighteenth century; casually introduced by Hogarth, it was practised with great wit and as a genre of its own by Thomas Rowlandson (1756–1827). The miniature-portrait, which had reached such a high level in the Elizabethan period, had further success in the eighteenth century with Richard Cosway (1742–1821). Water-colour painting was practised as an independent genre by such landscape artists as Alexander Cozens (about 1715–1786), his son Robert Cozens (1752–1797), Thomas Girtin (1775–1802), and the caricaturist Rowlandson.

North America

The architecture of the British colonies in North America, generally referred to as 'Colonial' (pl. 491), had its beginnings in the austere wooden buildings of New England in the late seventeenth and early eighteenth

491 *House of the Washington Family, Mount Vernon (Virginia). Before 1743*

centuries. It was an architecture of necessity rather than luxury, replacing the first dwellings of the settlers, which were hardly more than rude shelters. The earliest frame houses in Massachusetts with their overhanging second stories and their construction combining both adobe and clapboard are derived from the middle class urban architecture of medieval England.

The Georgian architecture of the later Colonial period (1720–1790) was a style that admirably expressed the new prosperity and security of the colonists. Typical of the American imitations of the Georgian Palladian style in England are the Longfellow House in Cambridge, Massachusetts (1759) and 'Westover' in Virginia. These are only two of the distinguished examples of this American Baroque style which was followed in all the colonies. In ecclesiastical architecture the Wren style found its way to America in such building as Christ Church, Philadelphia (1766), and King's Chapel in Boston (1749). To this same style belong such famous buildings as Independence Hall in Philadelphia and Faneuil Hall in Boston.

The establishment of the Republic necessitated a monumental architecture to serve as a symbol of the new democracy and to house its multiple branches of government. One of the leading sponsors of architecture in the Federal period (1790–1820) was Thomas Jefferson (1734–1826), whose espousal of the forms of Roman architecture inaugurated the neo-Classical revival in the United States. The principal monuments to Jefferson and his theories are the Capitol at Richmond, the first temple building, inspired by the Maison Carrée at Nîmes, and the University of Virginia, a series of temple pavilions disposed on the plan of a village green, an arrangement anticipated in Joseph J. Ramée's design for Union College in Schenectady. In the first of these enterprises Jefferson was assisted by C. L. Clérisseau, the teacher of Robert Adam. The style of the Adam brothers was the inspiration for Samuel McIntyre (1757–1811) of Salem.

As late as 1800, owing to the limited economy of the Colonies as well as the Puritans' prejudice against idolatry and their regard for art as luxury, portraiture was the only accepted form of expression in painting. Like the architecture of the Colonial period, the portraits of the seventeenth and eighteenth centuries were reflections of various European manners ranging from a provincial prolongation of the work of Tudor limners to American imitations of the formulas of Lely and van Dyck. John Smibert (1688–1751) purveyed a wooden version of the seventeenth century Continental manner with an emphasis on likeness rather than grace. A certain elegance, with more flattering portraiture and attention to the richness of textures, made its appearance in the work of Robert Feke (1705–1750). His portraits, as well as those of Joseph Blackburn (1700–1765), reveal the same expression of luxury and refinement evident in the Georgian houses of the Tory aristocracy. The culmination of the Colonial style is found in the painting of John Singleton Copley (1737–1815). With what little training he was able to acquire from men like Blackburn, Copley devised a manner notable not only for the striking candor and conviction of characterization, but also for the magic realism in the precise delineation of textures that gives his portraits something of the precise, crystalline definition of still-life paintings. In their completely straight-forward, objective recording of the sitter's appearance, Copley's portraits are among the most American pictures ever painted. Benjamin West (1738–1820), often called the 'Father of American Painting', spent most of his mature career in London, where, thanks to his early indoctrination by Raphael Mengs and Sir Joshua Reynolds, he became one of the originators of neo-Classicism in historical painting. His importance resides more in his teaching of generations of American artists who for more than fifty years flocked to his London studio. Among West's pupils were John Trumbull (1756–1843), portraitist and painter of scenes of the Revolution, Charles Willson Peale (1741–1827), inventor, painter, and founder of the Pennsylvania Academy of Fine Arts, and Gilbert Stuart (1755–1828). Stuart, no less incisive than Copley in his ability to catch a telling likeness, brought to American art of the post-Revolutionary period his own version of the facile grace and ideality and the magnificent technical bravura of the best of the English eighteenth-century portraitists.

France

Architecture

Religious activity (Oratorians, Jesuits, and Order of the Visitation), the nobility's desire for display, the rise of a new parliamentary and administrative middle-class, private and royal initiative, and town-planning schemes all resulted in an enormous demand for new architecture in the seventeenth century. At the dawn of the century the Jesuits introduced their new type of aisleless church and Etienne Martellange (1569–1641)

492 Colonnade of the Louvre. After designs by Le Vau, Le Brun and Claude Perrault. Begun 1665

built many structures in this style (Le Puy, 1605; La Flèche, 1607; Avignon, 1617; St-Paul-St-Louis, Paris, 1627). This was the most generally used plan (Val-de-Grâce; church of the Sorbonne, etc.) but it did not completely replace the Gothic type with aisles and ambulatory (St-Sulpice, Paris). The plain decoration in all these churches was strictly functional; marble facings were confined to certain parts of the church, and until the eighteenth century these buildings reflected the sober outlook of the first Roman style of the Counter-Reformation. There was a heavy demand for lay buildings, 'châteaux' or large country-residences, and for 'hôtels' or large town-houses. The château, which followed the medieval closed-in design until about 1640, tended after that date to open on to the country-side and to cluster round a central building. The Louis XIV period found a pleasing design for town-houses, the hôtel built between a courtyard and a garden; the façade did not give aggressively on to the street as in Italy, but withdrew behind a surrounding wall pierced by a large gateway. In the eighteenth century, when the refinement of social life and taste for privacy led to rooms each having a specific function, architects found various elegant solutions for the problem of how to lay out and relate the different parts or wings. In the seventeenth century, pride of place in both château and hôtel was given to the *galerie* or hall (used for banquets, receptions and balls), a long room containing all the finest decorations and furnishings in the building; this was changed under Louis XV. The organic grouping of the main elements of a township round a central square, together with the regulation of traffic by building arterial thoroughfares, the siting of public buildings – in a word everything we now mean by town-planning – all this began in the early seventeenth century when Henry IV created the first 'royal square', laid out as a kind of royal monument, in the Place des Vosges (originally Place Royale) followed by the Place Dauphine. This feature persisted in Paris

493 Versailles. Palace and Park (aerial view)

under Louis XIV (Place Vendôme, Place des Victoires) and under
Louis XV (Place Louis XV now Place de la Concorde), after which it
was imitated all over France and spread into other countries.

Baroque decoration, derived from the ornamental Fontainebleau style
which tended to stifle classicism in Henry IV's reign, sat heavily on many
civic buildings in Louis XIII's reign (Hôtel Sully, Paris; Hôtel de Ville,
Lyon). Architecture was purified and decoration handled more rationally
after 1640 thanks to the classical outlook of Jacques Le Mercier (1585
–1654), responsible for the present Sorbonne; François Mansart (1598–
1666), the author of the church of the Val-de-Grâce in Paris and the
château of Maisons-Laffitte; and Louis Le Vau (1612–1670) who designed
for Fouquet, then superintendent of finance, Vaux-le-Vicomte, the forerunner of Versailles. André Le Nôtre (1613–1700) planned its gardens.

With the more personal rule of Louis XIV, activities tended to centre
on the king. A superintendent or minister of works (the first of whom
was Colbert) now supervised public enterprises, for which an official
architect (Jules Hardouin-Mansart) and a 'first painter' (Le Brun) produced designs. The founding of the Academy of Painting and Sculpture
in 1648, the French Academy at Rome in 1666, the Academy of Architecture in 1671 and the setting up of the Goblins furniture and tapestry factory in 1662, all served to tighten official control of the fine arts
through teaching, the dictatorship of the academies and centralized production.

Louis XIV first turned his attention to the dynastic palace of the
Louvre, whose enlargement was taken in hand, Claude Perrault constructing the façade of the Colonnade (pl. 492) to a team design. This masterpiece of French classicism, the Parthenon of French architecture, amounted to a protest against the Baroque style of Bernini whom Louis XIV had
invited to France to submit plans for its completion. But it was the more
personal undertaking at Versailles which ended by absorbing the finest

efforts of his reign (pl. 493). Versailles was begun in 1668 and finished in 1690, after plans made by Le Vau and subsequently Jules Hardouin-Mansart (1646–1708) the nephew of François Mansart, in a park which had been already laid out by Le Nôtre between 1661 and 1665. With the host of statues of characters from mythology, in the gardens, and its luxurious Galerie des Glaces, 239½ feet in length, its ceilings painted by Le Brun, its huge imposing apartments faced with marble, Versailles was intended as a kind of Olympian residence, set round the solar symbol of

494 Jules Hardouin-Mansart. Church of the Invalides, Paris. 1677–1701

Apollo and designed for the glorification of the king (pl. 515). The park was planned in what we now call the 'French garden' style, in which nature is arranged architecturally. The chequer-work of avenues based on a main vista or perspective enclose stretches of water and *broderie* or trimmed boxwood and little glades or open-air 'rooms' for all kinds of entertainment and containing architectural furnishings. Statues stand all over the park; great jets play in the fountains which, in repose, are called 'mirrors of water'. In the park, a short distance away from the palace, Louis XIV had a charming 'rest' house built by Mansart, the Grand Trianon which is in limestone and pink marble.

The monuments and gardens of Versailles were imitated all over

495 Nicolas Ledoux. Rotunda of La Villette, Paris. 1785–1789

Europe in the eighteenth century; in Italy (Caserta, Colorno), in Spain (Buen Retiro, la Granja, Royal Palace at Madrid), in Sweden and in Russia (around Leningrad), but such imitations were most numerous in Austria and Germany. As late as the nineteenth century Ludwig II of Bavaria had a replica of the Galerie des Glaces built into one of his castles.

496 Jacques-Ange Gabriel. Petit Trianon, Versailles. 1762

Jules Hardouin-Mansart was also responsible for the chapel at Versailles (1700–1710) which was finished by his nephew Robert de Cotte, and above all the church for the Invalides in Paris (1677, pl. 494), which has the most elegant dome built in the seventeenth century, in which the vertical movement is well related to the relative weights of the different stories.

In the eighteenth century external architecture offers an increasingly strong contrast with internal decoration and furnishing. In spite of one or two digressions towards the Rococo (such as the urban planning of Nancy by Boffrand and Héré) there was a more rational approach and the architect Jacques-François Blondel, in his famous book *L'Architecture française* (1752–1756) was justified in boasting of the classicism of the French school. Jacques-Ange Gabriel (1698–1792) summed up the national classicism in his works, deriving from Perrault's Louvre Colonnade (Place de la Bourse, Bordeaux, 1747; Place de la Concorde, Paris, 1754; Petit Trianon, Versailles, 1762, pl. 496). This trend developed further under Louis XVI, owing to the influence brought from Rome by Soufflot (1713 –1780) who was under the spell of St Peter's (Pantheon, Paris, 1764), while the most important factor was the archaeological tendency which, after the discoveries made in Greece, Tuscany and Herculaneum, led to an emulation of the pure Greek and Etruscan styles. Roman Corinthian was abandoned in favour of the Doric and Ionic of Greece, and the fashion was for severe, ungarnished walls (Brogniart, Chalgrin, Gondouin, Louis, Ledoux, pl. 495). This trend was further encouraged by English influence, resulting in Palladianism. But the 'anglomania' also acted in the opposite direction, driving out the classical French garden in favour of the meandering, rustic English garden with its romantic implications.

The interior decoration of rooms, since the sixteenth century, had consisted of wooden panels applied to the walls, except under Louis XIV when a certain amount of marble was used. During the Regency, with the growing fashion for small apartments, the style of decoration was based more on Rococo curves, a tendency towards elaborateness which increased under Louis XV and began to take asymmetrical forms. Two interior designers, Oppenordt (1672–1742) and Meissonier (1695–1750) specialized in this *rocaille* decoration which was supplanted in about 1760 by a return to the straight line. The vogue for neo-Greek brought in decorations with Pompeian arabesques in stucco or paint; but in spite of its Classical origins this type of decoration remained somewhat heavy.

Sculpture

French sculpture in the seventeenth century is a remarkable instance of French resistance to European Baroque. The statues in the park at Versailles, which match so well in their classical balance with the antique pieces, are in astonishing contrast with the violent movement of Le Brun's paintings in the Galerie des Glaces. Pierre Puget (1622–1694, pl. 497), who has been described as 'the French Michelangelo', is the exception proving the rule; for his work is easily explained by his Marseilles origins, his contacts with art-circles in Genoa and Rome, his training in ornamental art and as a decorator of the royal galleys. The sculptors of Louis XIII's reign, Simon Guillain, Jean Warin, Jacques Sarrazin (1588–1660), Gilles Guérin, the Anguier brothers, have a slightly rough, realistic honesty in the tradition of Germain Pilon. The classicism of Antoine Coysevox (1640–1720) and François Girardon (1628–1715) and of the Versailles sculptors goes back, rather, to the elegant idealism of Jean Goujon. In *Apollo and the Nymphs of Thetis* (pl. 498), it is remarkable how Girardon, reaching back across the centuries, rediscovered that grace and power of gesture which so perfectly suggests the god's grandeur on the pediment of Olympia. Some of Girardon's statues are the nearest to Phidias that have been made in the West; with him, French sculpture turned back to the ancient Greek plastic code at the very height of its Roman Baroque phase. Antoine Coyse-

497 *Pierre Puget. Milo of Crotona. 1671–1682. Paris*

498 Girardon and
Renaudin. Apollo
and the Nymphs
of Thetis.
1665–1677
Versailles

vox (1640–1720) made some admirable portraits of the great men of
his time, in busts whose heroic dignity in no way detracts from the
sitter's personality (pl. 499). French sculpture in the seventeenth century
also produced a fine funerary art whose subdued reserve is in marked
contrast with the pompousness of Roman tombs.

Even more remarkable is the continuity of this classical tradition in
the eighteenth century, in spite of the steady infiltration of the Baroque
aesthetic. The brothers Nicolas and Guillaume Coustou (*The Horses of
Marly*, 1740–1747) and Robert Le Lorrain (1666–1743), were of a
distinguished line of Versailles sculptors. In Louis XV's reign Jean-
Baptiste Lemoyne (1704–1778), the brothers Sloditz and Adam and later
the portraitist Jean-Jacques Caffieri (1725–1791), were drawn by the

499 Antoine Coysevox. Bronze
Bust of the Grand Condé 1688.
Paris

500 Jean-Antoine Houdon.
Terra-cotta Bust of
Alexander Brongniart.
1777. Paris

sinuous grace of the Rococo, but Edme Bouchardon (1698–1762) rebuffed it with his deliberate classicism, which is somewhat cold and academic. Jean-Baptiste Pigalle (1714–1785, pl. 421) wavered between the two tendencies, but Jean-Antoine Houdon (1741–1824, pl. 500), the greatest sculptor of the century, who proved himself with his *Diana* to be in the direct line of descent from Jean Goujon, and whose terra-cottas are quivering with life, turned resolutely towards classicism. In the Louis XVI period, the neo-Classical purge led to an elegant formalism, with a touch of insipidness which was heightened by the Pompeian influence in Falconet (1716–1791), Pajou (1733–1809) and Julien Vassé (1716–1772). Clodion (1738–1814) popularized this form of art in his statuettes.

One of the finest themes of French sculpture in the seventeenth and eighteenth centuries was the royal statue, impressive equestrian images of the king of which all the numerous examples were unfortunately destroyed during the Revolution.

Painting

The seventeenth century saw the beginning of a state of things peculiar to French painting, when creative artists were driven into isolation by an 'official' art, with decorative and academic tendencies, amounting to a closed 'school'. The official style was created by Simon Vouet (1590–1647). Returning from a long stay in Rome in 1627, to find French painting still given to Mannerism, Vouet introduced the outsize mythological or religious painting in the Bolognese style. Jacques Blanchard

501 Poussin. Landscape with Orpheus and Eurydice. About 1655. Paris

502 Claude. Seaport: The Embarkation of the Queen of Sheba. 1648. London

and Laurent de la Hire at once absorbed this style, while François Perrier and Claude Vignon remained faithful to Mannerism. Eustache Le Sueur (1617–1655) went more directly to Raphael and Pietro da Cortona. In the reign of Louis XIV the taste for order and hierarchy made people see painting as an art governed by a set of rules and precepts, as taught by the Academy of Painting and Sculpture, founded in 1648 and officially recognized in 1663. Moreover, architecture now dominated the other arts, so that painting had to be content to play a decorative rôle. Charles Le Brun (1619–1690) was a pupil of Vouet, and after a stay in Rome from 1642 until 1645 he became practically a dictator over the arts during the reign of Louis XIV (pl. 514, 515). With an astonishingly large output, Le Brun took in hand all sorts of projects in architecture, furnishing, tapestry and sculpture; he organized the pompous, gala background which Louis XIV wanted as a setting for his glory. His great painted work is the ceiling of the Galerie des Glaces at Versailles, which he began in 1679. His loud, long-winded art is the nearest thing to the rhetoric of the Carracci to be found in France. A distinguished group of decorators gathered round him. Pierre Mignard (1612–1695), Le Brun's rival who succeeded him as the official painter, was also a follower of the Bolognese school. At the close of the reign Hyacinthe Rigaud (1659–1743) and Nicolas de Largillièrre (1656–1746) created a type of ceremonial portrait in keeping with the aesthetic and ethical outlook of the period, for which

the example was set by the king himself. Majestically clad in his courtier's uniform, the model is portrayed in all the symbols of his social status, appearing quite satisfied with the transfer of personality thus brought about (pl. 418).

The creative vein of French painting, apart from the 'schools' is to be found among artists who for the most part passed their lives in isolation, untouched by official developments. They all belong to the reign of Louis XIII. Two streams stand out in this very fertile class of artists; the classical and the realistic. The two great artists who created the French classical tradition in painting, Poussin and Claude Lorrain, spent their lives in Rome, far from the pomp and circumstance of the court, and equally aloof from the ostentatious style imposed on it by Bernini. They both pursued the mirage of antiquity, in Rome. Nicolas Poussin (1584 –1665) passed beyond Bolognese Baroque and was in the direct line of Italian classicism: Titian's generous humanism dominated his first Roman period (*Bacchanales; The Kingdom of Flora,* formerly Dresden); then

504 *Philippe de
Champaigne.
Mother Catherine
Agnès and Sister
Catherine de
Sainte-Suzanne
at Prayer
(L'Ex-Voto).
Paris*

505 Watteau. Love-Feast. About 1718. Dresden

Raphael gave him a more intellectual conception of his art so that his strictly-calculated compositions, in which form is the servant of the idea, are governed by the meaning of the subject (the *Seven Sacraments* series; *The Israelites gathering Manna in the Wilderness,* Louvre). Just when his art might have been spoiled by an overdose of rationalism, Poussin's love of nature came to his aid. From 1648 onward landscape took an increasingly important place in his work. He defined the ideal of classical landscape, which reduces the infinite complexity of the world to an intellectual unity, and humanized nature by associating it intimately with some moral theme, whether it be religious *(St Matthew and the Angel),* historical *(The Burial of Phocion),* philosophical *(Diogenes),* mythological *(Polyphemus)* or poetic *(Orpheus and Eurydice,* pl. 501).

The art of Claude Gelée, called Lorrain (1600–1682), who painted nothing but landscapes, sprang from that of the Northern painters established in Rome, the German Elsheimer and the Fleming Paul Bril, who were the first to work out the aesthetic of landscape composition. Claude's keen sensitiveness to nature expressed itself in wash-drawings. But for him nature was a human theme, a source of revery, just as for Poussin it was a matter for meditation. A native of the misty northern province of Lorraine, Claude was entranced by the diffusion of light in space, but satisfied himself with opening a window on to eternity in his paintings of ports, in which imposing buildings serve as a colonnade to the sea, which is tinted with the rays of dawn or sunset (pl. 502).

Other seventeenth-century artists revived the native realist tradition, interpreting the world as a source of human emotion. The revolution carried out by Caravaggio helped French art to rediscover its deep interest in the common people that had already been evident in the Middle Ages, seeing them as the vital source of the great elemental powers of the soul. The Lorraine painter Georges de La Tour (1593–1652) took directly from Caravaggio his passion for night-pieces and his way of interpreting biblical scenes through peasant characters; he painted ascetic canvases of deep mystical significance (pl. 419). The Le Nain brothers (Antoine, 1588–1648, Louis, 1593–1648 and Mathieu, 1607–1677) portrayed peasant life with a serious and almost priestly simplicity (pl. 503). This lofty sense of human dignity also permeates the work of a painter of Flemish origin, Philippe de Champaigne (1602–1674), who in spite of being a portraitist at Louis XIII's court, was unaffected by the official style and left some thoughtful studies of Jansenists (pl. 504).

An important evolution in taste is to be seen at the end of the seventeenth century. People were tiring of cerebral works and of an ideal beauty as defined by the Academy of Painting and Sculpture. This change took shape in the quarrel between the 'Poussinists' who favoured intellectual painting and the primacy of drawing over colour, and the 'Rubenists' who defended colour and sensual painting. The latter tendency triumphed after Mignard's death, when the lavish, brightly-coloured painting of Largillièrre – who was brought up in Antwerp – went straight

506 Nicolas de Largillière. Mlle. Duclos of the Comédie-Française as Ariadne. Chantilly

507 Fragonard. Fantasy Portrait (l'Abbé de Saint-Non). Paris

508 Boucher. The Sleeping Shepherdess. About 1755. Paris

back to Rubens, in the same way as Rigault's. The Rubens' Medici Gallery
in the Luxembourg was to play the part that hitherto belonged to the
Carracci's Farnese Gallery.

The intellectual work of the seventeenth century was followed, through
Antoine Watteau, a native of Valenciennes (1684–1721), by an art of
sensibility, addressed to the heart, more like sketching than painting, in
which a mood is evoked by a suggestive setting. He began by painting
small military scenes in the Dutch manner (*The Bivouac,* Leningrad). It
was no doubt Gillot who gave him his taste for scenes from the Comedia
dell'Arte when the Italian players, after Louis XIV's ban, reappeared in
Paris in 1716 (*Il Mezzetino,* Metropolitan Museum, New York; *Pierrot
and Columbine, Gilles,* both Louvre). But his fame was made particularly
by his *fêtes galantes* or pastorals, pictures with no defined subject, which
show lovers idling in a landscape – a sentimental theme which Rubens
had seen as a possible genre towards the end of his life (pl. 505).

It becomes more difficult to follow the two streams we have mentioned, in the later eighteenth century, when all painting tended more or
less towards decoration. Having lost sight of the intellectual mission
entrusted to it in the seventeenth century, painting now had little to aim
at but pleasure. Its job was to provide a pleasant background for existence. Two traditions may be seen in decorative painting, the first deriv-

509 Greuze. The Father's Curse. 1778. Paris

ing from Watteau, and the second from Italy While Watteau's immediate pupils Jean-Baptiste Pater (1696–1736) and Nicolas Lancret (1690–1745) made *fêtes galantes* with decorative themes, to set in woodwork panelling the tradition of painting for effects in the Italian manner was carried on by Jean-François de Troy (1679-1752), François Lemoyne (1688-1737), Charles Coypel (1694–1752) and especially François Boucher (1703–1770, pl. 508), but they treated history on a romantic level influenced by opera, and in a style that was overlaid with the mannered flourishes of Rococo. The portrait also indulged in this *galant* eroticism with Nicolas de Largillièrre (1656–1746, pl. 506) and Jean-Marc Nattier (1685–1766) who was the first to travesty themes from mythology for the benefit of his models; Diana, and Hebe the goddess of youth were the most frequent vehicles of his flattering symbolism. Honoré Fragonard (1762–1806) elegantly blended the influence of Tiepolo, Pietro da Cortona, Rubens and Rembrandt. He was the most gifted artist to exploit the *galant* manner and was beyond doubt the painter most characteristic of his century, of which he had all the happy-go-lucky optimism, the frivolous tastes, the erotic sensibility, the spontaneous fancy, the versatility, the variety of gifts, the lack of purpose, the charm, and the

510 Jean-Baptiste Oudry. Wolf-Hunt in the Forest. 1748. Nantes

511 Chardin. Still-Life. Paris

innate and refined breeding (pl. 507). Jean-Baptiste Greuze (1725–1805) was a very talented artist led astray by literature; he created an unsatisfactory type of composition which combined the *galant* erotic outlook with would-be edifying but sentimental intentions which he took from Rousseau and Diderot (pl. 509).

Fortunately the Northern schools infused sincerer feelings into French art. François Desportes (1661–1743) and Jean-Baptiste Oudry (1686–1755) were primarily decorative painters, the inventors of decorative still-lifes and hunting-scenes, but they showed a refreshing honesty in their protrayal of animals, as well as objects and landscapes (pl. 510). Trained as he was in the Dutch school, Jean-Baptiste Chardin (1699–1779) represents the strongest protest of the native French character against the elegant frivolity of the time. Like the Le Nain brothers he sought his inspiration in the rich life of the common people, in such homely scenes as *La Bénédicité* (*Grace before Meat,* Louvre) and *La Pourvoyeuse* (*The Return from Market,* Louvre); while in his still-lifes he painted commonplace things in everyday use, with the same restrained emotion as his scenes from domestic life (pl. 511). His grainy texture, with the paint laid on generously but never with the full brush, makes him one of the most impressive technical masters of painting. The realism of

Maurice Quentin de La Tour (1704 –1788), who worked in pastel, goes back through Robert de Nanteuil (1625–1678) to the psychological tradition of Clouet; there is something of Voltaire's critical outlook in his acute analysis (pl. 512). Mme Vigée-Lebrun (1755–1842) was to introduce both naturalness and the neo-Classical style into portraiture.

Landscape, which was composed like an operatic setting during Louis XV's reign, came closer to a sincere expression of nature under Louis XVI. Hubert Robert (1733 –1808) specialized in the painting of ruins, but many of his studies show a gift for observing the

512 Maurice Quentin de La Tour. Self-Portrait. Pastel. 1751. Amiens

picturesque (pl. 513). Louis-Gabriel Moreau (1740–1806) painted park-scenes which already had a Romantic flavour about them.

All these artists had a following of imitators and plagiarists – such a plethora of talents being characteristic of any civilization in its last stages.

At the end of the eighteenth century there was a strong reaction both in the moral and plastic sense against the *galant* academicism that Boucher had imposed. The reviving taste for classical composition, the idealistic conception of the beautiful and works of pure intellect, brought back Bolognese influence as well as Poussin's, resulting in a fresh wave of Greco-Roman influence which was stimulated by the discovery of Herculaneum and Pompeii. This tendency can be seen in Callet (1741

513 Hubert Robert. View of the Parc de Méréville. Paris

–1823), Vien (1716–1809), Vincent (1746–1816) and Suvée (1743–1807): it produced David's *Oath of the Horatii* which was practically the manifesto of a new art (pl. 524).

The Minor Arts

The minor arts assumed considerable importance in the seventeenth and eighteenth centuries, as a result of the refinement of social and private life which created a demand for furnishings. As France had shown Europe the way in perfecting the 'art of living', it is not surprising that the types of furnishings created in eighteenth-century France were imitated abroad.

The founding of the Manufacture royale des meubles de la Couronne – the Goblins – in 1662 was a determining factor in the success of French furnishings (pl. 514). The Manufacture de la Savonnerie, set up in 1604, specialized in making carpets, while the Beauvais factory, dating from 1664, made small-scale tapestries (in *petit-point*) which were often used for covering chairs.

In France the lavish decoration of interiors contrasted with the simplicity of the architecture. Rooms were covered with painted panelling and adorned with carvings and gilt. In the Regency period the large rooms and halls which still prevailed under Louis XIV were no longer fashionable, and apartments tended to be divided into smaller rooms (*pièces*) each of which was used for some special domestic or social activ-

514 Louis XIV visiting the Goblins Factory. Tapestry from the Histoire du Roi Series after Cartoons by Charles Le Brun

518 *Fauteuil cabriolet. Louis XV Style. Paris*

519 *Andrea Brustolon. Venetian Armchair. 18th c. Milan*

output of French porcelain from the various provincial potteries (Rouen, Nevers, Moustiers, Marseilles, Strassburg). The finest ceramics in England were those of Josiah Wedgwood, who at the Etruria factory set up in Staffordshire in 1768, made pieces in the neo-Classical style and even close imitations of the Greek. It was in Saxony in 1709 that it was first discovered how to make hard-paste porcelain in the Chinese manner, by using kaolin. The Meissen factory, which was at once set up by the Elector Frederick Augustus I, turned out luxurious table-ware and ornamental pieces in the Rococo style. Several other potteries were founded in Germany where the new process was exploited. France was

520 *Salon in the Archbishop's Palace, Bordeaux. Louis XV Style*

521 Salon in the Hôtel Necker, Geneva. Louis XVI Style

only able to produced hard-paste porcelain after 1769, when kaolin was discovered at Saint-Yriex (Limousin). The Sèvres factory dates from 1753. Portugal used ceramics for mural decorations; at first it was in polychrome, but in the eighteenth century it was confined to blue, as a result of which the tiles became known as *azulejos*.

The styles of the decorative arts in France under the *Ancien Régime* have been divided according to the various reigns from Louis XIII to the Revolution, but such a rough-and-ready classification is deceptive. The Regency style goes back to 1700, while the Louis XVI style dates from about 1755, long before the death of Louis XV in 1774. The sober and gloomy Louis XIII furniture reflects the architectural outlook of the sixteenth century. Louis XIV furniture was relieved by Baroque decorations set off with gilding, but never lost its stiff design. The Regency style, which was no more than the second phase of the Louis XIV style, adopted the shell-shaped ornamentation called *rocaille,* and curved outlines. Sinuosity of line and the use of asymmetrical *rocaille* both became more pronounced in the Louis XV style (pl. 520). This style produced a chair, the *fauteuil cabriolet* (armchair with cabriole legs, pl. 518) which was

522 Delft-ware Plate with Chinese Decoration. Paris

391

admirably suited for all the psychological and material uses required of a chair, and it is a masterpiece of refinement and civilization. The period as a whole, of which the tone was set by Mme de Pompadour, was the moment when French decoration most lent itself to the flowing gracefulness of the *rocaille,* a taste strengthened by Chinese influence, which was also responsible for the fashion for lacquered and highly-polished furniture.

The reaction against Rococo began to be felt in 1755, when the engraver Cochin, who had been to Italy in 1749, published his *Supplication aux orfèvres-ciseleurs et sculpteurs sur bois* in which he exhorted goldsmiths and wood-carvers to give up their 'excess of twisted, extravagant patterns' and to return to the straight line. The Marquis de Marigny, who supervised the arts between 1751 and 1773, helped Cochin's ideas to prevail. Furniture, like interior decoration, returned to the straight line (pl. 521) sometimes at the expense of functional logic. Interiors began to take fluted pilasters and pediments from external architecture, and arabesque decorations in imitation of those unearthed at Herculaneum and Pompeii became all the fashion. The return to the straight line, for all that, did not mean a return to simplicity; under Louis XVI both decorations and furniture remained fairly ornamental, and it was the so-called 'Directoire' style, after the *Ancien Régime,* which brought with it a crisis of puritanism.

Intent on the scientific mastery of the forces of nature, the modern world
has seen a slackening of that impressive creative tension which, from its
early beginnings, had led Western civilization to seek a representation of
the world in works of art. However, acting as heir to a Europe which
found itself suddenly without a single major talent, France still managed
to rear a school of painting which in the course of the century was to
produce great masters worthy of those of the past. These men, whom we
now grant a foremost place in history, and who for the most part were
despised by their contemporaries, help us to forget the horde of medio-
crities who were showered with official honours and awards during their
brief period of fame, and in whom an upstart, self-satisfied society found
a comforting reflection of its own worthlessness. A handful of geniuses
gave our common heritage of art many a significant utterance that can
be placed beside the great literary works of the century; but the medio-
crities were none the less the true expression of their age. The now forgotten architects, sculptors, painters and decorative artists showed general
tendencies which together made a 'style', and that style was international.
Delacroix, Courbet, Manet, Gauguin had no parallel in the rest of Europe.
But Paul Delaroche of Paris, Karl von Piloty of Munich, Louis Galliat
of Brussels, and Alexander Ivanov in Russia were 'brother geniuses'; a
common conception of history is to be found in the French Horace
Vernet, the German Alfred Rethel, or Nicaise de Keyser of Antwerp,
all of whom painted battle-scenes. It was such artists as these, bolstered
up by society, who together formed a school cutting across all national
frontiers: Horace Vernet had his imitators in Belgium, while the Lyons
school of religious decorators was inspired by the German Nazarenes.

This international unity had its source in a common point of departure,
the neo-Classicism which resulted between 1750 and 1800 from the con-
verging efforts of all the schools in Europe. Western civilization, whenever it passes through a crisis, always looks for salvation towards its
mother-civilization, that is to say Classical antiquity. That is what happened in the Carolingian period, when the Emperor's initiative sought
to put an end to the anarchy of the barbarians; it occurred again in the
Quattrocento, when Italy had prepared the way for a new culture which
she was about to offer the world in place of the declining Gothic. But Bramante's and Raphael's classicism, which emerged from that effort, was
at once thwarted by the unexpected triumph of the Baroque aesthetic.
This time, it was France and England that were to cling to classicism. In
about 1750, the English, French, Germans and Italians, in their wish to
avoid the blind alley into which Rococo was leading, saw no choice but
to appeal to that Classical art which is ever the stand-by of the Western

aesthetic. The discovery of Etruscan, Campanian and Greek sites revealed far purer models than were to be found in Roman art. England, encouraged by its own Palladian tastes, gave Europe the lead in its intuitional desire for an Attic architecture. The representational arts began to seek their principles in ancient statuary and painting. If it is true that David was forestalled by a few English academicians, he gave these aspirations a dignity of forms which at once caught the imagination of the whole of Europe.

David, who swept away all the theatrical trappings in which antiquity had been smothered for two hundred years, replacing them by the genuine costumes and settings of Greece and Rome, holds a place in painting not unlike Mantegna's, who threw aside the medieval coats of mail used for representing Roman emperors and gave them the *laurica* and the *paludamentum*. David gave a final form to the aesthetic which was to rule over Europe and the official French school throughout the century: the superiority of line and volume over colour, and of thought over sensation. The picture, whose arrangement was dictated by intellectual data, by subject, was thought of as a painted bas-relief, while cold tones without any modulation of colour-scale were used to stress the statuesque effect. Whereas David's art tends to give the illusion of volume, that of his pupil Ingres, inspired by the Grecian vase, flattened its shapes to suggest all the gracefulness of the arabesque.

Meanwhile, at the very time when Ingres was creating his linear style, a few German painters in Rome in 1810 grouped themselves together under the name of Nazarenes, in the monastery of S. Isidoro. They were after a fresh aesthetic formula which they sought not in the ancients but in the early Renaissance. Deceived by the apparent smoothness of Perugino's and Raphael's early work, their mystical enthusiasm led them to adopt the form and composition of these masters, so as to create – no doubt without realizing it – a new academicism inspired by the platitudes of fresco painting. This movement had repercussions all over Europe; signs of it can still be seen in the Paris churches. Thirty years later a group of English painters renewed this aesthetic, which they called 'pre-Raphaelitism' and injected it with a certain amount of realism.

The neo-Classical aesthetic, which resulted from the enthusiasm stirred up by the rediscovery of Greek art, together with the intention of counteracting Rococo, unfortunately found itself quite out of key with the general evolution of thought and sensibility which was urging the West to discover a new form of human consciousness in the shape of Romanticism. Temperamentally uneasy, the artists of the period found themselves being offered sculpture as their model; while they felt inclined to convey the passions through art, they were offered an idealistic aesthetic; at a moment when they were interested in the Middle Ages, they were asked to shape everything according to Classical patterns. A great confusion came out of all these clashes. The first generation of Romantic

523 *Karl Friedrich Schinkel. The Guard-House, Berlin. 1816*

artists, whom we might call the 'pre-Romantics', were armed with a brand-new neo-Classical technique and wore themselves out in their efforts to make statues gesticulate or dream (pl. 528, 529). Such was William Blake (1757–1827), who was haunted by Dante, Milton and Michelangelo, and his friend the Anglo-Swiss painter Henry Fuseli (1741 –1828), whose inspiration was related to Goya's but who was racked in the strait-jacket of neo-Classicism from which Goya alone of that generation was able to break loose, creating a romantic technique which, incidentally, had no future. In France, Prud'hon (1758–1823) got round the difficulty by swamping his statues in shade, while Girodet (1767– 1824) tried to blend the inspiration of Ossian and Chateaubriand with David's heroic style. In Germany Philipp Otto Runge (1777–1810) tightened his line and modelling and forced his colour in his attempts to wring a human note from the frozen style.

A technique at all suitable for the Romantic outlook could only be found by turning to the Venetian school, which had used colour for its emotional value; or more especially to Rubens, a painter who was despised by the academies. It was in David's very studio that a man of genius, Gros, rediscovered that forgotten language, which he used side by side with the Davidian principles of bas-relief composition. Two artists who came to the fore in 1820, Géricault and Delacroix, added the English element to the example given by Gros. Géricault still saw his painting with a sculptor's eye, but Delacroix rediscovered the principles of sym-

phonic and spatial painting common to Tintoretto, Veronese and Rubens; this was the true Romantic plastic code, though apart from a few minor artists who imitated Delacroix without understanding him, it found no serious following. The development of Romanticism was thwarted at the outset, not by any doctrinal dictatorship, but by the banalities of Realism. Realism pandered to the lazy imagination of the middle class, by making art a means of reproducing the material world which was all they cared

525 Romanticism. Delacroix. Death of Sardanapalus. Salon of 1827. Paris

526 *Realism.*
Courbet. The
Painter's Studio
(detail). Salon
of 1855. Paris

about; between 1830 and 1850 it contaminated both neo-Classicism and Romanticism to produce in architecture, painting and all the ornamental crafts a sort of utilitarian art which the French called 'Louis-Philippe' and the Germans 'Biedermeier' – an art for shopkeepers. Thanks to this impure aesthetic born of the uneasy alliance between neo-Classicism and Realism, romantic subjects found favour with the public. This was the art turned out in France by Paul Delaroche, Louis Boulanger, Horace Vernet, Ary Scheffer; in Germany by the Düsseldorf school; in Belgium by Louis Gallait, Gustave Wappers, Nicaise de Keyser, while in Brussels, Antoine Wiertz, who thought he was a new Michelangelo, merely proved his incapacity for creating a technique at all equal to his pretensions. Meissonier in France and Henri de Brakelaer in Belgium amused

527 *Impressionism.*
Manet. Le
Déjeuner sur
l'herbe. Salon
des Refusés,
1863. Paris

The Pre-Romantics

528 Goya. The Sleep of Reason   529 Fuseli. The Nightmare. About 1782.
   gives birth to Monsters   Basle
   (Capricho 43). 1792. Madrid

the bourgeoisie with a lifelikeness which, when applied to the past, revived genre painting.

This paradoxical state of things explains why in France, the only country where artists had enough genius to rise above the prevailing mediocrity, creative ability could only make itself felt by revolutionary tactics. The repeated failures of the official humbugs of art merely strengthened their resistance, so that Impressionism found it even harder to achieve recognition than Romanticism and Realism had done.

Four major movements show the continuity of French genius in the course of the nineteenth century: neo-Classicism, Romanticism, Realism (which might better be called Naturalism) and Impressionism. Although they sprang from a series of reactions the one against the other, seen historically they amount to a continuous evolution, leading from fiction to nature, from the 'intellectual construction' to the 'record of sensations', from an ideal beauty to the observed fact. Landscape, which invaded painting more and more to the point of becoming its chief end, had not such serious obstacles to face as subject-painting. Fortunately, antiquity could offer no ready-made models for landscape-painters to imitate, though to make up for it they were urged to copy Poussin. But while reducing nature to a dictionary of forms, neo-Poussinism did not forbid its direct study, and this outlet enabled Corot to develop from the neo-Classical stem. The landscape-painters, freed from the tyranny of the

bas-relief, were able to find a technique suitable for Romantic expressionism, while taking lessons in craftsmanship from the Dutch school; this
line was pursued independently by two contemporaries, the Englishman
John Crome (born 1768) and Frenchman Georges Michel (born 1763). In
France the '1830' or Barbizon school following this neo-Dutch tradition,
conveyed the infiniteness of nature in the loneliness of forests, the organic
strength of trees, the solidity of the land. The intensive use of water-
colour enabled the English school to discover means of translating light
and atmospheric values. John Constable enriched the palette, while Turner wavered between a visionary art in the Romantic manner, and the
pure expression of optical sensations – the path which Impressionism
was to follow in France.

Impressionism inherited all the technical researches of the century, and
found in *peinture claire* (abolishing black and brown and painting on a
white canvas) the technique that had been so desperately sought after; no
more line, no more volume, nothing but the direct message of pure colour.
Impressionism was a belated victory of painting over bas-relief. Created
by Manet and Claude Monet, and enthusiastically taken up by many
artists who form a genuine group, a school, their technique was to serve
the purpose of the different aesthetics which emerged towards the end
of the century. While Puvis de Chavannes tried to revive classicism by
giving it a symbolic value, the nineteenth century closed in an apotheosis
of light and colour, blessed with that profusion of talents which is always
a sure sign of the triumph of a genuine mode of expression.

1. ART IN FRANCE

Architecture and Sculpture

The nineteenth century discovered no form of architecture to call its
own. Until 1850 France followed the austere neo-Classical manner developed at the end of the eighteenth century by Brongniart, Chalgrin and
Ledoux. Percier and Fontaine created the Empire style which was a
majestic version of the Louis XVI style, but the latter showed itself
mainly in the decorative and furnishing arts. The shortness of Napoleon's
reign and the protracted wars prevented the great schemes that were drawn
up for Paris from being completed: all that was carried out were the Arc
de Triomphe du Carrousel, the Bourse and the Colonne Vendôme. The rue
de Rivoli, the Madeleine (a copy of the Corinthian temple-form, at first
intended as a 'temple of glory'), and the Arc de Triomphe de l'Etoile
were only finished under the Restoration and the July Monarchy. All
these works are marked by a taste for the colossal. During the Restoration
and Louis-Philippe's reign, the neo-Classical style underlined its native

530 *Charles Garnier. Staircase of the Opéra, Paris. 1860–1875*

soberness to the point of poverty. Napoleon III gave up neo-Greek austerity in favour of a pompous style more or less inspired by Versailles, corresponding with the lavish tastes of the Second Empire bourgeoisie. Paris was replanned by Baron Haussmann, who drove great thoroughfares through the old city and set up public buildings which are unfortunately in the worst of taste. The main undertaking under Napoleon III were the completion of the Louvre, entrusted to Visconti and Lefuel, and the Opéra (1860–1875, pl. 530) by Charles Garnier (1825–1898), a theatre glittering with paint, marble and gilt. Towards 1890 the taste for the baroque which was making itself felt under all this exaggeration was frankly admitted in the so-called 'Art Nouveau' style, a strange but short-lived revival of the plant-form ornamentation of Flamboyant Gothic. Under the influence of Viollet-le-Duc (1814–1879), Gothic architecture came into fashion again for church building under the Second Empire. The study of the principles of architecture encouraged the fashion for steel-construction, not only in civil engineering but in architecture.

531 *Françoise Rude. The Volunteers of 1792 (La Marseillaise, detail). Relief on the Arc de Triomphe de l'Etoile, Paris. 1832–1834*

532 *Jean-Baptiste Carpeaux. Bust of Mlle Fiacre. Paris*

XIII Claude Monet. Fields in the Spring. Stuttgart

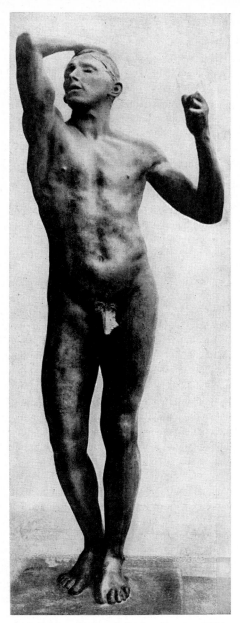

533 Rodin. *L'Age d'Airain. Bronze. 1876*

Sculpture suffered throughout the century from its submission to antiquity. The Empire and Restoration sculptors Bosio, Lemot, Cortot, were competent decorators. François Rude (1784–1855), whose masterpiece was the *Departure of the Volunteers of 1792* (*La Marseillaise,* pl. 531) on the Arc de Triomphe, Place de l'Etoile, founded an heroic and monumental style, corresponding in sculpture to what Gros did for painting, but he did not found a school. David d'Angers (1788–1856) was a portrait-sculptor, romantic in intention but not in form. It was by abandoning academic models and studying animals at first hand that Barye (1796–1875) found a fresh vigour yet without breaking the laws of classical modelling. However, it was Carpeaux (1827–1875), preceded by the experiments in modelling made by the painter and lithographer Daumier (1808–1879) who freed sculpture from the static convention and sought effects of fluidity, movement and life directly observed from nature (pl. 532). The century at last found its Romantic expressionism in the neo-Baroque of Auguste Rodin (1840–1917), whose feverish art, tormented by grandiose conceptions, has left works of rhetoric which are not suitable for monumental expression (pl. 533). Right through the century a host of sculptors who carried out hundreds of public monuments, followed the neo-Classical aesthetic with as little hesitation as they had ability. The least mediocre of them was perhaps Pradier (1790–1852).

Painting

Painting alone escaped the general bankruptcy, partly because it lends itself to individual expression, whereas architecture and sculpture are fundamentally public, social arts. The neo-Classical school represented by Ingres, David and their dull but over-plentiful following still thought of painting as being subordinate to its decorative function. It submitted all the elements of the picture to a hierarchy dictated by the intellect and immobilized it through a coldness of form allowing no freedom of interpretation. The Romantics freed painting from these shackles, and in the hands of a few artists down the century, painting was entrusted with all the secrets of the human heart and became a means of exploring the mysteries of nature.

A convert to Bonapartism, the revolutionary and regicide Louis David (1748–1825) sought in contemporary events (*Crowning of Napoleon,* Louvre, 1807; *Distribution of Eagles,* Versailles, 1810) subjects well adapted to the heroic style based on antique sculpture, which he perfected with the *Oath of the Horatii* (1784, pl. 524) and the *Rape of the Sabines* (1799). His capacity for objectiveness, his noble conception of the human form, make him one of the greatest portraitists of the French school (pl. 534). He developed a sober and sound craftmanship, painting in pure colours in well-blended *demi-pâtes* which leave no trace of the

brush-stroke, yet without freezing his colours like his pupils or imitators such as Vincent, Régnault, Girodet, Gérard, Guérin. Pierre-Paul Prud'hon (1758–1823) had a contrast of lights and shades which helped him to link neo-Classicism with the elegaic romantic manner of the eighteenth century.

In the second quarter of the century the champion of ideal beauty was Jean-Dominique Ingres (1780–1867), a pupil of David, who, however, spent a period in Italy from 1806 to 1824 where the influence of Raphael and Greek vases overcame his leaning towards antique statuary, so that he came to prefer the arabesque to volume. Lacking David's sense of the

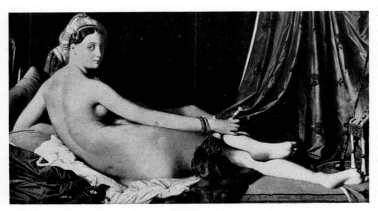

536 Ingres. Reclining Odalisque. Salon of 1819. Paris

heroic, Ingres had a very mediocre imagination and so his large compositions are cold and empty (*Vow of Louis XIII*, Montauban, 1824; *Apotheosis of Homer*, Louvre, 1827; *Martyrdom of St Symphorian*, Autun,
1834). With a longing for harmony that was instinctive rather than
intellectual, he achieved it empirically by making a laborious selection
of the features provided by his model: his best works are his smaller and
more limited canvases – his portraits, his nudes (pl. 536) and his admirable
drawings (pl. 535). Ingres, who was director of the French Academy at
Rome from 1834 to 1841 had a sterilizing influence on official art. He
was responsible for a second-rate line of decorative painters, of whom the
most representative was Hippolyte Flandrin (1809–1864) of Lyons. However, officialdom and public taste also favoured those painters who
sought to hide their meagre imagination in an uninspired Realism, such
as Horace Vernet (1789–1863) who filled the museum at Versailles with
acres of battle-scenes, or the genre-painter Meissonier (1815–1890). Paul

*539 Delacroix. Study for Liberty
guiding the People. Drawing. Paris*

540 Corot. The Studio. Paris

Delaroche (1797–1856) tried to give Classical atmosphere to his historical
realism. Thomas Couture (1815–1879) reacted against this decadence by
taking some of his stylistic principles from the Bologna school and
Veronese, and it was he who set the tone for the Second Empire decorators.

The classicist idea of nature as something to be arranged and moral-
ized about like a theatrical setting, was maintained till about 1850 by a
series of official painters (Bertin and Bidault, for instance). Jean-Baptiste-
Camille Corot (1796–1874) followed the system of composing landscapes
in the studio, all his life; but he was the only one of the classical school
to make anything worth while of his outdoor studies. In his wanderings
across Italy and France, he painted the abiding essence of the land civilized by man's presence, which can be felt in the slightest idiosyncrasy,
every tree or path having a human rather than a haphazard, natural,
significance. His poetic sensitiveness is seen in the increasing emphasis
given to pictures containing figures, which became pretexts for revery
and feeling (pl. 540).

The origin of Romantic paintings is to be found in Jean-Antoine Gros
(1771–1835) a pupil of David, who without in the least toning down
their violence, painted battle-scenes which David's aesthetic would have
condemned according to the strict tenets of ideal beauty (*Napoleon with
the Plague Victims of Jaffa*, Louvre, 1804, pl. 537; *Battle of Aboukir*,
Versailles, 1805; *Battle of Eylau*, Louvre, 1810). Deriving from the bas-
relief composition of David, he found a more eloquent use of colour in

541 *Théodore
Rousseau.
Village of
Becquigny
(Picardy).
Salon of
1864.
New York*

Rubens and the Venetians. The struggle between his Romantic aspirations and the doctrinal tyranny of his school caused Gros such anguish that he ended by committing suicide. Théodore Géricault (1791–1824) belongs to the Empire school through his cult of energy, but he introduced English influence into France. Even more than Gros whom he so much admired, he was obsessed by suffering and death (*Raft of the Medusa*, Louvre, 1819): his early death robbed the school of a great painter's maturity (pl. 538).

Eugène Delacroix (1798–1863), a portraitist who excelled equally in

542 *Daumier. Don Quichotte.
Munich*

historical pieces, still-lifes, landscapes and animal-painting, aspired to the ranks of those universal geniuses who made painting an encyclopaedia of man and nature. He received a classical training from Guérin; but it was in Rubens, the Venetians and Constable that he sought the principles of expression through all the resources of colour, based on the vibration of shadows. A trip to Morocco gave him a glimpse of Oriental life in 1832. In his youthful works the swirling composition that runs right across the field (pl. 539) follows no laws but those of life itself, and his dramatic intensity was never afraid of extravagance *(Massacre of Scio*, Louvre, 1824; *Death of Sardanapalus*, Louvre, 1829, pl. 525). However, in his matury he tended

543 Monet.
The Houses of
Parliament,
London. Private
Collection

to integrate Romantic expressionism into the formal system of the classicists (*Trajan giving Judgement*, Rouen, 1840; *Fall of Constantinople*, Louvre, 1841). These tendencies made him take themes from antiquity for his major decorations in the Senate Library and the Chambre des Députés (1838–1847), and the Louvre. The Chapelle des Saints-Anges which he painted in St Sulpice between 1853 and 1861 was his artistic and philosophical testament. Théodore Chassériau (1819–1856) tried to reconcile Ingres's manner with Romanticism.

A fresh eagerness for feeling and knowledge brought man into contact with a many-sided universe whose infinite variety and depth had been hidden under an outdated humanism. Georges Michel (1763–1843) sought

544 Camille
Pissarro.
A Corner
of the
Hermitage,
Pontoise.
1874.
Winterthur

545 Sisley. The Horse-Pond at Marly in the Snow. 1875. Paris

some echo of this in the open fields in the northern suburbs of Paris. It was in the Fontainebleau forest, in the neighbourhood of the little village of Barbizon, that the Romantic landscape-painters tried to follow the technical example of the Dutch and English. Théodore Rousseau (1812 –1867, pl. 541), Jules Dupré (1811–1899), Narcisse Diaz (1807–1876) reached closer to the mystery of nature. But apart from Rousseau, whose objective vision tried to pass beyond appearance into the inner meaning of things, they all saw nature as something passionate, stormy, uneasy and dramatic – like their own souls.

Under the *Ancien Régime* art was the handmaid of a king or aristocracy, but the nineteenth century restored to it something of the moral urgency of expression that it had in the Middle Ages. Millet, Daumier, Courbet, indeed all those who towards 1848 gloried in the title of 'Realists', were always chiefly attracted by the human drama, and in their search for man they explored the masses, the common people in whom human nature has a timeless, enduring quality. Jean-François Millet (1814–1875) exalted the dignity of rustic toil, the source of human life, with a religious and almost ritualistic seriousness that recalls the treatment of the *Months* in medieval cathedrals. Honoré Daumier (1808 –1879) recorded with profound compassion the abject poverty of the new industrial masses in the towns; like Courbet he was an ardent socialist and in his lithographs gave a scathing condemnation of middle-class selfishness. Daumier's impetuous painting, with its violent impasto, is perhaps the most successfully 'romantic' of the century (pl. 542). Gustave Courbet (1819–1877) gave the bourgeois of his time the scandalous

408

546 *Renoir. Le Déjeuner. 1879. Frankfurt*

picture of a tough, primitive humanity, close to the soil and to nature, and in his paintings he exalted the mud and even the muck of farm and field. Compared with Corot, who represents the pure French tradition for which painting is either an act of mind, or a revelation of the heart, Courbet was a painter of raw sensation and represents a crisis, a turning-point for the French school. Throwing away both the patient craftsmanship of the classicists and the ingenious, cunning resources of colour discovered by Delacroix, he founded an entirely instinctive manner of paint-

ing that consisted of applying one impasto on another by means of the
palette-knife (pl. 526).

Rejecting fiction and everything they could not see with their own
eyes in everyday life, the Realists of 1848 none the less saved something
of Romanticism, – that is to say the heroic tone, the tendency to exalt
the greatness and anguish of the human situation. Round about 1860 we
can see how a transition was made from this romantic and plebian naturalism to an analytical realism, the refined, urban realism of Manet and
the Impressionists.

It was at the *Salon des Refusés* of 1863 that the painters who founded
the Impressionist school first became aware of their common aims. They
grouped themselves round Edouard Manet (1833–1883) who caused a
scandal in this *Salon* with his *Déjeuner sur l'herbe* which shows a group
of art-students picnicking with a naked girl – a model (pl. 527). Manet
showed the way by freeing painting from all irrelevant anecdotal and
literary elements; he saw things entirely as pictorial values. After a 'black'
period, so-called because it was inspired by Spanish painting, which
lasted until 1870, he deliberately concentrated on scenes from the everyday life of his own time and took to *peinture claire,* and abolished blacks
and browns. Except for Manet, the group of innovators, who were systematically barred from the official *Salons,* formed themselves into a society
for showing their own works. At the first show, which caused an enormous scandal in 1874, a journalist dubbed these artists 'Impressionists'
after the title of one of Monet's canvases, the *Impression, soleil levant*
(Musée Marmottan, Paris). Claude Monet (1840–1926) proved to be the
real leader of the Impressionist revolution (colour pl. XIII) which had

410

been implied also in the work of Boudin (1824–1898), a native of Normandy and of the Dutchman Jongkind (1819–1891) who had settled in France. Monet ended by seeing the world as no more than an interplay of appearances in perpetual movement, and delighted in analyzing the infinite variations of light on the same view (*Argenteuil,* *1872–1875; Débâcles des glaces* or *Ice Breaking-Up, 1879–1880; Rouen Cathedral,* 1893; *Views of London,* 1902, *Nymphéas* or *Water-Lilies,* 1899–1926). Monet subjected all that usually serves to define shapes, such as contour, modelling, shadow, to an intense light, so that nothing remains on the canvas but patches of colour (pl. 543). Observing that each tint

548 Degas. Absinth. About 1876–1877. Paris

in nature contains several other colours, and is again modified by the reflection of surrounding colors as well as by the quality of the light that falls on it, Monet broke up the whole tone-scale of colour graduation by building up his canvas in touches of pure colour. The Englishman Alfred Sisley (1839–1899) was less remonte from the traditional vision, in his paintings of skies and rivers of the Ile-de-France region (pl. 545). Camille

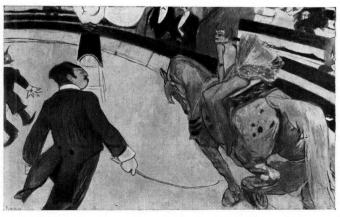

549 Toulouse-Lautrec. Au Cirque Fernando. 1888. Chicago

550 Cézanne. Les Grandes Baigneuses. About 1900–1905. Philadelphia

Pissarro (1830–1903) gave Impressionism the atmosphere of a French village (pl. 544); Berthe Morisot (1841–1895) tried to render the human figure in the *plein-airiste* manner, like her brother-in-law Manet. After his experiments with the light-magic created by the Impressionist school (*Le Déjeuner*, Frankfurt, 1879, pl. 546; *Moulin de la Galette*, Louvre, 1876; *Le Déjeuner des canotiers*, Philips Memorial Gallery, Washington, 1881), Pierre-Auguste Renoir (1841–1919) tried to pass beyond it. After his Impressionist phase he imposed a stricter discipline on himself, in order to regain a sense of form and volume, going so far as to seek his inspiration in Ingres and even a bas-relief by Girardon (*Les Grandes Baigneuses*, Tyson Collection, Philadelphia, 1885). After making sure of his grasp of all the technical resources he needed, he then began to portray mankind in a golden-age natural setting, reinvigorated by a primitive nakedness which he thought could help man to rediscover a pagan innocence (*Judgement of Paris*, Stang Collection, Oslo, pl. 547). While all the nineteenth-century artists painted opaquely, he was almost the only one besides Delacroix, one of his masters, to use colour in fluid and transparent glazes which give his painting a sensual depth that had been forgotten since Rubens.

551 Gauguin. Woman with Mangos (Te Arii Vahine). 1896. Private Collection

The sunshine of Impressionism drove out the gloomy dreams of the Romantics, and after Courbet's dramatic vision a dazzling sensation of the joy of existence invaded painting. However, Edgar Degas (1834–1917) and Henri de Toulouse-Lautrec (1864–1901) still retained all the disillusionment of Romanticism, if not its inspiring energy. Gripped by a pitiless lucidity, they set out to destroy deep-seated human illusions, and with all Ingres' acuteness of line they analyzed the manners and vices of their contemporaries with a hard objectivity (pl. 548, 549).

552 Seurat. Dimanche à la Grande Jatte. Exhibited 1886. Chicago

553 Van Gogh. Cornfield and Cypresses. London

The French mind, which dislikes excess of any kind, could not remain satisfied for long with the buoyant unrestraint of the Impressionists, or their faith in fleeting aspects of things. Several artists tried to impose an intellectual order on art again, a trend which between 1884 and 1890 crystallized into a deliberate reaction. Paul Cézanne (1839–1906), from Aix-en-Provence, aimed at a classical poise without giving up direct observation; he called this *'refaire Poussin sur nature'* (doing as Poussin did, but after nature). After a first sombre, so-called 'black' phase of aggressive Romanticism, ending in 1872, he tried Impressionism at Auvers-sur-Oise, but gave it up in about 1880. He now wanted to re-discover some classical sense of form, while desiring to convey volume and space by means of colour alone. He carried out this purpose slowly in a series of still-lifes, then in landscape (colour pl. XIV), and finally in large figure-compositions (pl. 550); his finest landscapes were inspired by the view of Sainte-Victoire, a mountain that dominates the Aix-en-Provence countryside. Georges Seurat (1859–1891), the founder of neo-Impressionism wanted to give a systematic, scientific basis, founded on the physicists' theories of light, to the break-down of the tone-scale which Monet had practized by pure instinct (pl. 552). Seurat invented a method-ical process for his painting which has been called 'Divisionism' or

'Pointillism'. This new aesthetic appealed to several artists, including Signac and for a short time Pissarro, after it appeared in 1886. Paul Gauguin (1848–1903) reacted mainly against the naturalistic element in Impressionism. Rejecting visual 'lifelikeness' he refused to see painting as representation, but rather as the expression of some inner vision. After some long periods spent at Pont-Aven in Britanny, where he founded a school of painters (1886–1890) he went off to Tahiti in 1890 in search of exotic surroundings more in keeping with his dreams. His art runs parallel with the literary Symbolist movement (pl. 551). The Symbolists also regarded Odilon Redon (1824–1916) as a kindred spirit, for like them he was a painter of dreams, as well as the academic Puvis de Chavannes (1824–1898), a monumental mural-painter whose work is the last manifestation of that ideal beauty, which in his hands became an allegorical interpretation of the world of the psyche. On the other hand, it was in favour of a fervent expressionism that the Dutch painter Vincent van Gogh (1853–1890) raised his moving protest against Impressionism, though he used their pure-colour technique (pl. 553).

It is with these artists, in revolt against the naturalism which had been the driving force in painting since the Romantics, that the nineteenth century ended, an extraordinary century which gave us at least twenty painters of genius, and showing a creative fertility unrivalled since the Italian Renaissance.

2. WESTERN ART OUTSIDE FRANCE

Architecture and Sculpture

The majority of nineteenth-century artists, except in France, have a following in their own countries, where they expressed something of the national temperament, but very few have a world-wide appeal or reputation.

All over Europe architecture showed the same developments as in France: it was neo-Classical until about 1850, after which it was unable to produce any new form and became 'eclectic', that is to say a hotch-potch of all the styles ever known in the West. The dignified Empire style did not produce its finest example in France, but at St Petersburg, where Alexander I seems to have set himself the task of fulfilling Napoleon's thwarted dreams; he replanned the city and gave it some imposing monuments worthy of the great river Neva. Inspired by French sources, this style developed from the ideas of Ledoux, Percier and Fontaine and was partly executed by French architects: Thomas de Thomon, who designed the Exchange (1805–1806) and Ricard de Montferrand, who based the cathedral of St Isaac of Dalmatia (1817) on Soufflot's Panthéon in Paris, and the Alexander Column (1829) on the Colonne

Vendôme. The Russian Zakharov built the Admiralty (1806–1810, pl. 554), and Voronikhin the cathedral of the Virgin of Kazan (1801-1811) which was inspired by St Peter's in Rome and its peristyle. The Italian Rossi continued this public style under Nicholas I, but with far less purity. Continuing the impetus given by Merlini under Stanislas Augustus, Poland, like Russia during the first half of the century, adopted a neo-Classical style, seeking effects of monumental grandeur.

Germany was notable for a tendency to archaeological pastiche, at first confined to neo-Hellenism but later imitating Renaissance and Gothic. The two main centres of architecture were Munich and Berlin. In Munich Leo von Klenze (1784–1864) built an imitation of the Propylaea and the first museums that were rationally planned (Glyptothek, 1816; Alte Pinakothek); he also set up a replica of the Parthenon in Regensburg (1830), Germanizing it by a dedication to the gods of Valhalla. Under Ludwig I Munich became a sort of architectural museum full of imitations of famous European monuments. In Prussia, Karl Friedrich Schinkel (1781–1841) imitated Soufflot's Panthéon at Potsdam (1830) and built the Guard-House (Neue Wache, pl. 523) in Berlin (1816) in the Greek Doric style, and the Altes Museum (1824) in the Ionic; but he also set the fashion for the Gothic revival which was to affect churches and castles. At the end of the century Germany witnessed a curious reappearance of native Rococo, which was to have repercussions in France (so-called 'Munich style' of the Petit Palais and the Grand Palais, in Paris, built for the Paris Exhibition, 1900). England, which was also at first inclined towards neo-Greek, found a national form in its revival of the native Gothic style, the laws of which A. W. N. Pugin (1812–1852) was carefully investigating. After the fire in 1834, the Palace of Westminster was rebuilt by Pugin and Charles Barry on an imposing scale and in a Perpendicular Gothic style of striking dignity (pl. 555). At the end of the century, in Barcelona, Antonio Gaudí planned one of the strangest and most fantastic buildings ever put together; a wild mixture of Gothic and Churrigueresque, it is the Spanish equivalent of Art Nouveau (pl. 636).

XIV Paul Cézanne. Val d'Arc. Private Collection

555 *Sir Charles Barry and Augustus Pugin. The Houses of Parliament, London.*
1836–1860

As for sculpture, few names are worth mentioning. The Italian Canova
(1757–1822) was the best interpreter of the neo-Classical aesthetic
(pl. 556). The Dane, Thorwaldsen (1777–1844) had a European reputation
but turned the neo-Greek into something quite cold and lifeless. Gottfried
Schadow (1764–1850) was a German Canova, though with more strength
and less gracefulness (pl. 557).

In the United States Thomas Jefferson's adoption of Roman forms was
only the beginning of a wholesale application of the neo-Classical formulas to every kind of building. This was a type of building in which the
plan of the interior was coerced into the preconceived Classical form of
the façade. Charles Bulfinch (1763–1844) added the severity of classicism
to the Georgian style in his capitols at Boston, Massachusetts, and Au-
gusta, Maine. The Greek Revival in America begins as early as 1798 with
Benjamin Latrobe's (1766–1820) Bank of Pennsylvania, which boasted
Ionic porticoes derived from the Erechtheum. Latrobe and Bulfinch were
responsible for the general disposition of the capitol at Washington based
on an earlier plan by William Thornton. Actually, the building with the
present dome was not completed until 1865. The plan of the city of
Washington had been drawn in 1791 by Major Pierre Charles l'Enfant.
The great period of florescence of the Greek Revival style was in the
second quarter of the nineteenth century, when temple houses and temple
banks sprang up around every village green from Maine to Florida and
westward to the frontier. In its nostalgic evocation of an earlier style this
revival was an aspect of Romanticism. It was not long before these bor-

556 Canova. *Pauline Bonaparte (detail). 1809. Rome*

557 *Gottfried Schadow. Hope. 1802. Berlin*

rowings from the Greco-Roman past were followed by imitations of Gothic architecture, again a symbolical rather than a functional adaptation of European originals.

Although a number of early sculptors like William Rush (1756–1833) were capable of a realism in portraiture similar to the work of the painters, for the most part the carving of the early nineteenth century in the United States is the plastic counterpart of the taste for classic forms in architecture. Horatio Greenough (1805–1852) was the designer of a colossal statue of Washington in the attitude of the Phidian *Zeus*. The Greek Revival in sculpture produced a veritable petrified forest of marbles derived from Canova and Thorwaldsen, manufactured for the American public by sculptors like Hiram Powers (1805–1873). The one original sculptor of the nineteenth century in the United States was William Rimmer (1816–1879), a strange, tortured spirit who executed a number of statues which in their suggestion of inner suffering through physical contortion anticipate the work of Rodin.

Painting

Painting had some prosperous schools in Europe, so far as the number of painters was concerned. Generally speaking, with the exception of England, romanticism failed to find its proper form and the first half-

418

century shows a steady decline of classicism, whereas the second half sank into the most dreary realism which was hardly redeemed by the imperfect assimilation of Impressionist features at the end of the century.

Germany has a strange paradox to offer. Entranced by the apparent serenity of classicism, Germany wilfully turned its back on its own genuine native tradition of expressionism, which would have enabled German art to find a pictorial medium for its romantic sensibility. In 1810 a group of artists gathered in Rome at the monastery of S. Isidoro, calling themselves the 'Nazarene school', turned Germany away from the neo-Classical tradition imposed by Winckelmann, while exalting the work of Perugino and the early Raphael. Overbeck (1789–1869) and Peter Cornelius (1783–1867) applied their new doctrine in a cycle of frescoes showing the story of Joseph, in the Casa Bartoldi in Rome, for which they were commissioned in 1816. They developed a style of frozen pastiche with flat hues and a hard line, which made itself felt all over Europe (pl. 558). To their Italian sources Overbeck, Peter Cornelius and Schnorr von Carolsfeld soon added archaic elements from fifteenth- and sixteenth-century German art, whose deep pathos they never grasped. The two best painters of the period in Germany were two free-lances, the portraitist Philipp Otto Runge (1777–1810) who approached very closely to expressionism, and the exquisite and intuitive landscape-painter Caspar David Friedrich (1774–1840, pl. 559) sometimes called the 'German van Eyck'. The school of historical painters at Düsseldorf (Wilhelm von Kaulbach, 1805–1874; Alfred Rethel, 1816–1859) took up the Nazarene style but gave it a Realist touch. The French Naturalism of 1848 came to Germany through Franz von Lenbach (1836–1904) and Wilhelm Leibl (1844–1900). Max Liebermann (1847–1935) was a disciple of the French Impressionists.

In Spain, Goya, the first half of whose career sets him in the eighteenth century, threw off his neo-Classical training and was a pioneer in his

558 Friedrich Overbeck. Joseph being sold by his Brothers. Berlin

559 Caspar David Friedrich. Moonrise over the Sea. 1823. Berlin

discovery of a technique more suitable to his romantic leanings, pl. 528). The misfortunes of Spain, which was torn by civil war, inspired him to paint some of the most dramatic works of the century, but his meteoric genius found no followers in the peninsula.

Britain, after making concessions to formalism through the portraitist Sir Thomas Lawrence (1769–1830), who painted all the great European statesmen, had the privilege of discovering the proper lines and medium for the Romantic landscape. In this the English painters were helped by the fashion for water-colour, which was used side by side with oils for open-air studies. John Crome (1768–1821) founded the school of landscape-painters known as the Norwich school, and turned to the Dutch for his conception of landscape. He had a very thorough craftsmanship, exploiting opacities to the full and drawing his effects from contrasts of light and shade (pl. 560). John Sell Cotman (1782–1842, pl. 561) was one of the Norwich group; first and foremost a water-colourist, he was passionately concerned for a landscape of flattened, carefully ordered planes. John Constable (1776–1837) developed a rich and varied palette and a bold execution ideally suited for portraying the fluidity of skies, in which he saw the very basis of landscape (*Weymouth Bay, Stoke-by-Neyland, Hampstead Heath with a Rainbow*, pl. 563); his brilliant technique was to have a decisive effect on the development of French Romanticism (*The Hay-Wain, The Leaping Horse*). In Joseph Mallord William Turner (1775–1821) a painter of genius and vision, an imagination that was given to reverie came into conflict with a gift for penetrating observation (*The Shipwreck, The Evening Star*). Obsessed by Claude Lorrain's historical and mythological scenes, he was a forerunner of the Impressionist 'cosmic' landscape, reduced to a whirl of water, sky or sunlight (pl. 564). Though cut off by an early death, Delacroix's friend, Richard Parkes Bonington (1802–1828, pl. 562) painted landscapes with an illuminated fluency. Samuel Palmer (1805–1881) based his small, intense visionary landscapes, some of the most remarkable in English painting, on the closest observation of nature.

Towards 1850, after having appeared to escape the aberrations that had befallen other national schools, England adventured into 'pre-Raphaelitism'. Like French Symbolism a little later, this movement was both literary and artistic. In 1848 a few writers, a sculptor and three painters, Dante Gabriel Rossetti (1828–1882), William Holman Hunt (1827–1890) and John Everett Millais (1829–1896, pl. 565) grouped themselves into a 'Brotherhood' in defence of a doctrine which made painting a visual version of literary material. Rebelling against the official worship of Raphael, the more fanatical of the group gave themselves to so strict a realism that they sometimes took years to complete a single picture. Pre-Raphaelitism also gave itself a moral aim, directed mainly against the standardization resulting from modern industry and mechanization; Ruskin defended the movement with passionate eloquence in his aesthetic writings. Other artists who were not members of the Brother-

560 *John Crome. The Poringland
    Oak. About 1818. London*
561 *John Sell Cotman.
    Kirk Viaduct. London*

562 Richard Parkes Bonington. *Fishing Village and the French Coast.*
Boston (Massachusetts)

hood followed its principles of realism, including Ford Madox Brown (1821–1893). Naturalism unsoiled by literary pretension or easy sentiment informs the drawings and few paintings of Charles Keene (1823–1891).

The ambitious work of the Swiss painter Arnold Böcklin (1827–1901, pl. 567) who enjoyed a great reputation in Germany, is not unrelated to pre-Raphaelitism in its literary pretensions, but it has also a certain Germanic harshness. In France the Symbolist aims of Gustave Moreau (1828–1898) were not furthered by the garish, pseudo-Romantic tricks he employed. The reliance of painting on literature is a striking example of the crisis through which Europe was passing, in its desperate search for a medium to convey its various aspirations, whether ideological, emotional or naturalistic.

The painters of the early nineteenth century in America, still following the lead of Europe, may be divided into representatives of classicism and romanticism. The cultural soil was too thin for the taste for neo-Classical historical painting to take permanent root, so that the failure of a man like John Vanderlyn (1776–1852), an American representative of the David style, was inevitable. Washington Allston (1779–1843), the first American painter of the imagination, is best remembered for his romantic landscapes and figure pieces.

A very American form of expression is genre painting, which came into its own during the thirties of the nineteenth century, William Sidney Mount (1807–1868) gave a vibrant interpretation of country activities on Long Island based on the technique of the Dutch 'Little Masters', and

563 Constable. *Hampstead Heath with a Rainbow. 1836. London*

George Caleb Bingham (1811–1879) was the pictorial counterpart of Mark Twain in his chronicling of life on the Mississippi.

The second half of the century witnessed a new period of maturity in American painting. Of the really great artists of this time, Winslow Homer (1836–1910) was a painter of the sea and a monumental illustrator of themes of the active American outdoor life: childhood games, hunting, fishing, and the drama of men against the sea. In Homer's paintings his concentration on a big central theme presented with specific realism transcends the literary content. Whereas Homer realized his seascapes with complete objectivity in an impressionistic technique based on value contrast rather than colour, Albert Pinkham Ryder (1847–1917) was a mystic painter of the sea, in his expressionistic distortion a forerunner of the art of the twentieth century: his patternized pictures of moon-drenched waters are the pictorial counterparts of Melville's descriptions of the great deep. Thomas Eakins (1844–1916) completes the trinity of artists with whom American painting came of age. He was a forceful, completely objective painter of portraits and athletic subject matter executed in the broad technique of the great Spanish artists of the seventeenth century.

Among the expatriate American painters were James Abbott McNeill Whistler (1834–1903), whose entire artistic career was passed in Paris and London. He was among the first to be influenced by the newly discovered Japanese prints; his distortion of spatial arrangement and subtlety of occult balance were far in advance of his contemporaries (pl. 566). Mary Cassatt (1845–1927), resident in France from 1879 until her death, worked in a manner reflecting Degas and Renoir. John Singer Sargent (1856–1925) was an artist of international reputation, a painter of superficial fashionable portraits in a facile and dazzling technique that went far to disguise their empty ideality.

Impressionism in America never attained the importance of its European prototype. George Inness (1825–1894), who actually denounced the Impressionist theory, was himself an American follower of Corot and the Barbizon school. Childe Hassam (1859–1935) and John Henry Twachtman (1853–1902), although described as Impressionists, suggested light in terms of value rather than the pure color of Monet and Pisarro.

By turning painting into the evocation of a sensation Whistler freed the English school from pre-Raphaelitism, and the New English Art Club, founded in 1886, at last absorbed Impressionism. Through Whistler, also, French naturalism and unity of feeling strengthened paintings of the London scene by Walter Greaves (1846–1931) and the intimate canvases of F. H. Potter (1845–1887). Whistler's example was the starting point for early evocations of seaside light and colour by Philip Wilson Steer (1860–1942), and for Walter Richard Sickert (1860–1942, pl. 684), a friend of both Degas and Lautrec, who painted in Dieppe, Paris, London and Venice, and prolonged Impressionism well into our century. Gwen John (1876–1939), pupil of Whistler and friend of Rodin, painted with

564 Turner. The Fighting Téméraire towed to her last Berth. 1838. London

565 Millais. Return of the
the Dove to the Ark.
1851. Oxford

566 Whistler. La Princesse
du Pays de la
Porcelaine. 1864.
Washington

simplicity and severe penetration the poor, the almswomen and nuns of
Meudon.

In Holland, Impressionism was represented by George Breitner (1857
–1923), who painted the Amsterdam canals.

3. THE MINOR ARTS

The decorative arts went through a progressive decadence during the
nineteenth century.

Until about 1820 the Empire style was a dignified version of the ancient
Pompeian decoration which had already been imitated but with greater
subtlety in the late eighteenth century, as well as in France under
Louis XVI. The Empire style was introduced under David's influence by
Georges Jacob (1739–1814), who in 1789 and 1790 made a whole set of
furniture to be used by David for his classical compositions. This sober
style crystallized towards the end of the century into the Directoire style,
and lasted a while under the Empire in domestic furnishing, parallel with
the official style of furnishing. Under the guidance of the architects Percier and Fontaine, Georges II Jacob (died 1803) and Jacob Desmalter
(1770–1841) acted as furnishers for the national palaces as well as for
highly-placed dignitaries, under the Directory and the Empire. They
were assisted by the bronze-worker Thomyre (1751–1843). They made
what was perhaps an excessive use of Greco-Roman, Etruscan and even
Egyptian patterns and motifs, which they applied in stucco on walls,
and in bronze on items of furniture (pl. 568).

Between 120 and 1830 the Restoration style evolved from the Empire
style, and was more rational, purer and much simpler in its decoration.

567 *Arnold Böcklin. Triton and Nereid.*
1875. *Berlin*

568 *Jacob Desmalter. Jewel-Cabinet made*
for the Empress Marie-Louise

The severity of this style was softened by the play of curved lines, while dark mahoganies were abandoned in favour of light timbers such as beechwood, ash, cedar, maple, and citron. Hangings and wallpapers were also in light colours, and *voile* curtains were fashionable. It was a period of great elegance of form.

Between 1830 and 1850 mahogany returned to favour with the French Louis-Philippe and German Biedermeier styles, both of them a mixture of the two preceding styles (Restoration and Empire), showing also a certain revival of Classical forms especially in easy-chairs which imitated the Roman magistrate's chair or *curule*. Interiors contained a great deal of upholstery and hangings, bright materials being used in preference to dark, and *voile* curtains rather than heavy textiles. Under Louis-Philippe there was a vogue for neo-Gothic interiors which have wrongly been dubbed 'Charles X style'. This Troubadour style produced clocks and fine bookbindings of a highly medieval flavour.

The Great Exhibition of 1851 in London and the Paris Universal Exhibition of 1855 showed the public how far the applied arts had degenerated. Attempts were made to put this right by giving artisans good examples to work from, which were housed in so-called 'craft' or 'industrial' museums set up for their benefit. This only made matters worse, resulting in only more copying and eclecticism; until 1890 or thereabouts it was an understood thing that a dining-room should be of the Henry II period, a bedroom Louis XV, a sitting-room Louis XVI. In official Second Empire furnishing, under the Empress Eugénie's guidance, eighteenth century styles were most imitated. Interior decoration made the utmost use of textiles in the form of heavy draperies and materials for upholsteries, thick, opaque curtains, thick carpets, padded chairs. Dark red was the prevailing colour for all these purposes.

XI. THE CIVILIZATIONS OF THE FAR EAST

All Western works of art are intended for a spectator: they are meant for another man's eyes and mind. They have to be readable; their parts must be clearly marked while remaining a coherent unity. They are essentially a defined significant form strictly related to space and time, as in the rhythmed colonnades of the Greek temple and the arrangement of its pediments; or as in the gravitation round a central point that governs a Byzantine church, or the perspective of Romanesque and Gothic naves which later passed into those painted canvases in which the spectator is invited to advance as down some avenue. The West worked towards the essential notion of a work of art, as the product of a specific activity addressed to a few members of an élite capable of appreciating it. It amounts to a dialogue between artist and spectator on an aesthetic theme.

In the hands of the artist of the Far East, form emerges as the manifestation of the being of the world itself, a symbol of universal powers or forces. It is not the result of a man's thought striving to master some definite aspect of nature. It is 'inspired', an artist's imaginative reflection of the eternal play of appearances; it aspires to the infinite, either through portraying an indeterminate flux, or, on the contrary, through the powerful concentration of its structure. At Mamallapuram, the famous bas-relief of the *Descent of the Ganges,* carved into the rock-face, is a river of images (pl. 569). In the same way Far-Eastern painting has no use for the idea of a frame, which governs ours; at Ajanta the various themes of the paintings are linked into one continuous action, as in some stage-play in which there are no intervals and the last act reintroduces the first. Kept in cylindrical cases, Chinese pictures unfold so to speak in time, they have to be read like musical compositions, and they suggest vague landscapes, fragments of the universal, which convey the mystery that flows, immanent, through all things. Round the sides of archaic Chinese bronzes there seethes a whole world in gestation, a chaos from which here and there forms seem to emerge, only to vanish before they can give enduring shape to fleeting appearances; they are monstrous shapes, apparitions from a world of fear. All these works are 'open' forms, that is to say they do not oppose their bold outline or definition to the invading fluidity of the universe, but are penetrated by it. They act like conductors to the cosmic flow, whereas Western works act as insulators; but the touch of the infinite is perhaps most intense in those Chinese objects which have naked contours over which the hand and the eye may glide – such as archaic jades with their hidden meanings, or the Sung vases with their slender curves, whose opalescent substance has the blue-green depth of the ocean itself.

569 *Descent of the Ganges, Mamallapuram (detail). Brahmanic. 7th c. A.D.*

This feeling that everything is no more than a moment in the cosmic flux of becoming, hardly encouraged the Orientals to develop architecture, which is the major art of the West where it governs all other art-forms, imposing its framework on them and allotting a particular function to each. The Chinese only went in for wooden constructions, which they later imitated in brick and ceramics. The Hindus, whose feeling for sculpture gave them a special gift for handling stone materials, did the same as the Chinese as soon as they took to building, bringing to it the primitive methods of timber construction which they perhaps borrowed from the Middle East. Then, being unequal to those abstract calculations which show how solids behave in space, and in which Greek, Roman, Romanesque and Gothic architects were fully proficient, they raised in corbelled layers colossal piles of blocks. This rudimentary form of building was primitive man's way of imitating one of the most impressive sights in the world, the mountain, which for the East is a symbol of the cosmos.

With its inorganic structure, this kind of monument knows nothing of the distribution of solids and spaces, or the concentration of decorative features and carved figures at vital points in the building so as to show off the pleasing completeness of the walls. Rock-faces in the East are profusely covered with ornamentation and carved figures; Chinese monuments are decked with multicoloured ceramics which make them look like enormous vases, while hundreds of figures swarm like ants on the pyramidal Hindu temples.

China and India are alike in their conception of a cosmic order in which man must live through a cycle in order to find his place. But the

428

two civilizations differ in the meaning they each give to the universal essence.

Few peoples have had so profound an intuition of the divine as the Hindus. On this earth in which everything is God, in order to find his salvation man must discover godliness in himeslf. The sight of endless creation unrelieved by seasonal change is a feature of tropical nature that has inspired the Hindu with a profound faith in existence. The Indian aesthetic is therefore 'naturalistic' in its essence. In the West, the Christian ideas of original sin, the Fall, and the periodical need for revolt against the idealism of schools and academies, have given this word 'naturalism' a harsh meaning which makes it hard for us to understand all the purity attached to it in the East. The West knows nothing of true naturalism, but is more at home with realism, an analytical attitude which isolates one or other aspect of the world only to fix it into some lifeless form. Perhaps Rubens and after him Renoir, managed to avoid this trap. But the flux of life flows through all Hindu art, one and indivisible, completely incarnate in all its potential strength, in the least of Hindu works. By a phenomenon which is unique in history, this art seems to have been born already complete, in a state of maturity, without going through all the conventions and stylizations so dear to the primitive mind. Of all the artistic civilizations, the Indian is the least stylized. What for the Greeks, Romans and Gothic artists was the fruit of a slow conquest of the external world, achieved only by throwing off primitive preconceptions and by dint of an unquenchable thirst for objective knowledge, was given to the Hindus from the very start. Right from the beginning, after a very short archaic period which is hardly noticeable, Sanchi art had come to terms with nature. On the contrary, it was Hellenic influence, brought in through Greco-Buddhist art, which was to strengthen Gupta

570 Stucco Head from Tash-kurghan. Greco-Buddhist Art of Gandhara. 1st c. A.D.

571 Angel from a Buttress at Rheims. Gothic. About 1240

572 *Bodhisattva from Lung-men. Wei Dynasty. 6th c. New York*

573 *King of Judea. Attached Figure on the Royal Porch of Chartres Cathedral. About 1150*

stylization, though it was soon abandoned once more in favour of a return to more lifelike forms.

Indian naturalism, like Greek realism, was bound to lead to the increasing prestige of sculptural form, since it can express the physical presence of living things better than any other type of art. The Greek experiment in realism was entirely based on the male form, whose sharp edges and distinct planes lent themselves to the Greek sense of measurement and definition. But the Indian aesthetic is feminine. The female body is more suggestive of flesh itself than of volume; the indefinite transitions of its modelling suits the Hindu outlook which refuses, or fails, to see anything at all definite in the world. Exaggerating the female attributes, the Indian artists stressed whatever is capable of giving and sustaining life, and the bodies they portray seem to sway like fruit-laden trees and are symbols of plenty.

The evolution of Greek sculpture showed a progressive liberation from the wall, a triumph of three-dimensional form. Hindu art was late in producing sculpture in the round. Sculpted forms were not detached from the rock-face, nor on the other hand were they completely subservient to monumental values as in Romanesque; but they drew their life from the block of which they were still a part, the Hindus conceiving nothing as distinct from its surroundings, but seeing everything in every thing. In the Mamallapuram carving the surge of figures represents the moment when living form emerges from raw matter. That is why the Hindus have always been fond of drawing their works from the very bowels of the earth, hewing out caves and carving into mountains. The

430

574 *Buddhist Stele (detail).*
Wei Dynasty. 533–543. New York

575 *Prophet in Souillac*
Church. About 1150

Greek temple, being an expression of victorious humanism, stands on the acropolis like a statue on its pedestal, whereas Hindu works flow like living seed in the matrix of the earth. The powerful biological creativeness that is typical of India produced strange monuments which multiply like cells and which, like a tree in a forest, are fast throwing out new shoots, while all around them swarm other sanctuaries cast in the same image (pl. 576, 577).

Burdened with ritual and formalism of every kind, the life of the 'Celestials' is fundamentally little moved by religious aspirations. Chinese theology is another version, though transposed to the level of a very high culture, of a primitive state of mankind which precedes the religious outlook in the proper sense of the term. The Chinese do not worship gods, though they believe in genii and demons which are formal expressions of the principles governing the universe; for them a knowledge of magic rites enables man to intervene in the universal order and attune himself to it. The Westerner prides himself on the free-will that he regards as man's privilege and something that makes him the 'Lord of Creation', whereas for the Chinese free-will appears to be the root of all evil. Like some sorcerer's apprentice, man upsets the world's natural order, and the gift of intelligence, which he alone of the creatures is blessed with, becomes a failing if he uses it to exploit the world; for man ought to serve the world and make the best of his privilege by contributing to the universal order. Magic enables him to do this. It is remarkable that the highest metaphysical form of Chinese thought, Taoism, has its roots in magic ritual.

431

In the field of art, creation tends to take place without regard to nature, that is to say in spite of or against nature's example. Whereas Hindu art is a figure, Chinese art is a stylization. The hidden source of the Chinese soul is to be found in the art of the ancient period, in the bronze cauldrons which are drawn from the bowels of the earth, still charged with the magic potentialities of the rites they will be used for. The plastic form of that primitive art writhes with a satanic rhythm; it is the source of that bristling, jagged, cruel style which was to obsess China even in its works of architecture right through its long history.

The wealth of Chinese civilization lies in its many contradictions. The gust of naturalism that came from steppe art and from Indian art, the sense of the divine which was brought in by the Buddhist missionaries of the 'Great Vehicle' (Mahayana), these came into conflict with their obsession with the chimaera. When they came into contact with Buddhism, the Chinese, who had naturally little sense of the divine, yet managed to express its sublime spirituality even better than India itself had done. India, overwhelmed by naturalism, sought to translate the inner life of the Buddha by taking from Greco-Buddhist art a formalism which resulted in the somewhat conventional works of Gupta art. The Chinese stripped the Yun-kang and Lung-men statues of their fleshly, earthly attributes so that they convey with the utmost dignity the Bodhisattvas' inward contemplation or compassion. But the warlike China of the T'ang period turned away from these holy images and gave themselves to a brutal realism fraught with the more pragmatic element in Chinese

576 Lingaraja Temple, Bhuvanesvar (Orissa). About 1000

civilization. And to complete the gamut of human expression, the Sung period produced works full of the philosophical reverie, fundamentally atheistic, typical of decadent periods in which strength is ousted by an elegant, intellectual scepticism.

Because the Chinese had an attitude of independence towards nature, they had more than any other race an exalted sense of essential form, and language cannot describe something which is as far from nature as it is from abstraction. Those naked objects, those archaic jades and Sung ceramics are addressed to the aesthetic sense in all its purity, so that once again the object becomes symbolic – a symbol of the absolute.

1. INDIAN ART

Historical Background

A peninsula of over two and a half million square miles, India is cut off from direct communication with Central Asia by the huge ranges of the Himalayas and the Hindu Kush. Its great gateway is the Indus valley, which brings it into contact with Iran and what is now Afghanistan. Through this gate the Mesopotamian civilization penetrated in the proto-historic period, and in the historical period came the Hellenistic influences of the Greco-Iranian kingdoms, brought in by Alexander's invasion. The link with China leaves Kashmir to join the Iranian highways of the Oxus valley, passing through the Turkestan oases; it was by this route that Buddhism made its impact on Chinese civilization. Buddhism also spread eastwards through Burma, into Siam, Cambodia and Annam, and by sea along the Coromandel coast towards the Indian Archipelago and Java. This eastern region was the real colonial province of Indian art: Buddhism flourished there after its introduction in the third and fourth centuries, and continued to do so after it was driven out of India in the twelfth and thirteenth centuries.

Excavations have shown that the Indus valley (Mohenjo-Daro, Harappa) had a civilization that depended on Mesopotamia. It is difficult to date (perhaps 2000 B.C.) and its relationship to the native civilizations of which works have survived is obscure. The latter are relatively recent and are confined to a fairly short era (second century B.C. to seventeenth century A.D.). The Muslim invasion which swept into India in the eleventh century and penetrated deeply into the sub-continent in the following centuries, sterilized and gradually impoverished the native art, though it managed to retain all its spirit in the miniatures of the Rajput, Sikh and Delahani schools. A most surprising fact about India is that no trace remains of the period when the Indian mentality was formed, no doubt because monuments and other works were then made of timber. Between 1500 and 800 B.C. an Aryan invasion filtered into the peninsula via the Indus, driving the Dravidian natives down to the southern tip. These invaders gave India its earliest religion, Vedism, which is not unlike the other Iranian religions such as that of Persia. Vedism later took on more marked native characteristics and developed into Brahmanism. This religion is essentially based on the belief in a universal soul (Brahman) in which all individual souls find their fulfilment. But in order to rejoin the primordial Being the individual soul is condemned to move upwards through the scale of creatures by means of transmigration of souls *(samsara)* until it has attained the way of salvation and broken the chain of rebirths, when a final disincarnation ensures its identification with God.

The Aryans brought a language with them, Sanskrit, which shares a common origin with the languages of the other Aryan peoples who invaded Europe. These make up the Indo-European language group (Sanskrit, Persian, Greek, Latin and Germanic). Treatises were composed in Sanskrit which serve as the basis of the Indian religions. These are the Vedas, composed between about 1500 and 1000 B.C. and written down in about the sixth century B.C., then metaphysical speculations *(Brahmanas, Upanishads)*, precepts *(Sutras)*, and finally two great epic poems, the *Mahabharata* and the *Ramayana*. Perhaps the reason why Vedism left no form of art was that, like the religion of the Persians, it must have been very spiritual and opposed to the making of images. Vedism was later paganized to some degree, in the stage known as Hinduism, and on the contrary began to represent gods who were formerly conceptual but were now personified. The main gods are Brahma, the least individualized and the least often portrayed, Vishnu, a messianic god who returns to the earth in successive incarnations *(avatars)* and Siva, a cosmic deity who is both creative and destructive, the god of life and death whose mystic dance created the world and whose most famous representation shows him as lord of the dance (pl. 578).

Meanwhile, when Brahmanism with its polytheistic pantheism was being developed, another religion, Buddhism, which began as no more than a moral teaching, was founded in the sixth century B.C. by the son of a rajah of Nepal (eastern basin of the Ganges), Prince Siddhartha,

578 *Nataraja or Siva, Lord of the Dance. Brahmanic Art of the Deccan.*
11th c. Madras

known as the Buddha or Enlightened One. He believed that the way of
salvation lay in the suppression of the desire or thirst for existence, so
that the soul might break free of its predestined transmigrations, effacing
itself in the state of Nirvana. Legend gives every detail of the life of
Prince Siddhartha, from his previous incarnations *(jatakas),* his noble

birth, his youthful sensuality which he renounced in order to become a monk, when he took the name of 'Sakyamuni'. After attaining wisdom (*Bodhi* or Enlightenment), in spite of the attacks of the demon Mara, he went about preaching the truth until he died after achieving Nirvana. His ashes were distributed in eight funerary monuments or stupas. Buddha's disciples set up monasteries, where they followed an ascetic life according to their rule. In the first or second century a doctrinal schism arose and the religion split into two branches, the Hinayana (or Theravada), meaning Little Vehicle of Salvation, and the Mahayana or Great Vehicle. The Hinayana conforms to the basic doctrine of the Buddha, regarding him as a superman but not as a god; it seeks personal salvation through the exercises leading to Nirvana. The Mahayana deifies Buddha and is a religion of redemption and love, comparable with Christianity; it brought hope and appealed to millions all over Asia. The redeeming divinities of Mahayana are the Bodhisattvas, or future Buddhas who are so touched by compassion for human suffering that they renounce Nirvana until all the other beings in the world are saved.

India has had a strange destiny, for after creating in Buddhism the most spiritual of Eastern religions, she lost sight of it in the eighth and ninth centuries, falling into the paganism of an idolatrous renewal of Brahmanism, in the form of Hinduism. After reaching China in the sixth century, Buddhism found its strongest hold in the cultural colonies of India, that is to say Indo-China and the East Indies.

Evolution of Indian Art

The early history of India is complicated by the fact that the country was always divided into a number of kingdoms or principalities, except in one or two periods when political unity was more marked (Maurya Empire, about third century B.C. and Gupta Empire in the fourth and fifth centuries A.D.). In spite of these divisions India's artistic civilization shows a genuine unity because of the common cultural outlook imposed by the Aryans and the consistency of the tropical climate.

The first Indian art was of Buddhist inspiration, for primitive Vedism and Brahmanism left few works, or at least few have survived. It was the Maurya dynasty which helped this early art to spread all over India. In the third century B.C. the Emperor Asoka, who has been called the Constantine of Buddhism, built memorial columns in the Ganges valley (at Sarnath) and stupas in the places associated with events in Buddha's life, and his example was followed by his successors.

If we set aside India's protohistoric civilization, which has no obvious connection with what followed, the artistic history of the country may be divided into the following periods:

1. Primitive period and introduction of Buddhist art. Third century B. C. to first century A. D.

The kings of the Maurya and Sunga dynasties built memorials (Sarnath) and stupas (Bharhut, Sanchi) in the Ganges valley, which show the life of the Buddha in narrative form and with lavish naturalism though he himself was never represented in person (pl. 580). The stupa is a stone version of an older timber construction, and shows belated Achaemenian influence in its ornament. The same features are to be found in sanctuaries and convents carved in the rock in central India, in the Deccan (Nasik, Karli, pl. 582, Bhaja).

2. Buddhist art. Early Christian era to fifth century A. D.

Indian now developed on three different planes:

a) in the north-west provinces, bordering Iran, and in Gandhara (province of Peshawar) and Kapisa in what is now Afghanistan (sites excavated at Hadda, Bamiyan, Kapisa), an art called 'Greco-Buddhist' appeared under the Kushan dynasty between the first and fifth centuries, and is so called because it shows the application of Hellenistic principles to Buddhist statuary. Large numbers of sculptures in blue schist or slate as well as in stucco have been found in the small stupas in the Hadda monasteries (pl. 570). There the Buddha was shown in person for the first time, dressed in a Grecian type of mantle or pallium with clinging folds or swags, and in various symbolic postures which became typical of Buddhist iconography. The idealized face is of the Apollo type, although with some Indian traits: the lengthening of the ear-lobe, the *urna* or "third eye" between the brows, the *ushnisha* or cranial protuberance disguised as a top-knot resembling that of the Greek sun-god (pl. 579). Demons and genii are also to be found in this highly figurative iconography.

b) Parallel with Greco-Buddhist art, the native naturalistic aesthetic that had appeared earlier developed between the first and third centuries A. D. in the form of the Mathura or pre-Gupta style, representing the Buddha, and perhaps with some influence from the Greco-Buddhist idealist manner which gradually affected it. The architecture of central-Indian caves showed the same features as in the preceding period.

579 Head of the Buddha. Greco-Buddhist Art of Gandhara. Paris

580 Stupa at Sanchi. Buddhist. 2nd c. B.C. – 1st c. A.D.

c) In the south of India between the first and fourth centuries, that is to say in the Deccan, at Amaravati, in the Krishna valley, a sculptural style developed which, perhaps owing to Greco-Buddhist influence, lost something of the native, naturalistic heaviness and sought to portray movement; the figures became more elongated, while the ritual *tribhanga* pose of the body, moving in three ways simultaneously – a pose introduced in the Sanchi period – found a graceful suppleness.

3. *Gupta period*. Fourth to sixth century A.D.

The Gupta period saw the triumph of idealism over the naturalism and vitalism of the previous periods. In the sculptures in the round of the Ganges valley, and in the frescoes and bas-reliefs of the Ajanta caves in central India, artists sought to express a divine serenity, detachment and mystic love through forms that have a great classical poise and that have a precise canon behind them. Buddhist iconography was now fixed into several types which spread to overseas Indian territories. Rock architecture was still carried on, but there were some outdoor temples, too.

4. *Post-Gupta period*. Seventh and eighth centuries A.D.

The academic impoverishment of Buddhist sculpture in the post-Gupta period was made up for by a revival of Brahmanism, resulting in a renewed native taste for a wealth of forms, and a new tendency to the colossal in an effort to express the greatness of the deities. Artists had the courage to carve enormous rocks (*Descent of the Ganges,* Mamalla-puram, in the south-east, pl. 569; Cave Temple of Siva at Elephanta,

581 Rathas hewn out of Rocks, Mamallapuram. Brahmanic. 7th c.

Deccan, eighth century). Sometimes they gave these blocks an architectural form (*Rathas* or Shrines, Mamallapuram, seventh century, pl. 581), and did not shrink before tremendous labours of excavation (Kailasanath Temple, sculpted in the eighth century from a single block excavated at Ellura). This period begins to show examples of open-air architecture (as distinct from caves) executed in durable materials. Starting from the elements of timber-construction showing Iranian characteristics, architecture now became more and more Indianized.

5. Development of Brahmanic art.

While the Indus and Ganges regions were invaded by Islam and ceased being the great creative centre, the Indian spirit survived in the north east (Bengal and Orissa) and the Deccan. Cut off from the external influences which might have been profitable, Indian art became self-centred and quickly exhausted its creative potential. This period saw the development of temples, from simple *cella* into structures of a more complex plan. In the north, the *cella* was given height, becoming a bulb-shaped *sikhara* (Lingaraja Temple in Orissa; Khajraho, about 1000), while in the south it became the pyramidal *vimana* (Tanjore, eleventh century). Multiplied in the form of *gopurams* or porch-towers, with concentric halls (pl. 585) this pyramidal type of structure gave the design of the great Temple of Siva at Tanjore which later, in the fourteenth

439

century was enriched with a columned ambulatory or *mandapa* (Madura, the greatest temple in India, seventeenth century). The supreme endeavour of Indian medieval architecture was the building of the Sun Temple at Konarak (thirteenth century), which remained unfinished. The *sikhara,* which has collapsed, must have reached a height of about 394 feet, and its central hall is still some 230 feet high. Decoration lost all its plastic value, becoming no more than a monotonous ornamentation which in Mysore state assumed tormented, 'flamboyant' features. However, from the eleventh to the fourteenth century, Dravidian art still produced admirable bronze statues made in the round, of only moderate size, in which the sense of poise handed down from the Gupta aesthetic gives an elegant restraint to the intense urge to movement: the Nataraja or dancing Siva is, thanks to its subject, the finest expression of this equilibrium (pl. 578).

Architecture

The Hindu architecture made in durable materials is entirely for religious purposes. The ancient lay buildings, made of timber, have not survived. The Buddhist undertakings were of three types: the *chaitya,* the *vihara* and the stupa. Outdoor buildings (stupas) or those excavated in rock *(chaityas* and *viharas)* are a literal stone reconstruction of wooden architecture. The stupa, or reliquary (pl. 580), is a tumulus or dome of masonry, topped with one or more stone 'parasols' – symbols of dignity – and surrounded by a circular balustrade with four heavily-carved gateways which open to the four cardinal points. The *chaitya,* or Buddhist church, whose form perhaps originated in the West, is a basilica with a nave and ambulatory, ending in an apse which contains a small stupa or *dagoba* (pl. 582, 583). The *vihara,* or monastery, consists of cells grouped round a square courtyard containing a sanctuary, and can be hollowed in rock as at Ellura.

The Brahman temple strongly resembles the Egyptian temple. It consists in its essentials of a square cell or *vimana* which is the sanctuary holding the idol, entered by a vestibule to which a columned hall or *mandapa* was added for the worshippers. In its definitive form, one or a number of enclosures, pierced by towers *(gopurams),* were set round this nucleus, and they contained columned halls (pl. 585), extra sanctuaries and sacred pools bordered with arcades or galleries and steps (pl. 584). As is the case with Egyptian temples, Brahman temples were subject to indefinite extension, by the process of adding more and more and ever larger internal sections.

India did not develop the true arch or vault, so that the exclusive use of corbelled roofing led the architects to build in tiers so that they arrived at a pyramidal structure (pl. 584). The successive tiers were decorated with smaller versions of the edifice itself, which, as it were,

582 *Interior of the Chaitya-Hall, Karli. 2nd–1st c. B.C.*

bud all over the building or even swarm all round it as at Bhuvanesvar (pl. 576). In the Dravidian temples the composition follows a diminishing pattern, each *gopuram* becoming smaller and smaller towards the central *vimana*, which is the smallest of the towers. As a result, no overall view of the temple can be had except from a *gopuram*.

Indian architecture has not succeeded in creating any original decorative code. The decorative principles of the earliest monuments consisted of nothing more than taking over into stone the same forms as were used by the carpenter, and borrowing freely from the old Achaemenian system (bell-shaped capitals ending in a bulbous form, pl. 587, sometimes topped with a flat supporting beam, or with animals back-to-back; plinths are often in the shape of an animal, with fabulous beasts, gryphons, sphinxes, fishlike or birdlike sirens, centaurs, creatures affrontee, palm-leaf moulding, garlands, etc.). Among those forms which persisted for a long time from the early timber structures one might mention the pillar surmounted by a beam or bracket which supports the entablature, and above all the *kudus* (gable or dormer windows) which

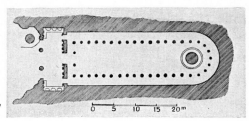

583 *Plan of the Chaitya-Hall, Karli*

0 5 10 15 20 m

584 *Vimana, Gopuram and Sacred Pool of the Siva Temple, Tinnevelly.*
Brahmanic. 15th c.

are one of the pervading features of the decoration (pl. 581). In the last
period of Dravidian art, the entire temple was overrun by figures
sculpted in the round which tended to oust ornamentation of other kinds.
The cornice-work was over-done and gave a confusing impression.

By comparison with sculpture, which evolved to a very high level,
Indian architecture never outgrew its archaism. Like the primitive
civilizations, India sought to convey an impression of strength, either
through immense excavatory works or through colossal piles of materials.
The inclination which was shown from earliest times for direct carving
either in the form of excavation (crypts) or in the round (rock-temples
of Mamallapuram) shows that the Hindu temperament tended to think

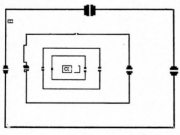

585 *Plan of the Enclosures,*
Gopurams and Sanctuary of the
Vishnu Temple, Srirangam.
Brahmanic. 16th c.

of architecture as something closely
related to a sculptured form; the Indian pantheistic genius discouraged
the labour of geometrical, abstract
calculation that architectural composition demands. With its ever-
increasing number of enclosures and
its decorations as recklessly plentiful as the growth of a virgin forest,
the Hindu temple, gathered round
its *vimana* as though round a pivot,
none the less answered the needs of
the Oriental temple, that had to be
an image of the cosmos which was

442

586 *Yakshini. Pillar from the Stupa at Bharhut. Buddhist. 2nd c. B.C. Calcutta*
587 *Pillars in Cave 31, Ellura. Brahmanic. 7th–8th c. A.D.*
588 *Yakshini. Pillar from the Balustrade of the Stupa at Mathura. Buddhist.*
   2nd c. A.D. Calcutta

thought of as having the form of a mountain. But the Khmers on the other hand were able to carry out the same programme in a way that implies a more proper conception of architecture.

The Figurative Arts

Sculpture is the major art of India. Her genius for naturalism expressed itself most completely through the carving of stone. The development of sculpture from the Bharhut bas-reliefs to Dravidian bronzes, shows a thorough exploitation of the formal possibilities of this art. Although it was not the main tradition and shows many signs of the Hellenistic aesthetic, yet Greco-Buddhist art finds a natural place in this development, for, in introducing the Greek example into Hindu sculpture, it quickened the evolution away from that archaism which stunted Indian architecture.

Hindu plastic art, however, never lost the mistrust of carving in the round which dated from early times; related to low-relief, it is a monumental form and it resembles that of the French medieval period rather more than it does Greek sculpture. But its function was not decorative,

443

it was not applied to the building or monument, but on the contrary absorbed it. Indeed, buildings became no more than pieces of sculpture carved on every side, without a single blank space on their walls.

With the summary planes of its modelling, its frontalism with figures so flattened on the block of stone that the spectator has no side-view to consider, the Bharhut style (pl. 586) has all the strength of an art in its first vitality; the forms recall the early Romanesque works in the ambulatory of St-Sernin at Toulouse (pl. 699). The perspective is shown by means of tiers or rows as in all ancient civilizations, whose first concern is the readability of forms (pl. 589). The art of the stupas of Sanchi has all the luxuriance of Romanesque in its first flowering: as in the twelfth century in Europe, the genius of the artist is seen revelling in its creative capacity, and inventing new variations on old themes borrowed from the Middle East, but now a rich sap, that of tropical life, flows into and rounds the forms. In the *yakshini* the canon of feminine Hindu beauty, which at Bharhut was still rather stiff, finds its full suppleness and sensuality, with the three-way movement of the body (*tribhanga*) expressing the rhythm of the dance, the fullness of the breasts, and the narrow hips on the broad pelvis. Plastically, the flattened modelling of the planes, avoiding profile, that was perhaps taken over from ivory-carvings, is sometimes accompanied in the animal and feminine figures by a tendency towards a rounded modelling, sensual and heavy like a ripe fruit. But – as in the finest Romanesque compositions, for instance at Moissac – the sculptor continued to respect the wall-surface, bringing it alive with the chisel rather than trying to produce a jutting relief. This final stage was reached in the Mathura style (first to fourth century A.D.), in which the voluptuous curves of the modelling have a fleshly quality that India was never to surpass (pl. 588). Parallel with the Mathura school, the Amaravati school (second to fourth century A.D.) conforms more strictly with the wall's plane surface and flattened modelling, but in its sinuous movement recalls the feverish Romanesque of Burgundy (pl. 590). The smile that graces these faces, the dancing rhythm of the figures both at Mathura and Amaravati convey all the optimism brought by the gospel of salvation.

589 Dream of Maya (Conception of the Buddha who enters his Mother as a young Elephant). Bharhut. 2nd c. B.C. Calcutta

590 *Women kneeling at the Buddha's Throne. Relief from Amaravati.
Buddhist. 2nd–3rd c.*

The Gupta aesthetic put an end to this feverishness, and may be
compared with early Gothic which shares the same moral and plastic
significance. Like the Gothic, it sprang from a desire to create holy images
and to convey divine serenity and compassion through restrained postures
and the simplified modelling of a classical style; just as Gothic created
the typical Western image of Christ, Gupta art determined the image of
the Buddha. Orientalists disagree as to whether the classical development happened spontaneously or whether, as seems likely, it was helped
by Greco-Buddhist art. The art of Hadda was certainly more attuned
to the West than to the East, and is perhaps the last smile of Greek art,
surviving in an outpost on the very edge of the ancient world. The

591 *Sleep of Vishnu. Relief in the Elephanta Caves. Brahmanic. 7th c.*

592 Buddha of Mathura. Buddhist. 4th–5th c.

extraordinary likeness between Hadda figures and those of thirteenth
century Gothic in France, proves the existence of enduring laws in the
creation of forms (pl. 570, 571), for at an interval of ten centuries the
meeting between a mystical religion and the plastic sense of the West
resulted in very similar forms.

The urge to abstractness gave Gupta statuary a rather dry stylization which might be called pseudo-Byzantine (frontal presentation, conventional modelling of draperies, facial impersonality, pl. 592). Perhaps Gandharian influence was also responsible for introducing an alien formalism which arrested the development of the native temperament. The mural paintings of the Gupta period were spared this influence, (Ajanta caves), and in them we see the highest expression of Buddhist spirituality (pl. 593). These works, which are now worn away and difficult to decipher have even more of the traditional Indian suppleness of movement than the statues. The gracefulness of the arabesque here assumes a mystical terderness. In keeping with the Oriental aesthetic,

593 The Great Bodhisattva. Wall-Painting in Cave I, Ajanta. Buddhist. 4th–5th c.

which sees everything unfolding or flowing, the different scenes shown in the same room or cave are all linked one to the other by figures or personages who play a part in two neighbouring subjects.

Brahmanic art had a means of expression at its disposal that had been enriched by centuries of experiment. It avoided Gupta abstractness and in its masterpieces at Elephanta, seventh century (pl. 591), Mamalla-puram, seventh century, and Ellura, seventh and eighth centuries, it rediscovered the strength that works of art always have in early phases of development while at the same time profiting from the plastic achievement of a mature classical art. But the evangelistic enthusiasm of Buddhist humanism gave way to the superhuman images common to primitive religions. In the tenth and eleventh centuries, at Orissa, the Hindu plastic system seems to have returned to the origins of Mathura art in works of overwhelming sensuality, while in the twelfth century, in the overladen bas-reliefs of Mysore the feverishness of a declining art became exacerbated in the same way as Flamboyant Gothic (pl. 594). After this, the major monumental sculpture withered into a decorative craft. However, from the tenth and almost into the seventeenth century, the Deccan produced admirable bronze statuettes in which an unexpected sense of arabesque restrains the usual lush roundness of the volumes. The firmness of line, the inner energy of the intense modelling, the depth of symbolism, together with an expansive feeling of life make some of the twelfth-century Nataraja figures – representing Siva's cosmic dance –

447

594 *Krishna playing the Flute. Brahmanic Art of Mysore. 12th c. Calcutta*

works of a formal perfection not often found in India, and they can be set beside the most refined creations of the Italian Renaissance or of Chinese art (pl. 578).

2. THE EXPANSION OF INDIAN ART

The cultural expansion of India by way of the sea-routes of the East Indies and through Indo-China has been compared with that of Greece. It is true that a similiar phenomenon is to be seen in both cases. India brought to the countries it influenced, not only religious forms of expression but also a classical vocabulary of images that was Aryan in spirit, that is to say profoundly naturalistic. But the native temperaments of the peoples concerned reacted on the imported culture, so that the Indian aesthetic was 'Orientalized': as it lost some of its original character its forms finally became Asiatic and inclined towards expressions that were not far removed from the Chinese. Generally speaking Hindu naturalism found itself opposed by the tendency towards stylization which characterizes the mentality behind all Asiatic civilizations – always aspiring to the abstract.

Javanese Art

The evolution described above is particularly noticeable in the art of Java. In the first period which lasted from the eighth to the tenth century, the artistic civilization that developed in the east of Java remained obedient to the Indian aesthetic, while imposing an even more purified classicism upon it. The temples, sanctuaries and pyramids (pl. 595), while being of modest dimensions, were restrained and balanced compositions in which a monumental conception imposes its own strict laws on sculptural form, whether it be Buddhist as at Barabudur, or Brahmanic as at Prambanam. The sculptor was pursuing the Gupta ideal of naturalism, while being held back by his impulse to idealize. The finest monument in Java is the

595 Temple at Candi Pawon. Javanese. 8th c.

Stupa of Barabudur (second half of seventh century), a structure quite unique of its kind, with its rising terraces surmounted by open bell-shaped *dagobas* or stupas, and with some 504 statues of the Dhayani Buddha set in niches, and bas-relief friezes telling the story of the Buddha in extraordinary detail, through 2000 pitcures which stretch over more than 3³/₄ miles. If the Dhayani Buddhas are suggestive of Gupta idealism, the friezes make one think more of the Ajanta frescoes; the mystical tenderness of the Great Vehicle was never expressed any-

596 The Buddha teaching. Stupa at Borobudur. Javanese. 2nd half of 8th c.

where with greater humanity and sweetness than in these youthful forms which have none of the lushness of the Indian canon but show a very graceful elongation (pl. 596). At Prambanam this art developed towards refinement and worldly preciosity. After a certain gap, due no doubt to a period of political upheaval, Javanese civilization revived in the west of the island in the eleventh century, in a renaissance which produced its finest works in the thirteenth and fourteenth centuries. The Indonesian tendency became the stronger and showed itself in hieratism, a fanciful stylization similar to the Chinese, and a taste for the monstrous. After the Muslim invasion this type of Javanese art retired to Bali, where it persists to this day.

Richly endowed with an imagination which, though unusually prolific of forms, seemed unable to conceive anything except at the prompting of what can be seen in nature, India was impotent when it came to making anything like a genuine architecture. The countries which depended on India and inherited a ready-made canon of ideas and imagery were capable of some speculation in the monumental field. Java produced some exquisitely pure monuments which were worthy of its own aesthetic, that seeks gracefulness rather than mere size. The Khmers built the most beautiful and impressive monumental works to be found in the Eastern hemisphere.

Khmer Art

If the Khmer kingdom seems to have existed since the third century, the earliest remaining monuments date from the sixth to the eighth century (so-called 'pre-Angkor art'). The great achievements of the kingdom date from the eighth century. In 802 Jayavarman II inaugurated on a mountain the cult of the king-god, lord of the world, from which no doubt sprang the notion of the temple-mountain which remained dear to the Khmers. Between 893 and 910 Yasovarman chose the site of Angkor for his capital, later to be enriched with more and more imposing monuments, of which the finest are the Temple of Angkor-Wat (first half of twelfth century) and the Bayon Temple (thirteenth century). Decadence set in rapidly after the Siamese invasion.

Of all the Oriental peoples, the Khmers alone showed a true genius for architecture. They understood how to plan cities according to definite principles, and how to make them into a harmonious monumental whole, and created a type of temple which may be compared with the finest architectural conceptions of the West. Being more positivistic than the Indians, who avoided any precision which might hinder their flights of thought, the Khmers took quite literally the idea that the temple should be an image of the cosmos, and therefore invented the temple in the form of a mountain. Taking the Indian *gopurams*, they had the idea of setting these out symmetrically and placing them in tiers on terraced pyramids,

597 Temple of Angkor Wat. Khmer. 1st half of 12th c.

in such a way that the whole architectural composition rose gradually towards the central *vimana* which contained the effigy of the king-god, wherein dwelt the king's soul in the form of the 'royal *lingham*' (phallic emblem). From this pivot of the mountain-temple other sanctuaries radiated, these being dedicated to ancestors (pl. 597). This central plan with its series of enclosures recalls that of medieval keeps and castles, and is a perfect symbol of the monarchic theocracy invented by the Khmers. The possibility of dedicating a temple to themselves led to competition between the sovereigns, and explains the prosperity of building in that kingdom.

All the elements of composition were ordered according to architectural requirements and principles. The towers were built in the shape of a cross to a coherent design; in some cases all the sides of a tower would be decorated with a gigantic head of monumental effect. These heads are a powerful symbol of the king, identified with the Lokesvara Bodhisattva and thus asserting his entry and fitting place in the pattern of the skies and of the kingdom.

598 Capital in a Gallery of the Temple of Angkor Wat. Khmer. 1st half of 12th c.

451

599 *Parade of the Troops of King Suryavarman II. Temple of Angkor Wat. Khmer. 1st half of 12th c.*

Inside the enclosures, galleries which served as libraries or halls of worship were arranged with a fine sense of perspective, and crowned with corbelled 'false vaulting' which gave the effect of a pointed barrel-vault. The Khmers worked out a system of ornamentation, whereas in India decoration never rose above an accumulation of heterogeneous forms, and they also restrained the carving and moulding of cornices which ran riot in Hindu architecture. They knew the proper principles of moulding, best calculated to enhance monumental effects. Such was their sense of the logic of architecture that in the pillars of the Angkor galleries they unwittingly reinvented the essential feature of the Doric column (pl. 598).

The Khmer sculptors spread their work almost slavishly as in the Indian temples, but with a proper regard for the needs of architectural design. The Khmers covered the walls inside the galleries with immense, flat bas-reliefs which respected the wall-surface but brought it to life (pl. 599). In these works, the forms follow a rhythmic pattern unknown to Indian art (pl. 600). The repetition of the same form in an indefinite series is a characteristic feature of the Asiatic mind. The flamboyant suppleness of contours and predominance of the arabesque (Apsara frieze) in Bayon art show the increasing expression of the Asiatic temperament and a strengthening of affinities with Chinese art.

Khmer art produced admirable statues in the round. The hieratism of the frontal attitudes, the stylization of a summary type of bas-relief, result in works that part company with Hindu naturalism and recall Egyptian art; they have an architectonic dignity and balance. In the

452

600 Frieze of Apsaras. Khmer: Bayon Style. 2nd half of 12th c. Paris

Bayon period the famous 'Angkor smile' graces the faces which, with closed eyes, express the fervour and bliss that the soul can achieve through the Buddha. This smile is to be found not only on Aryan and Indian faces, but also on faces which are more Asiatic, with almond-shaped eyes, waving eyebrows, thick and arched lips. An imagination given to the creation of monsters (*nagas, Garuda,* stylized lions) also related the art of Angkor to that of China; it was no doubt the Siamese invasion which prevented a more pronounced Asiatic influence.

The forms developed by the Tchampa (Annamese) are close to those of Khmer art. As for Siam, its main creation was its bronze sculpture, strongly hieratic, in which an Asian stylization was taken farther than in Java or Cambodia; its best pieces were produced from the thirteenth to the sixteenth century.

3. CHINESE ART

Historical Background

Although its immense coast-line opens China to the Yellow Sea and the China Sea, yet its civilization is of the continental type. Cut off from the rest of Asia by the high Tibetan plateau, China has always been focussed on the interior owing to the constant need for defence against the nomad peoples of the steppes who poured southwards through Mongolia. China only communicates with difficulty with the West by means of the oasis of Turkestan, the meeting-point of two different worlds through which the 'silk-road' ran, a route which goes through the Kashgar passes via Afghanistan to end at the gates of China at Tunhuang. The emperors were always concerned with holding the nomads at arms' length in the north and keeping the road open through Turkestan in the west. China is a fertile land, consisting of the alluvial plains of three great rivers stretching from north to south – the Yellow river (Huang-ho), the Blue river (Yang-tse), and the Si-kiang. This immense area, which at times came under a single emperor and was often divided into many states, has a great racial and religious unity which are ensured by a common language and method of writing. The history of China is one of alternating contraction and expansion. Whenever a dynasty managed to unify China under a single ruler, the need for quelling the barbarians resulted in an expansionist policy; but sooner or later an invasion of nomads, helped by internal strife, would come and shake the structure of the empire. Then the native dynasty would retreat to some internal province (Szechwan) or down to the south, while the barbarians, rapidly taking to Chinese ways, would give up their nomadic habits and found a settled state which might even work for the re-unification of China. This perpetual state of alarm and readiness has favoured Chinese civilization, since it discouraged the tendency to inertia rising from its respect for tradition, while infusing China periodically with new blood and strength and keeping it in contact with the outside world. The area of Chinese expansion stretches by sea towards Japan, and overland into Burma, Indo-China and the Indian archipelago, where it made contact with Hindu civilization.

Chinese religion is essentially based on a belief in the magical harmony between the human and universal orders, a harmony maintained by a ritual laid down by the emperor as head of the state. This religion, which is a rationalized form of a very early stage of human beliefs, sets man at the mercy of cosmic heavenly powers which are also delegated to the emperor who rules on earth. Ancestor-worship contributes to this universal harmony because the souls of the dead become intercessors. The moral code of this practical religion is also a civic code, formulated by Confucius whose thought inspired all the theories of the state developed by the intelligentsia or mandarins who followed him. It resulted in a philosophical humanism which underlies and cements the continuity of Chinese civilization.

However, the Chinese mind has also been tempted by various mysticisms which sharpened its more spiritual instincts. Taoism, attributed in its origins to Lao-tse, who lived in the sixth century B.C., urges that the soul must put off all material sensation so as to find in itself the principle of its pure essence, which is in harmony with the principle of universal order. This is the Tao. This mysticism, which had great influence on painting, was practised by monks. Introduced into China under the Han dynasty, in the first century of our era, Buddhism took root and was proclaimed the state religion by the Tartar dynasty of the Wei in the fifth century, in the form preached by the Great Vehicle. To the highly sophisticated Chinese, Buddhism brought the corrective of a religion of love based on a belief in the mercy of the Bodhisattvas, Maitreya, the Lord of Infinite Light and ruler of Paradise, and Avalokitesvara who in China became the goddess Kuan Yin, the very spirit of compassion. The so-called 'contemplative sect' (*dhyana* in Sanskrit, *tch'an* in Chinese) linked up with

Taoism and sought the essence of the Buddha in the human heart by intuitive means. Thus, through its various approaches, Chinese thought always tends towards a kind of monism, that is to say a belief in the unity, the oneness of all beings and all things in the universal essence, while regarding all differences and individualities as being no more than appearances, illusions of the senses. This intellectualism, together with an extreme refinement of the senses, makes the Chinese more inclined than any other race to prize purity of form above all else; for the Chinese the highest artistic pleasure is to be found in handling a jade piece whose extremely simple form and smoothness of touch, together with its supernatural meaning, uplift the soul in a kind of ecstasy which takes it beyond the world of appearances.

Evolution of Chinese Art

1. Prehistory

A number of sites in northern China give proof of the existence of a Neolithic pottery whose spiral decorations recall those of Aegaean or Central European pots. This confirms that there was some continuity in Neolithic civilizations.

2. Ancient China. Shang or Yin dynasty (sixteenth century B.C.), Chou dynasty (eleventh to third century B.C.)

The excavations at Hsiao-t'un in northern Honan, and at An-yang in north China, have brought up bronze vessels, inscribed and carved bones, jade objects, and a few marble figures of animals dating from the Shang period, the oldest historical dynasty. This symbolic art continued under the Chou dynasty (pl. 601) which ended in a feudal anarchy with the period known as the 'Warring States period' (fifth to third century), until Shih Huang Ti who founded the short-lived Ch'in dynasty (A.D. 221 –207) established a united China for the first time. The emperor was responsible for the building of the famous Great Wall of China which served as a barrier against the Mongol tribes. The art of this period may be considered as a highly cultured expression of the Bronze Age civilization, which at that time spread all over the Eurasian continent with the exception of the Mediterranean. The artist's activity was essentially bound up with a magic function, the objects he made being used for ritual purposes. These include bronze cauldrons or kettles of a strictly defined design and use, which were reserved for libations and sacrifices (pl. 602); inscribed bones used for divining; jade pieces for various uses, some being amulets, others symbols of power or strength (axes, knives, halberds) which were given to officials. The most remarkable were cosmic symbols used for sacrifices (a pierced disc meaning *pi*, a symbol of heaven (pl. 605), or a cylinder inserted in a rectangle meaning *tsong*, a symbol of the earth; a rectangular plaque standing upright and engraved with the Great Bear,

or *kuei* symbolizing a mountain). These articles have no decoration and owe their beauty to their purity of form and the quality of the jade, a hard stone which for the Chinese was a symbol of pure essence. The cauldrons are covered with a stylized decoration with a ritualistic, propitiatory meaning. The concentrated energy of these patterns makes itself felt in flamboyant curves in the Warring States and Ch'in periods.

3. Medieval China

Medieval China saw the vicissitudes of the great empire founded by the Ch'in. It begann with the strong monarchic, theocratic and cultural centralization of the Han emperors (202 B.C.–A.D. 220) which collapsed beneath barbarian invasions and gave way to a divided and chaotic China until the T'ang dynasty (618–906) managed to restore the empire. After a short period of anarchy (907–960) the Sung dynasty again unified the country, but only for a short time (960–1126) because it was soon conquered in the south by the Mongols (1127–1279). The Mongols again unified China but to their own advantage (Yuan dynasty, 1280–1368).

a) Han dynasty (202 B.C.–A.D. 220)

It was the Han dynasty which established the political and cultural unity of the Chinese Empire. This achievement meant the restoration of dynastic traditions as well as of Confucian philosophy, which had both been abolished by the Ch'in, according to a characteristic rhythm, since China always progresses by renewing its inspiration from the past. The Han policy of expansion into Asia opened China to the outside world and, through the North, brought in the influence of the animal art of the steppes (which had previously penetrated in the time of the Warring States), and through Turkestan, which General Pan Ch'ao had overrun, influences from Iran as well as the Buddhist religion. The Han capital cities were Chang-an (formerly Hsi-an-fu) and, later further east, Lo-yang, also in Honan, on the Yellow river.

After the long period of magic and symbolism of the Ancient period, the Han period allowed some relaxation which showed in the beginning of an art portraying figures (pl. 605). Han art tried to make great syntheses of forms freshly taken from nature, especially in terra-cotta sculpture for funerary use.

b) Political division: Period of the Six Dynasties (220–618 A.D.)

The Han Empire fell owing to revolution, and the Turco-Mongols invaded north China where they created new kingdoms, while national dynasties in the south carried on the native tradition. In the north the Tartar Wei dynasty, which came to regard itself as fully Chinese, made Buddhism the state religion in the fifth century (453). Buddhism brought with it a demand for idols which produced great monumental sculptures, whose themes and style were borrowed from Turkestan Buddhism, which in its turn sprang from a mixture of Greco-Buddhist, Iranian and Gupta styles. It was then that the caves of Yun-kang in Honan were sculpted (435–515), followed by those of Lung-men (495–515). In these rock-carvings and the Buddhistic styles of the same period, the feverish energy of the Chinese mind is sweetened to express only bliss and mystic ecstasy; it is the only time in Chinese art when a smile appears on the human face. The last supreme flowering of this mystic art occurred in the Sui period (589–617) under a dynasty which unified China for thirty years.

c) T'ang dynasty (618–906)

The sense of the divine was crushed by the realistic outlook of the T'ang period, which produced the most naturalistic art known to China. The positivism of this triumphant dynasty, which kept China in a state of political unity for a period of two hundred years, thanks to its military strength, expressed itself in the cult of sculpture in the round which now

602 *Bronze Ritual Kettle. Shang Dynasty. About 12th c. Washington*

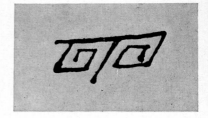

603 *T'ao-t'ieh. Drawing after a Bronze of the Chou Dynasty*

604 *Lei-wan. Drawing after a Bronze of the Chou Dynasty*

became the dominant art-medium (pl. 606). This form imposed its style on all other art, and, for instance, the decoration of mirrors in bronze is completely unbalanced by a powerful modelling out of proportion with the object. Painting also developed in this period. Generally speaking the T'ang aesthetic, strongly marked by outside influences as a result of imperial conquests, was rather foreign to the native Chinese genius.

4. Sung (960–1279) and Yuan (1280–1368) dynasties

After a period of anarchy the Sung emperors unified China, but not for long. Under the pacifist, traditionalist influence of the educated class, the Sung emperors gave up the T'ang policy of defensive aggression and were soon left with only south China, where they made Hang-chou their capital in 1127. These emperors had little sense of political realism and were dilettante aesthetes, 'crowned dreamers' who gave all their time to poetry and painting. The decadence of the arts of carving in relief is a sign of the decay of energy and realism, but painting, which now came to the forefront, offered a ready form of expression to intellectual, metaphysical speculation (pl. 614). In the capital at K'ai-feng-fu in Honan, and later at Hangchou, the emperor and his courtiers accumulated rich art-collections, while art-critics wrote the history of the artists of the past and showed their esteem for those of the present, there being an academy of fine arts (with sections for painting and calligraphy) to pay honour to the most famous artists. Subjects for paintings were given out for competition.

Softened by social refinements and the enjoyment of life, this society lost hold of its own future preservation. The formidable hordes of Genghis Khan found it easy to sweep away this effete empire, to unify the land once more under the rule of Mongolian emperors (the Yuan dynasty, which for a time brought China back to a more realistic art, with animal and military themes).

5. Modern China. Ming (1368–1644) and Ch'ing (1644–1912) dynasties

The really creative period of Chinese art ended with the Sung dynasty. The native dynasty of the Ming emperors, who overthrew the Mongols,

458

brought back a 'restoration' spirit with an emphasis on tradition resulting in an academic outlook in art which was only further strengthened under the Manchu Ch'ing dynasty. The European demand for Chinese pieces now hastened a decline by encouraging a tendency towards picturesque trinkets. Ceramics was the favorite art in the Ming and Ch'ing periods. Almost all the great Chinese monuments date from these dynasties, since few survived from the previous periods. In 1421 the Ming emperors transferred the capital from Nanking to Peking, a city which was founded in the tenth century by Mongolian settlers.

Archaic Art

As can be seen from the various articles and bronzes of the Shang, Chou and Ch'in periods, ancient Chinese art is a most remarkable example of the strength of expression that can be achieved in a range of forms extremely stylized in order to raise the image to a symbolic level. The characteristic Chinese genius for inventing non-representational shapes is found here at its highest intensity (pl. 602). These bronzes have a decoration whose purpose was to give the ritual utensil a magic power: the principal decorative features are the *t'ao-t'ieh*, a horned, jawless monster with popping eyes derived from a mixture of the ram or bull, the owl and the tiger (pl. 603), the *kuei* or dragon, the snake, the bird, and various types of spiral (some of which suggest the *lei-wan* or thunder-pattern which symbolizes rain, pl. 604). These signs could be transformed or combined in a thousand ways. Sometimes they are grouped symmetrically, though

605 *Pi. Symbol of Heaven. Han Dynasty. Private Collection*

606 *Head of a Bodhisattva from T'ien-lung Shan. T'ang Dynasty. 8th c.*

607 *Figures in the Yun-kang Caves. Wei Dynasty. 5th c.*

608 *Bodhisattva from the Lung-men Caves. Wei Dynasty. 6th c. Boston*

they consist of distinct elements which could be arranged like pieces of a jig-saw pattern, on a uniform background of carved spirals (*lei-wan*). They seem to spring out suddenly, threateningly, from the primordial chaos of matter, and in this maze the human mind finds no natural feature on which it can rest, and thus feels itself snatched into a demoniacal world devoid of human meaning; the broken stylization of line strengthens this impression of a merciless form of art. Made in a period of bloodshed and torture when human lives seemed worthless, these works are the most eloquent messages of the archaic periods when mankind lived in fear of cosmic powers. In spite of the temptations offered by realism, mysticism and humanism which it was to feel later, this sense of the power of a universe intent on crushing man is rooted deeply in the Chinese soul. The evolution of their bronzes shows a gradual weakening of this will to supernatural expression. As is usually the case, the artist's hand is most expressive when it is busy inventing, and the virtuosity that comes with experience weakens the value or impact of the message. The strongest examples of this style are thus the oldest, those of the Shang period (pl. 602). Though they were still powerful in the Chou period (pl. 601), the forms tend gradually, at the end of the dynasty, to decline into a purely decorative stylization, being only superficially inscribed on the bronze surface. This trend was completed in the Ch'in period, when the figures of animals carved in the round, inspired by steppe art, reached a further stage by giving the eye the reassuring shapes of living things.

Sculpture

The Chinese have never given sculpture much importance in the scale of artistic values. Whereas from the Han period onwards historians have piously recorded the names of painters whose works have long since vanished, the arts of relief have remained anonymous. They were practised by artisans who were all the less honoured because most of their works were at once hidden away in tombs. Sculpture had no place in the Chinese house, and as for the temples, it was only with Buddhism that any demand was felt for sculpture. However, all the arts of relief were practised successfully in the period of the great empires which created China. This sense for the most realistic of the arts, which exists and works in real space, is like a symbol of the positive outlook and energetic policy of the great dynasties. The animal and human forms taken by the funerary ceramics of the Han period show a fresh and bold desire to bring forms to life in space; the Chinese modeller shows only the essentials of his volumes without lingering over detail. In the Wei period the funerary statuettes became hieratic under the influence of the massive Buddhistic sculptures. The first Buddhistic works, the bas-reliefs of Yun-kang (453 –515, pl. 607), still retain something of the naturalistic vision of the Indian carvings that inspired them. But the Chinese gift for stylization set to work on the Indian data, showing a complete transformation of the Indian into the Chinese plastic code, in the art of the Lung-men caves (pl. 608). The modelling loses its roundness and becomes summary. The draperies fall into conventional folds that reach down to the feet in sharp waves, while the bodies are set in a frontal symmetry that eliminates

609 *Head of a Bodhisattva.*
Wei Dynasty. Late 5th-
Early 6th c.
Private Collection

610 *Head of a Bodhisattva.*
Sui Dynasty. Late 6th-Early
7th c. Private Collection

natural movement, all the forms being withdrawn and elongated in a hieratism that gives symbolic expression to the internity of the Buddha. These highly spiritualized works have been compared with those of Romanesque art; but perhaps they are even more like those of early Gothic, such as the statues on the Royal Porch of Chartres Cathedral, in which the de-materialized bodies are reduced to little more than a fragile stem supporting and ecstatic face (pl. 572, 573 and 609). The Sui period brought this style to its highest perfection, by detaching the figure from the wall and making it a work in the round. A hint of aristocratic mannerism that reminds one of the Gothic statues at Rheims, tends however to slacken its spiritual intensity a little (pl. 610). The T'ang period's will to power shows itself in an ostentatious fullness of the forms, a heavy vigorousness in the volumes (horsemen from the Tomb of the Emperor T'ai Tsung, pl. 611). The realism in the portrayal of animals, handed down from Sassanian art, came in by way of Turkestan, as did the growing taste for virile or warlike themes such as horsemen, warriors, guardians of tombs or *lokapalas*. The way in which muscles are accentuated (pl. 612) and the complete lack of stylization show that the triumphant China of the T'angs was given over to foreign influences, most of which filtered through from Turkestan, which China was then occupying. The Buddhist sculptures of T'ien-lung Shan, copies of Gupta art, amount to a rejection or betrayal of the national temperament (pl. 606), and it is the terra-cotta ceramists, producing funerary works, who seem to have been in closest touch with the traditional Chinese sense of arabesque (pl. 617). The Sung period marks the sharp decline of sculpture, when the image-maker strayed into a mass of mere picturesque detail, such as jewels, delicacy and softness of draperies, which have more to do with painting. The huge statues of animals which line the avenues leading to the tombs of the Ming emperors are clumsy versions of chimaeras and beasts, and merely served to show where emperors lay buried.

Painting

It is difficult for the public to appreciate Chinese painting, which along with the ancient bronzes best conveys the essence of the Chinese mentality, because of the few good specimens from the best periods that are to be found in museums and galleries, as well as their poor state of preservation, and the piecemeal presentation that becomes necessary for reproduction in books. When Chinese painting was not set on walls, it was done on rolls of paper or silk which were kept in special cases. According to whether they opened horizontally or vertically the scrolls were called (in Japanese) *makimono* or *kakemono*. The paintings were not intended to be seen at one glance, but to be read through systematically in the same way as handwriting.

Although the mural paintings that adorned the Han palaces no longer exist, we have some idea of them from the engraved funerary slabs that were copied from them; there is a feverish energy in those silhouettes which recall the black-figured Grecian vases (pl. 615). The *Scroll of Ku K'ai-chin* in the British Museum, which is a T'ang copy from the work of that fourth century artist, is evidence that the Chinese style of painting was already formed at that period. To make up for the scarcity of specimens up to the T'ang period, we have the large group of Buddhist mural paintings in the oasis of Tun-huang in Turkestan. These date from the seventh to the tenth century. Those which have been found in other oases (Turfan in Sinkiang, Miran, Dadan-Viliq) do not give a proper idea of the Chinese style, as they are strongly marked by Greco-Roman, Iranian and Indo-Gupta influences.

It was in the T'ang period that Chinese painting came into its own, at the same time as poetry, to which it was closely related. To judge from the few surviving examples, the artists seem to have been intent on defining forms by means of very precise outline both in landscape and figure-painting, as might be expected of the realistic outlook of their age.

In the Sung period, at the capital K'ai-feng-fu and later at Hangchou (Hangchow) – a city beautifully situated in the hills – the Taoist and Zen mystics had an influence which helped landscape towards a kind of metaphysical impressionism which was also reflected in poetry. Artists were trying to express the moods nature inspired in them, and the contemporary philosophy inclined them to feel the impermanence of things when they considered the world, and to probe behind appearances into the mystery of the universal essence into which everything merges. This 'cosmic dream' led them to compose landscapes of mountains and water, in which the mist-drenched forms seem to belong to a dissolving world (pl. 614). In the vertical composition of the *kakemono* the planes are arranged so that they appear one above the other and the landscape as a whole is viewed from a very high point by the artist. When the human figure is shown it is no bigger than an insect, unless the painter is trying

613 Liang K'ai. The Poet Li Ta'i-po. Ink on Paper. About 1200. Private Collection

612 Gatekeeper. T'ang Dynasty. 7th–10th c. Harvard

614 Attributed to Mi F (1051–1107). Landscap Ink on Silk. Washingto

to suggest the meditations of some Taoist or Buddhist in the seclusion of his mountain hermitage. Through this naturalistic form produced by a decadent period, the paintings somehow share the cosmic meaning of the primitive bronzes. The shapes of things float as though dissolved in space, just as in former times symbols were scattered across the sides of bronze vessels, and the steaming mists play the part of the diffused background that in former times was filled by monotonous series of spirals. In the foreground, the Sung landscapes often have some tormented outline of a tree that recalls the cruel, bristling arabesque of the monstrous visions of the Shang period. The painters, in their efforts to represent immateriality, gave up the naturalistic colouring of the T'ang artists and ultimately handled landscapes in a monochrome wash, relying on nothing but tone-values. In their treatment of human figures or the shapes of flowers and animals, very often a brief arabesque indicated by the merest stroke of the brush, suggests the presence of some evanescent form.

Many artists, whose names have been piously handed down by Chinese art-critics, specialized in painting, which was so honoured at court that some emperors, like Hui Tsung (1082–1135) who was overthrown by the barbarians, did not disdain to practise it. Among the most famous painters were Li Lungmien, Ma Yuan, Hsia Kuei, Liang K'ai (pl. 613) and Mu Ch'i, the last two being Taoist painters. This glimpse of a dream-world became a set formula in the Ming period, when artists were so lost in admiring their ancestors that they kept to the old recipes.

Ceramics and Lacquerwork

The industrial arts took an increasingly important place in Chinese civilization, which is one in which our distinction between major and minor arts loses all meaning. A taste for pure form naturally led the Chinese to love ceramics, a field in which they undertook endless experiments.

It was in the Han period – long after its first use in the Mediterranean – that the Chinese took to the potter's wheel. The Han artists, moved by that gift for synthesis that had already inspired the early sculptors, began to throw their clay into very beautiful contours which they covered with a yellow or green glaze, sometimes adding a relief or incized decoration on the shoulder or neck. Equally gifted with a plastic sense, the T'ang potters worked on the same lines but introduced polychrome decoration in bright colours, green, yellow, reddish-brown, cobalt blue. In the Sung period these refinements in colouring were followed by others in materials and shapes (pl. 616). The paste was ever thinner and finer, approaching porcelain, taking ivory-white tones or a milk-white, a reddish grey; but the so-called 'celadon' tones are the loveliest with their light bluish-green glazes, whose indefinable sea-like softness has a mysterious depth. The glazing often has a delicate incized decoration with a sweeping but simple effect. The way in which celadon lost its charm in the Ming period, when it became a stereotyped, stiff enamel, is enough to prove the Ming artists' loss of feeling for materials. They now replaced refinement of substance by a stress on effects, such as burnt glazings, 'shot' with streaks of colour, violent monochromes in ox-blood red, turquoise blue, aubergine, peach-yellow and the like. The finest vases are those with a blue decoration on a white ground which were imitated by the makers of Delft ware. Under the Ch'ing emperors the sides of vases, which were made in larger dimensions than before, were too readily used for figured decoration in polychrome. These vases are classified into 'families' ac-

615 *Tombstone (detail). Han Dynasty. 3rd c. B.C.–3rd c. A.D. Philadelphia*

616 *Celadon Bowl. Sung Dynasty. About 12th c. Boston*

*617 Princess with Handmaids, Dancers and Musicians. Terra-Cotta.
T'ang Dynasty (the two small Figures perhaps Wei Dynasty). Philadelphia*

cording to the dominant tone and the families are usually given in French: *famille verte, famille rose, famille rouge.* Little figurines and trinkets were also made in biscuit, the porcelain sometimes reaching an extraordinary, egg-shell thinness. The popularity of Chinese ware in Europe certainly helped to ruin this art by quickening the production of fanciful images and knick-knacks.

The same taste governed lacquered furniture, which was enlivened with decorative motifs or scenes from Chinese life from the late seventeenth century onwards. Chinese lacquers were even ordered for furniture made in Europe.

Architecture

In any study of the Chinese arts, architecture can only be treated as secondary, as a minor art. The Chinese are more deficient in architectural powers than in anything else, for they tend to think of forms in isolation as 'objects' and have little or no aptitude for making a whole or groups of wholes with an underlying composition governed by a rational distribution of forms. Their habit of building in light materials, such as brick and wood, means that no buildings earlier than the Sung period remain, and even Sung buildings are few and far between. China – unlike

618 Pa Li Chuan Pagoda (near Peking). Ming Dynasty. 1578

India – knew the principles of the vault and was thus able to erect important public works such as city gates, bridges and colossal walls or ramparts. The Chinese temple or pagoda is essentially a tower made of superimposed storeys, whose roofs are tilted upwards at the corners. Like the palace, the temple may be surrounded with annexes which stand in the enclosure without any apparent logical arrangement. From the Ming period onwards the buildings became covered with a garish polychrome ceramic (pl. 618), and architecture became practically a branch of decorative art. The Chinese have attached less importance to their houses than to their gardens, which are laid out like small images of the universe, having miniatures of various natural features such as mountains, rocks and lakes. These gardens were imitated in Europe in the eighteenth century, first in England and later in France.

4. THE EXPANSION OF CHINESE ART: JAPAN

In its spread southwards, Chinese art found itself checked by Indian art, which followed the preaching of Buddhism across the East Indies and Indo-China, in which territories Chinese art was obliged to come to terms with Indian art. The same happened in Tibet, whose position made it a meeting-place for both influences. In the eighth century Tibet took to a rather inferior form of Buddhist mysticism known as 'Tantrism' whose sensuality and demoniacal drive are still felt there to this day. Annam fell into the Chinese sphere of influence.

In the Pacific, on the other hand, Chinese civilization found in Japan a field where there was no danger of rivalry from other sources. The great religious and aesthetic currents which reached Japan, including those from India, all came by way of China, so that Japan became a kind of terminal of the Eurasian continent.

Japan emerged from its prehistoric state only in the sixth century, at the time when Buddhism found its way there and was at once absorbed by this awakening people, whereas China merely adapted it to her own traditions. The Buddhistic aesthetic, known to Japan through the art of the Wei and Sui dynasties resulted in statuary of a high level of mysticism, but its rather studied perfection of form robs it of depth (seventh to ninth century). The finest works of that time are the Nara period statues (eighth century) and the Horyuji frescoes which are like a belated echo of those of Ajanta (pl. 620). Meanwhile, the aggressive realism of the Japanese character was shown in statues of the four heavenly kings *(Shitenno)* (pl. 619). In the medieval period when Japan was split by feudal wars, the people discovered its warlike, chivalrous nature and began to break loose from the Chinese example in art; but Japan never ceased turning to China for inspiration, while tending to modify all that it borrowed in

619 Shitenno Head from the
Temple of Shinzakushi. 8th c.

620 Head of a Bodhisattva. Fresco
at Horyuji. Nara Period. 8th c.

accordance with its national outlook. The worship of Amida or Amitabha – the compassionate Buddha – and the influence of the mystical Zen sect gave Japan some inkling of Chinese philosophical pantheism, but this influence was too weak to make much impression on an art which was moving closer and closer to realism (Kochi sculptures, late twelfth century, painted portraits of the Tosa school). In the fourteenth and fifteenth centuries Japanese painting felt the rather tardy influence of the Sung aesthetic, but however skilfully the painters handled their washes of Chinese ink and overlaid their landscapes with mist, their firm, energetic draughtsmanship was out of keeping with their contemplative intentions (Sesshu, about 1420–1506; Soami, about 1430–1530; Sesson, end of fourteenth century). From the seventeenth century onwards Ming formalism also affected Japanese art which was now awakening to colour; the painters took readily to lacquer technique (Korin, 1605–1716, pl. 621). This kind of reverse interpretation of the Chinese aesthetic ended when the Japanese found a technique really suited to their temperament, a hard diagrammatic use of line, a preference for the concrete, a taste for bright, clearly defined colours, all of which fitted the Japanese for prints and engravings. Black and white engraving was in use in the sixteenth century, but the discovery of colour-printing in 1742 gave this form of art full scope. Torii Kiyonaga (1742–1813) brought ease of line and a freshness of colour to a sensuous art which portrayed feminine gracefulness; Utamaro (1754–1806) added a touch of eroticism in his studies of courtesans (pl. 622). Hokusai (1760–1849) was leader of the realist school. He brought a sharp eye to scenes from Japanese life and his country's magnificent landscape, which he portrayed with a tense dry line. In his *Thirty-*

*621 Korin. Lacquer Painting.
Private Collection*

*622 Utamara. Young Woman with a
Cage. Colour Print*

six Views of Fujiyama he began the 'record' or chronicle of a single site which goes even farther than Monet's mere variations on atmosphere; Hokusai's unquenchable curiosity also made him a keen observer of every gesture of everyday and working-class life (pl. 623). He published fifteen books of drawings, the *Mangwa,* which are a kind of journal of his life as an artist. Whereas Hokusai interpreted nature with a somewhat romantic, violent draughtsmanship, Hiroshige (1792–1858) was a poet who rid landscape of anecdote and abandoned himself to a dream of light and vastness, like an Impressionist (pl. 624). The Japanese print, incidentally, was to have a considerable influence on French painting in the second half of the nineteenth century.

Japan also depended on China for its architecture, and although stone materials were plentiful on the island, building was almost entirely carried out in wood, on account of earthquakes. For the same reason the

*623 Hokusai. Street-Scene.
Ink. Boston*

624 *Hiroshige.*
A Shower on
the Bridge.
Colour Print

paper-partitioned Japanese house is extremely flimsy. However, the Japanese have a wealth of fine materials and they outstripped the Chinese in their skilful use of timbers. The Japanese decorative arts, which are so admired in the West, are very unlike those of China which tend to the fantastic. The Japanese craftsman, with great skill, takes his ideas from nature, cleverly exploiting some natural shape for decorative purposes while respecting its objective truth. Always clinging to realism, the Japanese search for style shows itself in a certain formalism unknown to Chinese art, which is always open to the mystery of things.

In some respects the Asiatic situation of Japan is a paradox. Thanks to its strict realism, Japanese art, which began at the same time as Western art – with which it has a parallel historical development – is much nearer to modern European art than it is to Chinese, and it is to Japan rather than China that the West has turned for inspiration.

XII. ART NOW

A glance at the artistic atlas of the world today shows that the only regions that have remained creative artistically are those in which a scientific civilization has developed, in other words the Western countries. Asia is sterile, after being a fertile source of forms for thousands of years. European colonialism cannot be blamed for this decadence, for the vast country of China, which was never subdued, is no less poor in artistic genius than its neighbours. Japan is the only part of Asia which has shown a lively interest in our contemporary plastic arts, though it has nothing to contribute; but Japan deliberately adopted the mechanized civilization of the West, the Japanese showing remarkable affinities to our mentality while the rest of Asia pursued its own dreams.

Thus the accusation that science is fatal to art can only be maintained when art is too narrowly defined. The spirit of man is many-sided and at any given time it makes its mark in the realm of facts just as in art and ideas. Scientific creation and artistic invention are expressions of the same vital energy in our time.

Scientific civilization has produced a crop of new forms in a world that was rapidly becoming static. The revolution in building methods brought about by technical invention means the end of a time-honoured system of proportions based on the resistance of stone or wood. The conflict between old and new is particularly noticeable as regards Classical architecture, limited by the use of the flat architrave and the consequent need for numerous supports and the predominance of solid masses over empty spaces. By allowing wider spans, reinforced or ferro-concrete has brought architecture back to speculations on space that were the subject of experiment in the Middle Ages, thanks to a skilful handling of the vault and arch that freed the structure from its own weight. Architecture has

625 Picasso. Guernica. 1937. New York

Skyscrapers of Today and Yesterday

626 Ralph Walker. Chicago Tribune Building, Chicago. 1928

627 Tour de Beurre of Rouen Cathedral. Begun 1487

become vertical again, after being horizontal for a long period; the sky-scrapers of New York recall the competition for height that was so marked in the French cathedrals of the thirteenth century. The building has again been converted into an immense work of glass; it no longer rests on a solid foundation but on piles as slim as the pillars of Soissons Cathedral. Reducing the weight-carrying features to a few rib-like gir-ders, bridging immense gaps without visible support, suspending struc-tures over empty space, the modern architect seeks to surprise us by the airiness and daring of his colossal works. Like the master-builders of the thirteenth century, we sense his pride in defying gravity and proving the superiority of mind over matter. Moreover, history confirms the con-clusions we draw from such an analysis of forms. Contemporary archi-tecture, created by the use of steel and reinforced concrete, has taken lessons from the Middle Ages in its reaction against academic convention. Was it not an archaeologist who formulated the theory of Functionalism? Until very recently the New York skyscrapers, 'cathedrals of business', were vying with the towers of Gothic churches (pl. 626, 627).

However revolutionary it might appear, when the human mind invents it always starts from some hint given by works that only a generation ago were despised. The creators of the modern aesthetic took themselves for iconoclasts, and the war-cry of the Fauves and Cubists was 'Burn the museums'. But before the holocaust, the fire-raisers had a quick look round the museum to feast their eyes on their ancestors' works. If they pretended to walk scornfully past those of Raphael and Rubens, they were, on the contrary, passionately interested in China, archaic Greece, the medieval Romanesque, pre-Columbian America and even negro art (pl. 628, 629). The critics vied with the painters, and no art was more anxious to justify itself by pointing to the past than this modern art which was denounced as lunacy. Of course this 'past' had on no account

Influence of Negro Art

628 Picasso. Head of a Woman.
1908. Private Collection

629 Negro Sculpture from
Gabon. Private Collection

to be that of Classical antiquity, for contemporary art was based on the destruction of the aesthetic that Europe had lived on for four hundred years. Its appeals were made both to the medieval genius for formal invention that was never hidebound by realism, and to popular or folk-art (pl. 630, 631).

The modern world has to be credited with the discovery of the true value of artistic forms, a discovery that no other period managed to make, not even the China of the Sung period which had such a subtle capacity for aesthetic analysis. The language of forms had become a learned language with its own vocabulary and syntax, and art-historians pored over this dead language. The Fauves and Cubists were intent on achieving the 'pure' work of art, and tried to make it a living language. But at the same time an opposing current wanted the work of art to express the human passions, no longer – as in the past – by illustrating a 'subject', but in a modern manner, through the eloquence of forms alone. The revelations of recent psychology, by showing the human mind to have an irrational sub-structure, led certain artists, the Surrealists, to invent a new style of imagery whose symbolic process owed something to the Middle Ages.

The creation of the plastic language in use today was a cosmopolitan event. Perhaps this sharing of all the nations of the West in a common cultural endeavour heralds the political unity towards which we are painfully striving? Until now all the main stages of our artistic civilization have been dominated by some particular nation giving the lead to others: France, Flanders and Italy took turns in playing that part. France emerged from the nineteenth century proud of having kept her creative faculties intact while the arts were at such a low ebb in the rest of Europe.

Expressionism and Stylization

630 Rouault. Head of a
Woman.
Private Collection

631 Female Portrait from
Fayum. Coptic. 1st half
of 4th c. Paris

The school of Paris *(école de Paris)* has produced three groups of artists, France's lucid genius showing itself in the creation of movements, – Fauvism, Cubism and Surrealism – which are all based on intellectual speculation. On the other hand Expressionism, which was the main contribution of the Slav and Germanic countries, had a more emotional, passional basis. The emergence of the Slavs is a remarkable event which must be related to the awakening of Russia, which passed overnight from the Middle Ages into the modern world. Thrown into exile by an official doctrine which demanded a dull realistic imagery, the Russian artists are none the less genuine representatives of their own people, who no doubt will reclaim them sooner or later. It is the first time that Slav artists have thrown off their moribund Byzantinism to take part in the Western art-movement. Finally, Spanish romanticism was to provide its shock-troops, pioneers who brought a revolutionary violence into every movement they touched. Spain gave the world a man who has been astonishingly sensitive to all the forces animating his period: Pablo Picasso's work, so prolific and many-sided, would be enough in itself to interpret our age to future generations.

Even through the worst tragedies of modern times, – to which she was always the first to be exposed – France has never failed to maintain that sense of unity which she draws from her confidence in the supremacy of thought over all other human activities. Ignoring the terror of modern existence, Bonnard, Matisse, Braque, each in his own way pursued an art of contemplation whose aim (as Matisse consciously formulated it) is to reconcile man to himself by means of aesthetic harmony. The sense of urgency brought about by the most recent world-conflict was necessary

Fauvism and Folk-Art

632 Matisse. The embroidered
Blouse. 1945. Private Collection

633 Folk-Art from Poland

before younger French artists could create a tragic style which they are already beginning to forget, while in his poetic tapestries a Jean Lurçat is celebrating the victory of light and life. Spaniards, Slavs and Germans, on the contrary, gripped by a consciousness of drama, were expressing the stampede of demoniacal powers in the human soul, through an art of breathless cruelty. Picasso, the greatest of them all, carried this expressionistic language to its highest intensity of horror, and in those years of slaughter he was the conscience of a tortured world.

Expressionism is an instinctive form of art which, more than either Fauvism or Cubism, lends itself to the infinite variety of men's temperaments: it has therefore encouraged the revival of national schools which, together with the creation of the school of Paris, is the main event in twentieth century art, especially for the Northern European countries. Spreading to Latin America, a region once so tragically inspired by the blood-thirsty religions of the Indians, it has produced vigorous offshoots in Mexico and Brazil.

North America, full of confidence in human progress and refusing to take a dramatic view of the world, was bound to absorb Cubism and Surrealism which are the plastic and psychological expression of our time. The New York school is perhaps the nearest there is to the Paris school.

If the creative qualities of a period are to be judged by variety of expression, then none has been so rich as ours. We are witnessing no less than an artistic inflation. The feverish pursuit of change which originated in scientific development and competition, has now affected art. This need for advance has condemned the artist to an endless renewal of

475

style, and the individual is always producing new variants out of the plastic language invented by the pioneers of contemporary art, sometimes with the addition of features taken from the past. Our period, far from being sterilized by the abstractions of science, is one that thirsts for images. The forms of the past, as well as those that are being invented daily, are being consumed at an enormous rate, by a civilization that rapidly devours everything, including time, in its efforts to achieve the world of the future which scientific progress is constantly putting out of reach.

1. THE REVOLUTION IN ARCHITECTURE

The principle of architectural rationalism which makes the planning, appearance and decoration of a building depend entirely on its function, was formulated for the first time by the archaeologist and architect Viollet-le-Duc, who believed that this formula was demonstrated in Gothic architecture (*Entretiens sur l'architecture*, 1863–1872). A new material, steel, now allowed the rapid construction of the enormous covered spaces required by industry, such as stations, factories, stores, and exhibition-halls, which could be built by processes not unrelated to those of the Gothic cathedrals, since they resulted in a 'nerved' or ribbed architecture in which the wall, deprived of its weight-bearing function, could be replaced by partitions or glass. Steel construction had been extensively used in England for bridges and industrial buildings ever since the end of the eighteenth century (Coalbrook Bridge over the Severn, 1777–1779). It came into domestic architecture with the Brighton Pavilion by John Nash, in which steel was used with brick (1815–1820). The famous Crystal Palace, built for the 1851 exhibition, made entirely of glass with a steel framework, already fulfilled the modern ideal of transparent architecture (pl. 634). This work was built by Joseph Paxon (1801–1865) who, however, profited from a plan entered for the competition by the French architect Horeau, whose design was disallowed because it was submitted by a foreigner.

Horatio Greenough (1805–1852) was the first American to suggest that in architecture as in nature and the machine beauty resides in function rather than superficial or symbolic decoration. His idea found an eloquent illustration in the span of Brooklyn Bridge, the famous suspension bridge first conceived by the engineer, John Roebling, in 1857 and brought to completion by his son in 1883.

Practised occasionally before 1850 (Pont des Arts, Paris, 1803; Monnaie (Mint), Nantes, 1825), steel-architecture developed in France at about that date. Baltard built the Paris Halles (Central Market) in this style in 1855; Labrouste built the framework of the Bibliothèque Ste-Geneviève in 1843 and the main reading room of the Bibliothèque

476

Nationale in 1854. In 1866 Baltard began building the church of St-Augustin, a steel structure with stone revetments. Stations, factories and bridges benefited at once from the use of this new material, outstanding works being the Galerie des Machines (World Exhibition, 1889) by the architect Dutert and the engineer Condamin (147^1/$_2$ feet by 382 feet by 1355 feet), and the Eiffel Tower, which is 984 feet high. By his shrewd calculations and technical inventiveness, together with the remarkable simplicity and boldness of his methods of erection, the engineer Gustave Eiffel gave a sharp impetus to steel construction. Between 1877 and 1879 he built several such bridges and viaducts in Portugal, and between 1880 and 1884 he built the admirable Garabit Viaduct in France, which is perhaps his masterpiece (with a 541^1/$_2$ feet span and 400 feet elevation, pl. 635). The Eiffel Tower, erected quickly between 1887 and 1889, was his crowning achievement. It was intended as a kind of triumphal arch for the World Exhibition, celebrating the triumph of industrial civilization.

Meanwhile, public and private buildings continued to be built in stone, in a composite and over-decorative style which was usually Greco-Roman for civic and Gothic for religious purposes. The Palais de Justice at Brussels (1883) by Polaert, and the Petit-Palais in Paris, built by Girault for the Exhibition of 1900, are among the most pretentious of these efforts; but towards 1890 the Belgian architects Henry van de Velde, Victor Horta, and Hankar formulated the principles of Functionalism which forced the architect to show the structure of his building; while not condemning decoration, they wanted ornament to be based on nature as it was in medieval architecture. This idea led to the short-lived Art Nouveau, a kind of Baroque with undulating lines and plant-form decoration, which at that time seduced Guimard in Paris and Antonio Gaudí (1825–1926) who, in Barcelona, produced fantastic architectural

works inspired by rock-formations and which were swamped in lavish
decoration (unfinished church of the Sagrada Familia, 1878 onwards;
Güell Park; Casa Milá pl. 636).

The renewal of architecture was to be accomplished by a further step
in steel-construction with the help of reinforced concrete. The process
consists of casing steel girders or steel frames in concrete, thus preventing
oxydization of the metal. The elasticity of this material, which allows
great spaces to be bridged without supports, was to upset all the traditional rules of proportion based on lintel and vault construction. The new
process began to be used in England and France towards 1850; but it
was in France that it was developed rationally and had its greatest
success. The first attempts were made by the engineer François Coignet
(1852 onwards), the engineer Joseph-Louis Lambot, who at the 1855
World Exhibition showed a ship built according to this technique, and
the gardener Joseph Monier. Together with steel, concrete was readily
used for industrial buildings and artistic enterprises (road- and railway-
bridges) thanks to such daring engineers as Hennebrique, Bouissiron and
Freyssinet. The Exhibition of 1900 gave its blessing to concrete, just as
the exhibition in 1889 had established steel. In 1902 the architect Tony-
Garnier scandalized the Institut by sending, from the Villa Medici, a
plan for a whole industrial city in reinforced concrete. However, this
new material, which was widely used for industrial purposes from 1900
onwards, was slow in invading 'architecture'. From 1894 to 1904 Anatole
de Baudot, a pupil of Viollet-le-Duc, built the church of St-Jean de
Montmartre, Paris, with reinforced concrete and brick. The brothers
Auguste and Gustave Perret gave a final impetus to reinforced concrete
in their architectural programmes (house in the rue Franklin, Paris, 1902;
Théâtre des Champs-Elysées, 1911; church at Le Raincy, 1922, pl. 638);
however, they still observed the old system of proportions based on
Classical architecture. In 1904 a bold aesthetician, Paul Souriau, in his

636 *Antonio Gaudí. Casa Milá (la Pedrera), Barcelona. 1905–1910*

work *La Beauté Rationelle,* formulated the principles that would combine industrial efficiency with aesthetic value.

Meanwhile other architects both in Europe and the United States were concerned with freeing architecture from its Gothic and Greco-Roman fancy-dress through a disinterested study of the function of materials and their logical use. In Britain this tendency was particularly marked in domestic architecture. As early as 1859 William Morris (1834–1896), whose aim was to revive the domestic arts according to the principles laid down by Ruskin, commissioned Philip Webb (1830–1915) to build him the Red House at Bexley Heath, Kent, based on traditional English rural design. Richard Norman Shaw (1831–1912) and C. F. A. Voysey (1857–1941) followed this lead at the close of the century, as did the Scottish architect Charles Rennie Mackintosh (1869–1928), whose Glasgow School of Art was conceived in the same spirit in 1898. This revival of domestic architecture, with its reaction against eclecticism, was soon followed elsewhere. It caused a stir in Germany thanks to a book written by Hermann Muthesius in 1904, while it brought in its wake an entirely new outlook on town planning, first outlined in theory by Ebenezer Howard in his book *Garden Cities of Tomorrow.* Influenced by Ruskin's idea, Howard called for the spreading of residential areas on the outskirts of towns, so that the population would live in detached houses on estates ringed by 'green belts'. In Holland, H. P. Berlage carried out in the national material, brick, a work of satisfying plainness in the Amsterdam Stock-Exchange (1897–1903) and was followed by a new school whose most outstanding representative was Michael de Klerk. Functionalism was introduced into Germany by the Belgian savant Henry van de Velde (1863–1957, pl. 640), who was given the chair at Weimar University; German architects created the Werkbund at Darmstadt in 1908 in reaction against the Jugendstil, the German equivalent of Art Nouveau. From the aesthetic point of view, however, in the form of a spire (Woolworth Building) or a crown (Chicago Tribune Building, 1928, pl. 626).

The first experiments in 'modern' architecture before 1914 were not entirely free from the habit of ornamentation, nor from traditional proportions. It was after the first World War that a strictly-applied Functionalism established a truly modern art by creating new forms deduced from a rational study of technical needs, such as those of hospitals, banks, museums, factories, civic and administrative buildings, bridges, blocks of flats, private houses or town-planning. In Germany Walter Gropius founded the Bauhaus at Weimar in 1919 for this purpose (it was subsequently transferred to Dessau). Gropius, who is now in the United States, was inspired by a certain socialistic missionary zeal, and thought in terms of standardized production of building answering all the needs of great communities. In France, Le Corbusier, a Swiss of French extraction (born 1887), expounded his ideas in the review *Esprit nouveau* which he founded in 1920 with Ozenfant. Le Corbusier is an inexhaustible theorist, who coined the famous phrase '*une machine à habiter*' (a machine for living in) to define a house. In spite of this he saw beyond engineering and was not content with a purely materialistic Functionalism as Gropius was; he gave proper attention to architectural form, while basing it on strictly mathematical proportions. Le Corbusier's fundamental technical process is to rest his building on piles and girders that support flooring, there being no solid walls, only glass surfaces shaded by sun-screens (pl. 643). This architect is driven by a kind

641 Walter Gropius. Fagus Works, Alfeld an der Leine. 1911–1914

642 Frank Lloyd Wright. Kaufmann House, Bear Run (Pennsylvania). 1936

of mystical cult of sunlight and open air, and has drawn up plans for what he calls *cités radieuses* (radiant or sunlit cities) which would house a dense population while having only five per cent of the area built over. He has completed his Unité d'habitation (Housing-unit) at Marseilles, the first specimen of a thorough application of the idea of a functional dwelling based on a system of proportions depending entirely on the human body and its needs. This he calls the 'modulor' (from *module* meaning standard or unit; the modulor was first known as the 'proportioning grid').

Since 1914 French architects and engineers have vied with each other in their bold experiments. E. Freyssinet exploited the properties of parabolic curves in the aircraft hangars at Orly (1924, pl. 639), while Tony Garnier has built a number of civic buildings at Lyons; Mallet-Stevens, Roux-Spitz and André Lurçat make full use of the devices and proportions of the new architecture.

Functionalism is now universal. One of the most flourishing schools of architecture in Europe is in Holland, where J. P. Oud, Jan Wils and Dudok, who built Hilversum (pl. 644), combine reinforced concrete and brick with a simple but pleasing effect. In Brazil, Le Corbusier's visit in 1936 aroused great enthusiasm for architecture, an enthusiasm stim-

643 *Le Corbusier.*
Unité d'habition,
Marseilles.
1945–1953

ulated and satisfied by such talented artists as Lucio Costa, Burle-Marx
and Oscar Niemeyer. The first great undertaking to incorporate Le Corbusier's principles was the Ministry of Education Building at Rio de
Janiero, an immense stretch of glass fourteen stories high, built by a
group of Brazilian architects. Made of glass-bricks, with sun-screens, the
design was executed by Le Corbusier in 1936 (pl. 645). Modern architecture also made great strides forward in Latin America after the second
World War. In the cities whole groups of buildings were constructed
according to the new ideas: in Caracas (Venezuela), Bogota (Columbia)
and Mexico, where the impressive university town and the government

644 *Dudok. School at Boschdrift (near Hilversum). 1921*

quarter of the Pedigral, planned in accordance with Wright's principles, are examples.

All over the world ferro-concrete has outstripped steel building in the twentieth century, though it has not entirely replaced it. In the United States in particular, steel coated with concrete to prevent rust is commonly used. Such gigantic buildings as the Empire State Building, New York (1930), and the group of skyscrapers composing the Rockefeller Centre (1931–1939) are steel-built.

The American architects were drawn to the Gothic through the Anglo-Saxon tradition, and have tended to remain faithful to it. Manhattan, with its forest of towers and vertical rows of windows suggests some greatly-enlarged Tuscan town of the four-

645 Niemeyer, Costa and
Burle-Marx (design by
Le Corbusier). Ministry of
Education, Rio de Janeiro.
1936–1945

teenth century. As late as 1931 to 1932, in so practical a building as the Cornel Medical School and New York Hospital the central part has the look of a keep, and the high strips of glass, like lancet-windows, recall the machicolation of the Papal Palace at Avignon. But more recently this Gothic verticalism has been given up in favour of the system created by Frank Lloyd Wright, Gropius and Le Corbusier, which is to build in horizontal strata or layers. The UNO Building at Lake Success, erected by an international team, and the Brooklyn Veterans' Administration Hospital, New York, built by Skidmore, Owings and Merrill (1950), are obvious examples of the return to horizontal design.

2. THE SCHOOL OF PARIS

Painting

The renown achieved by the French school of painting in the nineteenth century attracted artists from all over the world after 1900. The invention of the plastic language of our age was thus a matter of universal rivalry in which the Spaniards, Slavs and Central-European artists played an important part. The intensified individualism which urges modern artists to create a personal style makes it hard to analyse contemporary art, for groups are now no sooner formed than scattered.

The first great movements in modern painting were, once more, of purely French origin. The Nabis (about 1890) and especially the Fauves

(1905) were violently opposed to naturalism but none the less derived from Impressionism since they both thought of the picture as pure colour: it demands little effort for us to pass from Gauguin and van Gogh to Matisse and Vlaminck. The essential principle of modern painting was formulated by the painter-aesthetician Maurice Denis, when he wrote in 1890 'Remember that before being a war-horse, a nude or some story or other, a picture is essentially a flat surface covered with coloured pigments arranged in a certain order'. The moderns discarded any dependence on subject or nature and made it their business to create 'pure painting'. Even when they wanted to translate some definite emotion, it was the form itself that had to be expressive, and not the representation or evocation of some touching theme. This aim was still not very noticeable in the group of painters who between 1890 and 1900 went under the name of the Nabis (Prophets): Pierre Bonnard (1867–1946, pl. 648); Edouard Vuillard (1868–1940); K.-X. Roussel (1867–1944) and Maurice Denis (1870–1943). Bonnard's entire work was dedicated to the lyricism of appearances, Vuillard's to *intimiste* interiors, while Roussel and Maurice Denis tended towards applied decoration. They all contrived to keep on good terms with nature. The movement which because of its uncompromising programme was dubbed *'fauve'* (wild) by Louis Vauxelles at the Salon d'Automne of 1905, on the contrary, broke completely with the whole naturalist tradition. Deliberately distorting the models which they continued to take from nature, all those connected with Fauvism sought to produce a shock effect on the spectator by sheer colour and brushwork. The numerous artists who began as Fauves were not long in deviating according to their own temperament. Only Henri Matisse (1869–1954) remained faithful to the original doctrine of pure painting (pl. 647), and in his old age even tended towards increasingly subtle, coloured abstraction (pl. 632). Others like Manguin (1874–1945), Camoin (born 1879), Puy (born 1876), Friesz (1897–1949), Marquet (1875–1947)

646 Henri
(le Douanier)
Rousseau.
Monkeys in the
Forest of
Orange-Trees.
Private
Collection

647 Matisse. Still-Life with Asphodels. Essen

– who painted some sensitive, atmospheric scenes of sea-ports (pl. 649) –
all moved imperceptibly towards an art of sensation like Impressionism
itself. The Dutchman van Dongen (born 1877) borders on Expressionism,
while after a short Fauve stage André Derain (1880–1954) returned to
a neo-traditional conception of painting. Marie Laurencin (born 1885)
managed to make a graceful stylization out of Cubism. Others used

648 *Bonnard. Nude. Private Collection*

extremes of colour to express tragic feeling, as in the case of Rouault (born 1871), a painter haunted by Christian anguish (pl. 630), and the dramatic landscape-painter Maurice de Vlaminck (born 1876). To these we may add the instinctive painter Maurice Utrillo (1883–1955), who interpreted disillusioned suburbs, although he had no historical connection with Fauvism and his tone-scale is quite different, being nearer the typical French feeling for 'values' (pl. 650). Instinctive or intuitive painting enjoyed great favour after the discovery of Henri Rousseau, called the Douanier (1844–1910), a self-educated painter who belonged to the Symbolist generation (pl. 646). Numerous self-made painters from the working classes were to follow his example, with a naive awkwardness in which the public thought they saw a return to the frankness of the primitives. They formed a group supported by Wilhelm Uhde, a German critic who had settled in Paris (Bombois, Vivin, Jean Eve, Boyer, Bauchant, Seraphine Louis).

The Cubist movement insisted still further on the self-sufficiency of the painted work. Cubism, which received its name from Henri Matisse at the Salon d'Automne of 1908, was the joint creation of the Spaniard Pablo Picasso (born 1881, pl. 628) and the French painter Braque (born

649 *Marquet.*
The Port of
Algiers. 1941.
Private
Collection

650 Utrillo. *The Church at Deuil. 1912.*
Private Collection

1882, pl. 651), who both quoted Cézanne's Constructivist aims in support of their own. The first, Picasso, gave this common effort his revolutionary violence, while Braque contributed his methodical approach. Between 1907 and 1914 they set out doggedly to invent a purely formal language. To the objects or figures they took from nature they brought an increasingly geometrical analysis which in the end reduced the painting to an interplay of surfaces and lines in which abstraction was deeply emphasized by ascetic colour, in which a greyish brown predominated.

651 Braque. *Man with a Guitar. 1911.*
Private Collection

652 Gris. *Chess-Board, Newspaper and Glasses.*
Private Collection

653 Delaunay. Three Windows, Tower and Wheel. 1912. Paris

With the support of the poet Guillaume Apollinaire's forceful publicity, Cubism developed a host of offshoots. The Spanish painter Juan Gris (1887–1927, pl. 652) and the Pole, Marcoussis (1883–1941) were alone with Braque in remaining faithful to orthodox Cubism. The French artists André Lhote (born 1885), Roger de la Fresnaye (1885–1925), Jacques Villon (born 1875), Metzinger (born 1883), and Gleizes (1881–1953) together created a 'colour-Cubism', starting from a stylization of the real, rather than breaking it down analytically. Robert Delaunay (1885–1941, pl. 653) gave this colour-Cubism a more abstract character by making the canvas a chromatic variation on contrasted colours, an aesthetic which Apollinaire labelled 'Orphism'. Certain artists, the *musicalistes,* used this technique in an effort to translate auditive sensations into painting (Valensi, Bourgogne, Blanc-Gatti, Belmont etc.). Futurism, which originated in Italy and tried to portray forms in motion on the canvas, was Parisian in its first and purest phase (1912) and learnt something from Cubism. The Vorticist movement, founded in London in 1914 by Wyndham Lewis, had affinities with both Futurism and Cubism.

The fifteen years before the first World War were marked by a remarkable mental tension, provoked perhaps by the desire to create a plastic language suitable to our times. After 1918 this new vocabulary was to be exploited for many different expressive purposes. There was a noticeable relaxation among all the pre-war pioneers, during the decade 1920 to 1930, possibly due to the feeling of well-being after the armistice, which resulted in a more conciliatory attitude to nature. This was

490

654 Dufy. The Paddock at Deauville. Water-Colour. Paris

Matisse's 'sensual' phase, while Braque went through a period of realism. Raoul Dufy (1877–1953) gave Fauvism a genial, picturesque tonality (pl. 654). As for Picasso, between 1918 and 1928 he adventured into harmonic experiments which sometimes he expressed in Cubist idiom (*The Three Musicians*, 1921), at other times in a naturalistic vocabulary (*Portrait of the Artist's Wife*, 1918).

It was also after the war that Fernand Léger (1881–1955), who created the *Effort moderne* movement, and Amédée Ozenfant (born 1886), the inventor of Purism, began developing a new plastic language out of Cubism. They aimed at creating a genuinely modern imagery, adaptable to the age of machines, which could be mass-produced. Propagandist pictures and images, commercial-art and advertising, window-dressing, stage-settings, all the spheres of modern life that call for visual forms were profoundly influenced by Léger's art (pl. 655) while interior decoration and posters also owe much to Ozenfant.

But there were some artists – mainly from Slavonic countries and some of Jewish origin – who brought a sense of pathos to the post-war world. This they conveyed in different ways: through melancholy (Moïse Kisling, Polish, 1891–1953; Amedeo Modigliani, Italian, 1884–1920, pl. 658; Jules Pascin, Bulgarian, 1885–1930), or through violent methods of expression (Chaim Soutine,

655 Léger. Woman with a Vase. 1924. Private Collection

491

656 *Chagall. The Funeral. 1909. Private Collection*

Lithuanian, 1894–1943, pl. 657). This expressionist tendency, which in Germany rapidly became a kind of school but which in Paris had only appeared haphazardly before 1914, blossomed out in France between the wars. The Russian Jew Marc Chagall (born 1887) gave the Paris school something of the Slavonic uneasiness of mind, in a kind of super-naturalism which blends the worlds of dream and reality (pl. 656). The name 'expressionist' was also given to a generation of French painters who were all born in about 1890 (Henri le Fauconnier, 1881–1946;

657 *Soutine. The old Actress. 1924. Private Collection*

658 *Modigliani. Seated Nude. 1917. Private Collection*

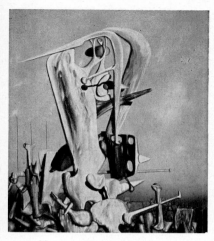

659 Tanguy. *Ma vie blanche et noire.*
1944. *Private Collection*

660 Chirico. *The disquieting
Muses. 1916. Private Collection*

Edouard Goerg, born 1893; Amédée de la Patellière, 1890–1932; Marcel
Gromaire, born 1892). These painters are closer to Flemish folk-expres-
sionism than to the pathos-loaded expressionism peculiar to the Slavs
and Central Europe.

In its reaction against the demand for the autonomy of painting so
typical of the pre-war movements, the decade 1920 to 1930 therefore
shows a tendency to relate the picture to some inspiration outside itself,
whether the external source or referent be the material world or human
sensibility. The Surrealist movement, which is the most original school
to have emerged since the first World War, and which is as important
as Cubism, points in the same direction. Surrealism derived from Dadaism,
an ephemeral movement of absolute negation, a protest against reason
itself, which sprang from the feeling of anguish created by the first
World War and which appeared during it, simultaneously at Zurich
(Tristan Tzara, a Rumanian poet, Hans Arp from Alsace, the Germans
Hülsenbeck and Hugo Ball) and in New York (Picabia from Spain,
Marcel Duchamp from France), as well as in Cologne and Berlin. Its
lines converged on Paris in 1919, but through the joint action of Aragon
and André Breton, two French poets, Dadist nihilism was soon liquidated.
On its ruins they founded Surrealism, a word derived from Guillaume
Apollinaire's early play, *Les Mamelles de Tirésias.* Taking over from
Dada all its hostility to rationalism, but drawing on the Freudian theory
of psychoanalysis, literary and plastic Surrealism tries to grasp elements
of the unconscious depths of the human mind and bring them to the surface, by expressing them in forms or words with a suitable symbolic ap-

661 Ernst. St Cecilia. 1923

paratus. Far from being an abstract tendency, Surrealism is on the contrary an 'imagery' in all its essentials, and perhaps its mistake lies precisely in having often neglected the purely plastic values of its works by sacrificing them to the symbolic power of the image. This movement so deeply reflected the sensibility of our time that it united artists from all over the world: Swiss (Paul Klee, 1879–1940), German (Max Ernst, born 1891, pl. 661; Wolfgang Paalen, born 1905), French (Marcel Duchamp, born 1887; Yves Tanguy, 1900–1955, pl. 659; André Masson, born 1896),

662 Miró. Circus. 1934. Paris

Spanish (Joan Miró, born 1893, pl. 662; Salvador Dali, born 1904, pl. 663), Italian (Giorgio di Chirico, born 1888, pl. 660), American (Man Ray, born 1890, pl. 664) and Cuban (Wilfredo Lam).

Now a world-wide movement, this new symbolism is being constantly renewed by the contribution of new generations of artists. Owing to the upheaval caused by the second World War, its principal centre now is perhaps New York, although André Breton has returned to Paris.

While Matisse, Braque and Picasso seemed to be showing a more indulgent attitude towards nature during the twenties, other artists who had already taken up that position before the first World War continued in maintaining it (Dunoyer de Segonzac, born 1884; Luc-Albert Moreau, 1882–1948; Jean-Louis Boussingault, 1883–1943). The young artists who were born about 1900 and began to express themselves towards 1930 took courage from this example and tried a pictorial realism which events were soon to eliminate. Some sought to comply with bourgeois tastes by making mild adaptations of Matisse, Bonnard, Vuillard, Derain (Terechkovitch, Cavaillès, Limouse, Brianchon, Chapelain-Midy). Others, with more success, followed their own bent (Aujame, Planson, Oudot, Poncelet, Despierre). Others tried to make an aesthetic out of an austere kind of realism (*Forces Nouvelles* group, founded in 1935: Jean Lasne, Humbolt, Rohner). Under the name 'neo-Humanism' the critic Waldemar George advocated a sort of pseudo-classicism in which the human form played an essential rôle. A Frenchman, Christian Berard, and some artists of Central-European origin (Berman, Léonid, Joseph Floch, Hosiasson, Helmuth Koll) assembled under this banner.

But realism was rejoicing too soon in its triumph. An international group founded in 1931 under the title *Abstraction-Création* called for an absolutely abstract art which would take none of its data from nature. It demanded non-representational forms, whether imaginary or mathematical. This group included Piet Mondrian (1886–1944, pl. 665), Theo van Doesburg, Hans Arp, Albert Gleizes, Valmier, Hélion, Gorin, Herbin and Ben Nicholson.

Meanwhile Matisse, after his trip to Indonesia in 1931, and the murals he painted for the American collector Barnes (*la Danse*, 1933), began to return to a more 'purist' art which he carried increasingly in that direction for the rest of his life (Chapel of the Rosary for the Dominican convent at Vence, 1948–1951).

After a short abstract period, Braque made a smooth synthesis of his naturalistic inspiration and his original Cubism (pl. 666). But the sensation of anguish provoked by the Spanish War and the approaching World War, drove Pablo Picasso, the painter who has in him the greatest measure of the grieving soul of our age, to invent a new expressionistic

663 Dali. *Apparition on a Beach. 1938. Hartford (Connecticut)*

XV Edvard Munch. House at Aasgaardstrand. Private Collection

style which achieved greater violence than any had been capable of before (colour pl. XVI). For over ten years this inspired painter expressed the cruelty that had been unleashed on the world, by means of broken composition, jagged line, intensified colour, showing murdered figures whose reassembled limbs result in grimacing monsters (*Guernica*, 1937, pl. 625). Out of this cruel style a new expressionism was to emerge in France during the war, attracting such artists as Bernard Lorjou, André Marchand, Francis Gruber (1912–1948).

However, while these artists emphasized expression, the mental stress arising from the conflict produced an unforeseen revival of pure painting, in the form of violently-coloured compositions with an abstract bias (Le Moal, Bazaine, Manessier, Pignon) or with a more or less emphatic stylization of reality (Gischia, Fougeron, Tailleux, Estève, Lapicque, Desnoyers, Robin). The blended influences of Delaunay, Villon, La Fresnaye, Matisse and the Romanesque fresco-painters all gave something to this movement. During the last few years some artists, going still further in this direction, have reduced their compositions to a play of lines and blobs *(tâches)* of colour, directed by instinct alone. Through this rejection of a conscious, formal aesthetic, they hope to find the underlying laws of art (Salon de Mai).

This return to abstract art found itself countered at the same time by another tendency, in the renewal of an old colour-technique which had been forgotten for over two centuries and was now revived by Jean Lurçat (born 1892). Freed from any allegiance to a school by his experiments in a new technique, Jean Lurçat reinvented a style of imagery which achieves a synthesis of natural forms with the strict plastic demands of our time and the pure poetic inspiration that leads from Symbolism to Surrealism. The painter-poet has the multitudinous forms of the world

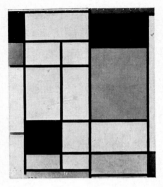

665 *Mondrian. Composition.*
Private Collection

666 *Braque. Still-Life. 1942.*
Private Collection.

at his disposal, and Jean Lurçat evokes them in cycles of images whose associations are thoroughly motivated by plastic requirements as well as by lyrical metaphor.

To sum up the main features in the complex evolution of the school of Paris in the past fifty years, it might be said that the 1905 to 1914 period tended to restore the prestige of pure form which had been weakened by Impressionist naturalism. The post-1918 period saw the image exalted once again, whether in an expressionist sense or a symbolic sense (Surrealism), but often at the expense of form. The art of Jean Lurçat, which incarnates the form in the image, suggests the opening of a new era in painting.

Sculpture

If contemporary sculpture cannot compete with painting in its variety of expression, this is inherent in the very nature of the art, which demands a costly and painful training and which is more dependent on social conditions than is painting. The demand for sculpture has been almost entirely from official quarters, and public authorities have continued to support a school of academic artists who merely prolong the canons of the nineteenth century without the slightest change.

Moreover, rationalistic architecture has discouraged sculpture. It is a paradox that this art should be driven away from buildings at the very time when it was rediscovering the monumental sense that it had lost with Carpeaux and Rodin, both of whom were seduced by the fluidity of painting. In the same way as painting, modern sculpture has evolved towards a definition of its true laws, and has therefore sought density of

667 Maillol. Nymph. Bronze

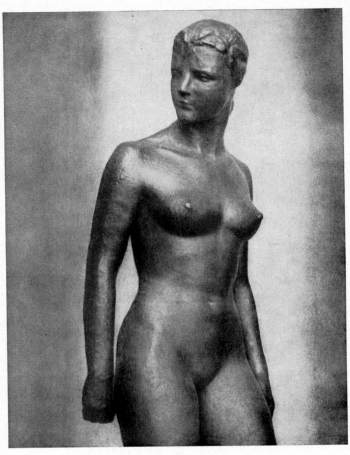

668 *Despiau. Asia (detail). Bronze. 1927*

volumes and balanced masses. If Antoine Bourdelle (1861–1929), who was a pupil of Rodin, still belonged to the nineteenth century thanks to his heroic vision, at the same time he tried to find the secret of architectonic poise in the archaic styles of Greece. It was to the Greek plastic example that our sculptors turned in their search for the lost sense of sculptural density. It inspired the meridional artist Aristide Maillol (1861–1944) whose researches were exclusively confined to the female nude. He did not forget Renoir's opulent forms and attained a fine balance between life and beauty. Had he been given more commissions he could have been a great monumental sculptor (pl. 667). Charles Despiau (1874–1946), an-

669 *Duchamp-Villon.*
   Nude. About 1912

other southern artist who turned to Greece, revived a long but forgotten French tradition in his portrait-busts, though his method of grasping character was synthetic rather than analytic (pl. 668). Joseph Bernard (1866–1931), unlike Bourdelle and Despiau, sought the gracefulness of the arabesque, not the density of compact forms. Pompon (1855–1933), the Spaniard Mateo Hernandez (1888–1949) and Joseph Constant (born 1891) earned a reputation for concentrated, sober reliefs in their animal-sculptures.

If the French painters led the way in the onslaught on nature, they lagged behind in sculpture in this respect, no doubt because in the nineteenth century sculpture had been given up to academicism and romantic sentimentality, and what was now required was a return to the model. Most of the artists who translated Cubism into metal or stone were from other countries. Some went no further than a geometrical stylization of reality, like the French artist Duchamp-Villon (1876–1919, pl. 669), or the Russian Chana Orloff (born 1888), though others adventured more boldly into the domain of abstract forms. The Frenchman Henri Laurens (born 1885) who both paints and sculpts, started from a kind of bas-

671 Lipschitz. Melancholy. Bronze. 1930. Private Collection

672 Gargallo Harlequin. Bronze. Paris

670 Zadkine. The City destroyed. Bronze. Rotterdam

relief rendering of Braque's pictures to end with compact, involved forms. The Rumanian Constantin Brancusi (born 1876) has invented smooth, egg-like shapes of an absolute simplicity; Ossip Zadkine (born 1890, pl. 670) breaks up the elements of relief and then fuses them into a solid composition; the Russian Jacques Lipschitz (born 1891, pl. 671) together with the Ukrainian Archipenko (born 1887) and the Spaniards Pablo Gargallo (1881–1934, pl. 672) and Julio Gonzales (1876–1942) are all baroque artists whose aim is to create form vibrating in space. Painters such as Matisse, Braque and especially Picasso have often tackled sculptural problems, like Degas before them. The Alsatian Hans (Jean) Arp (born 1887) and the Swiss Giacometti (born 1877) do not hesitate to give their non-representational pieces a surrealist meaning. A revival of non-representational sculpture is in progress in France at the present time, parallel with neo-Cubism in painting (Adam, Béothy, Brauner, Vitullo): some of them such as Jean Preyrissac go so far as emulating the American Calder's 'mobile' constructions. However, Paris has produced a whole school of representational figure-sculptors following on the example of Maillol and Despiau. Wlérick (1882–1944), Auguste Guénot (born 1882) and the Spaniard Manolo (1872–1945) are Maillol's most faithful disciples. Gimond (born 1894) is a scrupulous portrait-artist, Couturier (born 1905) is developing a sense of the monumental. Auricoste (born 1908), Yencesse (born 1900) and Saupique (born 1889) all go back to much earlier French traditions.

3. THE NATIONAL SCHOOLS

One of the most remarkable events of the twentieth century is the revival of national schools. While a cosmopolitan art has been developing in France, but without the French tradition as its stabilizing factor, the other European countries whose artistic schools were sterilized for over a hundred years by the tyranny of neo-Classicism and of French Realism, have finally asserted their independence and given expression to their native temperament, pushing it even to extremes. After the first World War, the new aesthetic which emerged in France spread to North and South America, where it was quickly absorbed and original talents began to spring up.

The most notable feature in this movement is the awakening of the Northern spirit as opposed to the Latin, as can be seen in Germany, Switzerland, Scandinavia, Belgium and Holland.

Nineteenth-century Germany was gripped by an academic outlook which was completely hostile to the national temperament, and this is one of the most astonishing paradoxes in the history of art. But between 1890 and 1900 Germany rediscovered expressionism, a manner which corresponds to something profoundly rooted in the national soul and which had provided the great tradition of Germany's finest period, the Middle Ages and the Renaissance. While the French Fauves and Cubists were busy defining pure painting, an art completely free of contingent elements, Germany sacrificed every consideration of form to the expression of its dramatic, tortured spirit, sometimes with brutal overemphasis. In 1892, at the time of an exhibition in Berlin of work by the Norwegian artist, Munch, which was to lead to the so-called 'Berlin Secession', Germany had abandoned neo-Classicism for a kind of realism inspired by Courbet (Menzel, Leibl) which was still not what she needed. The Expressionist lead was given by the surrounding Northern countries, by the Swiss Ferdinand Hodler (1853–1918) who painted gigantic epic pieces in clashing colours (pl. 673), the Norwegian Edvard Munch (1863–1944, pl. 674, colour pl. XV), and the Dutchman van Gogh. The Secession painters sought to free themselves from academic convention by turning to Impressionism, but if Max Liebermann (1847–1935, pl. 675)

673 Hodler. *Warrior in the Fray.*
1897. Geneva

674 Munch. The sick Girl. 1896. Oslo

went far towards assimilating it, Max Slevogt (born 1868) and Lovis Corinth (1858–1925) both interpreted it with a dramatic feverishness that is alien to it. Towards 1905, when Fauvism was emerging in France, Expressionism was becoming more fully conscious of itself in the *Brücke* (Bridge) group which was founded in Dresden in 1904 by artists including Ernst Ludwig Kirchner (1880–1938), Karl Schmidt-Rottluff (born 1884), Erich Heckel (born 1883), Emil Nolde (born 1867), Max Pechstein (1881–1955) and Otto Mueller (1874–1930). By means of harsh colour, rough drawing, dramatic choice of subject and a return to the 'primitive' by echoing negro sculpture, all these artists unleashed a kind of inward frenzy which sometimes became irrational. In Austria Oskar Kokoschka (born 1886, pl. 676), who painted portraits and landscapes, expressed this anguish in the human face as well as in the 'face' of nature. While the *Brücke* dissolved in 1913, a new group, the *Blaue Reiter* (Blue Horseman), which was founded in Munich in 1911 and was

675 Liebermann. The Jakobs-Terrasse at Nienstedten. 1902. Hamburg

supported by the Sturm Gallery in Berlin in 1912, was approaching non-representational art, but differently from Cubism, in a manner which amounts to a negation of appearances: Franz Marc (1880–1916), August Macke (1887–1914), the Swiss Paul Klee (1879–1940, pl. 677) and Heinrich Campendonck (born 1889). The most representative artist of this group was Wassily Kandinsky (1886–1944), a Russian artist whose abstracts evoke some strange world which refuses the limitations of geometry (pl. 678). The Bauhaus, a grouping together of the schools of fine arts and crafts, founded in Weimar in 1919, which gave a great impetus to architecture, saw the possibility of a more constructive abstract art, more closely related to Cubism (Lyonel Feininger, 1871–1956; Oskar Schlemmer, 1880–1943; Willi Baumeister, 1889–1955). After the war Germany produced another aesthetic, the *Neue Sachlichkeit* (New Objectivism) which demanded an uncompromising, intensified realism that was set at the service of a revolutionary imagery related to Surrealism (Otto Dix, born 1891; Georg Grosz, born 1893; Oskar Schlemmer, 1888–1943; Max Beckmann, 1884–1950). The German school of sculpture was strongly marked by the influence of Maillol and Despiau (Wilhelm Lehmbruck, 1881–1919; Ernst Barlach, who was also a draughtsman, 1870–1938, pl. 679).

By another paradox, when Nazism appealed to the Germans to rediscover their soul in the name of the 'Aryan' tradition, it condemned as degenerate the very Expressionism which had been based on all that was

676 Kokoschka. The Tempest (Die Windsbraut). 1914. Basle

most characteristic of the race, and the political movement imposed in its stead a propagandist imagery expressed in terms of puerile realism. The artists fled the country and the modern German movement came to nothing.

Meanwhile Impressionism helped Belgium to throw off a stifling realism. Between 1884 and 1889 the *Société des Vingt* gave exhibitions of the modern French masters in Brussels. With different emphasis according to their temperament, Theo van Rysselberghe (1862–1926), Vogels (1836–1896), Evenpoel (1872–1899), Oleffe (1867–1932), Opsomer (born 1878) and the fine painter Rick Wouters (1886–1916) used the Impressionist 'rainbow-palette' of light tones. But the real founder of the modern Belgian school was the English-born James Ensor (1860–1949), who already in 1888 with his *Entry of Christ into Bruxelles in 1889* (pl. 682) disturbed this sense of rapture with his visionary art, his violent tonality, his grimacing masks which recall Hieronymus Bosch. This tendency to view reality as the outward sign of a hidden world, which at that time could be seen in the Symbolist writings of Maeterlinck, resulted in a coherent movement which has been called the 'Laethem-Saint-Martin school', after the name of the Flemish village where between 1900 and 1910 a number

677 Klee. The Niesen. 1915. Berne

678 Kandinsky. Study for Composition No. 7. 1913. Berne

679 Barlach. Man out walking. 1912.

of artists formed a group round the sculptor George Minne (1866–1940). Flemish Expressionism has two main streams. First there is the mystical tendency towards Symbolism, which is best represented by George Minne, Albert Servaes (born 1883), Gustave van de Woestyne (born 1881). Then there is a rustic, folk or popular tendency with a stress on the health, joviality and robust physique of the Flemings, or else the grandeur of Flemish landscape. This stream is composed of Tytgat (born 1879), van den Berghe (born 1883), Gustave de Smet (born 1877), Valerius de Saedler (born 1867) and Constant Permecke (1886–1951, pl. 683), the last of these creating an elemental, colossal vision of man and nature out of the Flemish land and its people.

After Impressionism (George Breitner, 1857–1923) Holland also turned to Expressionism, with some hesitation over its plastic technique which rapidly threw Dutch painting into a harsh realism not unlike that of the *Neue Sachlichkeit* in Germany (Jan Sluyters, born 1881; Charles Toorop, 1857–1927; A. C. Willink, born 1900).

680 *Marini. Horse and Rider. 1947. Collection of the Artist*

England hesitated longer, after being profoundly marked by Impressionism through the charming painter Walter Richard Sickert (1860 –1942, pl. 684). In 1910 and 1912 paintings of the school of Paris were exhibited in London at the Grafton Galleries. In 1914 Wyndham Lewis (1884–1957), painter and theorist of a constructive alliance of the 'wild

681 Moore. Family Group. 1946. Private Collection

body' and the eye as compass of the intelligence, founded the Vorticist movement. In the late twenties the Seven and Five group brought together artists of decisive influence in England: Christopher Wood (1901–1930), indebted in his naive landscapes to Fauvist principles, Ben Nicholson (born 1894), later a member of the *Abstraction-Création* group in Paris, Ivon Hitchens (born 1893), in landscapes influenced by Matisse, and Henry Moore (born 1898, pl. 681), whose evolving, inventive idiom of an organic abstraction has made him the most influential of living Euro-

682 Ensor.
Entry of
Christ into
Brussels in
1889
(detail).
1888.
Knokke-le-
Zoute

pean sculptors. Graham Sutherland (born 1903, pl. 685) is in some degree Moore's idiomatic counterpart in painting. Edward Burra (born 1905) has painted sardonic images of violence also akin to the German *Neue Sachlichkeit*.

The Latin countries other than France have had a less impressive artistic record than the Nordic countries. Spain was robbed of a living national school because its best artists went to Paris: the first, 'Blue', period of Pablo Picasso (1902–1905, pl. 686), the acknowledged leader of the whole movement, may be considered as entirely Spanish. The romantic Spanish temperament lends itself readily to Expressionism (José Gutierrez Solana, who recalls Goya), but other artists come close to Cubism (Ismail de la Serna) or Surrealism (Manuel Angelico Ortiz and

683 Permeke.
The two
Brothers.
1923. Basle

685 Sutherland. Entrance to a Lane.
1939. London

684 Sickert. Interior of St Mark's, Venice. London

the sculptor Alberto). Portugal has produced a great sculptor in Franco, who is gifted with a sense of the monumental which is rare in our century. Italy produced a very original movement in Futurism, which was formed in Milan in 1910 by the poet Marinetti. Its first exhibition was held in 1912. The Futurist aesthetic exalted the clear-cut forms produced by machinery, and aimed at expressing dynamic force by a kind of plastic simultaneity of consecutive events (Gino Severini, born 1883, pl. 687; Prampolini; Carlo Carrà, born 1881, pl. 688; Giacomo Balla, born 1871; the sculptor Boccioni, 1882–1916). When Futurism returned to Italy it lost its original character and became confused with a vague idea of modernism. Gino Severini became a decorator, Prampolini a Cubist, Carlo Carrà a Surrealist, Tato exalted aviation, which of course was the pet glory of Fascism, with a realist imagery, while Massimo Campigli (born 1895) and Mario Tozzi both sought inspiration in the painting of antiquity. Two great artists springing from the school of Paris are the Tuscan Amedeo Modigliani (pl. 658), who had all the sensitive and nostalgic gracefulness of the Sienese painters, and Giorgio di Chirico (born 1888, pl. 660), who was a forerunner of Surrealism with his symbolic paintings composed of features taken from the antique and from the Quattrocento. More recently, Marino Marini (born 1901) has found something of the terse energy of primitive volumes (pl. 680).

The history of twentieth-century painting in the United States, following a trend already established in the nineteenth century, is the history

512

XVI Pablo Picasso.
The Meal.
Collection of the
Artist

686 Picasso. The old Jew. 1903. Moscow

of many individual artists rather than of groups or schools. Self-consti-
tuted groups or schools do occasionally appear but lack the solidarity and
continuity of schools in the European sense. One such group was 'The
Eight', which numbered painters like Robert Henri (1865–1929) and

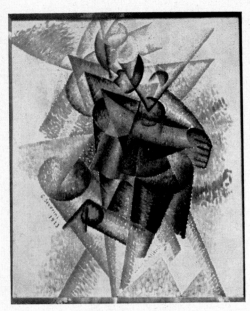

687 Severini. Argentine Tango. 1913.
Private Collection

John Sloan (1871–1953), whose art, based on observation of the realities of urban life, was a protest against the academic tradition. A follower of Henri and his ideals was George Bellows (1882–1925), painter of eloquent and sensitive portraits, dynamic boxing subjects, and elegiac landscapes. Post-Impressionism was slow to reach America. Marsden Hartley (1877–1942) and Max Weber (born 1881, pl. 690), who were both sponsored by Alfred Stieglitz, the distinguished photographer, introduced American variations on Cubism and Expressionism to New York as far back as the year 1910.

The turning point in modern American art was the Armory Show of 1913, a vast array of paintings and sculpture brought together to illustrate the most modern trends in Europe and America. This exhibition, organized by Walt Kuhn and Arthur B. Davies, was a sensation and a revelation to the American public.

So many factors contributed to the transformation of American art into the modern idiom of the Fauves and Cubists that it would be impossible to relate them all. Perhaps most influential of all was Stieglitz and his group at the '291' gallery; new assertions of freedom and defiance of the academicians brought about the founding of the Society of Independent Artists in 1917 and the first Independent Show of 1910.

Aggressive representatives of artistic isolationism were the Regionalist artists of the thirties, Thomas H. Benton (born 1889), Grant Wood (1892–1942) and John Stuart Curry (1897–1946). Among the artists who gave an American interpretation of post-Impressionist ideals was John Marin (1870–1953), who in a very personal calligraphic water-colour style sought to suggest dynamic change in the face of reality. Marsden Hartley developed into a twentieth-century Ryder in his expressionistic painting of the sea and its people. Lionel Feininger (born 1871), an offshoot of the modern German school, presented a formula of romantic, decorative abstraction.

A group sometimes described as 'Cubist-Realists' includes Charles Sheeler (born 1883), recorder in sharp focus of the cold face of the industrial landscape, and Charles Demuth (1883–1935), whose sensitive re-workings of Cubism are second only to his very personal flower studies. In his fondness for clean, unencumbered surfaces, the Surrealist Peter Blume (born 1906) is an outgrowth of this trend.

American landscape painting has its distinguished representative in the twentieth century with Charles Burchfield (born 1893), whose work, almost exclusively in water-colour, has been concerned with a romantic interpretation of the midwestern scene and the animation of motifs in nature through expressionistic devices. Edward Hopper (born 1882) in figure painting as well as in urban landscape reveals the American and the American scene in terms of sharp, cold illumination that intensifies the loneliness of his theme.

At mid-century the division of American painting into the work of many individuals and small, loosely associated groups continued. The New York school, numbering such *avant-garde* artists as Jackson Pollock and Robert Motherwell, represents a phase of non-objective expressionism

688 Carrà. Noon by the Sea. 1928

with a complete suppression of any kind of representation. Opposed to this group is the violent colouristic expressionism and social protest of Jack Levine (born 1915) and Hyman Bloom (born 1913). Ben Shahn (born 1898) has given his impressions of the rights and wrongs of democracy in forms combining realism with the simplicity of the primitive. A list of the more interesting American abstract painters would include the pioneer, Arthur Dove (1880–1946), Karl Knaths (born 1891), Rice Pereira (born 1907) and Stuart Davis (born 1894).

In the American sculpture of the early twentieth century, the Renaissance idiom of Augustus St-Gaudens (1848–1907), without his peculiarly lyric interpretation of form, continued with Daniel Chester French (1850–1931). John Flannagan (1895–1942) with his vision of the image in the rock was one of the most powerful carvers to appear in the first half of the twentieth century. Alexander Calder's (born 1898) abstract revolving metal compositions or 'mobiles', the artistic counterpart of the American love of the gadget, have won their creator an international reputation (pl. 689).

The Latin American republics have rapidly assimilated the whole plastic vocabulary of modern art, helped by the fundamental richness of the folk tradition which has been revitalized by European contributions. The 'neo-Latins' have produced some most original works. The two schools

691 Portinari. Gaucho
(destroyed). 1942.
Rio de Janeiro

690 Weber. Geranium. 1911.
New York

showing the greatest variety of talents are those of Argentine and Brazil.
In Uruguay, Pedro Figari (1861–1938) is an exquisite colourist and a
witty reporter of local life. Torres García (born 1874) has been influenced
by pre-Columbian art. The most remarkable development in the region
is the emergence in Mexico and Brazil of a monumental expressionism
reflecting the vitality and power of the masses, and which has found its
medium in enormous mural paintings. The revolutionary movement in
Mexico has inspired a number of painters. Of these, Diego Rivera (1880
–1957) developed an imagery of the awakening proletariat in his vast
compositions; José Clemente Orozco (1883–1949) and Rufino Tamayo
(born 1899) are more expressionistic; Alfaro Siqueiros (1898–1950) has
found an impressive source of inspiration in the ancient Indian tradition.
In Brazil, Lasar Segall (born 1890) has transplanted Slavic melancholy
into a new civilization, while Candido Portinari (born 1903) has created
a powerful style suitable for monumental works; during the recent war
Portinari successfully took up Picasso's expressionism and with its help
gave moving utterance to the anguish that then swept the world (pl. 691).

4. THE MINOR ARTS

Towards 1890, with Horta in Belgium and Galle in France, a reaction
set in against copying Classical styles in furniture, in favour of a new
style based directly on natural forms. Emile Galle (1846–1904), who
founded the Nancy school, designed furniture, vases and jewellery in

floral patterns with a latent symbolic meaning, whose lavish curves recall
the Flamboyant Gothic. This is what is known as Art Nouveau (pl. 692).
Louis Majorelle (1859–1926) developed this style in furniture, and it had
particular success in pottery (Delaherche, Emile Lenoble, Emile Decœur)
and in glass-ware (René Lalique, Daum).

The Baroque style fell out of favour towards 1910, when it was simplified by means of purer curves and plainer decoration, the result being
a style which became established at the Paris Exhibition of Decorative
Arts in 1925 (Paul Follot, pl. 693, Maurice Dufrène, Paul Poiret). This
style made great use of textiles, the materials taking their geometrical
patterns from Cubism, or having a stylized or geometrical design based
on the floral style of 1900. Brandt and Subes made some fine wrought-
ironwork in this manner. The best pieces of furniture – and perhaps the
only ones that are not already dated – are those of Ruhlmann, which
have a very pure contour deriving from the Louis XVI and English styles
and which are constructed of fine timbers.

Shortly after the 1925 exhibition there was a reaction against curves,
when Le Corbusier's influence imposed a functional style with straight
lines and no decoration. This style was already to be seen in Germany
before 1914, and it was shown in Paris in 1910 at the German Werkbund
Exhibition. This sober style was only established in Paris in 1930 (Francis
Jourdain, Pierre Chareau, Djo Bourgeois, pl. 694, Louis Sognot). The
influence of modern machinery resulted in the invention of furniture in
metal tubing (René Herbst). Towards 1937 a further reaction ousted the
'architect's' style, producing a 'decorator's' style which was less austere,
some of the new school (Arbus, Serge Roche) going as far as using stylized
Rococo shapes.

The first half of the twentieth century witnessed a considerable development in scenic art. This movement began in Paris, with Bakst's
scenery for the Russian Ballet in 1909.

693 *Paul Follot. Dining-Room. 1921*

Since about 1940 tapestry-making, which had for a long time been in a state of decadence, was revived with impressive results at the private workshops at Aubusson. Although Raoul Dufy and Marcel Gromaire were attracted to it and created some fine works, the painter Jean Lurçat (born 1892, pl. 695) was the moving spirit. He brought a 'modern's' rationalistic outlook to bear on the technical processes and formal laws of the art of tapestry as they had been in its finest period in the fourteenth and fifteenth centuries, and was finally in a position to impose his own aesthetic ideals on it. This renovation of an applied art, which calls for craftsmanship and appeals to a wide public, offers a much-needed change from the modern esoteric tendency which confines art-appreciation to an élite. Several individual styles have found their expression in this adaptable medium, from the lyricism of Lurçat, Picard le Doux and Marc Saint-Saens to the expressionism of Vogensky and the pure abstracts of Mategot.

694 *Djo Bourgeois. Interior. 1932*

There has also been a noticeable tendency in recent years, among established artists, towards applying their skill in the field of the industrial arts. Pablo Picasso gave an impetus to the search for new possibilities in pottery with his pieces fired at Vallauris in Provence since 1948. Fernand Léger, Joan Miró, Jean Lurçat and Marc Chagall have all followed his example. Henri Matisse has designed not only a chapel but all its accessories, from the architecture itself down to the stained glass, and ceramic decorations (Chapel of the Rosary, Vence). Two Dominicans, Frs. Couturier and Régamey, headed a campaign to admit modern art into the churches, the most remarkable success of its kind being the chapel at Assy-Passy, where Pierre Bonnard, Jean Lurçat, Fernand Léger, Henri Matisse, Braque, Bazaine and Germaine Richier all collaborated in the decoration.

CONCLUSION

While art-historians have been gradually taking stock of the manifold aspects of works of art of all times and places, it is inevitable that they should be constantly concerned with the problem of what a work of art is, and what the conditions are under which art may come into being.

For the first historians, the work of art threw more light than any other human creation on the individual: the Italian, Vasari (1550), and the Fleming, Carel van Mander (1600), both approached art from the biographical point of view.

However, it gradually began to be thought that the production of a work of art is determined by 'the material, moral and intellectual climate in which a man lives and dies' (Taine). Originally suggested to some extent by a belief in astrology, this notion was already to be found in Winckelmann's *History of Ancient Art* (*Geschichte der Kunst des Altertums*, 1764) and the Abbate Lanzi's history of Italian painting (*Storia pittorica della Italia*, 1789); the Swiss scholar Jacob Burckhardt applied it brilliantly in his *Civilization of the Renaissance in Italy* (*Kultur der Renaissance in Italien*, 1860). None the less, Hippolyte Taine in his *Philosophy of Art* (first English edition 1865) was mistaken in turning it into a systematic approach which swept all before it in the late nineteenth century.

Other historians, by stressing psychological more than geographical or historical factors, have believed the work of art to contain the most significant evidence of the spiritual outlook of a given period. This leads to the idea embodied in the work receiving more attention than the form itself, as in the case of Emile Mâle's work on religious art in France in the twelfth century (*L'Art religieux du XIIᵉ siècle en France,* 1899). Even more recently the Czech critic, Max Dvořák, writing in German, defended the same thesis in his study of the formation of Baroque.

Since the racial problem caused so much disagreement in the second half of the nineteenth century, it is not surprising to note its repercussions on art. Following on the French writer Courajod, the Austrian scholar Josef Strygowski thought he found the most fruitful powers of artistic creation in the Nordic race. After working for years in the field of Western and neighbouring Asiatic art, he astonished the art-historians of his time in 1901 with his book *Orient oder Rom?* in which he attributed the development of Byzantine art to the Eastern civilizations rather than to the genius of the Romans. Whereas Courajod gave a psychological and strictly ethnical meaning to the term 'race', Strygowski also gave it a geographical significance. For him, the history of Western art showed an endless struggle between two centres of world culture: that of the South, which he centred on the Equator; and that of the North, beginning near

*696 Titian. Assumption.
In the Frari, Venice.
1516–1518*

*697 Rubens. Assumption.
Brussels*

the North Pole, – a zone which would appear to be particularly favourable to artistic creation, thanks to the artistic gifts of the peoples who
settled in it and whose origins Strygowski sought Eastwards, at first in
Armenia, then in the East, and finally in the Siberian steppes. Whereas
the South generated 'academic' forms which served a temporal or religious
hierarchy, the Northern peoples had an imaginative capacity for creating
pure forms for their own sake. After defining the psychological make-up
of these 'Nordic' peoples, Strygowski tried to show their contribution to
the different Mediterranean civilizations which they had fertilized.

By reducing history to such postulates, Strygowski invented a chrono-
logical method which consisted in ignoring historical facts and dating
artistic forms according to a supposed logical succession. In particular,
he saw folk-art as a reflection of basic primordial forms and not as the
degenerate survival of advanced cultures. Strygowski's theories have an
epic touch which appeals to the imagination; but as they have no proper
connection with realities his later views particularly may be dismissed as
romantic speculations.

The end of the century showed a weakening grip on the concrete and
the rational (which is its correlative), and this came to a head in the
philosophy of Bergson, deeply influencing both the art and the politics of
our time. Art-historians, following a certain 'finalist' tendency which
showed itself particularly in neo-vitalist doctrines, began to seek the
determining factors in the work of art no longer in circumstances outside

the work, but in the artistic activity itself. They credited this activity with a capacity for development or expansion of its own, to be understood like life in terms of a 'creative evolution' working towards a more efficient use of its inherent properties.

It is not surprising that Germany was the first country to consider the work of art in these terms, for whereas French thought in the nineteenth century tended to be positivistic, German philosophy was more idealistic. The *Kunstwollen* formulated by Alois Riegl in 1895 in his *Stilfragen*, that 'will-to-art' which he postulated as the active principle behind all artistic development, is an *idée-force* or dynamic theory characteristic of German philosophy. In 1908, in a violent attack on the ideas developed by Semper in his work on style (*Der Stil in den technischen und tektonischen Künsten*, 1879), Alois Riegl argued that the art of the later Roman Empire (Byzantine art) resulted from the appearance of a new form of artistic expression and not merely a decay in technical processes, the latter being themselves determined by a 'will-to-art' in the proper sense of the term. This work is one of capital importance, being the first to recognize the creative value behind the artistic decline of ancient classical forms that resulted in the primitive forms of the Middle Ages.

Everything happened in a way which suggests that as soon as a new principle was discovered, the successive generations of artists were only concerned with developing it to the full, blindly obeying its implicit laws until they brought it to its inevitable end. Gothic architecture, as the present writer tried to show in a work on Mont Saint-Michel in 1934, is perhaps the most perfect example of an art obeying an unavoidable law of growth.

At the end of the nineteenth century a Swiss Professor, Heinrich Wölfflin, made a most valuable contribution to art-history, by defining the psychological concepts 'classical' and 'baroque' for the first time (*Die*

698 *Head of the Calf-Bearer. 600–590 B.C. Athens*

699 *Head of an Apostle. Late 11th c. Toulouse*

klassische Kunst, transl. as *Classic Art*). This he did apart from historical uses or applications of the terms, by confronting and opposing two artistic attitudes that correspond to two mutually hostile attitudes to life. Classicism, which attempts to strike a balance between form as it is conceived by the intellect on the one hand and the direct observation of nature on the other, expresses itself in centred compositions and through a strict arrangement of component parts, each of which retains its distinct unity; classical forms are ponderable and static, and obey the laws of gravity, while movements are governed by rhythms and may be reduced to a harmonic cadence (pl. 696). Baroque, on the other hand, expresses uneasiness and a longing for freedom, and shows itself in open compositions, fragments of the world rather than a world in themselves, which overflow the limits of the frame. Baroque forms are imponderable, weightless, they soar into space, which they cut across with movements that set the eye moving in every direction, far beyond what they actually show. The unity of baroque compositions is not of an intellectual order, but it is organic, living, comprehensive, resulting in a close dependence of the forms one upon the other (pl. 697). In its extreme form the pursuit of depth leads to forms being completely dissolved into their surroundings (Monet's *Nymphéas*). Classicism means cohesion, it reduces nature to the human scale. It is a state of being, while baroque is a state of becoming, a dispersion, so enamoured of nature that it absorbs man into the cosmic rhythm. Baroque tries to depict human passion, grief and pain (pl. 708–710), love and death, all the ages of man; whereas classicism is only interested in the mature man at the height of his powers, when all his faculties are controlled by reason. The favourite medium of baroque is

700 *Greek Statue. 1st half of 5th c. B.C. Rome*

701 *Angel of the Annunciation on Chartres Cathedral. Early 13th c.*

702 *Aphrodite (school of Praxiteles). 4th c. B.C. Naples*

703 *Madonna in Troyes Cathedral. 14th c.*

painting or music, while classicism express itself most fully in architecture and sculpture. In extreme baroque, architecture tends to abandon abstract principles, becoming as it were plant-like, closely wedded to the organic forms of nature (Manueline art, pl. 347).

An archaeologist who developed Riegl's fundamental ideas and took as his point of departure the astonishing parallel he found between the evolution of Greek and Romano-Gothic sculpture, the hellenist Déonna, director of the Geneva Museum, suggested that there are endlessly recurring 'artistic cycles'. This thesis has been taken up and cleverly developed by two French aestheticians, Elie Faure (*Esprit des formes*, 1927) and Henri Focillon (*Vie des formes*, 1934). These different works have satisfactorily defined the complete evolutionary cycle of a style as passing through the following stages:

Primitive, Archaic Stage, corresponding to the Experimental Age

In this immature stage man is still unable to make a clear distinction between his own soul and that of the world. The myriad forms of the world appear to him as being in a state of continuous creation and interchangeable with one another. Style is governed by certain mental data that the artist projects into his work. These impose certain schematic and ornamental deformations on nature (pl. 698, 699 and 714–717), but they gradually diminish as man's powers of observation awaken, as he begins to be aware of the reality of the external world and finds that he can act on it rationally.

525

Classical Stage, corresponding to the Age of Maturity

This stage represents an equilibrium between the soul's receptiveness, now open to the external world, and the creative power of the mind, – the mind informing the soul of its concepts and ideas and thus controlling observation and spontaneous sensation. These two currents in the human being, the one so to speak directed upwards and the other downwards, come together in the imagination, to their common advantage; they help the imagination to respect appearances and at the same time to perceive the harmony underlying their apparent disorder.

Academic and Mannerist Stages

These two stages may be reached after any great creative period, even after baroque; but they are particularly noticeable after a period of classicism. The soul's ability to absorb the manifold forms of the world now becomes inhibited by the artist's undue respect for the forms created by the previous generation.

A sense of weariness now pushes the weaker spirits towards academicism, or a conformity in which they obey conventional rules deduced from the art of the great masters and feel excused from having to invent anything themselves. But the more gifted artists revolt against the feeling of impotence and create what we call the 'mannerist' phase to which all styles are liable. With his mind obsessed and arrested by conventional memorized forms, his soul impoverished by the sudden lowering of vitality that cuts it off from the outside world, the artist can only create a

704 *Amenophis IV making an Offering to the Sun. Cairo*

705 *El Greco. Resurrection (detail). Madrid*

706 *Figure from a Frieze on the Altar of Pergamus (reversed). 2nd c. B.C. Berlin*

707 *Sluter. Madonna in the former Chartreuse of Champol, Dijon. 1391*

world of his own, a substitute for the real one around him. This anaemia results in artificiality and drives artists to extremes, for instance such deformities as the exaggerated lengthening of the body pl. 374, 704, 705) or frantic gestures, feverish attitudes and caricatured expression.

This sickness of styles is one of the most constant phenomena in the history of art. It is particularly noticeable in the Greek fourth century, in the French fourteenth century (pl. 702, 703) and in the second half of the sixteenth century when it afflicted the whole of Europe as a result of the nervous shock given by the Renaissance. It can also be seen in the Florentine school at the end of the fifteenth century, in Chinese sculpture under the Sung dynasty, or in Art Nouveau, an artificial style which arose out of exasperation against the conventionality of architecture in the nineteenth century, and which at the same time has none of the powerful rhythm of baroque. One of the most remarkable examples of the mannerist crisis would seem to be the eccentric art of the eighteenth Egyptian dynasty, at the time of Amenophis IV (pl. 704).

The mannerist phenomenon has created works which are by no means negligible, and which have acted as stimulants to the nervous sensibility of our own period. But the artists belonging to a mannerist generation rarely manage to break through the circle of impotence in which they are held. The cry that came from the very soul of Alonso Berruguete (pl. 402), the mystical outpourings of El Greco (pl. 405) and the feverish discovery of the truth of things by the artists of Tell el Amarna none the less show that the mannerist way of feeling may reach sublime heights.

527

The normal end of mannerism – its cure – lies in baroque. Once the spirit is again in contact with the world, the imagination drinks deeply of its forms, and at the very source, with an eagerness born of long deprivation. The cosmos itself seems to be throbbing in the soul, filling it with inspiring emotion.

For Germanic thinkers, baroque is the essential creative power that animates so many primitive works as well as those of so-called 'baroque' periods. According to them, it originates with the Nordic peoples and their Asiatic ancestors or offshoots, but the Southern peoples are always trying to smother it under their academic mentality. The concept of a baroque style as a 'resultant', a consequence and final expression of stylistic evolution, spelling the decline of certain techniques such as architecture and the minor arts, but on the other hand encouraging painting, holds good particularly with the art of the West. But there is also an 'immanent' baroque instinct with its reserves in the East, which is also found in such Western countries as Spain and Germany. The meeting of 'resultant' with

708 *Head of Laocoon. About 50 B.C.*

709 *Juan de Juni. St Jerome in S. Francesco, Rioseco (detail, inspired by the Laocoon Group). 1534*

710 *Head of Christ in St-Laurent, Eu. 15th c.*

'immanent' baroque results in an ultra-baroque, for example Flamboyant and Rococo in Spain and Germany, or American post-conquest art.

In the development of his *homo ludens* theory (1951), Professor Johan Huizinga of Utrecht produced a general vindication of the 'formalist' standpoint of the first half of the twentieth century. To him the work of art appeared as an expression of that 'urge to play' *(Spieltriebs)*, whose self-sufficiency and spontaneity form an essential human characteristic. Today, however, there is a tendency to reject this Olympian interpretation of artistic activity, which is now seen as being subject to other influences beside the pure *Kunstwollen*. As long ago as 1872 the German Robert Vischer put forward his theory of *Einfühlung*, or 'symbolic sympathy', which was derived from the Idealist aesthetic of Kant and Hegel. According to Vischer this instinctive tendency causes the artist, on the one hand, to evoke those forms from the real world which he feels are analogous to his inner inspirations, and, on the other, to create his own world of forms, a hand-writing that exteriorizes and clarifies his deepest feelings.

During the last five years or so the study of art as a human activity has tended to draw steadily closer to psychology (study of the conscious) or to psychoanalysis (study of the unconscious). Contemporary developments in abstract art show a tendency to render artistic forms independently of their representational, thematic or philosophical content, and even of their historical associations. These forms are seen as a system of signs and symbols with almost magical significance, which make the fundamental rhythms of the human soul, individual or collective, well up from the depths to the surface. This tendency, closer to psychoanalysis, which explains hidden meanings, than to psychology, the interpreter of the conscious mind, is shown in recent works by André Malraux, which together form his *Psychologie de l'art* (1947–1950).

In 1946, the present author drew attention in his *Crépuscule des images* to the profound correspondence between the forms of contemporary art and the 'morphology' of our times. Moreover, as much in the realms of scientific thought and of poetry as in the world of action, the artist finds himself more often than not playing a prophetic rôle and anticipating the course of events.

The impossibility of 'explaining' the work of art and the fact that it has a language peculiar to itself alone have been strongly emphasized by André Malraux and still more so by André Breton (*L'Art magique*). Breton, the leader of the Surrealist movement, rejects as useless all means of expression which are not derived from magic, and he considers it one of the merits of our times to have rediscovered the sense of this profound message. The theory of archetypes in Jungian psychoanalysis favours such interpretations.

711 Detail of a Cycladic Vase. Bronze Age. Athens
712 Detail of a Stele at Vallstenarum (Gotland). About 400 B.C.
713 Ornament from the Book of Durrow. Anglo-Irish

The spiral-motif, which probably originated in Crete, spread throughout the barbarian world, appears in Anglo-Irish work, and survives in contemporary Breton folk-art.

While the historians, aestheticians, psychologists and psychoanalysts have been investigating the work of art along these lines, paying special attention to primitive art, Bernard Berenson, who at the beginning of our century gave the decisive impetus to the discovery of early Italian painting, has remained stubbornly faithful to the assumption of the superiority of classicism and to the traditional interpretations dating back to before Riegl and Wölfflin (*Aesthetics and History*, 1950).

A study of the great laws governing artistic creation has been made by the historians of Western art and of the art of adjacent Asiatic countries. Our knowledge of the arts of the Far East was pursued quite independently, but if one wants to have an overall view of the great styles that have swept the world, it would be advisable to consider whatever morphology might be deduced from Western and Eastern art together. René Grousset, in his *Bilan de l'histoire* (1948) wrote the first great synthesis of the Western and Eastern cultures, taking works of art into account, though as evidence of civilization rather than for their own sake.

There are many analogies of form between the arts of the East and West, and some aspects of these have already been mentioned. The principles behind the birth and development of forms are the same all over the world, but it is apparent that the rhythm of formal evolution as defined by Riegl, Déonna, Elie Faure and Henri Focillon can strictly only be applied to the arts of the West. In the Far East many stages appear to be missing. India seems to have begun straight away at the stage of naturalism, without having passed through the ideomorphism or stylization common to primitive arts. In China the normal evolution – through primitivism, classicism and baroque – can be clearly seen running through the Wei, T'ang and Sung dynasties, but there is an inexplicable gap between the primitivism of the earliest periods and the sudden realistic work of the Han dynasty.

The resemblance between forms that emerge at immense distances from each other may have various explanations. However great the distance may be, it does not cut out all possibility of influence; for instance Chinese figures could be brought into the West across the silk-road that crossed Turkestan and Iran, carrying artistic forms to Byzantium and Islam. Or a remote common origin might explain similarities between peoples who have been separated over a long period of history; perhaps this explains the strange resemblance between the forms of pre-Columbian art on the American continent, and the much older forms of early China. It has also been known to happen that without any possibility of influence, similar circumstances produce similar artistic forms at enormous distances of time and space, the most famous of these parallels being that of Gandharan Greco-Buddhist art, which anticipated Gothic spiritually by a thousand years. In sociology this phenomenon is known as 'convergence'.

The frequency with which these resemblances recur tempts the historian to see or to seek profound unifying principles in the infinite variety of civilizations all over the world. If we try to take an overall view of the forms of art created by mankind, we see that after a phase of uniformity common to all the earth in the Neolithic period, the world seems to have become divided into three parts: two zones showing evolved civilizations which are clearly defined in geography, both of them being on the Eurasian continent, the third being a zone of archaic civilizations scattered over Africa, America and Polynesia.

The two zones of evolved civilizations, one covering the East and the other the West of the Eurasian continent, both exploited the plastic arts as far as they could take them. The differences between these two regions should not blind us to the resemblance between their underlying rhythms. In each of these two zones, indeed, two distinct poles are to be seen, based on opposite centres, the first tending to remind man of his attachment to the universe and his submission to supernatural powers; the second urging him, on the contrary, to free himself from those powers and rely on his own strength, so that he might possess the world and himself by means of thought.

In the primitive period of Mediterranean civilization, after the very earliest stage of immaturity Mesopotamia showed itself to be progressive as compared with a static Egypt. Then, in Classical antiquity, Asia Minor began to play its part as the enduring 'reservoir' of immanent powers as opposed to the Greco-Roman sense of progress. Asia Minor maintained the rights of God against Greek and Roman anthropomorphism, and restored God to the Mediterranean peoples. The Middle Ages saw an opposition between unchangeable Byzantium and the belated but impressive rise of the West. The same struggle was taken into the interior of Western Europe when Renaissance rationalism was checked by the resistance of Gothic irrationalism. At that time Germany seemed to have inherited from Asia its function of serving as a reservoir for irrational forces, in the same way as Spain which had become strongly marked by Orientalism owing to Islam: the Churrigueresque of the Spanish eighteenth century is of the same stock as the late Gothic of fifteenth- and sixteenth-century Germany. The struggle and the mingling of these two forces accounts for the extraordinary wealth of the so-called 'Baroque period'.

If we now look to the Far East, the same pattern may be observed there. But before considering that part of the world it is important to remember that the creative evolution came to a standstill there in the fifteenth century, for the prolongation of Chinese art thereafter represents a decadent crystallization or fixity, while that of India was arrested by Islam.

India, a creator of great metaphysical ideas as well as of a philosophy which quickly developed into a religion with universal implications, in the form of Buddhism – India is in a way the 'West' of the Eastern Hemisphere. Compared with India, China has remained culturally archaic in spite of a highly-developed civilization, and may be called a force for tradition. Were it not for the mystery of Han art, whose origins cannot be traced, it might be suggested that the influence of Buddhist India freed China from its prolonged primitivism, so great and so marked was the effect of Gupta art on the Chinese in the Wei dynasty, when Buddhism came to China. Just like ancient Greece, into a still primitive world – that is to say one whose art was ideomorphic and magical – India brought the awakening of naturalism, a sense of the concrete, a sense of the figure, in a word a physical, corporeal art, which perhaps she herself

714 Greek Vase (detail). Early 6th c. B.C. Athens
715 Buddhist Stele (detail). Wei Dynasty. A.D. 533–543
716 Christ from the Tympanum in La Madelaine, Vézelay (detail). About 1130
717 Rock-Drawing at Ramsunberg (Norway). About 1000

The urge towards stylization in the early stages of different civilizations makes them all produce similar formal patterns, though at considerable removes in both space and time.

had created under the influence of the last faint repercussions of Hellenism that were brought across Iran and Bactria into Gandhara. It was at Gandhara that the two worlds met, the point where the two great cultures dating back to the antiquity of man, recognized their blood-relationship. In his book *De la Grèce à l'Orient* (1948) René Grousset has described the astonishing adventure of Hellenism as it spread its roots and multiplied until at last it reached Japan.

This phase of lively Buddhist progress in India proved to be brief, because it rapidly succumbed to the upsurge of irrational forces provoked by Hinduism, a decadent form of the earlier Brahmanism. Dravidian India may be seen as a denial of Gupta India. The seed of India was to germinate in China. But even in the period of its highest philosophical refinement, China remained strongly fettered by its need for magic: its symbol is the chimaera, and the dragon that emerges from the broken tortuous patterns of archaic Chinese bronzes leaps from the sky in Sung paintings. It is extraordinary that though they have such a high metaphysical level, Sung landscapes show no sign of perspective, which is the particular expression of the Western will to progress. But in the Gupta period (Ajanta paintings), India had long since taken perspective to the same stage as it reached in the Hellenistic period, that is to say a perspective with several vanishing-points.

When the Spaniards reached America at the end of the fifteenth century, they discovered a world at a stage of civilization which must have been much the same as that of ancient China. When we consider the art of the so-called 'pre-Columbian' peoples, it is surprising that though they had reached a high quality as regards form, they had still not passed beyond the primitive stage in the evolution of styles. The cause for this must no doubt be sought in the isolation of the American continent. Sociologists have shown that closed societies, confined to what are called 'segregation territories', become static and die out. Here we put our finger on one of the most profound laws in the evolution of mankind. Man is necessary to man, there is no progress without contact between races and exchanges of influence, for man becomes more aware of himself by the impact of others, than by any amount of self-sufficiency. Other races have remained even farther behind in their evolution, perhaps because they were isolated even longer than the American tribes. This is the case with the primitives of Africa, Polynesia, the Polar regions and the Atlantic coast of South America, which are still at the Neolithic or even the Palaeolithic stage. The hunter civilization of the Perigordian age is still to be seen among the aboriginals of central Australia, who throughout their history had probably never seen other men before the Europeans arrived.

If we now compare the two great zones of the Eurasian continent, the East and the West, it can be seen that altogether they both have a history which shows a tension between the irrational and the rational, and that the internal evolution of each of them has been governed by it. No doubt the artistic manifestations of mankind are countless, but the archetypes towards which they tend are few. The law behind the creation of styles seems to draw its fundamental impulse from a tension between two hostiles forces. Thus art-history confirms the findings of modern psychology, which tends to see the principle of ambivalence beneath all the manifestations of the individual human being.

INDEX

The numbers in italic are those of the black and white illustrations
National schools of art, the different movements etc. are in capitals,
place-names in italic, and personal names in ordinary type

Aachen, 145, 148, 277; *147, 166*
Abbate, Nicolò dell', 293
Abusir, 15
ACHAEMENIAN ART. See PERSIA
Adam, Robert, 365, 370; *483, 517*
AEGEAN CIVILIZATIONS, 29–30; historical background, 50–1
See also MINOAN, MYCENAEAN ART
Aegina, 77, 85; *72, 87*
AFRICAN ART, 64–5
Agasias, *70, 76*
Agra, India, 213; *273*
Albani, Francesco, 327
Alberti, Leon Battista, 229–30, 246
Albertinelli, Mariotto, 290
Aleijadinho, 346
Alessi, 324
Allori, 327
Allston, Washington, 422
Altdorfer, Albrecht, 302; *393*
Alvares, Alfonso, 310
Amadeo, Giovanni Antonio, 231
Amiens, 176, 194; *220, 233*
Ammanati, Bartolomeo, 291, 324
Amorgos, 85
Andokides, 99
Andrieu, France, 194
d'Angers, David, 402
Anguier brothers, 376
Ani, Italy, 350

Antellami, Benedetto, 170; *210*
Anthemius of Tralles, 134
Antwerp, 274, 297, 298, 332, 334; *385*
Apelles, 96
Arca, Niccolo dell', 237, 308
Arnolfo di Cambio, 199; *253*
Arp, Hans, 493, 496, 502
Arruda, Diogo de, 347
Arruda, Francisco de, 269; *346*
Asam brothers, 350, 351
Asselijn, Jan, 360
Assisi, Italy, 197, 201, 324; *428*
ASSYRIAN ART, 47–9
Athens, 75–8, 81–2, 92; *78, 80–3, 91–3, 100*
Augsburg, Germany, 150, 301; *391*
Aulnay, France, 193
AUSTRIA: Italian architectural influence, 346; Baroque art, 348–9; *462–3*
Autun, France, 163, 165; *192*
Avignon, France, 187, 263; *339*
AZTEC ART, 57–53

Baburen, Theodor van 360
Babylon, 39; *33–4*
Baço, Jacomart, 268
Bagdad, 48; *39*
Baldovinetti, Alessio, 242, 264

Baltard, 476, 477
Bamberg, Germany, 171 –2, 194; *216, 246, 250*
Banco, Nanni di, 234
Bandinelli, Baccio, 291
Barcelona, 266, 416; *636*
Barlach, 505; *679*
Barye, 402
Baschenis, Evaristo, 329
BASILICAS: 127–30, 133; survival of basilican plan, 133, 144, 147, 169–71
Bassani, the, 292
Bautista, Sanchez and Juan, 336
Beauneveu, André, 252
Beauvais, France, 177, 194; *221*
Beer family, 350
Behzad, 221–2
BELGIAN CONGO, *59*
Belem, Portugal, 269, 310; *346*
BELGIUM, revival of national school in, 506–8
Bellini, Gentile, 247
Bellini, Giovanni, 274–8, 261, 263; *317*
Bellini, Jacopo, 228, 247
Bellotto, Bernardo, 355
Benin, 65; *57*
Berchem, Nicolaes, 360
Berckheyde, Gerrit Adriaensz., 360
Berecci, Bartolomeo, 313
Berlin, 350, 416; *523*
Berlage, H. P., 479
Berlinghieri, 200; *258*
Bermejo, Bartolomé, 268
Bernard, Joseph, 501

535

Bernini, Giovanni Lorenzo, 324, 326; *432*
Berruguete, Alonso, 307 –8; *402*
Berruguete, Pedro, 268; *244*
Bertoldo, 236
Bingham, George Caleb, 423
Blackburn, Joseph, 371
Blake, William, 395
Blanchard, Jacques, 378
Bloemaert, Abraham, 360
Blondel, Jacques-François, 375
Böcklin, Arnold, 422; *567*
BOLIVIA, Baroque art in, 345
Boltraffio, 288
Bonington, Richard Parkes, 421; *562*
Bonnard, 474, 486, 495; *648*
Bontemps, Pierre, 295
Bordeaux, France, 520
Borromini, Francesco, 324, 325; *431*
Bosch Hieronymus, 298, 300; *387*
Boschaert, Abraham, 358
Botticelli, Sandro, 242 –4; *308*
Bouchardon, Edme, 378
Boucher, François, 384; *508*
Boudin, 411
Boulanger, Louis, 397
Boulogne, Valentin de, 329
Bourdelle, Antoine, 500
Bourdichon, Jean, 295
Bourgeois, Djo, 510; *694*
Bouts, Dieric, 223, 255, 261; *327*
Boytac, 269
Brakelaer, Henri de, 397--8

Bramante, Donato, 229, 271–2, 277, 310, 322, 363; *352, 358*
Braque, 488–90, 495–7; *651, 665*
BRAZIL: Baroque art in, 345–6, *460;* Expressionism in, 475; modern architecture, 483–4, *645*
Breitner, George, 425
Brekelenkam, Quiringh, 359
Breton, André, 495
Brianchon, 495
Bril, Paul, 381
BRITISH ART. See ENGLISH AND BRITISH ART
Broeucq, Jacques du, 297
Brongniart, 399
Bronzino, 290, 298; *374*
Brouwer, Adriaen, 335–6
Brown, Ford Madox, 422
Bruant, L., *424*
Bruegel, Jan, the Elder, 335; *445*
Bruegel, Pieter, the Elder, 272, 275, 299–300, 336; *390*
Brunelleschi, 228, 233; *289, 294*
Brussels, 332; *441*
Brustolon, Andrea, *519*
Brygos, 99; *102*
Bulfinch, Charles, 417
Burgkmair, Hans, 301
Burle-Marx, 484; *645*
Bustamente, Bartolomé, 307
BYZANTINE ART, 121–2; Assyrian influence, 48; iconoclastic crisis, 123; historical background, 131–3; architecture, 133–6, *145–51;* figurative arts, 136–8, *154* –6, 184; in Slavonic

countries, 139–40; the minor arts, 140–1; its influence on the West, 141, 144, 170
Byzantium (Constantinople, Istanbul), 132 –3, 213, 277; *145, 148* *–50, 184*

Caen, France, 162; *196*
Caffieri, Jean-Jacques, 377
Cairo, 272
Calder, Alexander, 516; *689*
Callet, 386–7
Callicrates, 77
Cameron, Charles, 354
Camoin, 486
Campen, Jacob van, *472*
Canaletto, 331, 355
Cano, Alonso, 339
Canova, 417–18; *556*
Caracci family, 275, 320, 327–8; *433*
Caravaggio, Michelangelo Merisi, 275, 288, 320, 328–9, 340, 382; *435–6*
Carchemish, 47; 37
CAROLINGIAN ART, 145–50
Carolsfeld, Schnorr von, 419
Carpaccio, Vittore, 247; *315*
Carpeaux, Jean-Baptiste, 402; *532*
Carpets, eastern, 217–18, *275;* French, 387
Carrà, Carlo, 512, *688*
Carraciolo, 329
Casas y Novoa, Fernando de, 338; *448*
Castagno, Andrea del, 242, 244, 261; *285*
Castilho, Juan de, 269, 310
Cassatt, Mary, 424

CASTLES: Romanesque and Gothic, 177, *227;* Muslim, 209
CATACOMBS, ART OF THE, 125–7
Cavallini, Pietro, 201
CAVE PAINTINGS: Europe, 12–19; Sahara and Rhodesia, 65
Cellefrouin, France, 187
Cellini, Benvenuto, 291; *414*
CERAMICS: prehistoric, 19; Muslim, 220; Italian Renaissance, 314–15; European countries, 17th–18th cents., 389–91; Chinese, 465–6
Cézanne, Paul, 414; *550*
Cesena, Italy, 160
Chagall, Marc, 492; *656*
CHALDEAN ART. See MESOPOTAMIAN ART
Chalgrin, 399
Chambiges, Martin, *321*
Champaigne, Philippe de, 382; *504*
Chantereine, Nicolas, 310
Chardin, Jean-Baptiste, 385–6; *511*
Charlieu, France, 179
Chartres, 156, 176, 183, 185–6; *183, 223, 226, 231, 234, 573, 701*
Chassériau, Theodore, 407
Châteaumeillant, France, 188
CHÂTEAUX: French Renaissance, 292–3; 17th cent., 372
Chavanne, Puvis de, 399, 415
Cheops, Egypt, 32; 18
Chichen Itza, 60; 52

CHINESE ART: historical background, 453–5; evolution, 455–9; archaic art, 459–60; sculpture, 461–2; painting, 463–4; ceramics and lacquerwork, 465–6; expansion (see JAPANESE ART)
Chirico, Giorgio di, 495; *660*
Chodowiecki, Daniel, 351
Christus, Petrus, 255
Churriguera, José de, 319, 336–7
CHURRIGUERESQUE ARCHITECTURE, 319, 326, 336, 338
Cimabue, 200; *185*
Cividale, 14; *164*
Civitale, Matteo, 236
Claesz, Pieter, 358
Claude Lorrain, 380–2; *502*
Clérisseau, C. L., 370
Cleve, Joos van, 297
Clodion, 378
CLOISONNÉ WORK: Saxon, *48;* Byzantine, 141; of Goths and Franks, 142–3; in Lombardy, 145
Clouet, François, 296; *384*
Clouet, Jean, 296; *383*
Cluny, France, 158, 162–3; *199*
Cochin, 317, 392
Coello, Sanchez, 308, 342
Cologne, Germany, 150, 171–2, 194, 260–1; *214, 247*
Colombe, Michel, 228, 262, 295
Colonia, Hans de, 266
Colonio, Simon de, 266

COLUMBIA: Baroque art, 345; modern architecture, 484
Compostela. See *Santiago de Compostela*
Constable, John, 399, 420–1; *563*
Constantinople. See *Byzantium*
Copley, John Singleton, 371
COPTIC ART, 64–5
Coques, Gonzales, 335
Cordoba, Spain, 208, 210, 216, 220, 337; *264, 266*
Corinth, 75, 98; *77*
Cornejo, Pedro Duque, 337
Cornelisz, Jacob, 297
Cornelius, Peter, 419
Corot, Jean-Baptiste Camille, 398, 405; *540*
Correggio, 280, 288, 290; *373*
Cortona, Pietro da, 324
Cosimo, Piero di, 242
Cosmati family, 170
Cossa, Francesco, 245
Costa, Lorenzo, 245
Costa, Lucio, 484; *645*
Cosway, Richard, 369
Cotman, John Sell, 420; *561*
Cotte, Robert de, 375
Coucy, Château de, 177; *227*
Courbet, Gustave, 393, 408–10, 503; *526*
Cousin, Jean, 316
Coustou, Nicolas and Guillaume, 377
Coutances, France, 179; *228*
Couture, Thomas, 405
Coypel, Charles, 384
Coysevox, Antoine, 376–7; *499*
Cozens, Alexander and Robert, 369

Cracow, Poland, 259, 313; *410*

Cranach, Lucas, 302; *395*

Crayer, Gaspard de, 335

Cresilas, 92; *94*

Crespi, Daniele, 329

Crespi, Giuseppe Maria, 330

Crivelli, Carlo, 247

Crome, John, 399, 420; *560*

Cruz, Pantoja de la, 308

Ctesiphon, 112–13; *124*

CUBISM, 472–6, 485 ff.

Cueva Remigia, Spain, 7

CURVILINEAR STYLE, 189, 250

Cusco, Peru, 62, 345; *55–6*

Cuvilliés, 350

DADAISM, 483

Daddi, Bernardo, 202

Dali, Salvador, 495; *663*

Dalman, Luis, 268

Danzig, 257; *329*

Daumier, Honoré, 402, 408; *542*

David, Gerard, 228

David, Jacques Louis, 367, 387, 394, 425; *524, 535*

DECORATED STYLE, 189, 250

Degas, Edgar, 413; *548*

Delacroix, Eugène, 393, 395–7, 406–7, 409, 412; *525, 539*

Delaroche, Paul, 393, 397, 405

Delaunay, Robert, 490; *653*

Delcour, Jean, 332

DELFT POTTERIES, 389; *522*

Delorme, Philibert, 294 –5; *381*

Denis, Maurice, 486

Derain, 495

Deschamps, 179

Desmalter, Jacob, 425; *568*

Despiau, Charles, 499; *669*

Desportes, François, 385

Deutsch, Nicolas Manuel, 302

Diaz, Narcisse, 408

Diepenbeeck, van, 335

Dolci, Carlo, 327

Dolny, Kazmierz, *411*

Dominichino, 327

Donatello, 157, 228–9, 233–6, 245, 247, 291, 307–8; *298–9*

Donner, Georg Raphael, 350; *464*

Dossi, Dosso, 292

Dou, Gerard, 359, 363

Douris, 99

Dresden, Germany, 350; *461*

Dubois, Ambroise, 296

Dubreuil, Toussaint, 296

Duccio, 140, 157, 200; *259*

Duccio, Agostino di, 236

Duchamp, Marcel, 493–4

Duchamp-Villon, 501; *667*

Duck, Jacob, 359

Dudok, 483; *644*

Dufy, Raoul, 519; *654*

Dumonstier, Pierre, Etienne and Daniel, 296

Dupré, Jules, 408

Duquesnoy, 332

Dura-Europos, 115–16; *127*

Dürer, Albrecht, 275, 303–5; *357, 396–7*

DÜSSELDORF SCHOOL, 397, 419

DUTCH ART. See HOLLAND

Dutert, 477

Eakins, Thomas, 423

Earls Barton, Northants, 147; *170*

EFFORT MODERNE MOVEMENT, 491

Egas, Enrique de, 206, 306

EGYPTIAN ART, 26 –9; images, 23–4; historical background, 30–4; architecture, 33 –4, *18–22;* mural art, 36–7, *26;* minor arts, 37–8, *27;* Coptic art, 64–5; *631;* Roman period, 116; book illustration; Hellenistic period, 139

Eiffel, Gustave, 477; *635*

El Greco, 275, 310, 342; *403–4, 705*

Elsheimer, 381

Ely, 167, 192; *204*

EMPIRE STYLE, 425

l'Enfant, Major Pierre Charles, 417

ENGLISH AND BRITISH ART: Gothic churches, 187 –94, *239–44;* minor Gothic arts,, 194; Renaissance art, 311, *405–7;* 17th cent. architecture, 363–5, *483 –4, 517;* 17th and 18th cent. painting, 365–9, *485–90;* ceramics, 390; 19th cent. Gothic revival, 416, *555;* 19th cent. painting, 420–1, *561, 563–6;* later 19th and early 20th cent. painting, 424–5; revival of national school, 509–11

Ensor, James, 506; *682*

Epidauros, 78; *79, 84*

Ermannsdorff, Friedrich Wilhelm von, 352

Ernst, Max, 494; *661*

ETRUSCAN ART,
101–2
Euphronios, 99
Eve, Jean, 488
Evreux, France, 238
Exekias, *104*
EXPRESSIONISM,
474–6, 503
Eworth, Hans, 311; *406*
Eyck, Hubert van, 253–
–4; *281*
Eyck, Jan van, 223, 253
–5, 357; *281, 325*

Fabriano, Gentile da,
223, 242; *303*
Faidherbe, Lucas, 332
Falconet, 255, 378
Fancelli, Domenico, 307
FAUVISM, 472–6,
485 ff.
Feichtmayer, J. M., *465*
Feke, Robert, 371
Fernandez, Alejo, 269
Fiesole, Italy, 207
Figueroa family, 337
Fili, Russia, 352; 467
Fioravanti, Aristoteles,
313
Fischer, Johann Michael,
350; *462*
Fischer von Erlach, Jo-
hann Bernard, 348–9
FLAMBOYANT
STYLE, 177, 180, 189,
197–8, 223, 250–2,
262, 266, 332; *321*
Flandrin, Hippolyte,
404
FLEMISH ART: 15th
cent., 252–6, *323–8;*
Baroque, 332–6, *441*
–6
Florence, 157, 173, 197,
200–1, 229, 232, 235,
239; *289–90,* 292, 294
–5, 301
FLORENTINE
SCHOOL, 238–45,
276

Floris, Cornelis, 297;
385
Floris, Frans, 298
Follot, Paul, *693*
Fontaine, 415
Fontenay, France, 198
FORCES NOUVELLES
GROUP, 495
Fouquet, Jean, 228, 263
–4; *340*
Fra Angelico, 223, 228,
238–9, 242; *305*
Fra Bartolommeo, 290
Fragonard, Honoré, 384
–5; *507*
Francesco, Piero della,
244–5; *311–12*
FRANKS: Oriental in-
fluence upon, 141;
their cloisonné work,
142–3
Freiburg, Germany, 194;
245
Freminet, Martin, 296
FRENCH ART: Carol-
ingian, 145–50, *147,
165–70;* Romanesque,
151 ff., 161–2, *175–83,
186–201;* Gothic,
172 ff., *217, 219–38;*
earlier Renaissance,
261–5, *337–48;* later
Renaissance, 293–6,
379–84; 17th cent. architecture, 371–6, *492
–6;* 17th and 18th
cent. sculpture, *497–
500;* 17th and 18th
cent. painting, 378–87,
501–13; minor arts
17th–18th cent., 387–
92, *514–15, 518, 520
–1;* 19th cent. archi-
tecture and sculpture,
399–402, *530–3;* 19th
cent. painting, 402–15,
534–53; the Empire
and Restoration styles,
425–6; emergence
from 19th cent., 473

See also PARIS, THE
SCHOOL OF
FRESCOES: Byzantine,
138; Russian, 138; in
5th cent. Gaul, 144
Freyssinet, E., 483; *629*
Friedrich, Caspar David,
419; *559*
Friesz, 486
FURNITURE: Renais-
sance, 314, *412–13;*
French, 388, 391–2,
518; other countries,
17th–18th cents., 388
–9, *516, 519*
Fyt, 335
Fuseli, Henry, 395; *529*

Gabon, 629
Gabriel, Jacques-Ange,
375; *496*
Gaddi, Taddeo, 202
Gainsborough, Thomas,
365–6, 368; *488*
Galle, Emilie, 517–18
Gallegos, Fernando, 268
Galliat, Louis, 393, 397
Gargallo, Pablo, 502;
672
Garnier, Charles, 400;
530
Gaudí, Antonio, 416;
636
Gauguin, Paul, 393, 415,
486; *511*
GAUL: art of illumina-
tion, 143; basilicas,
144
Geneva, 521
Gentileschi, Orazio, 329
Géricault, Théodore,
395, 406; *538*
GERMAN ART: Roma-
nesque, 170–2, *213–17;*
Gothic, 194–6, *245–51;*
15th cent., 256–61,
329–36; Renaissance,
301–5, *391–9;* Baroque,
346–52, *461–5;* pot-
teries, 390; 19th cent.

architecture, 416; 19th cent. painting, 419; revival of national school, 503–6

Ghiberti, Lorenzo, 233–4; *297*

Ghirlandaio, 228, 242, 263

Ghislandi, Vittore, 331

Giambologna, 291; *376*

Gilbert, Cass, 481

Giordano, Luca, 330

Giorgio, Francesco di, 230

Giorgio, Maestro, *415*

Giorgione, 248, 280, 286–7; *370*

Giotto, 157, 201–3, 328; *261–2*

Giovanni, Matteo di, 244

Girardon, François, 376; *498*

Girault, 477

Girodet, 395

Girtin, Thomas, 369

Giusti, Giovanni, 295

Gloucester, 251; *322*

Goblins factory, 387; *514*

Goerg, Edouard, 493

Goes, Hugo van der, 256

Gogh, Vincent van, 415, 486, 503; *553*

GOTHIC ART: characteristics, 155–7; arise during Romanesque period, 162; birth in the Ile-de-France, and its spread, 172–3; creation of Gothic in France, 173; French architecture, 174–82, *219–25, 228–9;* arts of colour and minor arts, 185–7, *236–8;* architecture and sculpture outside France, 187–98, *238–55;* the resistance to Gothic (Italy), 197–203, *253–62*

GOTHS: Roman and Byzantine influences on, 141; cloisonné work, 142–3

Goujon, Jean, 294–5, 376, 378; *380, 382*

Goya y Lucientes, francisco José de, 330, 343, 419–20; *456, 528*

Goyen, Jan van, 360

Gozzoli, Benozzo, 242, 249

Graf, Urs, 302; *394*

Gravelot, 365

Greaves, Walter, 424

GREEK ART: historical background, 67–74; its three phases, 74–9; architecture, 79–83, *77–84;* sculpture, 83–96, *64–76, 85–99, 698, 700, 702, 706, 708;* painting, 96, *99;* ceramics, 98–101, *100–7*

Greenough, Horace, 418, 476

Greuze, Jean-Baptiste, 385; *509*

Grien, Hans Baldung, 302

Gris, Juan, 490; *652*

Gromaire, Marcel, 493

Gropius, Walter, 480–2; *641*

Gruber, Francis, 497

Grünewald, Matthias, 302; *398*

Gros, Jean-Antoine, 405–6; *537*

Guardi, Francesco, 331; *439*

Guarini, 325

Güas, Juan de, 266

Gubbio, Italy, 249, 315; *415*

Guercino, 327–8; *434*

Guérin, Gilles, 376

Guillain, Simon, 376

Hague, the, 472

Halberstadt, Germany, 172; *218*

Hals, Frans, 360–1; *476, 478*

Hamilton, Gavin, 367

Hankar, Paul, 477

Hassam, Childe, 424

Hawksmoor, Nicholas, 364

Heda, Willem, 358

Heem, Jan Davidsz. de, 358

Heemskeerk, Maerten van, 298; *389*

Herlin, Friedrich, 261

Hernando, Gregorio, 338; *449*

Herrera, Juan de, 307, 310, 336; *422*

Heyden, Jan van der, 360

Hildebrandt, Lukas von, 349

Hildesheim, 150; *172, 174*

Hilliard, Nicholas, 311; *407*

Hilversum, Holland, 483; *644*

Hiroshige, 469; *624*

Histiaea, 87; *89*

HITTITE ART, 45, 47; *37.* See also MESO-POTAMIAN ART

Hobbema, Meindert, 360

Hodler, Ferdinand, 503; *673*

Hogarth, William, 367, 369; *485*

Hokusai, 468–9; *623*

Holbein, Hans, the Elder, 228, 261, 301

Holbein, Hans, the Younger, 303, 311; *399*

HOLLAND: painting, 355–63, *472–82;* modern architecture, 483;

540

revival of national school, 503
Homer, Winslow, 423
Honthorst, Gerard van, 329, 360
Hooch, Pieter de, 359
Hoppner, John, 366
Horeau, 476
Horta, Victor, 477
Houdon, Jean-Antoine, 378; *500*
Howard, Ebenezer, 479
Hsia Kuei, 464
Hugo d'Oignies, 172
Huguet, Jaume, 268
Hunt, William Holman, 421
Huy, Gottfried von, 172
Huy, Reinier von, 172

Ictinus, *77*
Ile-de-France, 157, 179, 183, 188, 314
ILLUMINATION, ART OF, 143, 168, 186; *236*
IMPRESSIONISTS, 410 –14, 424–5
INCA ART, 58–63; *55–6*
Indaco (Jacobo Fiorentino), 307
INDIAN ART: Muslim, 212–13, *273;* Hindu miniatures, 222, *280;* historical background, 433–6; evolution, 436 –40; architecture, 440 –3; figurative arts, 443–8; repercussions, 448–53
Ingres, Jean-Dominique, 384, 403–4; *535–6*
Inness, George, 424
Isidorus of Miletus, 134–5
Isidorus the Younger, 135
Issoire, France, 180, 195
ITALIAN ART: painting in Gothic period,

186; resistance to Gothic, 197–203, *253 –62;* earlier Renaissance architecture, 228 –32; earlier Renaissance sculpture, 232–7; earlier Renaissance painting, 237–49; minor arts, 249–50; 16th cent. painting, 280–91; 16th cent. sculpture, 283–4, 291; Baroque architecture and sculpture, 323–6; Baroque painting, 327–31
Iuvara, Filippo, 325
Ivanov, Alexander, 393

Jacob, Georges (1739–1814), 425
Jacob, Georges (d. 1803), 425
Jansens, Abraham, 332
JAPANESE ART, 467–70
JAVANESE ART, 448 –50
Jefferson, Thomas, 370, 417
John, Gwen, 424–5
Jones, Inigo, 363–4
Jongkind, 411
Juni, Juan de, 308; *709*

Kalff, Willem, 358
Kandinsky, Wassily, 505; *678*
Karnak, Egypt, 32; *19, 22*
Kaulbach, Wilhelm von, 419
Kayser, Nicaise de, 392, 397
Keene, Charles, 422
Kells, Ireland, 143–4; *62*
Kent, William, 365
Khargur Tahl, Libyan Desert, 8
KHMER ART, 450–3

Khorsabad, 25, 44, 47; *13, 32, 38*
Kirby, Northants, 405
Kisling, Moise, 491
Klee, Paul, 494, 505; *677*
Klenze, Leo von, 416
Klerk, Michael de, 478
Knobelsdorff, von, 350
Kokoschka, 504; *676*
Koninck, Philips, 360
Korin, 468; *621*
Krafft, Adam, 259
Kubatchi, Caucasus, 263

La Cruz, Pantoja de, 342
La Fresnaye, Roger de, 490
La Hire, Laurent de, 379
La Patellière, Amédée, 493
La Mothe, Vallin de, 354
La Tour, Georges de, 320, 363, 383; *419*
La Tour, Maurice Quentin de, 366, 386; *512*
Lagash, 39; *35*
Lagneau, Pierre, 296
Lam, Wilfredo, 495
Lambot, Joseph-Louis, 478
Lancret, Nicolas, 384
Lanfranco, Giovanni, 327
Langhans, K. Gotthard, 352
Laon, France, 175–6; *222*
Largillière, Nicolas de, 379, 384; *506*
Lascaux, France, 13, 14; *1, 6*
Lastman, Pieter, 360
LATIN AMERICA: Baroque art, 345–6, *459–60;* modern architecture, 483–4, *645;* modern art, 516–17
Latrobe, Benjamin, 417
Laurana, Luciano, 230
Laurano, Francesco, 236

Laurens, Henri, 501–2
Lawrence, Sir Thomas, 366–7, 420
Le Blond, 353
Le Brun, Charles, 379, 514–15
Le Corbusier, 483–4; 643
Le Fauconnier, Henri, 492
Le Lorrain, Robert, 377
Le Nain, Antoine, Louis and Mathieu, 320, 336, 382; 503
Le Nôtre, André, 373–4
Le Sueur, Eustache, 379
Le Vau, Louis, 373
Ledoux, Nicolas, 399, 415; 495
Lefuel, 400
Leibl, Wilhelm, 419
Léger, Fernand, 491; 655
Lely, Sir Peter, 365, 371
Lemoyne, François, 384
Lemoyne, Jean-Baptiste, 377
Lenbach, Franz von, 419
Leningrad, 352; 468–9, 554
Leonardo da Vinci, 274, 280, 288; 349, 351, 364
Leoni, Pompeo, 308
Le Raincy, France, 478; 638
Lescot, Pierre, 294; 380
Lespugue, Venus of, 14; 3
Leu, Hans, 302
Levitski, Dimitri, 354
Lewis, Wyndham, 509
Leyden, Lucas van, 298
Leyden, Nicolas Gerhaert van, 257
Leyster, Judith, 359
Li Lung Mien, 464
Liang K'ai, 464; 613
Liebermann, Max, 419, 503; 675
Life of the Virgin, Master of the, 261

Ligorio, Pirro, 279; 360, 362
Limbourg, Pol, Hennequin and Hermann de, 252–3; 324
Lincoln, 188–9, 194; 239, 241
Lippi, Fra Filippo, 242, 244
Lipschitz, Jacques, 502
Loches, France, 186
Lochner, Stefan, 260
Lombardo, Pietro, 231
London, 363, 476; 484, 517, 555, 634
Longhena, Baldassare, 324; 430
Longhi, Alessandro, 331
Loos, Adolf, 480; 637
Lora, Francesco della, 313
Lorenzetti, Pietro and Ambrogio, 140, 203
Loret, France, 15; 5
Lorjou, Bernard, 497
Lotto, Lorenzo, 292
LOW COUNTRIES: Renaissance art, 297–300
    See also FLEMISH ART; HOLLAND
Lodovice, 343; 423
Luini, Bernardino, 288
Lurçat, Jean, 475, 497, 519–20; 695
Luristan, 56; 49
Luxor, Egypt, 20
Lyon, Corneille de, 296
Lyons, France, 314; 177
Lysippus, 78, 93; 69
Lyversburg Passion, Master of the, 261

Ma Yuan, 464
Mabuse, 297–8
Machuca, Pedro, 307
Mackintosh, Charles R., 479
McIntyre, Samuel, 370
Maderna, Carlo, 324

Madrid, 400, 422
Mafra, Portugal, 423
Magnasco, Alessandro, 330; 438
Maiano, Benedetto da, 230, 236
Maiano, Giuliano da, 230–1
Maillol, Aristide, 500; 667
Manet, Edouard, 393, 399, 410; 527
Manguin, 486
Mannerists, Mannerism, 273–4, 276, 288, 290–1, 296–8, 308, 310–11, 315, 332, 379
Mansart, François, 373–4
Mansart, Jules Hardouin, 373, 375; 424, 494, 515
Mantegna, Andrea, 245–8, 298; 313–14
Mantua, Italy, 229–30, 279; 296
MANUELINE STYLE, 269
Marchand, André, 497
Marcoussis, 490
Maria-Laach, Germany, 171; 213
Marini, 680
Marquet, 486–7; 649
Martellange, Etienne, 371
Martini, Simone, 203; 260
Masaccio, 157, 238–40, 244; 306
Masolino, 238; 304
Masson, André, 494
Massys, Quentin, 297; 386
Mateo, Maestre, 169
Matisse, 474, 486, 488, 491, 495; 647
Maulpertsch, Franz, 351
MAYA ART, 58–63
Mazo, Juan Bautista de, 342

Mazzoni, Guido, 311
Mchatta, Transjordan, 117, 209; *269*
Medici family, 227
Medina-az-Zahra Spain, 210; *270*
Meidias, 100
Meissonier (1695–1750), 376
Meissonier (1815–90), 397, 404
Memling, Hans, 228, 256, 261, 263; *286*
Mena, Pedro de, 339
Mengs, Raphael, 352, 371; *466*
Merrier, Philippe, 365
MESOPOTAMIAN ART: images, 24; the Chaldean genius, 39–42; architecture, 43–5; sculpture, 46; Mohammedan metalwork originates in, 220 See also SASSANIAN ART
Messina, Antonella da, 248; *315*
Metsu, Gabriel, 359
Metzinger, 490
Meulen, van der, 335
MEXICO: art of early civilizations, 28–9; Baroque art, 345; Expressionism in, 475
Mi Fei, *614*
Michel, Georges, 399, 407–8
Michelangelo, 96, 232–5, 239–40, 248, 272, 274, 277–8, 280, 283–6, 288, 290–2, 298, 307, 324, 327; *353, 356, 359–60, 368–9*
Michelozzo, 229; *295*
Mieris, van, 363
Mignard, Pierre, 379
Mignon, Abraham, 358
Milan, 149, 169, 198, 271, 280, 325; *349*

Millais, John Everett, 421; *565*
Millet, Jean-Françios, 408
MINIATURES:Persian, 221–2; English, 311
Mino da Fiesole, 236
MINOAN ART, 51–3
Miranda, Juan Carreño de, 342
Miró, Joan, 495; *662*
Modena, Italy, 169–70; *208*
Modigliani, Amedeo, 491, 512; *658*
Moissac, France, 164–5; *200*
Momper, Joos de, 336
Monaco, Don Lorenzo, 238
Montañes, Martinez, 339; *450*
Mondrian,Piet, 496; *665*
Monet, Claude, 399, 410–11, 414; *543*
Monier, Joseph, 478
Montferrand, Ricard de, 415
Montereau, Pierre de, 176
Mor, Anthonis (or Antonio Moro), 298, 308, 311; *388*
Moore, Henry, 510; *681*
Moreau, Gustave, 422
Moreau, Louis-Gabriel, 386
Moretto, 292
Morisot, Berthe, 412
Moroni, Giovanni Battista, 292
Morris, William, 479
MOSAICS: Byzantine, 137; Cosmati work, 170
Moscow, 138; *157 b, 408–9*
Moulins, Master of, 228, 263; *287*

Mount, William Sidney, 422
Mount Vernon, Virginia, 491
Mu Ch'i, 464
Multscher, Hans, 257–8, 260
Munch, Edvard, 503; *674*
Murillo, Bartolomé Esteban, 340–1; *453*
MUSLIM ART: characteristics, 205–9; evolution of, 209–22; architecture, 213–17; minor arts, 217–21
Mycenae, 53; *44–5*
MYCENAEAN ART, 53–4
Myron, 77, 92, 98; *90*

NABIS, THE, 485–6
Nanteuil, Robert de, 386
Nash, John, 476
Nasoni, Nicolo, 343
Naumberg, Germany, 171, 194, 196; *249, 251*
NAZARENES, 393, 394
NEO CLASSICISM, 367, 394–5, 397, 399–400, 415
NEO-IMPRESSIONISM, 414
Neroccio, 244
Netscher, Caspar, 363
Neuilly-en-Donjon, France, 178
Neumann, Johann Baltazar, 350; *463*
New Guinea, 58, 60
NEW YORK SCHOOL, 475
Niemeyer, Oscar, 483; *645*
Nikosthenes, 99
Nîmes, Provence, 104; *112, 114*
Noort, Adam van, 332–3, 335

NORTH AMERICA: colonial architecture, and the early Republic's art, 369–71
Notke, Bernd, 258
Novi, Alevisio, 313

OCEANIC ART, 65–6
d'Oggiono, Marco, 288
Oliver, Isaac, 311
Olympia, 75, 85, 92; *86, 88*
Oporto, Portugal, 343–4; *457–8*
Oppenordt, 376
Orcagna, Andrea, 199, 202–3
Orley, Bernaerd van, 298
Orloff, Chana, 501
ORPHISM, 490
Orvieto, Italy, 197, 199, 249; *254*
Oseberg, 57; *50*
Ostade, Adriaen and Isaack van, 359
Osterly Park, 483
Ottobeuren, Austria, 462
OTTOMAN TURKS, ART OF, 213–14
OTTONIAN ART, 150
Oud, J. P., 483
Oudry, Jean-Baptiste, 385, 388; *510*
Overbeck, Friedrich, 419; *558*
Ozenfant, Amédée, 491

Paalen, Wolfgang, 494
Pacher, Michael, 258, 261; *336*
Padovano, Giovanni Maria, 314
Paeonius, 92
Pajou, 378
Palermo, 132, 138, 217; *136, 276*
PALLADIAN STYLE, 364–5, 375

Palladio, Andrea, 279, 297; *363*
Palmer, Samuel, 421
Percier, 415
Pannini, Giovanni Paolo, 330
Paolo, Giovanni di, 244
Paray-le-Monial, France, 197
Paris: Gothic art, 175–7, 186–7, *224, 230;* Renaissance art, 294–5, *380–2;* Baroque art, *424;* 17th cent., buildings, 372–4, *492, 494 –5;* 19th cent. buildings, 399–400, 476–7, *530–1;* Haussmann's replanning, 400; Eiffel Tower, 477
PARIS, THE SCHOOL OF, 474–6; painting, 485–98; sculpture, 498 –502
Parmigiano, 288, 290; *375*
Parrhasios, 96
Pascin, Jules, 491
Pater, Jean-Baptiste, 384
Patinir, Joachim, 298, 336
Pavia, Italy, 169, 231, 274; *293*
Paxton, Joseph, 476; *634*
Peale, Charles Wilson, 371
Penicaud family, 316; *414 b.*
Périgueux, France, 159, 163; *190*
Permeke, 683
PERPENDICULAR STYLE, 194, 250, 257; *322*
Perréal, Jean, 295
Perrault, Claude, 373, 375
Perret, Auguste and Gustave, 478; *638*
Perrier, François, 379

Perroneau, 366
PERSIA: Achaemenian period, 49–50, 137, *40, 132–3;* Muslim art, 212, 217–18, 220, *275;* other influences, 214; ceramics, 220; miniatures, 221–2, *279*
PERU: Inca art, 58–63; Baroque art, 345
Perugino, 248, 256, 263; *287*
Peruzzi, Baldassare, 278
Pesne, Antoine, 351
Peterborough, 205
Phidias, 77, 88–92, 99– 100; *67, 92*
Piazzetta, 331
Picabia, 493
Picasso, Pablo, 474–5, 495, 510; *625, 628, 686*
Pietro, Sano di, 244
Pigalle, Jean-Baptiste, 378; *421*
Piloty, Karl von, 393
Pinaigrier, Robert, 316
Pinturicchio, 249
Pisa, 169, 200; *209*
Pisanello, 17, 140, 221, 223, 237, 250; *302, 320*
Pisano, Andrea, 199, 233
Pisano, Giovanni, 199; *257*
Pisano, Nicola, 157, 198 –9, 201–2; *256*
Pisano, Nino, 199
Pissaro, Camille, 411–12, 415; *544*
PLATERSQUE ART, 306–7, 337
Pleydenwurf, Hans, 261
Poelenburgh, Cornelis van, 360
Polaert, 477
POLISH ART: Renaissance, 313–14, *410–11;* Baroque, 346
Pollack, Jan, 261

Pollaiuolo, Antonio, 236, 242, 244
Pollaiuolo Piero, 242
Polycleitus, 77, 92, 98; *68, 73*
Polygnotus, 96, 100
Polymedes, *64*
Pompeii, 79, 96, 104; *116–17, 119, 129, 140*
Poniatowski, Stanislas, 355
Pontormo, 290
Pöppelmann, Daniel, 350; *461*
Pordenone, 288
Porta, Guglielmo della, 291
Porta, Giacomo della, 324; *360, 426–7*
Portinari, Candido, 517; *691*
PORTUGUESE ART: Manueline architecture, 269; painting, 269; Renaissance art, 310; Baroque, *457–8*; modern, 512
Pot, Hendrijk, *416*
Potter, F. H., 424
Potter, Paulus, 359
Poussin, Nicolas, 380; *501*
Powers, Hiram, 418
Pozzo, Andrea, 327
Pradier, 402
Praeneste, 122
Prandtauer, Jakob, 349
Praxiteles, 78, 92–3; *74, 702*
Predis, Ambrogio de, 288
PRE-RAPHAELITE BROTHERHOOD, 421
Pugin, A. W. N., 416
Primaticcio, 290, 293, 295, 316; *379*
Prud'hon, 395
Pucelle, Jean, 186; *236*
Puget, Pierre, 376; *497*

PURISM, 491
Puy, 486

Quarenghi, Giacomo, 354
Quarton (or Charonton), Enguerrand, 263
Quellin, Erasmus, 335
Quercia, Jacopo della, 232–3
Quesnel, Pierre, François and Nicolas, 296

Raeburn, Sir Henry, 366; *486*
Rainaldi, Girolamo, 324
Ramée, Joseph J., 370
Ramsay, Allan, 366
Raphael, 234, 239, 274, 278–83, 290–1, 324, 327; *355, 365–7*
Rastrelli, Bartolommeo, 353–4; *468, 470*
Ravenna, 131–3, 135–7, 147; *131–2, 146, 151, 153*
Ray, Man, 495; *664*
Rembrandt, 320, 360–3; *479–81*
Renaudin, *498*
Reni, Guido, 327
Renoir, Pierre-Auguste, 412, 429; *546–7*
RESTORATION STYLE, 425–6
Rethel, Alfred, 393, 419
Reynolds, Sir Joshua, 365–6, 371; *486*
Rheims, 148, 176, 179–80; *225, 232, 571*
Ribalta, Francisco, 339–40
Ribera, Jusepe de, 329, 340; *451*
Ribera, Pedro, 337
Richardson, Henry Hobson, 480
Riccio, Andrea, 291
Riemenschneider, Til-

man, 228, 259, 301; *331*
Rigaud, Hyacinthe, 379; *418*
Rimmer, William, 418
Rinaldi, Antonio, 354
Risueno, José, 339
Rivera, Diego, 517
Rizzo, Antonio, 231, 236
Robbia, Luca della, 235–6
Robert, Hubert, 386
Roberti, Ercole de', 245
Rodin, Auguste, 402; *533*
Rodriguez, Ventura, 338
Roebling, John, 476
Rohr, 464
ROMAN ART: Etruscan influence, 101–2; Republican period, 102; the great period of building, 102–3; architecture, 104–12, *110–18;* sculpture, 112, *118, 120–2*
ROMANESQUE ART: sources among nomadic peoples, 57; notion of order, and its characteristics, 151–4; birth of, 157; architecture, 158–66, *186–201, 203 –9, 213–15;* sculpture, 164–6, *175, 178–82, 201–1, 206;* painting and minor arts, 166–7; outside France, 167 –72, *202–17;* its differences from Muslim art, 206
Romano, Giulio, 279, 291; *361*
Romney, George, 366
Rome: Greek fresco, 96, *99;* buildings, Republic and early Empire, 102–3, 109, 112, *110– 11, 113, 118, 120–1;*

early Christian art, 125–7, *130*, *137–9;* basilicas, 127–30, *141–2;* Cosmati mosaic work, 170; Renaissance art, 229, 276–8, *352–3, 358 –60, 365, 367–8;* Baroque, 323–4, 328–9, *426–7, 429, 431, 466*

Rosselino, Antonio, 236; *301*

Rossellino, Bernardo, 230

Rossetti, D. G., 421

Rosso, 291, 294

Roualt, *630*

Rouen, Jean de, 310

Rouen, 179; *627*

Rousseau, Henri (le Douanier), 488; *646*

Rousseau, Théodore, 408; *541*

Roussel, K.-X., 486

Rowlandson, Thomas, 369

Rubens, Peter Paul, 319, 330, 332–6, 395, 429; *442–3, 696*

Rublev, Andrei, 139–40; *157 b.*

Rude, Françoise, 402; *531*

Ruffo, Marco, 313

Ruisdael, Jacob van, 360; *477*

Runge, Philipp Otto, 395, 419

Rush, William, 418

RUSSIA: Byzantine art, 133, 136, 138–40; Renaissance art, 312; Baroque art, 352–4, *467 –70;* 19th cent. architecture, 415–16

Ruysdael, Salomon van, 360

Ry, Simon Louis du, 352

Ryder, Albert Pinkham, 423

Saenredam, Pieter, 360; *475*

St-Benoit-sur-Loire, 201

St-Denis, 172, 295; *235*

St-Gall, 147–8; *165, 167*

St-Laurent, 710

St Petersburg. See *Leningrad*

St Severin, Master of, 261

Salisbury, 188–9, 194; *242–3*

Salviati, 327

Salzillo family, 339

Samothrace, 94; 98

Sandrart, Joachim von, 329

Sangallo, Antonio da, the Younger, *359*

Sangallo, Giuliano da, 231

Sansovino, Jacopo, 279, 291, 301

Santiago de Compostela, Spain, 163, 168–9, 307, 337–8; *203, 206, 448*

Sargent, J. S., 424

SARMATIAN ART, 56–7

Sarrazin, Jean, 376

Sarto, Andrea del, 290

Sarvistan, 125

SASSANIAN ART, 112 –15
    See also MESOPO-TAMIAN ART

Sassetta, 243–4; *309*

Savery, Roelandt, 336, 358

Savoldo, 292

Scamozzi, 279

Schadow, Gottfried, 417; *557*

Scheffer, Ary, 397

Schinkel, Karl Friedrich, 416; *523*

Schlüter, Andreas, 350

Schongauer, Martin, 261, 305; *335*

Scopas, 78, 92

Scorel, Jan van, 298

SCYTHIAN ART, 54, 56

Sées, France, 229

Segonzac, Dunoyer de, 495

Selommes, France, 161

Senlis, France, 175; *182*

Sens, France, 172, 188, *321*

Serlio, 279, 293, 297

Serrurier, G., *692*

Sesshu, 468

Sesson, 468

Sesto, Cesare da, 288

Settignano, Desiderio da, 236

Seurat, Georges, 414–15; *552*

Severini, Gino, 512; *687*

Shami, Teheran, 126

Shaw, Richard Norman, 479

Siberechts, Jan, 336

Sickert, Walter R., 424

Signac, 415

Sisley, Alfred, 411

Signorelli, Luca, 248–9; *318*

Siloé, Diego de, 306

Siloé, Gil, 268, 306; *345*

Simonetti, 325

Sinan, 213

Sloditz brothers, 377

Sluter, Claus, 157, 196, 252–3; *323, 707*

Smibert, John, 371

Snayers, 335

Snyders, Franz, 335; *444*

Saomi, 468

Sodoma, 288

Soest, Konrad von, *333*

Soissons, France, 219

Solari, Giovanni, 231

Solario, Pietro Antonio, 313

Solimena, 330

Sopotchani, Jugoslavia, 132–3, 138, *154*

ufflot, 375
uillac, France, 165;
575
utine, Chaim, 491–2;
657
?AIN: Visigothic art,
144; Romaesque art,
168–9, 202–3, 206;
Gothic art, 196–7;
Muslim art, 205, 208–
10, 212, 221, 264–7;
270; 15th cent. art,
266–7, 343–5; Renais-
sance art, 305–11, 400
–4; Baroque art, 336–
43, 447–56; 19th cent.
painting, 419–20;
modern, 511
Speyer, Germany, 171,
215
Spiegler, F. J., 465
Starov, Ivan Yegoro-
vich, 354; 469
Steen, Jan, 359
Stonehenge, 20; 9
Stoss, Veit, 258–9; 330
Strassburg, 257; 248
Strozzi, Bernardo, 330;
437
Stuart, Gilbert, 371
Stubbs, George, 369;
490
Sullivan, L. H., 480–1
SUMERIAN ART, 27,
39, 42
See also MESOPO-
TAMIAN ART
SURREALIST MOVE-
MENT, 493 ff.
Susa, 38, 49–50, 98, 210,
220; 30, 40, 133
Sutherland, Graham,
510; 685
Sutton Hoo, 143; 48
Suvée, 387
SWITZERLAND, re-
vival of national
school in, 503
Syracuse, 75; 107

Tahull, 202
Tanguy, Yves, 494; 659
TAPESTRIES: Brussels,
316; Beauvais, 387–8
Taq-i-Bustan, 115; 123
Tehran, Persia, 218; 277
Tell el Amarna, 36; 25
Teniers, David, 335
Ter Borch, Gerhard,
359; 474
Ter Brugghen, Hendrik,
329, 360
Thomon, Thomas de,
415
Thomyre, 425
Thornhill, Sir James,
365
Thornton, William, 417
Thorwaldsen, 417–18
Thulden, van, 335
Thumb family, 350
Tiepolo, Giambattista,
331, 350; 440
Tintoretto, 272, 288
Tiryns, 52; 43
Titian, 248, 271, 280,
286, 292, 322, 327;
371, 377, 696
Tivoli, 102; 362
Toledo, Juan Bautista
de, 422
TOLTEC ART, 58–63
Tomar, Portugal, 269,
310; 347
Tony-Garnier, 478
Torralva, Diego, 310
Torii Kiyonaga, 468
Torrigiano, Pietro, 307,
311
Toulouse, 163–4, 169,
179; 189, 699
Toulouse-Lautrec,
Henri de, 413; 549
Tours, France, 148, 263;
337
Trier, 104; 109
Troost, Cornelius, 363
Troy, Jean-François de,
384

Troyes, France, 179;
703
Trumbull, John, 371
Tsarskoe Selo, 354; 470
Tura, Cosimo, 245; 310
Turner, J. M. W., 399,
421; 564
Turriano, João, 343
Tutilo, 167
Twatchman, J. H., 424
Tzara, Tristan, 493

Ubeda, Spain, 401
Ucello, Paolo, 223, 239–
42, 244, 261; 307
Udine, Giovanni da, 283
UNITED STATES:
19th cent. architecture
and sculpture, 417–18;
19th cent. painting,
422–4; the New York
School, 474; modern
architecture, 480–1;
revival of national
school, 512–16
See also NORTH
AMERICA
Utamaro, 468; 622
Utrillo, Maurice, 650

Valdès Leal, Juan de,
341–2; 420
Valencia, Spain, 220,
337, 339; 447
Valkenborch, 336
Valladolid, Spain, 267,
305–7, 338; 343
Vandaelvira, 306
Vanderlyn, John, 422
Van Dyck, Sir Anthony,
330, 335, 365, 371;
417
Vanvitelli, Luigi, 325
Vaphio, 51; 42
Vasari, 327
Vassé, Julien, 378
Vatican City, 277; 365,
367–8
Vázquez, Lorenzo, 306

Vecchio, Palma, 286, 288; *372*
Veccieta, Lorenzo, 236
Veenius (or van Veen), Otto, 332-3, 335
Veii, 108
Velazquez, Diego, 320, 341-2, 363; *454-5*
Velde, Henry van de, 477, 479; *640*
VENETIAN SCHOOL, 247, 286-92, 331,
Venice, 132, 231-2, 279; *157 a, 291, 363, 430*
Verdun, Nikolaus von, 172
Vergara, Ignacio, *447*
Vergos, Pablo, 268
Verhaecht, Tobias, 336
Vermeer, Jan, 320, 363; *482*
Vernet, Horace, 393, 397, 404
Vernet, Joseph, 369
Veronese, 291-2; *378*
Verrochio, Andrea del, 236, 242; *300*
Versailles, 319, 373-5; *493, 496, 515*
Vézelay, France, 165; *181, 191*
Vien, 387
Vigée-Lebrun, Mme, 386
Vignola, 278-9, 293, 297; *426-7*
Vignon, Claude, 379
Viheir-ed-Din, 213
Villanueva, Juan de, 338

Villon, Jacques, 490; *669*
Vincent, 387
Vinckebooms, David, 335
Viollet-le-Duc, 476, 478
Vischer, Peter, 301; *392*
Visconti, 400
VISIGOTHIC ART, 144
Vitruvius, 102, 277, 297, 338
Vivarini, Antonio, 247
Vivarini, Bartolomeo, 247
Vlaminck, Maurice de, 486, 488
Vos, Cornelius de, 335
Vos, Paul de, 336
Vouet, Simon, 378
Voysey, C. F. A., 479
Vranck, Sebastian, 335
Vries, Hans Vredeman de, 297
Vuillard, Edouard, 486, 495
Vuolvinio, 173

Wappers, Gustave, 397
Warin, Jean, 376
Warsaw, 35; *471*
Watteau, Antoine, 365 -6, 383-4; *505*
Webb, Philip, 479
Weber, Max, 514
Weingarten, 425
Wells, 188, 194; *240*
West, Benjamin, 367, 371

Westminster Abbey, 1 194, 251, 311; *244*
Weyden, Rogier van de 223, 255, 261; *325*
Whistler, J. A. M., 4 -4; *566*
Wiertz, Antoine, 397
Willendorf, Venus of, 14; *2*
William of Sens, 188
Wils, Jan, 483
Wilton, Diptych, *237*
Wittingau, Master of, *332*
Witz, Konrad, 223, 26 -1; *284, 334*
Wohlgemuth, Michael, 261
Wood, John, 365
Wren, Sir Christopher, 363-4; *484*
Wright, Frank Lloyd, 481; *642*
Wurzburg, Austria, 350; *463*

Zadkine, Ossip, 502; *670*
Zakharoff, Adrian, 416; *554*
Zeuxis, Zevio, Stefano da, 237; *282*
Zimmermann brothers, 350
Zoffany, John, 369
Zuccaro, Federico, 309
Zurbarán, Francisco de, 320, 340-1, 363; *452*
Zwiefalten, 465